Study Guide

for

Aronson, Wilson, and Akert

Social Psychology

Seventh Edition

prepared by

Cynthia K. Shinabarger Reed
Tarrant County College

Prentice Hall

Boston   Columbus   Indianapolis   New York   San Francisco   Upper Saddle River
Amsterdam   Cape Town   Dubai   London   Madrid   Milan   Munich   Paris   Montreal   Toronto
Delhi   Mexico City   Sao Paulo   Sydney   Hong Kong   Seoul   Singapore   Taipei   Tokyo

Prentice Hall
is an imprint of

www.pearsonhighered.com

ISBN-10: 0-13-814482-6
ISBN-13: 978-0-13-814482-1

TABLE OF CONTENTS

PREFACE TO THE STUDENT

Thank you for using this study guide. I hope you find that it assists you in your social psychology class. This supplement to the textbook will help you study and prepare to take exams and write papers. I would like to describe the sections for each chapter that you will see in this book and give you some tips for using the guide for maximizing your chances for success in the class.

The chapters begin with a Chapter Overview and a Chapter Outline that correspond with the text. These provide you with a framework in which to fit in the details that you will discover in the chapters. Outlines are great memory tools as they help to organize material making it easier to remember. I recommend that you write out your own outline of the chapter and then compare it to the one in this study guide. Writing your own outline will help you begin to get the information into your long-term memory.

The next section contains the Learning Objectives for the chapter. Use these both to instruct you regarding the important points in the text and as a way to monitor your progress in a chapter. You may not be tested on all of these objectives, but using these to direct your reading and comprehension of the chapters will help you get ready for an exam on any given chapter. Page numbers are indicated for each objective. Therefore, if something sounds unfamiliar, you can refer to the text.

The Key Terms sections contain terms that are given special attention in the text. I recommend that you know these well. Most instructors consider knowledge of terminology to be a vital objective of the course. Try to do more than memorize the definitions of these terms. Define them in your own words. Apply them to your life (or your friends' lives). You will improve your recall for the test and acquire language to describe our social world to others.

The next section consists of a Guided Review including a Practice Test, Short Answer Review, and Essay Review. Measure your knowledge of the material by taking these tests. All the answers to the test questions can be found at the end of each chapter. Page numbers are provided to reference any material that you need to review.

The Essay Review and the Study Questions sections are designed to help you answer essay questions and to help you apply the information to real life. They also can be helpful for stimulating paper topic ideas. Try to answer these questions even if you only take multiple choice exams in your class. Answering these questions can show you how the material is connected and applied. Read these questions and assess your ability to answer them effectively. The Exit Tests are provided as a way to assess your knowledge once more, after you have thoroughly studied the chapter and completed the rest of the study guide sections.

Finally, good luck in your social psychology class! I hope you enjoy learning about the topics in social psychology. I also hope the information you learn will help you achieve success in your academic, personal, and professional pursuits.

Cynthia K. Shinabarger Reed, Ph.D.
Tarrant County College

v

CHAPTER 1

Introducing Social Psychology

CHAPTER 1 OVERVIEW

The first chapter is an introduction to the field and perspective of social psychology. At the heart of social psychology is **social influence**. We are all influenced by other people.

A main focus of this chapter is to tell you what **social psychology** is and what it is not. In the first part of the chapter, you will discover similarities between social psychology and other disciplines such as **sociology**, while noting the important differences that set social psychology apart from fields that study similar phenomena. For example, it may be obvious why social psychology is different from folk wisdom, but distinguishing the differences in perspective between sociology and **personality psychology** is more challenging. This chapter also addresses how **construals** influence social situations.

The second part of the chapter examines the importance of **social influence**. When we underestimate the power of social influence, we gain a false sense of security. The **fundamental attribution error** refers to our tendency to overestimate the extent to which people's behavior is due to internal, dispositional factors, and to underestimate the role of situational factors. **Behaviorism** focuses on the objective properties of a situation, such as how rewarding it is to people, and then documents the behaviors that follow from these objective properties. **Gestalt psychology** stresses the importance of studying the subjective way in which an object appears in people's minds, rather than objective, physical attributes of the object.

The third part of the chapter addresses where construals come from and describes two fundamental approaches to the study of social behavior — the **self-esteem approach** and the **social cognition approach**. To master the rest of the text, it is very important to know the basic assumptions of each approach. These approaches are based on two basic human motives, the need to maintain **self-esteem** and the need to be accurate. Most people have a strong need to maintain reasonably high self-esteem — that is, to see themselves as good, competent, and decent. To maintain our self-esteem we may justify our past behavior. **Social cognition** refers to how people think about themselves and the social world; more specifically, how people select, interpret, remember, and use social information to make judgments and decisions. Sometimes our expectations about the social world interfere with perceiving it accurately. Although the need to maintain a positive view of ourselves (the self-esteem approach) and the need to view the world accurately (the social cognition approach) are the most important of our social motives, they are not the only motives influencing people's thoughts and behaviors. Biological drives can be powerful motivators, as well as fear or the promise of love, favors, and other rewards involving social exchange. The need for control is also a significant motive.

The application of social psychology to solving social problems is considered in the last part of the chapter. Social psychologists have examined issues such as how to: induce people to conserve natural resources, educate people to practice safer sex, understand the relationship between viewing violence on television and the violent behavior of television viewers, develop effective negotiation strategies for the reduction of international conflict, find ways to reduce racial prejudice, and help people adjust to life changes.

CHAPTER 1 OUTLINE

I. What Is Social Psychology?
• Social influence is at the heart of social psychology.
• Other people can influence our behavior or our thoughts and our feelings through direct attempts at persuasion, or more indirectly, through their presence and the transmission of cultural values.
• **Social psychology** is defined as the scientific study of the way that the thoughts, feelings, and actions of people are influenced by the real or imagined presence of other people.

A. The Power of Social Interpretation
• Social psychology is distinct from other social sciences because of its emphasis on **construal**, or the way in which people perceive, comprehend, and interpret the social world.
• Social psychology is distinct from folk wisdom because it is empirical.

B. How Else Can We Understand Social Influence?
• We can ask people directly about what influenced their behavior, but people are not always aware of the origins of their own responses and feelings.
1. Journalists, Instant Experts, and Social Critics
• Common sense explanations such as those cited by journalists, social critics, and novelists are known as folk wisdom.
• Folk wisdom tends to be wrong or oversimplified. Specifically, it tends to underestimate the power of the situation. The examples of Jonestown, Waco, and Heaven's Gate are cited. In each case, people looked for someone to blame; this makes people feel better but is no substitute for understanding the complexities of the situations that produced those events.
• Much can be learned from folk wisdom; however, different pieces of folk wisdom can contradict each other, and there is no easy way to determine which of them is correct. Contradictory aphorisms are cited as examples.
2. Philosophy
• Social psychology differs from philosophy because it is empirical. Social psychologists make *hypotheses*, or educated guesses, about the specific situations under which different generalizations about human behavior hold, then design experiments to tease out these situations.

C. Social Psychology Compared with Personality Psychology
• **Personality psychology** focuses on **individual differences** in human behavior (those aspects of people's personalities that make them different from other people), while **social psychology** focuses more on how similar social situations affect different people.
• Social psychologists believe that explaining behavior primarily in terms of personality factors can be superficial because it leads to a serious underestimation of the role played by social influence. The fact that most people fail to take the situation into account has a profound impact on how people relate to one another.
• Social psychology is compared to sociology and personality psychology in Table 1.1.

D. Social Psychology Compared with Sociology
• Although social psychology shares areas of interest with sociology, economics, and political science, it focuses on a more micro level of analysis than these other social sciences, being concerned with individuals rather than societies.
• Social psychology is more concerned than other social sciences with trying to derive universal properties of human behavior.
• **Sociology** is concerned with such topics as social class, social structure, and social institutions.
• Sociology looks toward society at large.

II. The Power of Social Influence
• People are prone to the **fundamental attribution error**: the tendency to overestimate the extent to which people's behavior is due to internal, dispositional factors and to underestimate the role of the situational factors.

A. Underestimating the Power of Social Influence
• The fundamental attribution error can lead to developing a sense of false security—we assume problematic behavior could never happen to us and thus we do not guard against its occurring.
• In a demonstration of the fundamental attribution error, Ross & Samuels (1993) found that college students' personalities, as rated by the resident assistants in their dormitories, did not determine how cooperative or competitive they were in a laboratory game. The name of the game—whether it was called the Wall Street Game or the Community Game—did, however, make a tremendous difference (see Figure 1.1). Two-thirds of the students responded competitively when the game was called Wall Street Game compared with only one-third when it was called Community Game.

B. The Subjectivity of the Social Situation
• What do we mean by the social situation?
• **Behaviorism** is a school of psychology maintaining that, to understand human behavior, one need only consider the reinforcing properties of the environment (how positive and negative events in the environment are associated with specific behaviors). Behaviorists tried to define social situations objectively, focusing on the reinforcements received in response to behavior.
• Because behaviorism does not deal with cognition, thinking, and feeling, this approach has proven inadequate for a complete understanding of the social world. We have learned that it is important to look at the situation from the viewpoint of the people in it to see how they construe the world around them.
• This emphasis on construal has its roots in **Gestalt psychology**, a school of psychology stressing the importance of studying the subjective way in which an object appears in people's minds, rather than the objective, physical attributes of the object.
• Kurt Lewin, the founding father of modern experimental social psychology, was the first to apply Gestalt principles from the study of perception to the social domain (how people perceive other people and their motives, intentions and behaviors).

III. Where Construals Come From: Basic Human Motives
• Social psychologists have found that two motives are of primary importance in determining our thoughts and behavior: the need to be accurate and the need to feel good about ourselves.
• Sometimes both of these motives pull us in the same direction. But often we find ourselves in situations where these two motives pull us in opposite directions—where to perceive the world accurately requires us to face the fact that we have behaved foolishly or immorally.
• Leon Festinger realized that it is when these two motives pull us in opposite directions that we can learn the most about psychological processes.

A. The Self-Esteem Approach: The Need to Feel Good about Ourselves
• **Self-esteem** is people's evaluation of their own self-worth, or the extent to which people see themselves as good, competent, and decent. Most people have a strong need to maintain high self-esteem. This need can clash with the need for accuracy, leading people to distort their perceptions of the world.
1. Justifying Past Behavior
• In order to preserve self-esteem, people may distort their perceptions of reality. Such distortions are more "spins" on the facts than they are total delusions.
2. Suffering and Self-Justification

• Social psychological research demonstrates that when people volunteer to undergo a painful or embarrassing initiation in order to join a group (e.g., a fraternity hazing), they need to justify the experience in order to avoid feeling foolish. One way they do this is to decide that the initiation was worth it because the group is so wonderful.

• Under certain conditions, then, the need for self-justification can lead people to do surprising or paradoxical things (e.g., preferring things for which they have suffered to those which are associated with ease and pleasure).

B. The Social Cognition Approach: The Need to Be Accurate
• Although people may bend the facts to serve their self-esteem needs, they usually do not distort reality. In fact, human reasoning skills are extraordinary.
   1. Social Cognition
• **Social cognition** is the study of how people think about themselves and the social world; more specifically, how people select, interpret, remember, and use social information.
• This approach views people as amateur sleuths seeking to understand and predict their social world. However, coming up with an accurate picture of the social world may be difficult because there are many relevant facts and we have only limited time. For example, when asked to judge which is better for you, Lucky Charms or 100% Natural from Quaker, most people will choose 100% Natural, however, it contains far more fat than Lucky Charms. Even though Lucky Charms has a bit more sugar, it is a more healthy choice than 100% Natural.
   2. Expectations about the Social World
• Our expectations can sometimes get in the way of our accurately perceiving the world. In the *self-fulfilling prophecy*, our expectations about another person's behavior result (via the mechanism of influencing our behavior toward the target) in changing the target's behavior.

C. Additional Motives
   •Although the need for self-justification and accuracy are the dominant motives influencing social behavior, our behavior is also influenced by biological drives, social motives, and the need for control.

IV. Social Psychology and Social Problems
• While social psychologists are often motivated by simple curiosity to study social behavior, they are also frequently motivated by the desire to help resolve social problems such as increasing conservation of natural resources, increasing the practice of safe sex, understanding the relationship between viewing television violence and aggressive behavior, developing effective negotiation strategies for the reduction of international conflict, finding ways to reduce racial prejudice, and helping people adjust to life changes.
• Social psychologists helped the government change an ad campaign to promote safe sex that was based on increasing fear of contracting AIDS, noting that fear promotes denial and flies in the face of the need to preserve self-esteem.

LEARNING OBJECTIVES

After you have read Chapter 1, you should be able to do the following:

1. Define social influence and state why it is of interest to social psychologists. (p. 3)

2. Define social psychology. (p. 3)

3. Define construals. Indicate why social psychologists study these rather than simply the objective environments of people. (pp. 4-5)

4. Indicate how the approach taken by social psychologists is different from that of social critics, journalists, and philosophers. Describe why the social psychological approach may lead to more accurate predictions about human behavior compared to these other approaches. (pp. 6-8)

5. Define the term *individual differences*. Identify how personality psychology differs from social psychology. (pp. 9-10)

6. Identify the goal of social psychology. (p. 10)

7. Compare and contrast social psychology with sociology and personality psychology. (pp. 9-11)

8. Define the term *fundamental attribution error*. Identify the consequences of making this error and underestimating the power of social influence. (pp. 11-12)

9. Explain how social psychology is influenced by behaviorism and Gestalt psychology. Identify what each school of psychology has contributed to social psychology. (pp. 12-14)

10. Identify the two basic motives that underlie the origins of people's construals. (p. 14)

11. Identify the approaches associated with the two basic human motives. Define the term *self-esteem*. Define the term *social cognition*. Describe the assumptions of each approach. (pp. 15-17)

12. Identify the factors that interfere with our attempts to be accurate. (pp. 17-18)

13. Identify other motives that influence the formation of people's construals. (p. 18)

14. Identify some social problems that social psychologists research and try to remedy. (pp. 18-19)

KEY TERMS

Correctly identify the definition of each key term. Place the name of the correct term in the space provided.

1. _____ The effect that the words, actions, or mere presence of other people have on our thoughts, feelings, attitudes, or behavior. (p. 3)

2. _____ The scientific study of the way in which people's thoughts, feelings, and behaviors are influenced by the real or imagined presence of other people. (p. 3)

3. _____ The way in which people perceive, comprehend, and interpret the social world. (p. 4)

4. _____ The aspects of people's personalities that make them different from other people. (p. 8)

5. _____ The tendency to overestimate the extent to which people's behavior is due to internal, dispositional factors, and to underestimate the role of situational factors. (p. 11)

6. _____ A school of psychology maintaining that to understand human behavior, one need only consider the reinforcing properties of the environment—that is, how positive and negative events in the environment are associated with specific behaviors. (p. 12)

7. _____ A school of psychology stressing the importance of studying the subjective way in which an object appears in people's minds, rather than objective, physical attributes of the object. (p. 13)

8. _____ People's evaluations of their own self-worth—that is, the extent to which they view themselves as good, competent, and decent. (p. 15)

9. _____ How people think about themselves and the social world; more specifically, how people select, interpret, remember, and use social information to make judgments and decisions. (p. 17)

GUIDED REVIEW

PRACTICE TEST

1. Social psychology is not concerned with social situations in any objective sense, but with how people are influenced by:
   a) their construal of the social environment.
   b) abstract social rules and customs.
   c) social situations they've encountered in the past.
   d) their interactions with other people in social situations.

2. One problem with relying entirely on folk wisdom such as "birds of a feather flock together" is that
   a) it is never accurate.
   b) for some people one saying applies while for others the opposite is applicable.
   c) more often than not, sayings from folk wisdom disagree with one another.
   d) such sayings were developed in different cultures that taught contrasting values.

3. Psychologists interested in the effects of different personality traits on aggressive behavior are referred to as:
   a) personality psychologists.
   b) social psychologists.
   c) behaviorist psychologists.
   d) Gestalt psychologists.

4. Why is it difficult for social psychologists to convince people that their behavior is greatly influenced by the social environment?
   a) because people outside of social psychology are rarely interested in the causes of social behavior
   b) because people are motivated to perceive the world accurately
   c) because people are inclined to commit the fundamental attribution error in explaining behavior
   d) all of the above

5. Behavioral psychologists like Watson and Skinner believed that all human behavior could be understood by examining:
   a) rewards and punishments in the individual's environment.
   b) the impact of broad social and cultural factors on the individual.
   c) how the individual thinks and feels about rewards and punishments.
   d) how the individual is rewarded and punished for having various thoughts and feelings.

6. Research on hazing shows that members like a group better if they had endured unpleasant procedures to get into the group than if they had not. These findings are best accounted for by:
   a) self-justification.
   b) the fundamental attribution error.
   c) principles of reinforcement.
   d) the self-fulfilling prophecy.

7. According to the social cognition approach,
   a) people try to view the world as accurately as possible.
   b) people do their best to understand and predict the social world.
   c) coming up with an accurate picture of the social world is often difficult.
   d) all of the above

8. Social psychologists are primarily concerned that their ideas about human social behavior:
   a) withstand empirical testing.
   b) obey philosophical principles.
   c) adhere to conventional wisdom.
   d) make sense intuitively.

9. Sociologists focus on _____ for explanations of human behavior whereas social psychologists focus on _____ for such explanations.
   a) society; the individual
   b) society; people's past experiences
   c) people's past experiences; the individual
   d) the individual; society

10. When we commit the fundamental attribution error in explaining people's behavior, we _____ the power of personality traits and _____ the power of social influence.
    a) overestimate; underestimate
    b) overestimate; overestimate
    c) underestimate; overestimate
    d) underestimate; underestimate

11. By emphasizing the way in which people construe the social world, social psychology has its direct roots more in the tradition of _____ than in behaviorism.
    a) sociology
    b) personality psychology
    c) developmental psychology
    d) Gestalt psychology

12. Whereas the _____ approach emphasizes that behavior is motivated by the desire to feel good about ourselves, the _____ approach emphasizes the need to be accurate.
    a) self-esteem; rational
    b) emotional; rational
    c) social cognition; emotional
    d) self-esteem; social cognition

13. Researchers who attempt to understand social behavior from the perspective of social cognition assume that we:
    a) have a limitless capacity to process information.
    b) try to view the world as accurately as possible.
    c) logically suspend our judgments until we have gathered all the relevant facts.
    d) are primarily motivated to view ourselves as rational.

14. You expect that people at a party will not enjoy your company. Consequently, you spare them the misery of talking with you by being brief and cutting short their conversations with you. Later you learn that your company was not enjoyed. What social psychological phenomenon has occurred in this situation?
    a) social cognition
    b) self-justification
    c) reinforcement
    d) self-fulfilling prophecy

15. Which of the following is NOT an example of social influence?
    a) A salesperson convinces someone to buy a set of encyclopedias.
    b) At a party a man feels jealous because his date talks more to his friend than to him.
    c) A student says "thank you" when her professor hands her an exam she doesn't want to take.
    d) A friend tends to be optimistic and views situations in a positive light.

16. Conflicting answers to questions about basic human nature are most likely to be found:
    a) from one generation to the next.
    b) in folk wisdom and philosophy.
    c) from one culture to another.
    d) in personality and social psychology.

17. Which question about aggression is a sociologist most likely to ask?
    a) What universal property of all humans causes them to be aggressive?
    b) What is it about a particular society that produces aggression in its members?
    c) To what extent is human aggression inborn?
    d) Why are humans more aggressive than are other animal species?

18. A personality psychologist interested in studying happiness would most likely wonder:
    a) whether some people are generally happier than others.
    b) what the psychological processes are that cause people to be happy.
    c) if people in the U. S. are happier than people in China.
    d) whether happy workers are productive workers.

19. Rather than study how the physical attributes of an object combine to form an impression, Gestalt psychologists study:
    a) the whole object itself as it exists in objective reality.
    b) people's subjective perception of the whole object.
    c) the isolated parts without regard to their combination.
    d) parts of the whole that go unnoticed but enter the unconscious mind.

20. To determine the origin of a construal, social psychologists look to:
    a) the social situation itself.
    b) an individual's upbringing and family background.
    c) basic human motives.
    d) broad societal and cultural factors.

21. According to social psychologists, an individual's behavior in a given situation is best predicted from knowing:
     a) how that individual has behaved in past situations.
     b) the nature of the present situation.
     c) how that individual construes the present situation.
     d) the individual's personality traits.

22. When people observe others behaving in a given situation, they tend to jump to the conclusion that the person rather than the situation caused the behavior. In this, people are most like a(n):
     a) social psychologist.
     b) personality psychologist.
     c) sociologist.
     d) anthropologist.

23. Which of the following would be the most likely to claim that people blindly follow leaders because they are reinforced for such compliance?
     a) Gestalt psychologists
     b) personality psychologists
     c) behavioral psychologists
     d) social psychologists

24. According to Gestalt psychology:
     a) "The whole is nothing more than the sum of its parts."
     b) "The whole is different from the sum of its parts."
     c) "Opposites attract."
     d) "When the whole is construed, some parts will be deleted."

25. When the need to feel good about oneself clashes with the need to be accurate, people tend to:
     a) put a slightly different spin on the facts so that they are seen in the best possible light.
     b) deny the existence of all information that reflects badly on them.
     c) suffer from low self-esteem and continue to see the world accurately.
     d) remain in conflict since they are willing neither to distort reality nor to perceive themselves negatively.

26. A social psychologist notices that a large number of her students report getting nervous when they have to give presentations in class. In trying to determine the causes of this emotional reaction, the social psychologist will tend to examine:
     a) the dispositional qualities that these students share.
     b) her own commonsense view of why these students become nervous.
     c) the situational factors that could lead to this emotional reaction.
     d) clinical reasons that might explain why students experience nervousness.

27. Which two basic human motives do social psychologists focus on the most?
     a) the desire to reproduce and the desire to maintain one's self-esteem
     b) the desire to reproduce and the desire to achieve a sense of inner peace and harmony
     c) the desire to maintain one's self-esteem and the desire to achieve a sense of inner peace and harmony
     d) the desire to maintain one's self-esteem and the desire to view the world as accurately as possible

28. Which of the following is true about Kurt Lewin?
    a) He was a well-known behaviorist.
    b) He applied Gestalt principles to social perception.
    c) He argued that most social behaviors were caused by individual's personalities.
    d) all of the above

29. Rosenthal and Jacobson's (1968) study in which students were identified as "bloomers" illustrates:
    a) the self-esteem approach to understanding human motivation.
    b) the fact that teachers are solely focused on dispositional attributes such as students' abilities.
    c) that expectations have profound impact on social behavior and perception.
    d) the pitfalls of considering social psychology as a science.

30. Identifying universal properties of human nature that make everyone susceptible to social influence, regardless of social class or culture is the goal of:
    a) social psychology.
    b) personality psychology.
    c) sociology.
    d) philosophy.

31. One of the goals of social psychologists is to make educated guesses called _____ about the specific situations under which one outcome or the other would occur.
    a) independent variables
    b) hypotenuses
    c) theories
    d) hypotheses

32. In the study by Ross in which Stanford University students played a game called the Wall Street Game or the Community Game, Ross found the _____ determined whether the student played competitively or cooperatively.
    a) student's personality
    b) name of the game
    c) student's housing situation (whether they lived at home or in a dormitory)
    d) student's birth order (whether they were a first born, middle, or youngest child)

33. In the study by Ross in which Stanford University students played a game called the Wall Street Game or the Community Game, Ross found that when the name Wall Street Game was used approximately _____ of the students played competitively.
    a) one-fourth
    b) one-third
    c) one-half
    d) two-thirds

34. Rosenthal and Jacobson's (1968) study in which students were labeled as "bloomers" illustrated which of the following?
    a) construals
    b) the need to be accurate
    c) self-fulfilling prophecy
    d) fundamental attribution error

35. In addition to the need to maintain a positive view of ourselves and the need to view the world accurately, which of the following is also a source of construals?
    a) need for control
    b) dominance motive
    c) superiority motive
    d) need for cognition

36. What makes predicting behavior so challenging for social psychologists?
    a) Psychology is a young science and does not have clearly established guidelines for how to predict behavior.
    b) Psychologists are attempting to predict the behavior of highly sophisticated organisms in a variety of complex situations.
    c) People rarely behave in predictable ways.
    d) Patterns of human behavior radically change from one generation to the next.

37. The creativity and analytical thinking of _____ are a major part of the foundation of contemporary psychology.
    a) psychiatrists
    b) sociologists
    c) philosophers
    d) anthropologists

38. Behaviorists choose not to deal with
    a) cognition.
    b) thinking.
    c) feeling.
    d) all of the above

39. The process of denial stems from the
    a) need to maintain self-esteem.
    b) desire to be accurate.
    c) need for control.
    d) desire to be dominate.

40. A special kind of construal is what Lee Ross calls _____ — the conviction all of us have that we perceive things as they really are.
    a) naïve construal
    b) naïve realism
    c) unrealistic construal
    d) fantasy construal

SHORT ANSWER REVIEW

At the very heart of social psychology is the phenomenon of (1) _____ (p. 6). We are

all influenced by other people. Direct attempts at social influence form a major part of social psychology.

Social influence is broader than an attempt by one person to change another person's (2)

_____ (p.6). Social influence extends beyond behavior—it includes our thoughts and feelings as well as our overt acts. Each of us is immersed in a social and (3) _____ context. Social psychology is the scientific study of the way in which people's (4) _____ (p. 6), feelings and behaviors are influenced by the real or (5) _____ (p. 6) presence of other people.

Other disciplines are also interested in how people are influenced by their social environment. Social psychology is distinct, however, primarily because it is concerned not so much with social situations in any objective sense but rather with how people are influenced by their interpretation, or (6) _____ (p. 7), of their social environment. Given the importance placed on the way people (7) _____ (p. 7) the social world, social psychologists pay special attention to the origins of these interpretations. Another distinctive feature of social psychology is that it is an (8) _____ (p. 8) based science. As scientists, our goal is to find (9) _____ (p. 8) answers to a wide array of important questions.

A great deal can be learned about social behavior from journalists, social critics, and novelists. There is, however, at least one problem with relying entirely on such sources: More often than not, they disagree with one another, and there is no way of determining which of them is (10) _____ (p. 10).

Throughout history, (11) _____ (p. 11) has been a major source of insight about human nature. Social psychologists address many of the same questions that philosophers address, but we attempt to look at these questions (12) _____ (p. 11). One of the tasks of the social psychologist is to make (13) _____ _____ (p. 11) called hypotheses.

When trying to explain social behavior, personality psychologists generally focus on (14) _____ _____ (p. 12), the aspects of people's personalities that make them different from others. Social psychologists, however, are convinced that (15) _____

13

(p. 12) behavior primarily through personality factors ignores a critical part of the story, the powerful role played by social influence.

Social psychology's focus on social behavior is shared by several other disciplines in the social sciences. Each of these examines the influence of social factors on human behavior, but important differences set social psychology apart, most notably in their (16) _____ _____ _____ (p. 13). For the social psychologist, the level of analysis is the individual in the context of a (17) _____ _____ (p. 13). Other social sciences are more concerned with broad social, economic, political, and historical factors that influence events in a given society. (18) _____ (p. 13), for example, is concerned with such topics as social class, social structure, and social institutions. The goal of social psychology is to identify (19) _____ _____ (p. 13) of human nature that make everyone susceptible to social influence, regardless of social class or culture.

When trying to convince people that their behavior is greatly influenced by the social environment, the social psychologist is up against a formidable barrier: All of us tend to explain people's behavior in terms of their (20) _____ (p. 15). This barrier is known as the (21) _____ _____ _____ (p. 15), the tendency to explain our own and other people's behavior entirely in terms of personality traits, thereby underestimating the power of social influence. When we underestimate the power of social influence, we gain a feeling of false security.

We have argued that the social situation often has profound effects on human behavior. But what exactly do we mean by the social situation? One strategy for defining it would be to specify the objective properties of the situation and then document the behaviors that follow from these objective properties. This was the approach taken by (22) _____ (p. 16), a school of psychology maintaining that to understand human behavior, one need only consider the reinforcing properties of the environment.

Behaviorists choose not to deal with issues like (23) _____ (p. 17) , thinking, and feeling

because they considered these concepts too vague and mentalistic and not sufficiently anchored to

observable behavior. We have learned that social behavior cannot be fully understood by confining our

observations to the physical properties of a situation. We need to look at the situation from the viewpoint

of the people in it, to see how they construe the world around them. This emphasis on construal, the way

people interpret the social situation, has its roots in an approach called (24) _____ (p. 17)

psychology. This perspective holds that we should study the (25) _____ (p. 17) way in which

an object appears in people's minds, rather than the way in which the objective, physical attributes of the

object combine.

Human beings are complex organisms; at a given moment, various intersecting motives underlie

our thoughts and behaviors. Over the years, social psychologists have found that two of these motives are

of primary importance: The need to feel (26) _____ _____ _____ (p.

19) and the need to be (27) _____ (p. 19). Most people have a strong need to maintain

reasonably high (28) _____ _____ (p. 20), to see themselves as good, competent,

and decent. Acknowledging major deficiencies in ourselves is very difficult, even when the cost is seeing

the world inaccurately. It is often possible for normal people to put a slightly different spin on the existing

facts, one that puts us in the best possible light. The fact that people distort their interpretation of (29)

_____ (p. 20) so that they might feel better about themselves is not surprising. Human beings

are motivated to maintain a positive picture of themselves, in part by (30) _____ (p. 21) their

past behavior.

Given the amazing cognitive abilities of our species, it makes sense that social psychologists, when

formulating theories of social behavior, would take into consideration the way in which human beings

think about the world. We call this the cognitive approach to social psychology, or (31)

_____ _____ (p. 22). Researchers who attempt to understand social behavior

from the perspective of social cognition begin with the assumption that all people try to view the world as

15

(32) _____ (p. 22) as possible. This is by no means easy, because we almost never know all the facts we need to accurately judge a given situation. Sometimes our (33) _____ about the social world interfere with perceiving it accurately. This can lead to a (34) _____

_____ (p. 23) as Rosenthal and Jacobson found in their study of school children labeled "bloomers."

In addition to the self-esteem approach and the social cognition approach our behavior can be influenced by other motives. These include (35) _____ (p. 24) drives, fear, the promise of love, favors, and other rewards involving social exchange. Another significant motive is the need for (36) _____ (p. 24).

Many social psychologists study the causes of social behavior in order to contribute to the solution of (37) _____ _____ (p. 24) such as how to induce people to conserve natural resources, how to reduce hostility and prejudice, and how to help people adjust to life changes.

ESSAY REVIEW

1.   Write an essay on social psychology which addresses the following questions:
   - What is social psychology?
   - What role do construals play in helping to explain social behavior?
   - How is social psychology different from personality psychology and sociology?

2.   Discuss the power of social influence including all of the following:
   - Identify and describe the formidable barrier that exists when trying to convince people that their behavior is greatly influenced by the social environment.
   - What happens when we underestimate the power of social influence?
   - Describe the study conducted by Ross at Stanford University that illustrated the power of the social situation.

3.   Differentiate between behaviorism and the Gestalt perspective.

4.   Describe where construals come from including:
   - The two motives social psychologists have found to be of primary importance.
   - The ways in which people sometimes avoid admitting the truth to feel better about themselves and how that applies to fraternity hazing?

5.   Write an essay on social cognition including:
   - The definition of social cognition.
   - A description of the Rosenthal and Jacobson (1968) study on "bloomers" and how the study illustrated social cognition.

EXIT TESTS

EXIT TEST 1

1. Social psychology is defined in your text as the scientific study of
    a) society and human behavior.
    b) behavior and mental processes.
    c) the way in which people's thoughts, feelings, and behaviors are influenced by the real or imagined presence of other people.
    d) humanity.

2. Laura looks at her colleagues from across the room. She smiles and waves at Judy but does not acknowledge Kay. Judy believes that Laura does not see Kay, but Kay believes that Laura is mad at her. This best illustrates a difference in
    a) attitudes.
    b) construals.
    c) social cognitions.
    d) social labeling.

3. When Dr. Keith observes differences in behavior among her students, she assumes these differences in behavior are caused by individual differences of the students and not social factors. Dr. Keith is most likely a
    a) personality psychologist.
    b) social psychologist.
    c) behaviorist psychologist.
    d) sociologist.

4. Mark observes a parent handling a child roughly in the grocery store. He assumes the parent is a "child abuser" rather than considering the possibility that the parent may have just had a very stressful day. Mark's behavior illustrates the
    a) fundamental attribution error.
    b) self-esteem approach.
    c) actor-observer bias.
    d) self-serving bias.

5. Dr. Walker believes that to understand behavior you need to understand the reinforcing properties of the person's environment. Dr. Walker is a
    a) sociologist.
    b) Gestalt psychologist.
    c) psychoanalytic psychologist.
    d) behaviorist.

6. David made a purchase from a salesperson in a furniture store. After his purchase, David kept talking with the salesperson even though it was obvious that the salesperson wanted to leave and assist other customers. When David's wife later confronted him and said that his behavior was rude, David replied, "I spent a lot of money there so he needs to listen to me." David is engaging in _____ so he will not feel badly about his behavior.
    a) self-justification
    b) the fundamental attribution error
    c) principles of reinforcement
    d) the self-fulfilling prophecy

7.   The self-fulfilling prophecy phenomenon shows that _____ the social world
      can interfere with perceiving it accurately.
      a)   attitudes about
      b)   expectations about
      c)   past experience in
      d)   all of the above

8.   In addition to the need to maintain a positive view of ourselves and the need to view the world
      accurately, biological drives are also a source of construals.
      a)   True
      b)   False

9.   Research has shown that when it comes to need for control
      a)   only people with mental illnesses are high in this need.
      b)   most people are low in this need and trust their future to fate.
      c)   people need to feel they exert some control over their environment.
      d)   only people who like to dominate others are high in this need.

10.   Social psychologists focus their efforts on research done just for the purpose of learning more
      about social behavior but do not conduct research to solve social problems since this is the goal of
      sociologists.
      a)   True
      b)   False

EXIT TEST 2

1.   Chloe had a very close friend named Danielle. A year ago Danielle stopped talking to Chloe and
      started avoiding her and Chloe does not know why. Danielle's actions have affected the way
      Chloe thinks, feels, and behaves. It has also had a negative impact on Chloe's attitudes regarding
      friendship. This situation best illustrates
      a)   construals.
      b)   social influence.
      c)   the self-fulfilling prophecy.
      d)   naïve realism.

2.   Social psychologists are interested in studying how and why our thoughts, feelings, and behaviors
      are shaped by
      a)   our own culture.
      b)   our family of origin.
      c)   social institutions.
      d)   the entire social environment.

3.   Construal refers to the way in which people perceive, _____, and interpret the social world.
      a)   comprehend
      b)   distort
      c)   accept
      d)   redefine

4. One distinctive feature of social psychology is that it is not an experimentally based science.
    a) True
    (b) False

5. Social psychology is similar to sociology but the two fields are different in that
    a) social psychology is experimentally based and sociology is not.
    b) sociology is experimentally based and social psychology is not.
    (c) social psychology focuses on the individual and sociology focuses on society at large.
    d) sociology focuses on the individual and social psychology focuses on society at large.

6. The fundamental attribution error is the tendency to overestimate the extent to which people's behavior is due to internal, _____ factors and to underestimate the role of _____ factors.
    a) psychological; social
    b) biological; cultural
    c) situational; dispositional
    (d) dispositional; situational

7. Dr. Sadowski is a family therapist. When she treats families with problems she focuses on how each family member interprets the social situations of the family. Dr. Sadowski has most likely been influenced by
    (a) Gestalt psychology.
    b) behaviorism.
    c) personality psychology.
    d) sociology.

8. The _____ perspective begins with the assumption that people try to view the world as accurately as possible.
    a) correctionist
    b) Gestalt
    (c) social cognition
    d) behaviorist

9. Rosenthal and Jacobson's (1968) study in which students were labeled as "bloomers" illustrated the fundamental attribution error and showed that expectations about the social world can interfere with
    a) attitude formation.
    (b) perceiving it accurately.
    c) relationships between social groups.
    d) all of the above.

10. At a psychological level, we can be motivated by all of the following EXCEPT
    a) fear.
    (b) biological drives.
    c) the promise of love.
    d) rewards involving social exchange.

Study Activities

1. Linda, a social psychologist, and Mark, a sociologist, take a walk in a park where they witness a fight between two youths. What explanations are Linda and Mark likely to offer for the aggressive behavior they observed?

2. Compare the self-esteem and social cognition approaches to the study of social behavior. What assumptions are made by each approach?

3. What is the critical distinction between social psychology and folk wisdom? What is the advantage of social psychology's approach to social behavior?

4. Describe an instance of the self-fulfilling prophecy from your own experiences.

5. Discuss ways in which you are influenced by both the real and imagined presence of others.

6. What is the fundamental attribution error? Why do people commit this error when they try to explain other people's behavior? Provide examples of the fundamental attribution error and discuss some consequences of committing the fundamental attribution error.

7. Do you think behaviorism or Gestalt psychology provides a better explanation for behavior? Explain your choice.

8. What is self-justification and why do people engage in it? What consequence may self-justification have? Provide an example of self-justification from your own experience.

9. What is an assumption of the social cognition approach? What interferes with a person's desire to be accurate?

10. What are some of the motives besides the desire to be accurate and the desire to feel good about ourselves that influence our behavior? Give examples from your own experience of when some of these motives have influenced your behavior.

Chapter 1 Answers

Practice Test

1. A (p. 4)
2. C (p. 7)
3. A (p. 8)
4. C (p. 11)
5. A (p. 12)
6. A (p. 15)
7. D (p. 17)
8. A (p. 5)
9. A (pp. 10-11)
10. A (p. 11)
11. D (p. 13)
12. D (pp. 15, 17)
13. B (p. 17)
14. D (p. 18)
15. D (p. 3)
16. B (p. 7)
17. B (p. 10)
18. A (p. 8)
19. B (p. 13)
20. C (p. 14)
21. C (p. 4)
22. B (p. 8)
23. C (p. 12)
24. B (p. 13)
25. A (p. 15)
26. C (pp. 8-9)
27. D (p. 14)
28. B (p. 13)
29. C (pp. 17-18)
30. A (p. 10)
31. D (p. 8)
32. B (pp. 11-12)
33. D (p. 12)
34. C (pp. 17-18)
35. A (p. 18)
36. B (p. 5)
37. C (p. 7)
38. D (p. 12)
39. A (p. 19)
40. B (p. 5)

Short Answer Review

1.   social influence (p.3)
2.   behavior (p. 3)
3.   cultural (p. 3)
4.   thoughts (p. 3)
5.   imagined (p. 3)
6.   construal (p. 4)
7.   interpret (p. 4)
8.   experimentally (p. 5)
9.   objective (p. 5)
10.   correct (p. 7)
11.   philosophy (p. 7)
12.   scientifically (p. 7)
13.   educated guesses (p. 8)
14.   individual differences (p. 8)
15.   explaining (p. 8)
16.   level of analysis (p. 9)
17.   social situation (p. 10)
18.   Sociology (p. 10)
19.   universal properties (p. 10)
20.   personalities (p. 11)
21.   fundamental attribution error (p. 11)
22.   behaviorism (p. 12)
23.   cognition (p. 12)
24.   Gestalt (p. 13)
25.   subjective (p. 13)
26.   good about ourselves (p. 14)
27.   accurate (p. 14)
28.   self-esteem (p. 15)
29.   reality (p. 15)
30.   justifying (p. 16)
31.   social cognition (p. 17)
32.   accurately (p. 17)
33.   expectations (p. 17)
34.   self-fulfilling prophecy (p. 18)
35.   biological (p. 18)
36.   control (p. 18)
37.   social problems (p. 18)

Essay Review

1.   Your essay on social psychology should include:
     - Social psychology is the study of the way in which people's thoughts, feelings, and behaviors are influenced by the real or imagined presence of other people. (p. 3)
     - Construals are ways in which people perceive, comprehend, and interpret the social world. When we understand people's construals we can better understand why they react to their social environment the way they do. (p. 4)
     - When explaining social behavior, personality psychologists focus on individual differences—the aspects of people's personalities that make them different from others while social psychologists place more emphasis on the powerful role played by social influence. (p. 8)
     - The level of analysis is different for social psychologists and sociologists. Social psychology focuses on the individual while sociology looks toward society at large. (p. 10)

2.   Your essay on the power of social influence should include:
     - The barrier is known as the fundamental attribution error—the tendency to overestimate the extent to which people's behavior is due to internal, dispositional factors, and to underestimate the role of situational factors. (p. 11)
     - When we underestimate the power of social influence, we gain a feeling of false security. (p. 11)
     - Ross had students rated by their resident assistants in their dorm as to whether they were especially cooperative or competitive. Then the researchers had them play a game. The game was called either the Wall Street Game or the Community Game. The study found that a student's personality made no measurable difference in the student's behavior. When it was called the Wall Street Game, approximately two-thirds of the people responded competitively. When it was called the Community Game, only a third of the students responded competitively. (pp. 11-12)

3.   Your essay on these perspectives should include:
     - Behaviorism is a school of psychology maintaining that to understand human behavior, one need only consider the reinforcing properties of the environment—that is, how positive and negative events in the environment are associated with specific behaviors. (p. 12)
     - Gestalt psychology is a school of psychology stressing the importance of studying the subjective way in which an object appears in people's minds, rather than the objective, physical attributes of the object. (p. 13)

4.   Your discussion of where construals come from should include:
     - Social psychologists have found that the need to feel good about ourselves and the need to be accurate are of primary importance. (p. 14)
     - People may justify their past behavior in order to avoid the truth and feel better about themselves. If a person goes through a severe hazing to get into a fraternity but then finds being a member of the fraternity disappointing, the person will justify the decision to undergo the hazing by distorting the perception of the fraternity experience. (pp. 15-16)

5. Your essay on social cognition should include:
    - Social cognition refers to how people think about themselves and the social world; more specifically, how people select, interpret, remember, and use social information to make judgments and decisions. (p. 17)
    - It illustrated that expectations about the social world can interfere with perceiving it accurately. This was illustrated by the mere fact that the teachers were led to expect these students ("bloomers") to do well caused a reliable improvement in their performance. (p. 18)

Exit Test 1

1. C (p. 3)
2. B (p. 4)
3. A (p. 8)
4. A (p. 11)
5. D (p. 12)
6. A (p. 15)
7. B (p. 18)
8. A (p. 18)
9. C (p. 18)
10. B (p. 18)

Exit Test 2

1. B (p. 3)
2. D (p. 3)
3. A (p. 4)
4. B (p. 5)
5. C (p. 10)
6. D (p. 11)
7. A (p. 13)
8. C (p. 17)
9. B (p. 18)
10. B (p. 18)

Study Activities

1. Linda is most likely to identify psychological processes, like frustration, that produce aggression. Mark is likely to identify broad societal factors, like social class, that may affect aggression. (p. 10)

2. The self-esteem approach assumes that behavior is motivated by the desire to perceive ourselves favorably and that we may place a slightly different spin on reality to achieve this end. The social cognition approach assumes that we want to perceive the world accurately but that several obstacles may block this goal. (pp. 15-18)

3. Social psychology takes a scientific approach to the study of human behavior and folk wisdom does not. The scientific approach allows social psychology to explain the causes of behavior and demonstrate the conditions under which (sometimes opposite) behaviors will occur. (pp. 6-8)

4. Your example should reflect how an expectation actually caused a change in your social environment so that your expectation was confirmed. Expecting it to rain and finding that it does rain, for instance, is not an example of the self-fulfilling prophecy, because you did not cause it to rain. (p. 18)

5. Your essay should include instances of how pervasive social influence is and how we are not always aware of how it changes our behavior. (pp. 11-12)

6. The fundamental attribution error refers to the tendency to overestimate the extent to which people's behavior is due to internal, dispositional factors, and to underestimate the role of situational factors. We make this error because most of us go through life assuming that what really counts is an individual's personality. When we underestimate the power of social influence, we gain a feeling of false security. (pp. 11-12)

7. There is no right or wrong answer here. You could even say that both perspectives add to our understanding of human behavior. (pp. 12-13)

8. Self-justification involves making excuses for our past behaviors. We may put a different spin on what happened and even distort reality. People engage in self-justification in order to feel better about themselves. The consequence of this distortion is that learning from experience becomes very unlikely. (p. 15)

9. An assumption of the social cognition approach is that all people try to view the world as accurately as possible. Our expectations can interfere with perceiving the social world accurately. (pp. 17-18)

10. Additional motives include: biological drives, fear, the promise of love, favors and other rewards involving social exchange. (p. 18)

CHAPTER 2

Methodology: How Social Psychologists Do Research

CHAPTER 2 OVERVIEW

Chapter 2 contains the basic underlying principles of social psychological research. The reader is warned that the results of some of the experiments discussed will seem obvious because social psychology concerns topics with which we are all familiar. The thing to remember is that when we study human behavior, the results may appear to have been predictable—in retrospect. There is a well known human tendency called the **hindsight bias**, whereby people exaggerate how much they could have predicted an outcome *after* knowing that it occurred.

The first part of the chapter introduces you to the beginning of the research process, the formation of theories and hypotheses. Many studies stem from a researcher's dissatisfaction with existing theories and explanations. Social psychologists, like scientists in other disciplines, engage in a continual process of theory refinement: A theory is developed; specific hypotheses derived from that theory are tested; based on the results obtained, the theory is revised and new hypotheses are formulated.

The next part of the chapter discusses the types, advantages, and disadvantages of the observational method. The **observational method** is a technique whereby a researcher observes people and systematically records measurements or impressions of their behavior. One form of observational research is **ethnography**, the method by which researchers attempt to understand a group or culture by observing it from the inside, without imposing any preconceived notions they might have. To make sure that observations are not subjective, it is important to establish **interjudge reliability**, which is the level of agreement between two or more people who judge independently. The observational method is not limited to observations of real-life behavior. The researcher can also examine the accumulated documents, or archives, of a culture, a technique known as an **archival analysis**. There are limits to the observational method including: certain kinds of behaviors are difficult to observe, the researcher is at the mercy of the original compiler (with archival analysis), and the observational method can only be used to describe behavior but not to predict or explain it.

The third part of the chapter discusses the correlational method. The **correlational method** is a technique whereby two or more variables and the relationship between them are systematically measured. Researchers look at such relationships by calculating the **correlational coefficient**, a statistic that assesses how well you can predict one variable from another. The correlational method is often used in **surveys**, research in which a representative sample of people are asked questions about their attitudes or behavior. Surveys allow researchers to judge the relationship between variables that are difficult to observe and to sample representative segments of the population. **Random selection** can be used to ensure that a sample of people is representative of the population by giving everyone in the population an equal chance of being selected for the sample. A major shortcoming of the correlational method is that it tells us only that the two variables are related, whereas the goal of the social psychologist is to identify the *causes* of social behavior.

The fourth section explains the **experimental method**. This is the method in which the researcher randomly assigns participants to different conditions and ensures that these conditions are identical except for the independent variable. The **independent variable** is the variable a researcher changes or varies to see if it has an effect on some other variable. The **dependent variable** is the variable a researcher measures to see if it is influenced by the independent variable; the researcher hypothesizes that the dependent variable will depend on the level of the independent variable. By using **random assignment to condition,** researchers can be relatively certain that differences in the participants' personalities or backgrounds are distributed evenly across conditions. However, even with random assignment there is always the very small possibility that different characteristics of people did not distribute themselves evenly across conditions. The analyses of data come with a **probability level (*p*-value)**, which is a number, calculated with statistical techniques, that tells researchers how likely it is that the results of their experiment occurred by chance and not because of the independent variable.

The key to a good experiment is to maintain high **internal validity**, meaning we make sure that nothing besides the independent variable can affect the dependent variable. Also important is **external validity**, the extent to which the results of a study can be generalized to other situations and to other people. Research in social psychology is sometimes criticized for being conducted in artificial settings that cannot be generalized to real life. **Psychological realism** is the extent to which the psychological processes triggered in an experiment are similar to psychological processes that occur in everyday life. To maintain psychological realism a **cover story** may be used—a description of the purpose of a study, given to participants, that is different from its true purpose.

A good experiment is also generalizable across people. The only way to be certain that the results of an experiment represent the behavior of a particular population is to ensure that the participants are randomly selected from that population. Ideally, samples in experiments should be randomly selected but unfortunately, it is impractical and expensive to select random samples for most social psychology experiments.

One of the best ways to increase external validity is by conducting field experiments. In a **field experiment**, researchers study behavior outside of the laboratory, in its natural setting. There is almost always a trade-off between internal and external validity. We have the most control in a laboratory setting, but the laboratory may be unlike real life. The trade-off between internal and external validity has been referred to as the *basic dilemma of the social psychologist.* The way to resolve this dilemma is not to try to do it all in a single experiment.

Replications are the ultimate test of an experiment's external validity. **Replication** involves conducting the study again with different subject populations or in different settings. Often, when many studies on one problem are conducted, the results are somewhat variable. **Meta-analysis** is a statistical technique that averages the results of two or more studies to see if the effect of an independent variable is reliable.

The goal in **basic research** is to find the best answer to the question of why people behave as they do. **Applied research** refers to studies designed to solve a particular social problem. In social psychology the distinction between basic and applied research is fuzzy. Most social psychologists would agree that in order to solve a specific problem, we must understand the psychological processes responsible for it.

Social psychologists are always looking for new ways of investigating social behavior and in recent years some new approaches have received a good deal of attention. To find out how culturally dependent a psychological process is, social psychologists conduct cross-cultural research. **Cross-cultural research** is conducted with members of different cultures, to see whether the psychological processes of interest are present in both cultures or whether they are specific to the culture in which people were raised.

Evolutionary psychology attempts to explain social behavior in terms of genetic factors that evolved over time according to the principles of natural selection. **Natural selection** is the process by which heritable traits that promote survival in a particular environment are passed along to future generations, because organisms with that trait are more likely to produce offspring. The core idea of evolutionary psychology is that evolution occurs very slowly, such that social behaviors that are prevalent today are due at least in part to adaptations to environments in our distant pass.

Social psychologists have become increasingly interested in the connection between biological processes and social behavior. These include the study of hormones and behavior, the human immune system, and neurological processes in the human brain. Research in this area is in its infancy but promises to open up a whole new area of inquiry into the relationship of the brain to behavior.

Ethical issues in social psychology are discussed in the last section of the chapter. Psychological researchers must abide by strict guidelines to insure the welfare of participants in their research. To obtain **informed consent**, the researcher explains the nature of the experiment to participants before it begins and asks for their agreement to participate. **Deception** in social psychological research involves misleading participants about the true purpose of a study or the events that transpire. Deception is sometimes used so that participants will experience contrived events as if they were real. An **institutional review board (IRB)** is made up of at least one scientist, one nonscientist, and one member not affiliated with an institution who reviews all psychological research at that institution and decides whether it meets ethical guidelines. All research must be approved by the IRB before it is conducted. When deception is used in a study, the post-experimental interview, called the debriefing session, is both crucial and required. **Debriefing** is the process of explaining to the participants, at the end of the experiment, the true purpose of the study and exactly what transpired.

CHAPTER 2 OUTLINE

I. Social Psychology: An Empirical Science
• Empirical research allows us to test the validity of personal observations.
• Findings from social psychological research may appear obvious because they deal with familiar topics: social behavior and social influence.
• **Hindsight bias** is the tendency for people to exaggerate how much they could have predicted an outcome after knowing that it occurred.
• Social psychology relies on three types of methods—observational, correlational, and experimental—to provide empirical answers to questions about social behavior.

II. Formulating Hypotheses and Theories
• Research begins with a hunch, or *hypothesis*, that the researcher wants to test. Science is cumulative and people often generate hypotheses based on previous theories and research.

A. Inspiration from Earlier Theories and Research
• Many studies stem from a researcher's dissatisfaction with existing theories. For example, Festinger's cognitive dissonance theory was inspired by the inability of behaviorist theories to explain attitude change. In turn, his research inspired other researchers to generate and test alternative explanations, a process which led to revision and refinement of the theory.

B. Hypotheses Based on Personal Observations
• Social psychology deals with phenomena we encounter in everyday life. Researchers often observe something in their lives or the lives of others that they find curious and interesting, stimulating them to construct a theory about why this phenomenon occurred—and design a study to see if they are right. (e.g., Kitty Genovese and Latané & Darley's work on the *diffusion of responsibility*).
• Once researchers have a hypothesis, they can use the observational, correlational, and experimental methods to test it (see Table 2.1, p. 33).

III. The Observational Method: Describing Social Behavior

• The **observational method** is the technique whereby a researcher observes people and records measurements or impressions of their behavior.

• One example of an observational method is **ethnography**, the method by which researchers attempt to understand a group or culture by observing it from the inside, without imposing any preconceived notions they might have.

• The key to ethnography is to, as much as possible, avoid imposing one's preconceived notions in order to understand the point of view of the people being studied.

• Other times, researchers use observational methods to test a specific hypothesis. These studies use trained observers who code behavior according to a prearranged set of criteria.

• In such studies, it is important to establish **interjudge reliability**, the level of agreement between two or more people who independently observe and code a set of data. By showing that two or more judges independently come up with the same observations, researchers ensure that the observations are not the subjective, distorted impressions of one individual.

A. Archival Analysis

• **Archival analysis** is a form of the observational method whereby the researcher observes social behavior by examining accumulated documents of a culture (e.g., diaries, novels, magazines, and newspapers).

• In archival analysis, well-defined coding categories are created and applied to the archival source.

• Archival analysis can tell us a great deal about a society's values and beliefs. For example, archival analysis has been used to describe the content of "adults only" literature and photographs in America. Studies of pornography reveal high levels of depicted sexual violence by men against women, suggesting its appeal to readers.

B. Limits of the Observational Method

• Certain kinds of behavior are difficult to observe, because they occur rarely or in private.

• As is always the case with archival analysis, the researcher is at the mercy of the original compiler of the material.

• Perhaps the most important limitation is that social psychologists want to do more than describe behavior, they want to predict and explain it. To do so, other methods are more appropriate.

IV. The Correlational Method: Predicting Social Behavior

• A goal of social science is to understand the relationships between variables and to be able to predict when different kinds of social behavior will occur.

• The **correlational method** involves systematically measuring the relationship between two or more variables.

• The **correlation coefficient** is a statistical technique for calculating the degree of association between two variables. Positive correlations indicate that an increase in one variable is associated with an increase in the other, and negative correlations indicate that an increase in one variable is associated with a decrease in the other.

A. Surveys

• The correlational method is often used in surveys. **Surveys**, research in which a representative sample of people is asked (often anonymously) questions about their attitudes or behavior, are used when the variable of interest is not easily observable.

• The *sample* is the group of people actually tested. The validity of survey data depends on using samples that are representative of the population being studied. **Random selection**, in which everyone in the population has an equal chance of being selected, can ensure that a sample is representative.

• One possible problem with surveys is sampling errors (for example, the 1936 *Literary Digest* presidential poll fiasco, in which relying on telephone directories and automobile registries for the sample led to selecting a sample wealthier and more prone to vote Republican than voters in general).
• Survey questions that ask people to predict or explain their own behavior are likely to be inaccurate, as people often simply don't know the answer, but think they do.

B. Limits of the Correlational Method: Correlation Does Not Equal Causation
• The major shortcoming of the survey method is that it identifies only that two variables are related, whereas the goal of the social psychologist is to identify the *causes* of social behavior. We want to be able to say that A causes B, not just that A is correlated with B.

V. The Experimental Method: Answering Causal Questions
• Only the **experimental method**, in which the researcher randomly assigns participants to different conditions and ensures that these conditions are identical except for the independent variable, can determine causality.

A. Independent and Dependent Variables
• The **independent variable** is the variable a researcher changes or varies to see if it has an effect on some other variable. The **dependent variable** is the one measured by the researcher to see if changes depend on the level of the independent variable (see Figure 2.2, p. 44).
• Experiments can determine whether or not one variable is in fact *a* cause; however, this does not mean that such a variable is the only cause.

B. Internal Validity in Experiments
• An experiment has high **internal validity** when everything is the same in the different levels of the independent variable, except for the one factor of concern. Internal validity is established by controlling all extraneous variables and by using random assignment to conditions. In **random assignment to condition**, each participant has an equal probability of being assigned to any of the experimental conditions. Random assignment helps ensure that the participants in the two groups are unlikely to differ in any systematic way.
• Even with random assignment, there is a small probability that different characteristics of people are distributed differently across conditions. To guard against misinterpreting the results in such an event, scientists calculate the **probability level (*p*-value),** a number calculated with statistical techniques that tells researchers how likely it is that their experimental results would occur by chance. By convention, a *p*-value of less than or equal to 5 chances in 100 that an event would occur by chance is considered to be statistically significant.

C. External Validity in Experiments
• **External validity** is the extent to which the results of a study can be generalized to other situations and other people.
1. Generalizability across Situations
• Laboratory research in social psychology is sometimes criticized for being conducted in artificial settings. However, there are different ways in which an experiment can be realistic. An experiment is high in **psychological realism** to the extent to which the psychological processes triggered are similar to the psychological processes occurring in everyday life. Psychological realism often depends upon the creation of an effective **cover story**, or false description of the purpose of the study. Cover stories are used because if participants are forewarned about the true purpose of the study, they will plan their response, and we will not know how they would act in the real world. Thus cover stories increase psychological realism.

31

2. Generalizability across People
• The only way to be certain that the results of an experiment represent the behavior of a certain population is to randomly select from that population. However, this may be impractical and expensive. Social psychologists often assume that the psychological processes studied are basic components of human nature and thus similar across different populations. To be truly certain of this, however, studies should be replicated with different populations.

3. Field Research
• One of the best ways to increase external validity is by conducting field experiments. In **field experiments**, researchers study behavior outside of the laboratory, in its natural setting.
• There is often a trade-off between internal and external validity—making a situation more controlled makes it less realistic, and making it realistic makes it less controlled.

4. Replications
• This trade-off has been referred to as the *basic dilemma of the social psychologist* (Aronson & Carlsmith, 1968). The way to resolve this dilemma is not to try to do it all in a single experiment.
• **Replication** is repetition of a study, often with different populations or in different settings. This provides the ultimate test of an experiment's external validity.
• **Meta-analysis** is a statistical technique that averages the results of two or more studies to see if the effect of an independent variable is reliable.
• Most of the studies in the book have been replicated with different populations and/or settings.

D. Basic Versus Applied Research
• **Basic research** tries to find the best answer to the question of why people behave the way they do, purely to satisfy intellectual curiosity. **Applied research** tries to solve a specific social problem. However, in practice, the distinction between basic and applied research is often fuzzy.
• Most social psychologists would agree that in order to solve a specific social problem, we must understand the psychological processes responsible for it.

VI. NEW Frontiers in Social Psychological Research
• Social psychologists are always looking for new ways of investigating social behavior and in recent years some new approaches have received a good deal of attention.

A. Culture and Social Psychology
• **Cross-cultural research** is conducted with members of different cultures to see whether the psychological processes of interest are present in both cultures or whether they are specific to the culture in which people were raised.
• Some findings in social psychology are culture-dependent.
• Cross-cultural researchers always have to guard against imposing their own viewpoints and definitions, learned from their culture, onto another culture with which they are unfamiliar.

B. The Evolutionary Approach
• **Natural selection** is the process by which heritable traits that promote survival in a particular environment are passed along to future generations, because organisms with that trait are more likely to produce offspring.
• **Evolutionary psychology** attempts to explain social behavior in terms of genetic factors that evolved over time according to the principles of natural selection.
• The core idea of evolutionary psychology is that evolution occurs very slowly, such that social behaviors that are prevalent today are due at least in part to adaptations to environments in our distant past.

C. Social Neuroscience
• Social psychologists have become increasingly interested in the connection between biological processes and social behavior.
• These include the study of hormones and behavior, the human immune system, and neurological processes in the human brain.

E. The Basic Dilemma of the Social Psychologist
• One of the best ways to increase external validity is through **field experiments**, experiments conducted in real-world settings.
• There is often a trade-off between internal and external validity—making a situation more controlled makes it less realistic, and making it realistic makes it less controlled. This trade-off has been referred to as the *basic dilemma of the social psychologist* (Aronson & Carlsmith, 1968). The resolution to this dilemma is the use of replication in both laboratory and field settings.

VII. Ethical Issues in Social Psychology
• Social psychologists face the tension between wanting experiments to be realistic and wanting to avoid causing participants unnecessary stress and unpleasantness.
• The dilemma is less problematic when researchers can obtain **informed consent**, specifying the nature of the experiment and getting permission from the participants before the experiment is conducted. However, in some cases, full disclosure of the procedures would influence the nature of the results, and in this case, **deception** experiments are used, where only partial or misleading information about the procedures is given to participants in advance.

A. Guidelines for Ethical Research
• Ethical principles of psychologists in the conduct of research are summarized in Figure 2.3, p. 53.
• Any institution that seeks federal funding for psychological research is required to have an institutional review board that reviews research before it is conducted. An **institutional review board (IRB)** is a group made up of at least one scientist, one nonscientist, and one member not affiliated with an institution that reviews all psychological research at that institution and decides whether it meets ethical guidelines.
• These ethical principles specify, among other things, that researchers who do deception experiments conduct a **debriefing**, or explicit statement to the participant about what deception was used and why it was necessary. During the debriefing, researchers attempt to alleviate any discomfort that occurred during the session, and discuss the research with them. Studies examining the impact of deception experiments on participants have typically found that participants do not object to the mild discomfort that is typically produced, and in fact often find such experiments more interesting to participate in than non-deception experiments.

LEARNING OBJECTIVES

After you read Chapter 2, you should be able to do the following:

1. Explain why social psychological results sometimes appear obvious. (p. 24)

2. Describe the process of theory refinement. (p. 26)

3. Identify the origins of hypotheses. (p. 26)

4. Identify the three research methods that are used to test/explore hypotheses. (p. 26)

5. Identify the goal of the observational method. Describe ethnography, interjudge reliability and archival analysis. (pp. 27-29)

6. Describe the limitations of the observational method in general and a limitation unique to archival analysis. (p. 29)

7. Identify the goal of the correlational method. Discuss and define the characteristics of a correlation and a correlation coefficient. Describe what is meant by positive correlation and negative correlation. (pp. 29-30)

8. Identify the role of surveys and samples in conducting correlational research. Explain the importance of selecting samples randomly. Identify potential threats to obtaining accurate survey results. Define random selection. (pp. 30-31)

9. Distinguish between correlation and causation. (pp. 31-32)

10. Explain why the experimental method is the method of choice in most social psychological research. (p. 33)

11. Distinguish between independent and dependent variables. (p. 35)

12. Define internal validity. Identify factors that threaten the internal validity of an experiment. Define random assignment to conditions and explain why it is necessary to internal validity. Explain the difference between random assignment and random selection. (pp. 30, 36-37)

13. Define the term probability value and explain what a p-value tells us. Explain why probability levels are associated with statistics in experimental science. Describe the conditions under which results are considered statistically significant. (p. 36)

14. Define external validity. Identify the two kinds of generalizability that concern researchers. (pp. 37-38)

15. Define psychological realism. Discuss the role of the cover story in making experiments realistic. (pp. 37-38)

16. Compare and contrast lab experiments and field experiments. Describe the relationship between internal and external validity and each type of experimental setting. (pp. 38-39)

17. Describe the basic dilemma of the social psychologist. Identify a solution to this dilemma. (p. 39)

18. Explain what it means to replicate a study and identify what replications serve as the ultimate test for. (pp. 39-40)

19. Describe the meta-analysis technique. Identify the purpose and goal of this method. (p. 40)

20. Contrast the goals of basic and applied research. Discuss the relationship between these types of research. (pp. 40-41)

21. Identify the benefits and goals of cross-cultural research. Discuss precautions researchers should take when doing cross-cultural research. (pp. 41-42)

22. Explain natural selection and define evolutionary psychology. (p. 42)

23. Discuss the nature of research done by social neuroscientists. (p. 43)

24. Identify the ethical issues/concerns of social psychologists. Describe the ethical dilemma faced by social psychologists and the role of informed consent in resolving this dilemma. (pp. 43-44)

25. Identify what it means to use deception in an experiment. Identify the requirements set forth in the APA guidelines for treating participants ethically. (p. 44)

26. Describe the function of the Institutional Review Board (IRB). Explain the necessity and functions of a debriefing session. Discuss the effects on participants of being deceived. (p. 44)

KEY TERMS

1. _____ The tendency for people to exaggerate how much they could have predicted an outcome after knowing that it occurred. (p. 24)

2. _____ The technique whereby a researcher observes people and systematically records measurements or impressions of their behavior. (p. 27)

3. _____ The method by which researchers attempt to understand a group or culture by observing it from the inside, without imposing any preconceived notions they might have. (p. 27)

4. _____ The level of agreement between two or more people who independently observe and code a set of data; by showing that two or more judges independently come up with the same observations, researchers ensure that the observations are not the subjective, distorted impressions of one individual. (p. 27)

5. _____ A form of the observational method in which the researcher examines the accumulated documents, or archives, of a culture. (p. 27)

6. _____ The technique whereby two or more variables are systematically measured and the relationship between them is assessed. (p. 29)

7. _____ A statistical technique that assesses how well you can predict one variable from another. (p. 30)

8. _____ Research in which a representative sample of people are asked questions about their attitudes or behavior. (p. 30)

9. _____ A way of ensuring that a sample of people is representative of a population by giving everyone in the population an equal chance of being selected for the sample. (p. 30)

10. _____ The method in which the researcher randomly assigns participants to different conditions and ensures that these conditions are identical except for the independent variable. (p. 33)

11. _____ The variable a researcher changes or varies to see if it has an effect on some other variable. (p. 35)

12. _____ The variable a researcher measures to see if it is influenced by the independent variable. (p. 35)

13. _____ A process ensuring that all participants have an equal chance of taking part in any condition of an experiment. (p. 36)

14. _____ A number calculated with statistical techniques that tells researchers how likely it is that the results of their experiment occurred by chance and not because of the independent variable or variables. (p. 36)

15. _____ Making sure that nothing besides the independent variable can affect the dependent variable. (p. 36)

16. _____ The extent to which the results of a study can be generalized to other situations and to other people. (p. 37)

17. _____ The extent to which the psychological processes triggered in an experiment are similar to psychological processes that occur in everyday life. (p. 37)

18. _____ A description of the purpose of a study given to participants, that is different from its true purpose, used to maintain psychological realism. (p. 38)

19. _____ Experiments conducted in natural settings rather than in the laboratory. (p. 38)

20. _____ Repeating a study, often with different subject populations or in different settings. (p. 39)

21. _____ A statistical technique that averages the results of two or more studies to see if the effect of an independent variable is reliable. (p. 40)

22. _____ Studies that are designed to find the best answer to the question of why people behave as they do and that are conducted purely for reasons of intellectual curiosity. (p. 40)

23. _____ Studies designed to solve a particular social problem. (p. 40)

24. _____ Research conducted with members of different cultures, to see whether the psychological processes of interest are present in both cultures or whether they are specific to the culture in which people were raised. (p. 41)

25. _____ The process by which heritable traits that promote survival in a particular environment are passed along to future generations, because organisms with that trait are more likely to produce offspring. (p. 42)

26. _____ The attempt to explain social behavior in terms of genetic factors that evolved over time according to the principles of natural selection. (p. 42)

27. _____ Agreement to participate in an experiment, granted in full awareness of the nature of the experiment, which has been explained in advance. (p. 44)

28. _____ Misleading participants about the true purpose of a study or the events that will actually transpire. (p. 44)

29. _____ A group made up of at least one scientist, one nonscientist, and one member not affiliated with an institution that reviews all psychological research at that institution and decides whether it meets ethical guidelines. (p. 44)

30. _____ Explaining to participants, at the end of an experiment, the true purpose of the study and exactly what transpired. (p. 44)

GUIDED REVIEW

PRACTICE TEST

1. From dissonance theory, Leon Festinger was able to make specific predictions about when and how people would change their attitudes. We call these specific predictions:
    a) theories.
    b) hypotheses.
    c) observations.
    d) methods.

2. Using archival analyses, scientists describe a culture by:
    a) surveying a representative sample of members in a culture.
    b) observing the behavior of members in a culture.
    c) manipulating archives and measuring subsequent responses.
    d) examining documents like magazines, diaries, and suicide notes.

3. When INCREASES in the value of one variable are associated with DECREASES in the value of the other variable, then the variables are:
    a) positively correlated.
    b) negatively correlated.
    c) uncorrelated.
    d) independent.

4. As long as the sample is selected randomly, we can assume that the sampled responses:
    a) are a reasonable match to responses of the whole population.
    b) correlate with one another.
    c) reflect the true beliefs and opinions of the individuals sampled.
    d) are determined by chance factors.

5. From studies which indicate that viewing television violence is positively correlated with aggressive behavior in children, we can conclude that:
    a) watching violence on television may cause aggressive behavior.
    b) the aggressive personalities of some children may cause them to prefer violence on television.
    c) some third factor like a hostile home environment may cause some children to both prefer violence on television and to behave aggressively.
    d) the more children view violence on television the more aggressive their behavior becomes.

6. A "____ experiment" is identical in design to a laboratory experiment except that it is conducted in a real-life setting.
    a) situational
    b) field
    c) quasi
    d) real-life

7. How should research be conducted in order to resolve the basic dilemma of the social psychologist?
    a) By trying not to do it all in a single experiment but instead doing replications; conduct some experiments that have internal validity and others that have external validity.
    b) Conduct carefully designed experiments that have both internal and external validity.
    c) Do all research in the field.
    d) Conduct applied rather than basic research.

8. Which of the following is a statistical technique that allows researchers to test how reliable the effects of an independent variable are over many replications?
    a) correlation coefficient
    b) deception
    c) meta-analysis
    d) double blind

9. Two individuals independently observe the same behavior at a playground. If one reports seven instances of "aggression" and the other records seventeen such instances, then ____ will be low.
    a) interjudge reliability
    b) internal validity
    c) generalizability
    d) external validity

10. Height and weight are ____ correlated.
    a) negatively
    b) positively
    c) not
    d) insignificantly

11. Latané and Darley (1968) varied the number of witnesses to an emergency and measured helping behavior. In this experiment _____ was the independent variable and _____ was the dependent variable.
    a)   helping behavior; the number of witnesses
    b)   the number of witnesses; helping behavior
    c)   the emergency; helping behavior
    d)   number of witnesses; the emergency

12. When the only aspect that varies across conditions in an experiment is the independent variable(s), the experiment is said to have:
    a)   internal validity.
    b)   external validity.
    c)   reliability.
    d)   generalizability.

13. Social psychologists are most concerned with generalizability across:
    a)   independent and dependent variables.
    b)   theories and hypotheses.
    c)   identical experiments.
    d)   situations and people.

14. Matt is sitting in a room waiting to take part in a psychology experiment when smoke begins pouring out of a vent in the ceiling. Matt does not realize it, but this is actually part of the experiment. He becomes very concerned that there is actually a fire somewhere in the building. This experiment
    a)   does not have psychological realism.
    b)   has psychological realism.
    c)   is a field experiment.
    d)   cannot possibly have external validity.

15. The basic dilemma of the social psychologist is that:
    a)   there is usually a tradeoff in experiments between internal and external validity.
    b)   individual differences among participants can never be ruled out as alternative explanations for experimental results.
    c)   there is a tradeoff between mundane and psychological realism.
    d)   people behave differently when they are being observed.

16. While _____ research aims to solve a specific problem, _____ research tries to understand human social behavior purely for reasons of intellectual curiosity.
    a)   basic; applied
    b)   applied; basic
    c)   theoretical; practical
    d)   practical; theoretical

17. Which of the following is among the American Psychological Association's list of guidelines for conducting ethical research in psychology?
    a) The results of the study must be revealed during a debriefing.
    b) No research procedures may be used to deceive subjects about the true nature of the study.
    c) Psychologists have a primary obligation, and take reasonable precautions, to protect confidential information.
    d) All participants must agree to complete the experiment once it has begun.

18. What is the best research method to use to find out if watching violent pornography affects men's attitudes toward women?
    a) case study
    b) participant observation
    c) experiment
    d) survey

19. Why is the experiment considered the method of choice by most social psychologists?
    a) It is the least expensive method.
    b) It is the only method that describes human behavior.
    c) It is the only method that discovers correlational relationships between variables.
    d) It is the only method that allows the experimenter to make causal inferences.

20. Which of the following do social psychologists calculate to determine whether or not the results of their study are statistically significant?
    a) the significance level (s-value)
    b) the functional level (f-value)
    c) the probability level (p-value)
    d) the correlational value (c-value)

21. Dr. Gomez studies different cultures by becoming a part of the cultural group being investigated. Dr. Gomez most likely is using the _____ method.
    a) experiment
    b) case study
    c) ethnography
    d) archival analysis

22. The purpose of the cover story is:
    a) to deceive participants to make them give researchers data that supports their hypotheses.
    b) to maintain psychological realism.
    c) to decrease mundane realism.
    d) to increase external validity.

23. Which of the following is one of the new frontiers in social psychological research?
    a) cross-cultural research
    b) the evolutionary approach
    c) social neuroscience
    d) all of the above

24. What must follow the research study, especially when deception is used?
    a) informed consent
    b) debunking
    c) debriefing
    d) a cover story

25. Which statement is true regarding theory refinement in social psychology?
    a) Once a theory is developed, it cannot be modified.
    b) Social psychologists continuously refine theories based on their observations of how society is changing.
    c) Social psychologists continuously refine theories based on empirical tests of their theories.
    d) Once a hypothesis derived from a theory is disproved, the theory cannot be refined.

26. An experiment has external validity when:
    a) the only aspect that varies across conditions in the experiment is the independent variable.
    b) the experimental situation is similar to events that often happen in everyday life.
    c) the results of the experiment generalize across situations and people.
    d) the experiment satisfies the researcher's goal to solve a specific problem.

27. Dr. Sanchez conducted an experiment to find out how facial expressions affect impressions of people. Participants had a discussion with someone (the experimenter) who either smiled a lot, frowned a lot, or kept a neutral facial expression throughout the interaction. The participants then filled out a questionnaire to indicate their gender, ethnicity, and how much they liked the experimenter. The independent variable is _____ and the dependent variable is _____.
    a) gender; liking
    b) ethnicity; liking
    c) liking; facial expression
    d) facial expression; liking

28. Suppose that a study assessing the relationship between alcohol consumption and students' grade point average (GPA) found a negative correlation between the amount of alcohol that students drink and their GPA. The best conclusion from this study would be:
    a) something about drinking alcohol tends to make people have a lower GPA.
    b) something about drinking alcohol tends to make people have a higher GPA.
    c) if one knows how much alcohol a student drinks, one can predict quite well the student's GPA.
    d) having a high GPA tends to cause people to drink less.

29. Upon reading the results of a psychology study in her textbook, Debra thinks "the results of that study are so obvious. I knew that all along!" This illustrates which phenomena?
    a) a self-fulfilling prophecy
    b) the hindsight bias
    c) the fundamental attribution error
    d) retrospective memory

30. _____ refers to the process of ensuring each person in an experiment has an equal chance of taking part in any condition; _____ is a way of ensuring that the sample of people in a study is representative of a population.
    a) Random assignment; random selection
    b) Random selection; random assignment
    c) Self-selection; random selection
    d) Random selection; self-selection

31. A fundamental principle of social psychology is that many social problems can be studied _____.
    a) through casual observations
    b) ethnographically
    c) using only archival analysis
    d) scientifically

32. The key to _____ is to avoid, as much as possible, imposing one's preconceived notions in order to understand the point of view of the people being studied.
    a) the observational method
    b) ethnography
    c) interjudge reliability
    d) experimentation

33. Dr. Agger wants to study how images of women and men in magazine advertisements have changed over the last 50 years. Which research method should Dr. Agger use?
    a) archival analysis
    b) experimental method
    c) correlational method
    d) ethnography

34. _____ is the process by which heritable traits that promote survival in a particular environment are passed along to future generations, because organisms with that trait are more likely to produce offspring.
    a) Evolutionary psychology
    b) The evolutionary approach
    c) Natural selection
    d) Instinctual drift

35. _____ are a convenient way of measuring people's attitudes.
    a) Surveys
    b) Correlational studies
    c) Experiments
    d) Observations

36. The large survey conducted by the *Literary Digest* in 1936 asking people which candidate they planned to vote for in the upcoming presidential election, failed to make a correct prediction because they
    a) did not sample enough people.
    b) relied on correlations.
    c) did not randomly assign to conditions.
    d) relied on telephone directories and automobile registrations to obtain their sample and during the Depression most people could not afford telephones and cars.

37.   Correlation
    a)   always proves causation.
    b)   does not prove causation.
    c)   sometimes proves causation, if you collect enough data.
    d)   sometimes proves causation, if you calculate the probability level (*p*-value).

38.   The convention in science, including social psychology, is to consider results significant if the probability level is less than _____ in 100.
    a)   5
    b)   10
    c)   15
    d)   20

39.   A goal of many cross-cultural studies is to explore the differences between us by examining how culture influences
    a)   all behavior.
    b)   the behavior of people in groups.
    c)   basic social psychological processes.
    d)   personality traits.

40.   Dr. Reid is conducting a study on childfree couples just to learn more about them. Dr. Reid is conducting _____ research.
    a)   experimental
    b)   ethnographic
    c)   basic
    d)   applied

SHORT ANSWER REVIEW

A fundamental principle of social psychology is that many social problems can be studied (1)

_____ (p. 24). One thing to remember is that when we study human behavior, the results may

appear to have been predictable—in retrospect. There is a well-known human tendency called the (2)

_____ (p. 24), whereby people exaggerate how much they could have predicted an outcome

after knowing that it occurred. Social psychology is a scientific discipline with a well-developed set of

methods to answer questions about social behavior. These methods are of three types: the (3)

_____ (p. 24), the (4) _____ (p. 24), and the (5) _____ (p. 24).

Research begins with a hunch, or (6) _____ (p. 25), that the researcher wants to test.

Many studies stem from a researcher's dissatisfaction with (7) _____ (p. 25) and

explanations. After reading other people's work, a researcher might believe that he or she has a better way of explaining people's behavior. Social scientists engage in a continual process of (8) _____ (p. 26). A theory is developed; specific hypotheses derived from that theory are (9) _____ (p. 26); based on the results obtained, the theory is (10) _____ (p. 26) and new hypotheses are formulated. Social psychology deals with phenomenon we encounter in everyday life. Researchers often observe something in their lives or the (11) _____ (p. 26) that they find curious and interesting, stimulating them to construct a theory about why this phenomenon occurred—and to design a study to see if they are right.

If the goal of research is to describe what a particular group of people or type of behavior is like, the (12) _____ (p. 27) method is very helpful. This is the technique whereby a researcher observes people and records measurements or impressions of their (13) _____ (p. 27). One example of an observational method is ethnography, the method by which researchers attempt to understand a group or culture by observing it from the (14) _____ (p. 27). The goal is to understand the richness and complexity of the group by observing it in action. The key to ethnography is to avoid, as much as possible, imposing one's preconceived notions in order to understand the point of view of the people being studied. Sometimes, however, researchers have a specific hypothesis that they want to test using the observational method. When observations are made it is important to establish interjudge reliability, which is the level of (15) _____ (p. 27) between two or more people who independently observe and code a set of data.

The observational method is not limited to observations of real-life behavior. The researcher can also examine the (16) _____ (p. 27), or archives, of a culture, a technique known as an archival analysis. For example, diaries, novels, suicide notes, popular music lyrics, television shows, movies, magazines and newspaper articles, and advertising all tell us a great deal about how a society (17) _____ (p. 27). There are drawbacks to the observational method. Certain kinds of behavior are difficult to observe because they occur only rarely or occur only in (18) _____

(p. 29). With archival analysis the researcher is at the mercy of the original compiler of the material.

Perhaps most importantly, social psychologists want to do more than just (19) _____ (p. 29)

behavior, they want to predict and explain it.

A goal of social science is to understand relationships between (20) _____

(p. 29) and to be able to predict when different kinds of social behavior will occur. With the correlational

method, two variables are (21) _____ (p. 29), and the relationship between them is assessed.

Researchers look at such relationships by calculating the correlation coefficient, a (22) _____

(p. 30) that assesses how well you can predict one variable from another. A (23) _____ (p.

30) correlation means that increases in the value of one variable are associated with increases in the value

of the other variable. A negative correlation means that increases in the value of one variable are

associated with decreases in the value of the other.

The correlational method is often used in (24) _____ (p. 30), research in which a

representative sample of people are asked questions about their attitudes or behavior. Surveys have a

number of advantages, one of which is allowing researchers to judge the relationship between variables

that are (25) _____ (p. 30). Another advantage of surveys is the capability to sample (26)

_____ (p. 30) of the population. Researchers make sure to use a (27) _____ (p.

30) of people from the population at large, which is a way of ensuring that a sample of people is

representative of a population by giving everyone in the population an equal chance of being selected for

the sample. The major shortcoming of the correlational method is that it tells us only that two variables

are related, whereas the goal of the social psychologist is to identify the (28) _____ (p. 32) of

social behavior.

The only way to determine causal relationships is with the (29) _____ (p. 33)

method. Here, the researcher systematically orchestrates the event so that people experience it in one way or another way. The experimental method always involves a direct (30) _____ (p. 34) on the

part of the researcher. In an experiment, the independent variable is the variable a researcher changes or

varies to see if it has an (31) _____ (p. 35) on some other variable. The dependent variable is

the variable a researcher (32) _____ (p. 35) to see if it is influenced by the independent

variable.

Keeping everything but the independent variable the same in an experiment is referred to as (33)

_____ (p. 36). Random assignment to condition is a technique that allows experimenters to

minimize differences among (34) _____ (p. 36) as the cause of the results. The analyses of

data come with a (35) _____ (p. 36), which is a number, calculated with statistical

techniques, that tells researchers how likely it is that the results of their experiment occurred by chance

and not because of the independent variable. The key to a good experiment is to maintain high (36)

_____ (p. 36), which we can now define as making sure that the independent variable, and

only the independent variable, influences the dependent variable; this is accomplished by controlling all

extraneous variables and by randomly assigning people to different experimental conditions.

For all the advantages of the experimental method, there are some drawbacks. By virtue of

gaining enough control over the situation so as to randomly assign people to conditions and rule out the

effects of extraneous variables, the situation can become somewhat (37) _____ (p. 37) and

distant from real life. External validity is the extent to which the results of a study can be (38)

_____ (p. 37) to other situations and other people. Psychologists attempt to maximize the

study's (39) _____ (p. 37), which is the extent to which the psychological processes triggered

in an experiment are similar to psychological processes that occur in everyday life. Psychological realism

is heightened if people feel involved in a real event. To accomplish this, experimenters often tell

participants a cover story—a disguised version of the study's true (40) _____ (p. 38).

One of the best ways to increase (41) _____ (p. 38) is by conducting field experiments. In a field experiment, researchers study behavior outside of the laboratory in its natural setting. There is almost always a trade-off between internal and external validity. We have the most control in a (42) _____ (p. 39) setting, but the laboratory may be unlike real life. Real life can best be captured by doing a field experiment, but it is very difficult to control all (43) _____ (p. 39) variables in such studies. The trade-off between internal and external validity has been referred to as the (44) _____ (p. 39). The way to resolve this dilemma is not to try to do it all in a single experiment. (45) _____ (p. 39) are the ultimate test of an experiment's external validity. Only by conducting studies in different settings, with different populations, can we determine how generalizable the results are. Often when many studies on one problem are conducted, the results are somewhat variable. Fortunately, there is a statistical technique called (46) _____ (p. 40) that averages the results of two or more studies to see if the effect of an independent variable is reliable.

The goal in (47) _____ (p. 51) research is to find the best answer to the question of why people behave as they do, purely for reasons of intellectual curiosity. In contrast, applied research is geared toward solving a particular social problem.

Social psychologists are always looking for new ways of investigating social behavior and in recent years some new approaches have received a good deal of attention. To study the effects of culture on social psychological processes, social psychologists conduct (48) _____ (p. 41) research. (49) _____ (p. 42) attempts to explain social behavior in terms of genetic factors that evolved over time according to the principles of natural selection. Human beings are (50) _____ (p. 43) organisms and social psychologists have become increasingly interested in the connection between biological processes and social behavior.

Researchers are concerned about the health and welfare of the individuals participating in their experiments. Researchers are also in the process of discovering important information about human social behavior. To do this, experimenters may have to expose people to situations that can make them uncomfortable. The dilemma would be less problematic if researchers could obtain (51)

_____ (p. 44) from their participants before their participation. To obtain informed consent, the researcher explains the nature of the experiment to participants before it begins and asks for their agreement to participate. Sometimes deception is necessary in social psychological research. This involves misleading participants about the true nature and purpose of a study or the events that will transpire. To ensure that the dignity and safety of research participants are protected, the American Psychological Association has published a list of ethical principles that govern all research in psychology. In addition, any institution that seeks federal funding for psychological research is required to have an institutional review board (IRB) that reviews research before it is conducted. When deception is used in a study, the postexperimental interview, called the (52) _____ (p. 44) session, is crucial and must occur. Debriefing is the process of explaining to the participants, at the end of an experiment, the true purpose of the study and exactly what transpired.

ESSAY REVIEW

1. Write an essay describing how research begins and studies originate. Also describe the process of theory refinement.

2. Discuss the observational method and its types. Also define what is meant by interjudge reliability and explain why it is important.

3. Identify what the correlational method is. What is a correlation coefficient and what does it tell us? What is a limitation of the correlational method?

4. Describe the experimental method and the variables involved.

5. Identify the two types of validity important in experimental research. Define psychological realism.

EXIT TESTS

EXIT TEST 1

1. James has just learned about the case of Kitty Genovese and the bystander effect in his social
    psychology class. After learning this information James says, "Well, I could have told you that no
    one would do anything to help Kitty. It is obvious that everyone would assume someone else
    would call the police." James' belief illustrates the _____.
    a) expectancy effect
    b) predictable outcome effect
    c) hindsight bias
    d) clairvoyant effect

2. _____ is the method by which researchers attempt to understand a group or culture by observing
    it from the inside.
    a) Ethnography
    b) Participant observation
    c) Cross-cultural research
    d) The field experiment

3. When INCREASES in the value of one variable are associated with INCREASES in the value of
    the other variable, then the variables are:
    a) positively correlated.
    b) negatively correlated.
    c) uncorrelated.
    d) independent.

4. Dr. Chi wants to determine whether consuming products containing artificial sweeteners causes
    an increase in appetite. Which of the following methods should Dr. Chi use?
    a) observational method
    b) survey method
    c) correlational method
    d) experimental method

5. Dr. DePaepe is conducting a study to test a new drug for Alzheimer's disease. She is giving the
    drug to patients to see if it will decrease their symptoms of Alzheimer's. What is Dr. DePaepe's
    independent variable?
    a) the symptoms of Alzheimer's
    b) the patients
    c) the time of day the patient receives the drug
    d) the drug being tested

6. Which of the following can be used to increase internal validity in an experiment?
    a) random selection
    b) random assignment to condition
    c) study only one independent variable at a time
    d) study only one dependent variable at a time

7. The experimental method is the perfect research tool because it has no limitations.
    a) True
    b) False

Chapter 2

8. Dr. Munz is conducting an experiment in which he pumps smoke into a vent in a waiting room in order to see if the number of research participants in the room has an effect on whether or not any one research participant will go looking for help. Dr. Munz is concerned about whether the participants will believe the threat is real or will simply think "that researcher must be up to something." Dr. Munz is concerned about
   a) believability quotient.
   b) expectancy effect.
   c) psychological realism.
   d) mundane realism.

9. Dr. Milgram told his research participants that he was studying the effects of punishment on learning when he was really studying obedience. Dr. Milgram's deception is called a cover story.
   a) True
   b) False

10. Numerous studies have been conducted to study the effects of viewing television violence on aggressive behavior in children. These studies have had mixed results. To determine whether there really is a relationship between these variables which of the following should be used?
   a) correlational study
   b) a survey
   c) ethnographic research
   d) meta-analysis

EXIT TEST 2

1. Dr. Fritschner is studying how parents interact with their children by watching them in public places such as parks and fast food restaurants. Dr. Fritschner is using the _____ method.
   a) observational
   b) ethnographic
   c) correlational
   d) archival

2. One limitation of the correlational method is that it cannot be used to predict or explain behavior.
   a) True
   b) False

3. Dr. Williams wants to learn more about people's attitudes about, and behavior in, families. Which method should she use?
   a) correlational
   b) experimental
   c) survey
   d) archival

4. The Literary Digest conducted one of the first political polls in 1936 and correctly predicted the winner of the upcoming presidential election.
   a) True
   b) False

5. The experimental method always involves a direct intervention on the part of the researcher.
   a) True
   b) False

6. Dr. Hilgard is studying the effects of different hypnosis methods on the perception of pain. Dr. Hilgard's dependent variable is
   a) hypnosis.
   b) different types of hypnosis.
   c) the hypnotized participants.
   d) the perception of pain.

7. Dr. Kelley has analyzed data from her experiment and found that her probability level (*p*-value) is less than 5 in 100. She can conclude that
   a) 95% of her participants provided valid data.
   b) 5% of her participants provided valid data.
   c) her results are probably due to the independent variable.
   d) her results are probably due to an extraneous variable.

8. The only way to be certain that the results of an experiment represent the behavior of a particular population is to ensure that the participants
   a) are randomly assigned to conditions.
   b) are randomly selected from that population.
   c) make up at least 30% of the population.
   d) make up at least 40% of the population.

9. Conducting cross-cultural research simply involves traveling to another culture, translating materials into the local language, and replicating a study there.
   a) True
   b) False

10. To study the brain and its relation to behavior, psychologists use sophisticated technologies, including
    a) electrocardiogram (EKG) and functional magnetic resonance imaging (*f*MRI).
    b) electrocardiogram (EKG) and magnetic resonance imaging (MRI).
    c) electroencephalography (EEG) and electrocardiogram (EKG).
    d) electroencephalography (EEG) and functional magnetic resonance imaging (*f*MRI).

STUDY ACTIVITIES

1. Why must the independent variable be the only thing that varies between the groups in an experiment?

2. What is the primary limitation of carefully controlled laboratory experiments and how can this limitation be overcome?

3. Under what conditions can deception experiments be conducted, and what procedures must be followed if deception is used?

4. A local news program asks viewers to place a 50-cent call to the station in order to survey opinions on gun control. Near the end of the program a reporter announces "Our survey results indicate that community members overwhelmingly support gun control." Why should you be skeptical about the conclusion drawn?

5.   You are watching an infomercial for a new weight loss product. The announcer states that there is a strong correlation between use of the product and weight loss. Why should you be skeptical about the effectiveness of this product?

6.   Your psychology professor asks you to take part in an experiment on the effects of temperature on mood and you immediately agree. Have you given informed consent? Explain your answer.

7.   What is the purpose of debriefing?

8.   Identify the goal of, and key to, ethnography.

9.   Discuss the advantages of surveys and identify a potential problem with survey data.

10.   Go to your school library and look up a research article from a psychology journal on any topic. After reading the article, determine whether the article described a basic or applied study.

Chapter 2 Answers

Practice Test

1. B (p. 25)
2. D (p. 27)
3. B (p. 30)
4. A (p. 30)
5. D (p. 30)
6. B (p. 38)
7. A (p. 39)
8. C (p. 40)
9. A (p. 27)
10. B (p. 30)
11. B (p. 35)
12. A (p. 36)
13. D (pp. 37-38)
14. B (p. 37)
15. A (p. 39)
16. B (p. 40)
17. C (p. 44)
18. C (p. 33)
19. D (p. 33)
20. C (p. 36)
21. C (p. 27)
22. B (p. 38)
23. D (pp. 42-43)
24. C (p. 44)
25. C (p. 26)
26. C (p. 37)
27. D (p. 35)
28. C (p. 30)
29. B (p. 24)
30. A (pp. 36, 30)
31. D (p. 24)
32. B (p. 27)
33. A (p. 27)
34. C (p. 42)
35. A (p. 30)
36. D (p. 31)
37. B (p. 32)
38. A (p. 36)
39. C (p. 41)
40. C (p. 40)

Short Answer Review

1. scientifically (p. 24)
2. hindsight bias (p. 24)
3. observational method (p. 24)
4. correlational method (p. 24)

5.   experimental method (p. 24)
6.   hypothesis (p. 25)
7.   existing theories (p. 25)
8.   theory refinement (p. 26)
9.   tested (p. 26)
10.   revised (p. 26)
11.   lives of others (p. 26)
12.   observational (p. 27)
13.   behavior (p. 27)
14.   inside (p. 27)
15.   agreement (p. 27)
16.   accumulated documents (p. 27)
17.   views itself (p. 27)
18.   private (p. 29)
19.   describe (p. 29)
20.   variables (p. 29)
21.   systematically measured (p. 29)
22.   statistic (p. 30)
23.   positive (p. 30)
24.   surveys (p. 30)
25.   difficult to observe (p. 30)
26.   representative segments (p. 30)
27.   random selection (p. 30)
28.   causes (p. 32)
29.   experimental (p. 33)
30.   intervention (p. 34)
31.   effect (p. 35)
32.   measures (p. 35)
33.   internal validity (p. 36)
34.   participants (p. 36)
35.   probability level (p-value) (p. 36)
36.   internal validity (p. 36)
37.   artificial (p. 37)
38.   generalized (p. 37)
39.   psychological realism (p. 37)
40.   purpose (p. 38)
41.   external validity (p. 38)
42.   laboratory (p. 39)
43.   extraneous (p. 39)
44.   basic dilemma of the social psychologist (p. 39)
45.   Replications (p. 39)
46.   meta-analysis (p. 40)
47.   basic (p. 40)
48.   cross-cultural (p. 41)
49.   Evolutionary psychology (p. 42)
50.   biological (p. 43)
51.   informed consent (p. 44)
52.   debriefing (p. 44)

Essay Review

1.   Your essay should include:
- Research begins with a hunch, or hypothesis, that the researcher wants to test. (p. 25)
- Many studies stem from a researcher's dissatisfaction with existing theories and explanations. (p. 25)
- After reading other people's work, a researcher might believe he or she has a better way of explaining people's behavior. (p. 25)
- Social psychologists engage in a continual process of theory refinement: A theory is developed; specific hypotheses derived from that theory are tested; based on the results obtained, the theory is revised and new hypotheses are formulated. (p. 26)

2.   Your discussion of the observational method should include:
- The observational method is a technique whereby a researcher observes people and systematically records measurements or impressions of their behavior. (p. 27)
- Ethnography is a method by which researchers attempt to understand a group or culture by observing it from the inside, without imposing any preconceived notions they might have. (p. 27)
- Archival analysis is a form of the observational method in which the researcher examines the accumulated documents, or archives, of a culture. (p. 27)
- Interjudge reliability is the level of agreement between two or more people who independently observe and code a set of data. By showing that two or more judges independently come up with the same observations, researchers ensure that the observations are not the subjective, distorted impressions of one individual. (p. 27)

3.   Your essay on the correlational method should include:
- The correlational method is a technique whereby two or more variables are systematically measured and the relationship between them is assessed. (p. 29)
- A correlation coefficient is a statistical technique that assesses how well you can predict one variable from another. (p. 30)
- A positive correlation tells us that increases in the value of one variable are associated with increases in value of the other variable. A negative correlation means that increases in the value of one variable are associated with decreases in value of the other. (p. 30)
- The major shortcoming of the correlational method is that it tells us only that two variables are related, whereas the goal of the social psychologist is to identify the causes of social behavior. (p. 32)

4.   Your essay on the experimental method should include:
- The experimental method is the method in which the researcher randomly assigns participants to different conditions and ensures that these conditions are identical except for the independent variable. (p. 33)
- The independent variable is the variable a researcher changes or varies to see if it has an effect on some other variable. (p. 35)
- The dependent variable is the variable a researcher measures to see if it is influenced by the independent variable. (p. 35)

5.   Your essay on validity should include:
- Internal validity refers to making sure that nothing besides the independent variable can affect the dependent variable. (p. 36)
- External validity is the extent to which the results of a study can be generalized to other situations and to other people. (p. 37)
- Psychological realism is the extent to which the psychological processes triggered in an experiment are similar to psychological processes that occur in everyday life. (p. 37)

Exit Test 1

1.   C (p. 24)
2.   A (p. 27)
3.   A (p. 30)
4.   D (p. 33)
5.   D (p. 35)
6.   B (p. 36)
7.   B (p. 38-39)
8.   C (p. 37)
9.   A (p. 38)
10.   D (p. 40)

Exit Test 2

1.   A (p. 27)
2.   A (p. 32)
3.   C (p. 30)
4.   B (p. 31)
5.   A (p. 34)
6.   D (p. 35)
7.   C (p. 36)
8.   B (p. 30)
9.   B (p. 41)
10.   D (p. 43)

Study Activities

1.   Anything in addition to the independent variable that varies could also have caused your results to turn out the way they did. Therefore, the exact cause of your results cannot be known. (p. 36)

2.   The setting of highly controlled experiments is often artificial. Results from such experiments may not generalize to everyday life. By replicating the experiment in the field, this limitation can be overcome. (pp. 37-39)

3.   The APA guidelines tell us deception may be used only if no other means of testing the hypothesis is available and only if an Institutional Review Board rules that the experiment does not put participants at undo risk. Following the deception experiment, participants must be provided with a full description and explanation of all procedures including the necessity of deception during the debriefing. (pp. 44-45)

4.   You cannot generalize survey results to a population that is not represented by your sample. Members of the community who watch other local news programs, who were not home on this particular night, or who were unwilling to pay the fee and/or call the station are not represented here. (pp. 30-31)

5.   You should be skeptical because correlation does not equal causation. (p. 32)

6.   No. To give informed consent you have to be fully aware of the nature of the experiment which has to be explained to you in advance. (p. 44)

7.   The purpose of debriefing is to explain the true purpose of the experiment to the participant and inform the participant of any deception that was used. (p. 44)

8.   The goal of ethnography is to understand the richness and complexity of the group by observing it in action. The key to ethnography is to avoid, as much as possible, imposing one's preconceived notions in order to understand the point of view of the people being studied. (p. 27)

9.   One advantage of surveys is that researchers can judge the relationship between variables that are difficult to observe. Another advantage of surveys is the capability to sample representative segments of the population. A potential problem with survey data is the accuracy of the responses. (pp. 30-31)

10.   If the study was simply seeking to better understand behavior, it was a basic study. If the study was designed to solve a particular social problem, it was an applied study. Ask your instructor if you are unsure which one best describes your article. (p. 40)

CHAPTER 3

Social Cognition: How We Think about the Social World

CHAPTER 3 OVERVIEW

Chapter 3 informs readers of the procedures, strategies, and problems people exhibit when they perceive and judge the social world. The chapter begins with a discussion of **automatic thinking**; thinking that is nonconscious, unintentional, involuntary, and effortless. Automatic thinking helps us understand new situations by relating them to our prior experiences. We use **schemas**, mental structures that organize our knowledge about the social world, and influence the information we notice, think about, and remember. When applied to members of a social group, schemas are commonly referred to as stereotypes. In this case, schemas can have negative consequences. However, schemas are typically very useful for helping us organize and make sense of the world and to fill in the gaps of our knowledge. Schemas are particularly important when we encounter information that can be interpreted in a number of ways because they help us reduce ambiguity. Schemas also help people fill in the blanks when they are trying to remember things.

In ambiguous situations the schema that comes to mind and guides impressions can be affected by **accessibility**, the extent to which a schema and concepts are at the forefront of the mind and are therefore likely to be used when we are making judgments about the social world. Sometimes schemas are chronically accessible due to past experience, because they are related to a current goal, or they can be temporarily accessible because of recent experiences—a process known as **priming**.

People are not always passive recipients of information. They often act on their schemas in ways that change the extent to which these schemas are supported or contradicted. In fact, people can inadvertently make their schemas come true by the way they treat other people. A **self-fulfilling prophecy** is a case whereby people have an expectation about what another person is like, which influences how they act toward that person, which causes that person to behave consistently with people's original expectations, making the expectations come true. This is what happened in Rosenthal and Jacobson's (1968) study when they told some elementary school teachers that certain students were going to "bloom" academically in the coming school year. Although these students had been selected at random, their scores on IQ tests at the end of the school year indicated greater gains (compared to their scores before the school year began) than the other students who were not labeled "bloomers".

People often use mental shortcuts called **judgmental heuristics**. One such shortcut is the **availability heuristic** in which people base a judgment on the ease with which they can bring something to mind. The **representativeness heuristic** involves classifying something according to how similar it is to a typical case. When using this heuristic we sometimes ignore **base rate information**, information about the frequency of members of different categories in the population.

Part of the definition of automatic thinking is that it occurs unconsciously. If we had to rely on slow, conscious thinking alone we would be in a pickle because we often need to make very fast decisions about what is happening around us, what to pay attention to, and which of our goals to pursue. Most of the time, unconscious thinking is critical to navigating our way through the world. There is evidence that our unconscious minds can do better at some tasks than our conscious minds.

Although everyone uses schemas to understand the world, the *content* of our schemas is influenced by the culture in which we live. Schemas are a very important way by which cultures exert their influence; namely by instilling mental structures that influence the very way we understand and interpret the world. People in different cultures have fundamentally different schemas about themselves and the social world, with some interesting consequences. Culture can influence the kinds of thinking people automatically use to understand their worlds. People who grow up in Western cultures tend to have an **analytic thinking style,** a type of thinking in which people focus on the properties of objects without considering their surrounding context. People who grow up in East Asian cultures tend to have a **holistic thinking style,** a type of thinking in which people focus on the overall context, particularly the ways in which objects relate to each other.

The second major part of the chapter focuses on controlled social cognition. **Controlled thinking** is thinking that is conscious, intentional, voluntary, and effortful. People can usually turn on or turn off this type of thinking at will and are fully aware of what they are thinking. People have the capacity to think in a conscious, controlled way about only one thing at a time.

When we experience a negative event that was a "close call" we may engage in **counterfactual thinking**, mentally changing some aspect of the past as a way of imagining what might have been. Counterfactual thoughts can have a big influence on our emotional reactions to events. The easier it is to mentally undo an outcome, the stronger the emotional reaction to it. Counterfactual thinking is conscious and effortful; however it is not always intentional or voluntary. Counterfactual thinking can result in rumination, whereby people repetitively focus on negative things in their lives. Rumination has been found to be a contributor to depression. Instead of ruminating about something we might engage in **thought suppression**, the attempt to avoid thinking about something we would just as soon forget.

One purpose of controlled thinking is to provide checks and balances for automatic thinking. Controlled thinking takes over when unusual events occur. Often we have greater confidence in our judgments than we should. Anyone trying to improve human inference is up against an **overconfidence barrier**. One approach to address this directly is to get people to consider the possibility that they might be wrong, perhaps by getting them to consider a point of view opposite of their own. Another approach is to teach people directly some basic statistical and methodological principles about how to reason correctly, with the hope they will apply these principles in their everyday lives.

Looking back at the Amadou Diallo case presented at the beginning of the chapter, we can now see how automatic thinking may have played a role in his death. The police officer who shot him may have made an automatic assumption based on race.

CHAPTER 3 OUTLINE

• The Amadou Diallo case, in which police shot and killed Diallo when he reached for his wallet, (assuming he was reaching for a gun) is described as an example of how people often make automatic inferences about the world.
• **Social cognition** is the study of how people think about themselves and the social world, or more specifically, how people select, interpret, remember, and use social information to make judgments and decisions.
• There are two important modes of social cognition: automatic and controlled.

I. On Automatic Pilot: Low-Effort Thinking
• **Automatic thinking** is thinking that is nonconscious, unintentional, involuntary, and effortless.

A. People as Everyday Theorists: Automatic Thinking with Schemas
• In automatic thinking, people make quick judgments based on what they have seen before. Experience leads us to develop theories or schemas about what the world is like.
• **Schemas** are mental structures that people use to organize their knowledge about the world around themes or subjects. They influence what we notice, think about, and remember.

• We have schemas for ourselves, other people, social roles, and events. When applied to members of a specific group, schemas are referred to as *stereotypes*.

1. Stereotypes about Race and Weapons

Stereotypes can be applied rapidly and automatically when we encounter other people. Recent experiments have tested whether people's stereotypes about African Americans can influence their perception of whether a person is holding a weapon. Correll, Park, Judd, & Wittenbrink (2002) found when participants played a video game in which they were supposed to "shoot" a man if he was holding a gun and withhold fire if he was not, that participants were influenced by the race of the men in the pictures. As seen in Figure 3.1, p. 54, people were prone to make mistakes by shooting black men who were unarmed.

2. The Function of Schemas: Why Do We Have Them?

• Schemas are important for organizing and making sense of the world. We need continuity, to be able to relate new experiences to past ones. Sufferers of Korsakov's syndrome, who cannot form new memories, invent schemas where none exist to be able to impose order on their worlds.

• Schemas are particularly important when we encounter information that can be interpreted in a number of ways, because they provide us with a way of reducing ambiguity.

• Kelley's (1950) "warm/cold" study is described, in which students were given descriptions of a guest lecturer that differed only in the inclusion of "warm" or "cold." Students who were told the instructor was warm rated him higher, asked more questions, and participated in discussion more than those told he was cold.

• When what we see is relatively unambiguous, we do not need to use our schemas to help us interpret it. For example, in Kelley's study, one instructor was clearly extremely self-confident, and was rated as immodest in both the "warm" and the "cold" conditions. However, the warm/cold manipulation still influenced subjects' perceptions of the instructor's sense of humor, which was an inference based on more ambiguous information. Thus the more ambiguous the information, the more we use schemas to fill in the blanks.

• Our reliance on schemas is not "wrong" but often helpful. Relying on schemas becomes problematic when we cling too tightly to schemas that are inaccurate.

3. Which Schemas Are Applied? Accessibility and Priming

• Your impression of an ambiguous stimulus can be affected by **accessibility**, the extent to which schemas and concepts are at the forefront of people's minds and are therefore likely to be used when making judgments about the social world (Figure 3.2, p. 64).

• There are two kinds of accessibility: chronic, in which some schemas become chronically accessible due to the effects of past experience, and temporary, due to the effects of temporary and often arbitrary experiences. **Priming** is the process by which recent experiences increase the accessibility of a schema, trait, or concept.

• In an experiment by Higgins, Rholes, & Jones (1977), participants memorized lists of either positive or negative words, then in an ostensibly unrelated study read an ambiguous paragraph about a man named Donald. Those participants who read the positive traits formed a more positive impression (Figure 3.3, p. 65). However, the effect of trait positivity only occurred when the memorized traits were also applicable to the story. Thus, thoughts need to be both accessible and applicable to act as primes.

• Bargh & Pietromonaco (1982) demonstrated subliminal priming. Participants saw either words related to hostility or neutral words presented subliminally, then read a paragraph describing a person who behaved in a way that could be interpreted as hostile or not. Those who saw the hostile prime rated the character as more hostile.

4. Making Our Schemas Come True: The Self-Fulfilling Prophecy

• The **self-fulfilling prophecy** is the case whereby people (a) have an expectation about what another person is like, which (b) influences how they act toward that person, which (c) causes that

person to behave in a way consistent with the original expectations. The operation of this cycle is illustrated in Figure 3.5, p. 68.
• Self-fulfilling prophecies can have frightening consequences; for example, the self-fulfilling prophecy has been implicated in sex differences in academic achievement. Teachers tend to believe that boys are more likely to succeed than are girls, and research suggests that this difference in belief translates into teachers' differential behavior towards boys and girls. The Rosenthal and Jacobson "blooming children" study is described as a well-controlled experiment showing the effects of the self-fulfilling prophecy (Figure 3.6, p. 69).
• The self-fulfilling prophecy is not a deliberate attempt at schema confirmation, but is an example of automatic thinking that occurs inadvertently and unconsciously and often against a person's conscious attempts to treat others in an unbiased fashion. Self-fulfilling prophecies may be stronger when the perceiver is distracted.
• The fact the self-fulfilling prophecy occurs automatically makes schemas even more resistant to change because we see a good deal of false evidence (created by our own expectations) that confirms them.

5. Limits of Self-Fulfilling Prophecies
Recent research has shown that when interviewers are motivated to form an accurate impression and are not distracted, they are often able to put their expectations aside and see what the person is really like.

B. Mental Strategies and Shortcuts
• **Judgmental heuristics** are mental shortcuts people use to make judgments quickly and efficiently. Usually, these work quite well, although sometimes they lead to errors.

1. How Easily Does It Come to Mind? The Availability Heuristic
• The **availability heuristic** is a mental rule of thumb whereby people base a judgment on the ease with which they can bring something to mind.
• An example of medical diagnosis facilitated by availability is described.
• We use this heuristic to make inferences about ourselves as well as others. Schwarz et al. (1991) showed that people who were asked to provide six instances of their own assertiveness could do so easily and inferred they were highly assertive; those who were asked to provide twelve instances had difficulty and inferred they were low in assertiveness (Figure 3.7, p. 75).

2. How Similar Is A to B? The Representativeness Heuristic
• The **representativeness heuristic** is a mental shortcut whereby people classify something according to how similar it is to a typical case. This is not problematic in itself, but it becomes so when we rely only on similarity and ignore **base-rate information** about the frequency of members of different categories in the population. People tend to over-rely on the representativeness heuristic and under-rely on the base-rate.

C. The Power of Unconscious Thinking
•Part of the definition of automatic thinking is that it occurs unconsciously. If we had to rely on slow, conscious thinking alone we would be in a pickle because we often need to make very fast decisions about what is happening around us, what to pay attention to, and which of our goals to pursue. There is evidence that our unconscious minds can do better at some tasks than our conscious minds.
•Just because people think they are consciously controlling their actions does not necessarily mean they are. Daniel Wegner (2002, 2004) argues that the sense that people have of consciously willing an action can be an illusion, a feeling that we create when our actions were really controlled by either our automatic thinking or the external environment. Sometimes we overestimate the amount of control we have and sometimes we underestimate it.

D. Cultural Differences in Social Cognition
•Social psychologists have become increasingly interested in the influence of culture on social cognition.

1. Cultural Determinants of Schemas
• Much of the content of our schemas is culturally determined, based on what is important in our culture. In fact, much of the way that culture has an influence is by instilling mental structures that influence the way we understand and interpret the world.
• Bartlett (1932), for example, noted that the Bantu have extremely well-developed schemas for cattle, which are a central part of their economy and culture, and are able to remember complicated transactions involving them without written reminders—not because of overall superior memory, but because people have superior memory in the domains of their personal schemas.

2. Holistic Versus Analytic Thinking
• Culture can influence the kinds of thinking people automatically use to understand their worlds.
• People who grow up in Western cultures tend to have an **analytic thinking style,** a type of thinking in which people focus on the properties of objects without considering their surrounding context.
• People who grow up in East Asian cultures tend to have a **holistic thinking style,** a type of thinking in which people focus on the overall context, particularly the ways in which objects relate to each other.

II. Controlled Social Cognition: High-Effort Thinking
• Racial profiling is discussed as a consciously instituted, prejudicial strategy used by police departments.
• **Controlled thinking** is conscious, intentional, voluntary, and effortful. Controlled processing can be turned on and off at will. However, it takes motivation and effort to engage in controlled processing, so that we must be motivated and have the time and energy to engage in it.

A. Mentally Undoing the Past: Counterfactual Reasoning
• **Counterfactual thinking** is mentally changing ("undoing") some aspect of the past as a way of imagining what might have been. The easier it is to "undo" the past or imagine an alternative outcome, the stronger our emotional reaction to what actually occurred. Although in one sense this is rational, in another sense it is not, since the extent of our feeling depends not on actual probabilities but on the mental ease of imagining an alternative.
• Counterfactual thinking can have a big influence on people's emotional reactions to events. The easier it is to mentally undo an outcome, the stronger the emotional reaction to it. For example, researchers found that the more ways that people imagined a personal tragedy (loss of a spouse or child) being averted, the greater their distress.
• Counterfactual thinking can lead to paradoxical effects on our emotions; for example, Medvec, Madey, & Gilovich (1995) showed that silver medal winners at the Olympics appeared less happy than bronze medal winners, because silver medal winners could easily imagine having won the gold, while bronze medalists could easily imagine not having placed at all.
•Counterfactual thinking is conscious and effortful; however, it is not always intentional or voluntary. It may be hard to turn off and may result in rumination, whereby people repetitively focus on negative things in their lives. When people ruminate about bad outcomes, they can become more depressed; however, counterfactual thinking can potentially focus peoples' attention on ways that they can cope better in the future and give them heightened motivation and perceptions of control.

B. Thought Suppression and Ironic Processing
• Being preoccupied reduces our ability to engage in **thought suppression** (the attempt to avoid thinking about something we would just as soon forget). According to Wegner (1992, 1994), thought

suppression depends on two processes, one automatic and one controlled. The automatic process is *monitoring*, searching for evidence that the unwanted thought (e.g., "I want ice cream" when you are dieting) is about to intrude. Once the thought is detected the controlled *operating process* comes into play, finding a distraction. When people are tired or preoccupied, the operating process does not engage, but the monitoring process still does—leading, ironically, to high levels of unwanted thoughts.
• There can be an emotional and physical cost to thought suppression. Petrie et al. (1998) found that participants who suppressed thoughts about what they had written about personal topics showed decreased immune system functioning; while Major and Gramzow (1999) found that women who tried to suppress thoughts about an abortion reported greater psychological distress.

C. Improving Human Thinking
• One purpose of controlled thinking is to provide checks and balances for automatic processing.
• Often we have more confidence in our judgments than we should. To try to improve reasoning skills, we need to break through this **overconfidence barrier** and make people more humble about their abilities. One possibility is to break the barrier directly, by asking people to "consider the opposite" point of view to their own. Lord et al. (1984) have shown that this leads to fewer errors in judgment.
• Another approach is to directly teach people some basic statistic and methodological principles about correct reasoning, with the hope that they will apply these principles to their daily lives. Studies by Nisbett and his colleagues demonstrate that people's reasoning can be improved by college statistics classes, graduate courses in research design, and even brief, one-time lessons (see Figure 3.9, p. 86).

III. The Amadou Diallo Case Revisited
• Social psychologists disagree as to whether automatic or controlled processing is more important in human functioning. Some believe that controlled processing may be quite limited; others believe that it can be difficult but possible to gain conscious control over unwanted automatic responses.
• Both kinds of thinking are very useful. Both kinds of thinking can also lead to consequential errors.
• People are, on the one hand, very sophisticated social thinkers with amazing cognitive abilities; however, there is plenty of room for improvement because of the *mental contamination* provided by pervasive biases and errors. The authors suggest a "flawed scientist" model of humans as social thinkers, brilliant and often logical, but also blind to truths that don't fit their schemas, and sometimes acting in ways that make their schemas come true. The flawed scientist model could help to explain the death of Amadou Diallo. His death may have been the result of an automatic assumption by the police officers who shot him, based on his race.

LEARNING OBJECTIVES

After reading Chapter 3, you should be able to do the following:

1.   Identify the characteristics of automatic thinking. Discuss the advantages and disadvantages of automatic thinking. (pp. 52-55)

2.   Define a schema. Identify which mental processes are affected by the use of schemas. (p. 53)

3.   Identify the functions of schemas. Describe conditions when schemas are very important. (pp. 55-56)

4.   Define the processes of accessibility and priming. Describe the influence of accessibility and priming on schema use. (pp. 56-58)

5.   Explain how the self-fulfilling prophecy makes schemas resistant to change. Outline the steps involved in the self-perpetuating cycle of a self-fulfilling prophecy. (pp. 58-61)

6.   Define judgmental heuristics and the advantages and limitations of using these heuristics. (p. 63)

7.   Define the availability heuristic. Discuss reasons why the availability heuristic may result in faulty judgments. Identify conditions that increase the availability of information in memory. (pp. 63-66)

8.   Define the representativeness heuristic. Define base rate information. Discuss why the use of the representativeness heuristic results in the under-use of base rate information. (p. 66)

9.   Discuss some examples of automatic thinking that are common within many everyday behaviors, and identify how priming can influence a person's goals. (pp. 66-68)

10.   Describe the relationships among culture, schema content, and memory. (pp. 68-69)

11.   Explain the difference between analytic thinking style and holistic thinking style. (p. 69)

12.   Identify the characteristics of controlled thinking. (p. 73)

13.   Define counterfactual thinking. Give an example of a statement that is indicative of this type of reasoning. Discuss conditions that facilitate counterfactual thinking. Identify consequences, both positive and negative, of counterfactual reasoning. (pp. 73-74)

14.   Describe the two-part process involved in successful thought suppression. (pp. 74-75)

15.   Define the overconfidence barrier. Describe how this barrier can be overcome. Discuss the effectiveness of teaching people basic statistical and methodological reasoning principles. (pp. 75-77)

16.   Describe the portrayal of the social thinker. Define the meaning of the metaphor "flawed scientist" for the human thinker. (p. 78)

KEY TERMS

1.   _____   How people think about themselves and the social world, or more specifically, how people select, interpret, remember, and use social information to make judgments and decisions. (p. 51)

2.   _____   Thinking that is nonconscious, unintentional, involuntary and effortless. (p. 52)

3.   _____   Mental structures people use to organize their knowledge about the social world around themes or subjects and that influence the information people notice, think about, and remember. (p. 53)

4. _____ The extent to which schemas and concepts are at the forefront of people's minds and are therefore likely to be used when we are making judgments about the social world. (p. 56)

5. _____ The process by which recent experiences increase the accessibility of a schema, trait, or concept. (p. 56)

6. _____ The case whereby people have an expectation about what another person is like, which influences how they act toward that person, which causes that person to behave consistently with people's original expectations, making the expectations come true.
(p. 58)

7. _____ Mental shortcuts people use to make judgments quickly and efficiently. (p. 63)

8. _____ A mental rule of thumb whereby people base a judgment on the ease with which they can bring something to mind. (p. 63)

9. _____ A mental shortcut whereby people classify something according to how similar it is to a typical case. (p. 65)

10. _____ Information about the frequency of members of different categories in the population. (p. 65)

11. _____ A type of thinking in which people focus on the properties of objects without considering their surrounding context. (p. 69)

12. _____ A type of thinking in which people focus on the overall context, particularly the ways in which objects relate to each other. (p. 69)

13. _____ Thinking that is conscious, intentional, voluntary, and effortful. (p. 73)

14. _____ Mentally changing some aspect of the past as a way of imagining what might have been. (p. 73)

15. _____ The attempt to avoid thinking about something we would prefer to forget. (p. 74)

16. _____ The fact that people usually have too much confidence in the accuracy of their judgments. (p. 75)

GUIDED REVIEW

PRACTICE TEST

1. Social cognition is the study of:
   a) the way people think, feel, and act toward others.
   b) the way in which people's thoughts, feelings, and behaviors are influenced by the real or imagined presence of others.
   c) how people's behavior is motivated by the need to perceive and present themselves favorably.
   d) how people select, interpret, remember, and use information to make judgments and decisions .

2. Automatic thinking helps us understand new situations by relating them to
    a) our prior experiences.
    b) the experiences of others.
    c) conscious thoughts.
    d) cognitive frameworks.

3. Schemas are typically very useful for helping us
    a) organize the world.
    b) make sense of the world.
    c) fill in the gaps of our knowledge.
    d) all of the above.

4. In a study by Correll et al. (2002), nonblack participants playing a video game were most likely to press a button to "shoot" when the people in the photo were
    a) black, whether or not these people were holding a gun.
    b) black, but only if they were holding a gun.
    c) black, but only if there was more than one black person in the photo.
    d) Hispanic.

5. It is likely that the differences in academic performance between boys and girls can be explained solely by biological differences.
    a) True
    b) False

6. People who grow up in Western cultures ten to have a/an _____ thinking style.
    a) open
    b) centric
    c) analytic
    d) holistic

7. The self-fulfilling prophecy makes schemas resistant to change because:
    a) it distorts our perceptions of disconfirming evidence.
    b) it produces the evidence that confirms the schema.
    c) it provides a theme or topic around which a schema can be structured.
    d) all of the above

8. When we base our judgments on the ease with which we can bring something to mind, we are using the ____ heuristic.
    a) availability
    b) representativeness
    c) anchoring/adjustment
    d) retrievability

9. Given information about a specific person that contradicts base rate information, people tend to:
    a) ignore the information about the person and use only the base rate information.
    b) integrate the information about the individual and the base rate information.
    c) look for another heuristic.
    d) ignore the base rate, judging only how representative the information about the person is of a general category.

10.   Which of the following is most likely performed using controlled thinking?
        a)   tying one's shoes
        b)   calculating the answer to a difficult math problem
        c)   walking around one's house
        d)   using established stereotypes to form an impression of
                someone

11.   Because people think that their reasoning processes are less fallible than they actually are, anyone trying to improve people's accuracy is up against a(n):
        a)   certainty threshold.
        b)   perseverance effect.
        c)   illusory correlation.
        d)   overconfidence barrier.

12.   Kelley (1950) had students read different descriptions of a guest lecturer who they evaluated at the end of class. Results indicated that:
        a)   the descriptions influenced how students rated the lecturer's unambiguous behaviors.
        b)   the descriptions influenced students to such an extent that they failed to differentiate between ambiguous and unambiguous behaviors.
        c)   the descriptions had no effect on the students' ratings.
        d)   the descriptions influenced how students rated the lecturer's ambiguous behaviors.

13.   Which of the following is NOT an advantage of viewing the world through schema-tinted glasses?
        a)   Schemas allow us to interpret the meaning of ambiguous behavior.
        b)   Schemas facilitate the unbiased processing of information.
        c)   Schemas facilitate smooth social interactions.
        d)   Schemas allow us to deal with experiences in a manner that requires little cognitive effort.

14.   The process by which recent experiences increase accessibility of a schema is called:
        a)   retrieval.
        b)   priming.
        c)   availability.
        d)   perseverance.

15.   Any time people act on their schemas in a way that makes the schema "come true," a(n) _____ results.
        a)   stereotype
        b)   self-fulfilling prophecy
        c)   illusory correlation
        d)   perseverance effect

16.   Making judgments by comparing someone to a stereotype demonstrates the use of a(n) _____ heuristic.
        a)   anchoring
        b)   representativeness
        c)   adjustment
        d)   unavailable

17. Matt and Samantha are both trying to catch 10:00 AM flights but arrive at the airport too late. Matt finds out that his plane had been delayed and he missed it by only 2 minutes. Samantha's flight left on time and she missed it by 20 minutes. Based on what you've learned about counterfactual thinking, who will be more upset about missing their flight?
   a) Matt, because he can easily imagine getting to the airport a few minutes earlier
   b) Matt, because his flight was delayed
   c) Samantha, because her flight left on time
   d) Samantha, because she can easily imagine getting to the airport 20 minutes earlier

18. Counterfactual thinking is
   a) conscious and effortful.
   b) conscious and effortless.
   c) unconscious and effortful.
   d) unconscious and effortless.

19. Nonconscious and unintentional is to _____ thinking as conscious and effortful is to _____ thinking.
   a) automatic; controlled
   b) heuristic; automatic
   c) controlled; heuristic
   d) automatic; conditioned

20. In a study by Petrie et al. (1998) medical students were asked to suppress thoughts. The results found that
   a) thought suppression leads to depression.
   b) thought suppression leads to denial.
   c) people who suppressed thoughts showed a significant increase in immune system functioning.
   d) people who suppressed thoughts showed a significant decrease in immune system functioning.

21. Regarding our ability to engage in thought suppression, the _____ process is the automatic part of the system and the _____ process is the controlled part of the system.
   a) operating; checking
   b) distracting; monitoring
   c) monitoring; operating
   d) operating; monitoring

22. Which of the following is FALSE about thought suppression?
   a) It involves two processes, one automatic and the other controlled.
   b) It is more difficult to suppress unwanted thoughts when one is preoccupied or tired.
   c) It is healthier for people to suppress thoughts about negative events than to discuss them.
   d) It is healthier for people to discuss their problems than it is to suppress thoughts about them.

23. Natasha expects men to be rude. She meets her roommate's boyfriend, and he acts somewhat rude to Natasha because she is cold toward him. This is an example of the:
   a) hindsight bias.
   b) expectation bias.
   c) self-fulfilling prophecy.
   d) perseverance effect.

24. When applied to members of a social group such as a gender or race, schemas are commonly referred to as
    a) sexist and racist.
    b) biased.
    c) discrimination.
    d) stereotypes.

25. Counterfactual reasoning is clearly conscious and effortful.
    a) True
    b) False

26. Heuristics
    a) always lead to inaccurate inferences.
    b) always lead to accurate inferences.
    c) are sometimes adequate and sometimes inadequate.
    d) take more time than controlled thinking.

27. Categorizing things according to representativeness is often a perfectly reasonable thing to do.
    a) True
    b) False

28. Carol has just taken a personality test online. She was surprised at how accurately the feedback described her. Carol has probably just experienced
    a) a self-fulfilling prophecy.
    b) the Barnum effect
    c) an expectancy effect.
    d) an availability heuristic.

29. A highly accessible schema is one that:
    a) people can bring to mind easily.
    b) most people have developed.
    c) is very easy to develop.
    d) others will know is being used.

30. Higgins and colleagues (1977) study of participants' perceptions of "Donald" illustrates which of the following processes?
    a) the judgmental heuristic
    b) thought suppression
    c) schemas
    d) priming

31. The police officers who shot Amadou Diallo used _____ thinking.
    a) conscious
    b) effortful
    c) automatic
    d) illogical

32.	The term *schema* is very
	a)	hard to define because the word means different things to different people.
	b)	specific, it encompasses only our knowledge about our social world.
	c)	general, it encompasses our knowledge about many things.
	d)	specific, it encompasses only our knowledge about ourselves.

33.	People with Korsakov's syndrome
	a)	lose the ability to form new memories.
	b)	go to great lengths to try to impose meaning on their experiences.
	c)	invent schemas where none exist.
	d)	all of the above.

34.	The holistic thinking style is a type of thinking in which people focus on the properties of objects without considering their surrounding context.
	a)	True
	b)	False

35.	If you ask teachers which of their current students are most academically gifted or who their most outstanding students have been over the years, most of the students they mention are _____.
	a)	male
	b)	female
	c)	students who sit in the front row
	d)	good looking

36.	Self-fulfilling prophecies are more likely to occur when interviewers are _____.
	a)	inexperienced
	b)	happy
	c)	not paying careful attention to the person they are interviewing
	d)	angry

37.	Which of the following can explain why the Barnum effect occurs?
	a)	the judgmental heuristic
	b)	availability heuristic
	c)	representativeness heuristic
	d)	base rate information

38.	Larry was engaged in a conversation at a party when he suddenly noticed that someone across the room said his name. Larry has just experienced the _____.
	a)	acute hearing experience
	b)	representativeness heuristic
	c)	perceptual enhancement effect
	d)	cocktail party effect

39.	Facilitated communication
	a)	is currently used with the hearing impaired.
	b)	has been discredited.
	c)	is currently widely used with autistic children.
	d)	is currently widely used with the hearing impaired and autistic children.

40.   Nisbett found that after two years of graduate work
   a)   students in psychology and medicine improved on statistical reasoning problems more than students in law and chemistry did.
   b)   students in law and chemistry improved on statistical reasoning problems more than students in psychology and medicine.
   c)   students in psychology, medicine, chemistry, and law all performed equally well on statistical reasoning problems.
   d)   students in social psychology performed better on statistical reasoning problems than students in all other fields tested.

SHORT ANSWER REVIEW

People often size up a new situation very quickly: They figure out who is there, what is happening, and what might happen next. Automatic thinking is thought that is nonconscious, unintentional, (1) _____ (p. 52), and effortless. Automatic thinking helps us understand new situations by relating them to our prior (2) _____ (p. 53). We use mental structures called (3) _____ (p. 53) to organize our knowledge about the social world around themes or subjects that influence the information we notice, think about, and remember.

When applied to members of a social group, schemas are commonly referred to as (4) _____ (p. 53). Schemas are typically very useful for helping us (5) _____ (p. 54) and make sense of the social world and to fill in the gaps of our knowledge. Schemas are particularly useful when we are in (6) _____ (p. 55) situations because they help us figure out what is going on.

The social world is full of ambiguous information that is open to (7) _____ (p. 56). Schemas help us to interpret ambiguous situations. The schema that comes to mind and guides your impressions of ambiguous situations can be affected by (8) _____ (p. 56), the extent to which schemas and concepts are at the forefront of the mind and are therefore likely to be used when we are making judgments about the social world. (9) _____ (p. 57) is the process by which recent experiences increase the accessibility of a schema, trait, or concept. Priming is a good example of (10) _____ (p. 58) thinking because it occurs quickly, unintentionally, and unconsciously.

We can also act in ways that make our schemas come true. When this happens it is called a (11) _____ (p. 58).

People use mental shortcuts called (12) _____ (p. 63) to make judgments quickly and efficiently. The (13) _____ (p. 63) heuristic is a mental rule of thumb whereby people base a judgment on the ease with which they can bring something to mind. The representativeness heuristic is a mental shortcut whereby people classify something according to how similar it is to a (14) _____ (p. 65). Kahneman and Tversky found that people do not use (15) _____ (p. 65) information sufficiently when using the representativeness heuristic. Base rate information refers to information about the frequency of members of different categories in the (16) _____ (p. 65). Part of the definition of automatic thinking is that it occurs unconsciously. If we had to rely on slow, conscious thinking alone, we would be in a pickle because we often need to make very fast decisions about what is happening around us, what to pay attention to, and which of our (17) _____ (p. 67) to pursue.

Social psychologists have become increasingly interested in the influence of (18) _____ (p. 68) on social cognition. Although everyone uses schemas to understand the world, the (19) _____ (p. 68) of our schemas is influenced by the culture in which we live. People who grow up in Western cultures tend to have an analytic thinking style, a type of thinking in which people focus on the (20) _____ (p. 69) without considering their surrounding context. People who grow up in East Asian cultures tend to have a holistic thinking style, a type of thinking in which people focus on the (21) _____ (p. 69), particularly the ways in which objects relate to each other.

(22) _____ (p. 73) is defined as thinking that is conscious, intentional, voluntary, and effortful. People can usually turn on or turn off this type of thinking at will and are (23) _____ (p. 73) of what they are thinking. We sometimes engage in counterfactual thinking,

mentally (24) _____ (p. 73) some aspect of the past as a way of imagining what might have

been. Counterfactual thoughts can have a big influence on our (25) _____ (p. 82) to events.

The easier it is to (26) _____ (p. 73) an outcome, the stronger the emotional reaction to it.

Even when we want to stop dwelling on the past and move on to something else, it can be difficult to turn

off the kind of "if only" thinking that characterizes counterfactual thinking. This is not so good if

counterfactual thinking results in (27) _____ (p. 74), whereby people repetitively focus on

negative things in their lives. Rumination has been found to be a contributor to (28) _____ (p.

74). Instead of ruminating about something, we might simply do our best not to think about it. This is

called (29) _____ (p. 74), the attempt to avoid thinking about something we would just as

soon (30) _____ (p. 74).

One purpose of controlled thinking is to provide (31) _____ (p. 75) for automatic

thinking. Often we have greater (32) _____ (p. 75) in our judgments than we should. Anyone

trying to improve human inference is up against an (33) _____ (p. 75). Many people seem to

think that their reasoning processes are just fine the way they are and hence there is no need for any (34)

_____ (p. 75). One approach is to address this overconfidence barrier directly, getting people

to consider the possibility that they might be wrong. Another approach is to teach people directly some

basic (35) _____ (p. 76) principles about how to reason correctly.

ESSAY REVIEW

1. Define automatic thinking and explain how schemas are involved and the purpose they serve.

2. Explain the concept of accessibility and the reasons something can be accessible.

3. What is a self-fulfilling prophecy? Imagine that you are an employee working in a human resources department and you are responsible for conducting interviews. How could you use research on self-fulfilling prophecy to prevent its occurrence when you interview prospective employees?

4. Write an essay identifying what is meant by judgmental heuristics and the availability heuristic. How might the availability heuristic affect your performance if you were a physician?

5. What is meant by counterfactual thinking, how does it influence emotions, and how can it be used to explain why Olympic bronze medalists (third place) tend to be happier than those who win a silver medal (second place)?

EXIT TESTS

EXIT TEST 1

1. Mental structures that organize our knowledge about the social world are known as _____.
   a) cognitive frameworks
   b) stereotypes
   c) schemas
   d) heuristics

2. In a study by Correll, participants were more likely to press a button labeled "shoot" if the male in the picture _____, whether or not these people were holding a gun.
   a) was a teenager
   b) looked like a gang member
   c) was Hispanic
   d) was black

3. Having continuity, being able to relate new experiences to our past schemas, is so important that people who lose this ability invent schemas where none exist.
   a) True
   b) False

4. _____ are a central part of the Bantu economy and culture, and therefore the Bantu have well-developed schemas about them.
   a) Horses
   b) Cattle
   c) Pigs
   d) Sheep

5. Whitley has recently finished taking a course on abnormal psychology in which she learned about various types of mental illnesses. Today at the grocery store Whitley saw a woman talking with herself and acting strangely. Whitley decided the woman must have a mental illness. Whitley's judgment about the woman at the grocery has been influenced by
   a) priming.
   b) perceptual salience.
   c) prejudice.
   d) the perseverance effect.

6. Schemas increase the amount of social information we need to take in.
   a) True
   b) False

7. People use the availability heuristic to make judgments about other people, but they do not use it when making judgments about themselves.
   a) True
   b) False

8.   In a study by Shariff and Norenzayan (2001), they showed that _____ can be activated and
      influence people's behavior without their knowing it.
      a)   feelings
      b)   schemas
      c)   goals
      d)   attitudes

9.   Evidence suggests that racial profiling is a conscious policy decision in some police departments
      and not the result of automatic thinking.
      a)   True
      b)   False

10.   In thought suppression, the automatic part of the system is called the _____ process.
      a)   stopping
      b)   identifying
      c)   operating
      d)   monitoring

EXIT TEST 2

1.   The type of social cognition that is more effortful and deliberate is called _____thinking.
      a)   cognizant
      b)   controlled
      c)   decisive
      d)   Rodin

2.   A stereotype is
      a)   a type of schema.
      b)   completely unrelated to schemas.
      c)   an example of controlled thinking.
      d)   only used by prejudiced people.

3.   Something can be accessible because
      a)   the schema has become chronically accessible due to past experience.
      b)   it is related to a current goal.
      c)   the schema is temporarily accessible due to recent experiences.
      d)   all of the above

4.   Sadker and Sadker spent years observing teachers' behavior. One fifth grade teacher they
      observed did which of the following when explaining a difficult math problem?
      a)   She explained it to the smart children in the class and ignored everyone else.
      b)   She spoke very slowly and displayed the problem on a screen so everyone could see it.
      c)   She turned her back to the girls.
      d)   She turned her back to the boys.

5.   Which of the following people is more likely to notice changes in the background of pictures?
      a)   Rick, who is from New York
      b)   Kim, who is from East Asia
      c)   George, who is from Indiana
      d)   Sandra, who is from Texas

Chapter 3

6. When our expectations about someone cause us to treat them differently and in turn, bring about the behavior we expected, it is called the
   a) expectancy effect.
   b) perseverance effect.
   c) self-fulfilling prophecy.
   d) influential bias.

7. People in different cultures have fundamentally different schemas about themselves and the social world.
   a) True
   b) False

8. When we classify something according to how similar it is to a typical case we are using the _____ heuristic.
   a) representativeness
   b) availability
   c) anchoring/adjustment
   d) fundamental judgmental

9. Throughout history, people have assumed that the cure for a disease must resemble the
   a) most recent cure discovered for any disease.
   b) cure for a similar disease in animals.
   c) cure for other similar diseases.
   d) symptoms of the disease.

10. People are always able to consciously control their actions when they believe they are.
    a) True
    b) False

STUDY ACTIVITIES

1. What is social cognition? What do researchers in this area study?

2. Define automatic thinking and identify an advantage of it.

3. Why are schemas so important to study? What role do they play in people's understanding and interpretations of themselves and the social world? What are examples of cognitive processes that are influenced by schemas?

4. Describe the influence of culture on the content of schemas.

5. You have a friend who is a graduate student and was recently given her own section of Introduction to Psychology to teach as a graduate teaching assistant. The semester is almost over and your friend is concerned about the teaching evaluations her students will be completing to evaluate her teaching and the course. This is her first time teaching on her own and the evaluations can impact whether or not she is given other courses to teach in the future. Which heuristic should you remind your friend about and what might you suggest she do, based on information in the chapter, to improve her evaluations?

6. Identify the two approaches that have been demonstrated to reduce people's overconfidence.

7. How do automatic thinking and controlled thinking interact to allow for successful thought suppression?

8. What portrait of the social thinker has emerged? Why?

9. You were born and raised in the United States but you have recently developed a new friendship with another student who is from Korea. Explain how this new friend's thinking is probably different from yours.

10. Your brother has just read his horoscope in the newspaper and is amazed at how it perfectly describes what is going on in his life right now. Using what you have learned in this chapter, how would you explain to your brother why his horoscope seems so accurate?

Chapter 3 Answers

Practice Test

1.   D (p. 51)
2.   A (p. 53)
3.   D (p. 54)
4.   A (p. 54)
5.   B (pp. 58-59)
6.   C (p. 69)
7.   B (p. 61)
8.   A (p. 63)
9.   D (p. 65)
10.   B (p. 73)
11.   D (p. 75)
12.   D (p. 55)
13.   B (p. 62)
14.   B (p. 57)
15.   B (p. 58)
16.   B (p. 65)
17.   A (p. 73)
18.   A (p. 73)
19.   A (pp. 52, 73)
20.   D (p. 75)
21.   C (p. 74)
22.   C (pp. 74-75)
23.   C (p. 58)
24.   D (p. 53)
25.   A (p. 74)
26.   C (p. 63)
27.   A (p. 65)
28.   B (p. 66)
29.   A (p. 56)
30.   D (p. 57)
31.   C (p. 52)
32.   C (p. 53)
33.   D (pp. 54-55)
34.   B (p. 69)
35.   A (p. 59)
36.   C (p. 61)
37.   C (p. 66)
38.   D (p. 67)
39.   B (p. 72)
40.   A (p. 77)

Short Answer Review

1. involuntary (p. 52)
2. experiences (p. 53)
3. schemas (p. 53)
4. stereotypes (p. 53)
5. organize (p. 54)
6. confusing (p. 55)
7. interpretation (p. 56)
8. accessibility (p. 56)
9. priming (p. 57)
10. automatic (p. 58)
11. self-fulfilling prophecy (p. 58)
12. judgmental heuristics (p. 63)
13. availability (p. 63)
14. typical case (p. 65)
15. base rate (p. 65)
16. population (p. 65)
17. goals (p. 67)
18. culture (p. 68)
19. content (p. 68)
20. properties of objects (p. 69)
21. overall context (p. 69)
22. Controlled thinking (p. 73)
23. fully aware (p. 73)
24. changing (p. 73)
25. emotional reactions (p. 73)
26. mentally undo (p. 73)
27. rumination (p. 74)
28. depression (p. 74)
29. thought suppression (p. 74)
30. forget (p. 74)
31. checks and balances (p. 75)
32. confidence (p. 75)
33. overconfidence barrier (p. 75)
34. remedial action (p. 75)
35. statistical and methodological (p. 76)

Essay Review

1. Your essay on automatic thinking should include:
    - Automatic thinking is thinking that is nonconscious, unintentional, involuntary, and effortless. (p. 52)
    - People use schemas, which are mental structures that organize our knowledge about the social world. These mental structures influence the information we notice, think about, and remember. (p. 53)
    - Our schemas contain our basic knowledge and impressions that we use to organize what we know about the social world and interpret new situations. (p. 53)

2.   Your essay should include:
   - Accessibility is the extent to which schemas and concepts are at the forefront of people's minds and are therefore likely to be used when we are making judgments about the social world. (p. 56)
   - Some schemas are chronically accessible due to past experience. (p. 56)
   - Something can become accessible because it is related to a current goal. (p. 56)
   - Schemas can become temporarily accessible because of our recent experiences. This is called priming. (p. 56)

3.   Your essay on self-fulfilling prophecy should include:
   - A self-fulfilling prophecy is a case wherein people have an expectation about what another person is like, which influences how they act toward that person, which causes that person to behave consistently with people's original expectations, making the expectations come true. (p. 58)
   - Research has shown that self-fulfilling prophecies are most likely to occur when interviewers are not paying careful attention to the person they are interviewing. (p. 61)
   - Thus, I should be motivated to form an accurate impression and schedule each interview for a time of day when I can be free from distractions and take the time to form an accurate impression. (p. 61)

4.   Your essay on heuristics should include:
   - A judgmental heuristic is a mental shortcut people use to make judgments quickly and efficiently. (p. 63)
   - The availability heuristic is a mental rule of thumb whereby people base a judgment on the ease with which they can bring something to mind. (p. 63)
   - If I were a physician, the availability heuristic could affect my diagnoses. The symptoms of illnesses that occur frequently will be more easily remembered, making them more easily recognized. If a person has a rare disorder, the appropriate diagnosis is more likely to be missed because it will not be as accessible. (pp. 63-64)

5.   Your essay on counterfactual thinking should include:
   - Counterfactual thinking refers to mentally changing some aspect of the past as a way of imagining what might have been. (p. 73)
   - Counterfactual thoughts can have a big influence on our emotional reactions to events. The easier it is to mentally undo an outcome, the stronger the emotional reaction to it (p. 73)
   - The silver medalist might feel worse because he or she could more easily imagine having won the event and the gold medal, while the bronze medalist could more easily imagine not having placed at all and may be happy just to have a medal. (pp. 73-74)

Exit Test 1

1.   C (p. 53)
2.   D (p. 53)
3.   A (p. 54)
4.   B (p. 69)
5.   A (p. 57)
6.   B (p. 62)
7.   B (p. 64)
8.   C (p. 68)
9.   A (p. 73)
10.   D (p. 74)

Exit Test 2

1.   B (p. 52)
2.   A (p. 53)
3.   D (p. 56)
4.   C (p. 60)
5.   B (p. 69)
6.   C (p. 58)
7.   A (p. 69)
8.   A (p. 65)
9.   D (p. 66)
10.   B (p. 71)

Study Activities

1.   Social cognition refers to how people think about themselves and their social world. Researchers in this area study how people select, interpret, remember, and use social information to make judgments and decisions. (p. 51)

2.   Automatic thinking is thought that is nonconscious, unintentional, involuntary, and effortless. Automatic thinking helps us understand new situations by relating them to our prior experiences. (pp. 52-53)

3.   It is important to study schemas because they influence the information we notice, think about, and remember. Schemas contain our basic knowledge about other people, ourselves, social roles, and specific events. They contain our basic knowledge and impressions that we use to organize what we know about the social world and interpret new situations. (pp. 53-54)

4.   Cultures determine what schemas we learn and remember. What is valued in a particular culture is more likely to be a part of a well-developed schema. (pp. 68-69)

5.   The friend should be reminded about the availability heuristic, a mental rule of thumb whereby people base a judgment on the ease with which they can bring something to mind. I would suggest that before she give out the evaluations, she ask her students to list 10 ways the course could be improved. It will be difficult for students to think of ten things so they will conclude that it must be a great course. (pp. 63-66)

6. Asking people to consider the opposite point of view to their own makes people realize that there are other ways to construe the world. Another approach is to teach people directly some basic statistical and methodological principles about how to reason correctly. (pp. 75-76)

7. In thought suppression the automatic part of the system, the monitoring process, searches for evidence that the unwanted thought is about to intrude on consciousness. After the unwanted thought is detected, the more controlled part of the system, the operating process, comes into play. This is the effortful, conscious attempt to distract oneself by finding something else to think about. (p. 74)

8. Perhaps the best metaphor of human thinking is that people are "flawed scientists"—brilliant thinkers who are attempting to discover the nature of the social world in a logical manner but do not do so perfectly. People are often blind to truths that don't fit their schemas and sometimes treat others in ways that make their schemas come true—something that good scientists would never do. (p. 78)

9. Being from the U.S., I have an analytic thinking style so I tend to focus on the properties of objects and do not consider the surrounding context. My friend, coming from Korea, is more likely to have a holistic thinking style and focus on the overall context, especially the ways in which objects relate to each other. (p. 69)

10. You would tell your brother about the Barnum effect in which statements are so vague that they apply to virtually everyone. It is related to the representativeness heuristic. (p. 66)

CHAPTER 4

Social Perception: How We Come to Understand Other People

CHAPTER 4 OVERVIEW

The topic of Chapter 4 is social perception. **Social perception** is the study of how we form impressions of and make inferences about other people. The first section of the chapter describes the ability people have to decode and encode nonverbal behavior. **Nonverbal communication** refers to how people communicate, intentionally or unintentionally, without words. Facial expressions can communicate our emotions. All humans **encode** or express these emotions in the same way, and all humans can **decode** or interpret them with equal accuracy. Facial expressions of emotion are universal for six major emotional expressions: anger, happiness, surprise, fear, disgust, and sadness. These six emotions are also the first to appear in human development. Research has indicated that the emotion of *pride* exists cross-culturally. Pride is a particularly interesting emotional display because it involves a facial expression as well as body posture and gesture cues.

Decoding facial expressions accurately can be complicating for two reasons. People frequently display **affect blends**: One part of their face registers one emotion while another part registers a different emotion. A second reason why decoding facial expressions can be inaccurate has to do with culture. **Display rules** are particular to each culture and dictate what kinds of emotional expressions people are supposed to show. Gestures of the hands and arms are also a fascinating means of communication. **Emblems** are nonverbal gestures that have well-understood definitions within a given culture. Everyday life is made up of multichanneled nonverbal social interaction.

The next section of the chapter discusses implicit personality theories. An **implicit personality theory** is a type of schema people use to group various kinds of personality traits together. These theories are developed over time and with experience and they vary by culture.

The third section consists of research in the area of attribution theory. **Attribution theory** refers to a description of the way in which people explain the causes of their own behavior and other people's behavior. An **internal attribution** is an inference that a person is behaving in a certain way because of something about the person, such as attitude, character, or personality. An **external attribution** is an inference that a person is behaving a certain way because of something about the situation he or she is in; the assumption is that most people would respond the same way in that situation.

Social psychologists have proposed several attribution theories. For example, the **covariation model** focuses on how people make internal or external attributions to explain other people's behaviors. According to this model, this involves considering three types of information: **consensus** (the extent to which other people behave the same way toward the same stimulus as the actor does), **distinctiveness** (information about the extent to which one particular actor behaves in the same way to different stimuli), and **consistency** (information about the extent to which the behavior between one actor and one stimulus is the same across time and circumstances).

The pervasive, fundamental theory or schema most of us have about human behavior is that people do what they do because of the kind of people they are, not because of the situation they are in. The **correspondence bias** is the tendency to infer that people's behavior corresponds to (matches) their disposition (personality). One reason people fall prey to the correspondence bias is that when we try to explain someone's behavior, our focus of attention is usually on the person, not on the surrounding situation. People, not the situation, have **perceptual salience** for us; we pay attention to them, and we tend to think that they alone cause their behavior. We go through a two-step process when we make attributions. First, we assume that a person's behavior was due to something about that person and then we attempt to adjust this attribution by considering the situation the person was in.

For decades, it was taken for granted that the correspondence bias was universal. But social psychologists are focusing more on the role of culture in many aspects of social behavior. Research has indicated that differing cultural values affect the kind of information that people notice and pay attention to. People in individualistic cultures prefer dispositional attributions about others, relative to people in collectivistic cultures, who prefer situational attributions. However, it would be a mistake to think that members of collectivistic cultures don't ever make dispositional attributions. They do, it's just a matter of degree. People in collectivistic cultures are more likely to go beyond dispositional explanations, including information about the situation as well.

The correspondence bias applies unevenly. We are very likely to find internal causes for other people's behavior but we tend to explain our own behavior by looking at the situation. The **actor/observer difference** is the tendency to see other people's behavior as dispositionally caused but focusing more on the role of situational factors when explaining one's own behavior. One reason for this difference is perceptual salience. Just as we notice other people's behavior more than their situation, we notice our own situation more than our own behavior. The actor/observer difference also occurs because actors have more information about themselves than observers do.

Self-serving attributions are explanations for one's successes that credit internal, dispositional factors and explanations for one's failures that blame external, situational factors. People also alter their attributions to deal with other kinds of threats to their self-esteem. **Defensive attributions** are explanations for behavior that defend us from feelings of vulnerability and mortality. The **belief in a just world** is the assumption that people get what they deserve and deserve what they get.

Another main focus of this chapter is on the role of culture in other attributional biases. Social psychologists have examined the actor/observer difference in Korea and the United States. They found that Korean and American research participants did not differ in the attributions they made to themselves—the "actors." they both made situational attributions about their behavior. However, Americans were more likely to think another person's behavior was due to his or her disposition (the correspondence bias), while Koreans were more likely to think the other person's behavior was due to the situation. Researchers have examined the self-serving bias and found a strong cultural component to it as well. A recent meta-analysis found that the self-serving bias is strongest in the United States and some other Western countries—Canada, Australia, and New Zealand. In collectivist cultures like China, the reverse is true: People attribute failure to internal causes, not to external ones. Preliminary research suggests that in cultures with extremes of wealth and poverty, just world attributions are more common than in cultures where wealth is more evenly distributed.

CHAPTER 4 OUTLINE

I. Nonverbal Behavior
• **Social perception** is defined as the study of how we form impressions of and make inferences about other people.
• To learn about other people, we rely on information from their physical appearance, and verbal and nonverbal communication.
• **Nonverbal communication** is defined as the way in which people communicate, intentionally or unintentionally, without words—including through facial expressions, tone of voice, gestures, body position and movement, touch, and gaze.

• We share our ability to read nonverbal cues with other species. For example, dogs are adept at reading not only "dog nonverbals" but human nonverbals as well.
• Humans and primates have a special kind of brain cell called mirror neurons. These neurons respond when we perform an action and when we see someone else perform the same action. Mirror neurons appear to be the basis of our ability to feel empathy.
• Nonverbal cues serve many functions in communication. They help us express our emotions, our attitudes, and our personality. In addition, some nonverbal cues actually contradict the spoken words.

A. Facial Expressions of Emotion
• Facial expressions are a prime source of nonverbal communication.

1. Evolution and Facial Expressions
• Charles Darwin believed that human emotional expressions are universal—that all humans **encode** (express or emit nonverbal behavior) and **decode** (interpret the meaning of the nonverbal behavior of others) expressions in the same way.
• Modern research suggests that Darwin was right, for the six major emotional expressions: anger, happiness, surprise, fear, disgust, and sadness.
• For example, Ekman & Frieson's (1971) study with a preliterate tribe in New Guinea that had had no previous contact with Western civilization found that the tribes' people used similar expressions to Americans to display similar emotions, and that these tribes' people could accurately match pictures of Americans displaying emotions to relevant stories.
• The six major emotions are the first to appear in human development. Children as young as six months to a year express these emotions with the facial expressions we associate with adults. Even children who have been blind from birth are able to encode the basic emotions even though they have never seen them displayed by adults.
• Recent research on the facial expression of contempt suggests that it is recognized cross-culturally like the six major emotions discussed earlier. Research has also indicated that the emotion of *pride* exists cross-culturally.

2. Why Is Decoding Sometimes Inaccurate?
• Facial expressions may sometimes be hard to interpret accurately because people may display **affect blends**, facial expressions where one part of the face registers one emotion and another part registers a different emotion.
• A second reason why decoding facial expressions can be inaccurate has to do with culture.

B. Culture and the Channels of Nonverbal Communication
 Paul Ekman and his colleagues have studied the influence of culture on the facial display of emotions. They have concluded that **display rules** are particular to each culture and dictate what kinds of emotional expressions people are supposed to show.
• Eye contact and gaze are also powerful nonverbal cues.
• The use of personal space is a nonverbal behavior with wide cultural variation.
• **Emblems** are nonverbal gestures of the hands and arms that have well-understood definitions within a given culture.

C. Multichannel Nonverbal Communication
• In everyday life, we usually receive information from multiple channels simultaneously. The Social Interpretation Task (SIT; Archer & Akert, 1991), which uses videotaped naturally occurring interactions as stimuli, reveals that people are able to interpret such cues fairly accurately by making use of multiple cues.

• There is a dilemma of email communication: Words go out, but there are no nonverbal cues to give them additional meaning, creating a potential for misinterpretation.

II. Implicit Personality Theories: Filling In the Blanks
• An **implicit personality theory** is a type of schema people use to group various kinds of personality traits together. Like other schemas, using these theories help us form well-developed impressions of other people quickly.

A. Culture and Implicit Personality Theories
• Within a culture, many people share similar implicit personality theories. For example, our culture shares a "what is beautiful is good" stereotype, and Chinese culture has a stereotype that describes a person who maintains harmony in relationships as well as inner harmony.
• In a study by Hoffman et al. (1986), Chinese-English bilingual subjects formed different interpretations of the same person depending on whether they read the description in English (where an artistic impression was evoked) or in Chinese (where a *shi gû* (worldly, devoted to family, socially skilled, and reserved) impression was evoked by the very same description) (Figure 4.3, p. 94).

III. Causal Attribution: Answering the "Why" Question
• Although nonverbal behavior and implicit personality theories provide a guide to understanding others, there is still substantial ambiguity about why people act the way they do. **Attribution theory** describes the way in which people explain the causes of their own and other people's behavior.

A. The Nature of the Attribution Process
• Fritz Heider is considered the father of attribution theory. He believed that people are like amateur scientists, trying to understand other people's behavior by piecing together information until they arrive at a reasonable cause.
• He proposed a simple dichotomy for people's explanations: **internal attributions**, in which people infer that a person is behaving a certain way because of something about that person (e.g., a trait or attitude) versus **external attributions**, in which people infer that a person is behaving in a certain way because of the situation that he or she is in.
• Fincham et al. demonstrate that spouses in happy marriages make internal attributions for their partner's positive behaviors and external attributions for their partner's negative behaviors, while spouses in distressed marriages display the opposite pattern.
• Heider also noted that people seem to prefer internal attributions.

B. The Covariation Model: Internal versus External Attributions
• Kelley's (1967) theory of attributions focuses on how people decide whether to make an internal or an external attribution. Additionally, Kelley's covariation model focuses on instances where you have multiple observations of behavior.
• The **covariation model** states that in order to form an attribution about what caused a person's behavior, we systematically note the pattern between the presence (or absence) of possible causal factors and whether or not the behavior occurs. The possible causal factors we focus on are (1) **consensus information**, or information about the extent to which other people behave the same way towards the same stimulus as the actor does; (2) **distinctiveness information**, or information about the extent to which one particular actor behaves in the same way to different stimuli; and (3) **consistency information**, or information about the extent to which the behavior between one actor and one stimulus is the same across time and circumstances.
• People are most likely to make an internal attribution when consensus and distinctiveness are low but consistency is high; they are most likely to make an external attribution when consensus, distinctiveness, and consistency are all high (see example, Figure 4–4, p. 107).

•The covariation model assumes that people make causal attributions in a rational, logical fashion. Several studies generally confirm that people can indeed make attributions in the way that these models predict; with the exception that consensus information is not used as much as Kelley's model predicts.
• Correspondent inference theory and the covariation model portray people as systematic and logical. However, attributions can be distorted by self-serving motives and by biases in reasoning.

C. The Correspondence Bias: People as Personality Psychologists
• Rosa Parks, a black seamstress in Montgomery, Alabama, broke the law one day in December, 1955 when she refused to give up her seat to a white person. She was convicted of violating the segregation laws and fined. Her act was the precipitating event of the Civil Rights Movement. Rosa Parks died on October 24, 2005, at the age of 92. To commemorate her, the American Public Transportation Association called for December 1 to be the "Tribute to Rosa Parks Day." Busses in major cities across the country designated one seat, behind the driver, to be kept empty for the day in her honor. Signs were posted on the windows adjacent to the seat to alert riders. While most people honored the request to keep the seat empty, some riders did not. Other people on the bus made negative attributions about the character and attitudes of the people who sat in the special seat. However, a journalist began asking these people why they were sitting there and an alternative explanation emerged—they had not seen the sign.
• The **correspondence bias** is the tendency to infer that people's behavior corresponds to (matches) their disposition (personality). The correspondence bias is so pervasive that many social psychologists call it the fundamental attribution error.
• A classic experiment demonstrating this tendency was conducted by Jones and Harris (1967). Students read a pro- or anti-Castro essay ostensibly written by another student. Half of the participants were told that the author freely chose which position to take, while half were told that the author had no choice. Even in this latter condition, people still tended to believe that the author's essay reflected a true attitude (Figure 4.5, p. 110).
• Although oftentimes people's behavior is accounted for by internal dispositional factors, the label "fundamental attribution error" reflects that, when explaining behavior, people tend to underestimate the large effects that situations can have, even when these situational constraints are obvious.

1. The Role of Perceptual Salience in the Correspondence Bias
• One reason people make the fundamental attribution error is that observers focus their attention on actors, while the situational causes of the actor's behavior may be invisible. People, not the situation, have **perceptual salience** for us; we pay attention to them, and we tend to think that they alone cause their behavior.
• For example, Taylor & Fiske (1975) arranged six participants in assigned seats to manipulate how easily different participants could see each other (Figure 4.6, p. 111). They found that people rated the actor they could see most clearly as having the largest role in the conversation (Figure 4.7, p. 101).
• Thus perceptual salience, or the information that is the focus of people's attention, helps explain why the fundamental attribution error is prevalent.

2. The Two-Step Process of Making Attributions
• Gilbert's work suggests that there is a two-step process of attribution: when people analyze another's behavior, they typically make an internal attribution automatically (the first step in the process); they may then consciously choose to engage in the effortful second step in the process, where they think about possible situational reasons for the behavior. After engaging in the second step, they may adjust their original internal attribution to take account of situational factors (Figure 4.8, p. 103).
• Because this second step is more conscious and effortful, people may not get to it if they are distracted or preoccupied.

• People will be more likely to engage in the second step of attributional processing when they consciously think carefully before making a judgment, when they are motivated to be as accurate as possible, or if they are suspicious about the motives of the target.

• Recent research on videotaped police interrogations has shown that perceptual salience can trigger the correspondence bias, affecting how guilty the suspect is judged to be.

D. Culture and the Correspondence Bias

• North American and some other Western cultures stress individual autonomy. In contrast, East Asian cultures such as those in China, Japan, and Korea stress group autonomy. This raises the question of whether Western culture, which emphasizes individual freedom and autonomy, socialize its members to prefer dispositional attributions over situational ones?

• People in individualistic cultures do prefer dispositional attributions about others, relative to people in collectivistic cultures, who prefer situational attributions.

• Morris and Peng (1994) compared newspaper articles about two murders that appeared in English and Chinese language newspapers, and found that journalists writing in English made significantly more dispositional attributions about both the Chinese and Anglo-American murderer than did journalists writing in Chinese.

• A tendency to think dispositionally about others—the correspondence bias—appears in many cultures. However, members of collectivistic cultures are more aware of how the situation affects behavior and more likely to take situational effects into account.

• Cross-cultural research replicated the Jones & Harris (1967) study and shows that research participants in Korea, Japan, and China all fall prey to the fundamental attribution error just like Western participants.

• Cross-cultural demonstrations of the correspondence bias suggest that there really is something "fundamental" about the fundamental attribution error. People in all cultures display it; however, people from Eastern cultures also have more of an ability to override the dispositionalist tendency.

E. The Actor/Observer Difference

• The **actor/observer difference** is the tendency to see other people's behavior as dispositionally caused, while focusing more on the role of situational factors when explaining one's own behavior. This can lead to striking disagreements between people.

• **Perceptual Salience Revisited**

• One reason for the actor/observer difference is perceptual salience: actors notice the situations around them that influence them to act, while observers notice the actors.

• **The Role of Information Availability in the Actor/Observer Difference**

• The actor/observer difference also occurs because actors have more information about themselves (e.g., their behavior in other situations) than do observers.

F. Self-Serving Attributions

• Self-serving attributions are explanations for one's successes that credit internal, dispositional factors and explanations for one's failures that blame external, situational factors. Lau & Russell (1980) observed this pattern in the attributions professional athletes made for their performances.

• Roesch & Amirkham (1997) found that less experienced athletes, more highly skilled athletes, and athletes in solo sports are more likely to make self-serving attributions.

• One reason people make self-serving attributions is to maintain their self-esteem.

• A second reason is self-presentational, to maintain the perceptions others have of one.

• A third reason is because people have information about their behavior in other situations, which may lead to positive outcomes being expected and negative outcomes being unexpected (and thus attributed to the situation).

• **Defensive attributions** are explanations for behavior or outcomes (e.g., tragic events) that avoid feelings of vulnerability and mortality.

• One way we deal with tragic information about others is to make it seem like it could never happen to us. We do so through the **belief in a just world**, a form of defensive attribution wherein people assume that bad things happen to bad people and that good things happen to good people. Because most of us see ourselves as good, this reassures us that bad things will not happen to us.
• The belief in a just world can lead to blaming the victim for his or her misfortunes. This keeps anxious thoughts about one's own safety at bay.

IV. Culture and Other Attributional Biases

• Continuing to explore the link between culture and attributional biases, social psychologists have examined the self-serving bias and found a strong cultural component to it as well.
• In a meta-analysis of 266 studies conducted all over the world, Mezulis et al. (2004) found that the self-serving bias is strongest in the United States and some other Western countries—Canada, Australia, and New Zealand.
• With regard to the belief in a just world, Furnham (1993) argues that, in cultures where the belief is dominant, social and economic injustices are considered fair (the poor and disadvantaged have less because they deserve less). Preliminary work suggests that the just world belief is more predominant in cultures where there are greater extremes of wealth and poverty.

LEARNING OBJECTIVES

After reading Chapter 4, you should be able to do the following:

1.   Define social perception. (p. 84)

2.   Define nonverbal communication. Identify the different channels of nonverbal communication. (p. 84)

3.   Identify the various functions of nonverbal behavior and discuss the effects nonverbal communication can have on verbal communication. (p. 85)

4.   Discuss Darwin's theory of universal facial expressions of emotion and research that supports this theory. Define encode and decode. (pp. 86-87)

5.   Identify factors that decrease decoding accuracy. Define affect blends. Define display rules. Define emblems and list examples of them. Discuss cross-cultural differences in nonverbal communication. (pp. 88-89)

6.   Describe how we gather information from multichannel nonverbal communication. (p. 89)

7.   Discuss the email dilemma of communicating without nonverbal cues. (pp. 91-92)

8.   Define implicit personality theory and describe how it is influenced by culture. Identify the focus of attribution theory. (pp. 92-94)

9.   Describe the nature of the attribution process according to Fritz Heider. Distinguish between internal and external attributions. List examples of each type of attribution. (pp. 95-96)

Chapter 4

10. Describe the covariation model of Kelley and the process it attempts to describe. Identify and define the three kinds of information Kelley claims we use to make attributions. Identify the types of attributions we make when these kinds of information are combined in different ways. (pp. 96-98)

11. Define the correspondence bias/fundamental attribution error. Define perceptual salience. Describe the two-step process of attribution. Discuss why the fundamental attribution error is so prevalent. Describe people's intuitive beliefs about others' tendencies to make the fundamental attribution error. (pp. 98-102)

12. Describe the findings from research on the role of culture in the attribution process. Discuss cultural differences in the prevalence of the correspondence bias. (pp. 103-107)

13. Define the actor/observer difference. Discuss the causes of the actor/observer difference. Identify the influences of perceptual salience and information availability on the actor/observer difference. (pp. 107-108)

14. Define self-serving attributions. Identify self-serving attributions for success and for failure. Discuss why people make self-serving attributions. (pp. 109-110)

15. Discuss the motives underlying defensive attributions. Identify and define two forms of defensive attributions. Discuss the relationship between defensive attributions and "blaming the victim" of misfortune. (pp. 110-111)

16. Discuss cultural differences in the frequency of other attribution biases including the actor/observer difference, the self-serving bias, and the belief in the just world. (pp. 111-113)

KEY TERMS

Correctly identify the definition of each key term. Place the name of the correct term in the space provided.

1. _____ The study of how we form impressions of and make inferences about other people. (p. 84)

2. _____ The way in which people communicate, intentionally or unintentionally, without words. (p. 84)

3. _____ To express or emit nonverbal behavior. (p. 86)

4. _____ To interpret the meaning of the nonverbal behavior of other people. (p. 86)

5. _____ A facial expression in which one part of the face registers one emotion while another part of the face registers a different emotion. (p. 88)

6. _____ Culturally determined rules about which nonverbal behaviors are appropriate to display. (p. 88)

7. _____ Nonverbal gestures that have well-understood definitions within a given culture. (p. 89)

8. _____ A type of schema people use to group various kinds of personality traits together. (p. 92)

9. _____ A description of the way in which people explain the causes of their own and other people's behavior. (p. 95)

10. _____ The inference that a person is behaving in a certain way because of something about the person. (p. 95)

11. _____ The inference that a person is behaving a certain way because of something about the situation he or she is in. (p. 95)

12. _____ A theory that states that to form an attribution about what causes a person's behavior, we systematically note the pattern between the presence or absence of possible causal factors and whether or not the behavior occurs. (p. 96)

13. _____ Information about the extent to which other people behave the same way toward the same stimulus as the actor does. (p. 96)

14. _____ Information about the extent to which one particular actor behaves in the same way to different stimuli. (p. 97)

15. _____ Information about the extent to which the behavior between one actor and one stimulus is the same across time and circumstances. (p. 97)

16. _____ The tendency to infer that people's behavior corresponds to (matches) their disposition (personality). (p. 100)

17. _____ The seeming importance of information that is the focus of people's attention. (p. 101)

18. _____ Analyzing another person's behavior first by making an automatic internal attribution and only then thinking about possible situational reasons for the behavior, after which one may adjust the original internal attribution. (p. 102)

19. _____ The tendency to see other people's behavior as dispositionally caused but focusing more on the role of situational factors when explaining one's own behavior. (p. 107)

20. _____ Explanations for one's successes that credit internal, dispositional factors and explanations for one's failures that blame external, situational factors. (p. 109)

21. _____ Explanations for behavior that avoid feelings of vulnerability and mortality. (p. 110)

22. _____ A form of defensive attribution wherein people assume that bad things happen to bad people and that good things happen to good people. (p. 110)

GUIDED REVIEW

PRACTICE TEST

1.   Which of the following is an example of multi-channel nonverbal communication?
   a)   averting ones eyes while speaking with a flat tone and twisting on one foot
   b)   exhibiting sadness in one part of the face and disgust in another
   c)   interpreting a compliment as false flattery when you're in a bad mood
   d)   all of the above

2.   Greg has recently taken in a stray dog. If you make an external attribution for Greg's behavior, you will conclude that:
   a)   Greg likes dogs.
   b)   Greg felt sorry for the dog.
   c)   the dog is probably cute and friendly.
   d)   others will perceive Greg as an animal lover.

3.   The perception that our own behaviors are caused by the situation but that others' behaviors are dispositionally caused is known as the:
   a)   fundamental attribution error.
   b)   attribution difference.
   c)   actor/observer difference.
   d)   anchoring adjustment heuristic.

4.   A consequence of our belief in a just world is that we:
   a)   blame the victims of misfortune.
   b)   focus on situational causes of others' behavior.
   c)   make accurate attributions and impressions.
   d)   are more likely to attribute our own behavior to dispositional causes.

5.   Facial expressions, tone of voice, and the use of touch are all examples of:
   a)   context dependent attributional cues.
   b)   affect blends.
   c)   display rules.
   d)   nonverbal communication.

6.   Japanese women less often exhibit a wide, uninhibited smile than women in Western cultures because Japanese and Western cultures prescribe different:
   a)   display rules.
   b)   values.
   c)   affect blends.
   d)   implicit personality theories.

7.   Which of the following is an example of an emblem?
   a)   a road sign
   b)   the written explanation of a nonverbal cue
   c)   the "okay" sign created with the thumb and forefinger
   d)   averted eye gaze

8.	Research indicates that suppressed emotions are often
	a)	the cause of mood disorders.
	b)	totally invisible to family members.
	c)	"leaked" via a facial expression or body movement.
	d)	the cause of stomach disorders.

9.	The display of different emotions on different parts of the face is called a(n):
	a)	affect emblem.
	b)	nonverbal blend.
	c)	facial incongruity.
	d)	affect blend.

10.	According to Fritz Heider (1958), the attributions we make for people's behavior can be either _____ or _____.
	a)	target-based; category-based
	b)	internal; external
	c)	perceptual; physical
	d)	accurate; biased

11.	The study of how we form impressions and make judgments of others is called:
	a)	judgmental heuristics.
	b)	social perception.
	c)	attribution theory.
	d)	social cognition.

12.	The three types of information central to Kelley's (1967) covariation model are:
	a)	consensus, correspondence, and distinctiveness.
	b)	consensus, consistency, and correspondence.
	c)	correspondence, distinctiveness, and consistency.
	d)	consensus, distinctiveness, and consistency.

13.	Research on cultural differences in attribution styles indicates that people from individualistic cultures
	a)	are less skilled at forming impressions of behavior.
	b)	prefer dispositional explanations of behavior.
	c)	prefer situational explanations of behavior.
	d)	are reluctant to publicly state dispositional explanations of behavior.

14.	The automatic formation of an internal attribution followed by a situational one given time and effortful thought describes the:
	a)	fundamental attribution error.
	b)	multi-step process of attribution.
	c)	actor/observer difference.
	d)	two-step process of attribution.

15.	To express emotions is to _____ and to interpret emotions is to _____.
	a)	display; perceive
	b)	decode; encode
	c)	encode; decode
	d)	display; decode

16.   Lassiter and colleagues (2007) presented courtroom judges and police officers with a videotaped suspect (actually a confederate) who confessed to a crime. They found that
a)   for both the judges and police officers, the videotape that focused on the detective and the suspect produced significantly higher ratings of "voluntariness."
b)   for the police officers, the videotape that focused only on the detective produced significantly higher ratings of "voluntariness," but for the judges the videotape that focused equally on both the detective and suspect produced the highest ratings of "voluntariness"
c)   for both the judges and police officers, the videotape that focused only on the suspect produced significantly higher ratings of "voluntariness."
d)   for both the judges and police officers, the videotape that focused only on the detective produced significantly higher ratings of "voluntariness."

17.   Which of the following is FALSE regarding implicit personality theories?
a)   The implicit personality theories of different individuals can share common components.
b)   Implicit personality theories are influenced by cultural factors.
c)   Implicit personality theories influence how people form impressions of others.
d)   We are always consciously aware of using implicit personality theories.

18.   Which of the following focuses on how we make inferences about the causes of other people's behaviors?
a)   implicit personality theory
b)   attribution theory
c)   social role theory
d)   social perception theory

19.   According to Kelley's (1967) covariation model, when people use information about whether or not the actor acts the same way toward everyone, not just the target, they are using _____ information to make an attribution about the actor's behavior.
a)   distinctiveness
b)   consensus
c)   discriminating
d)   consistency

20   According to Kelley's (1967) covariation model, when people use information about whether or not others, not just the actor, act the same way toward the target, they are using _____ information to make an attribution about the actor's behavior.
a)   distinctiveness
b)   consensus
c)   discriminating
d)   consistency

21.   The six major emotions are the first to appear in human development.
a)   True
b)   False

22. Gyekye and Salminen (2004) asked industrial workers and their supervisors in Ghana, Africa, to assign causality for on-the-job accidents. Workers blamed _____ and supervisors blamed _____.
    a) weather conditions; the fact that the workers were often tired
    b) factors in the situation; weather conditions
    c) the supervisors; the workers
    d) factors in the situation; the workers

23. Which of the following is FALSE regarding the 2005 study conducted by Kruger et al. on email communication?
    a) Participants were very confident of their communicative abilities.
    b) Recipients were significantly less likely to get the emotional meaning if the message was communicated via email.
    c) Participant's friends did better at decoding the correct emotion than did complete strangers.
    d) All of the above are true.

24. Chinese students are expected to attribute their success to their own intelligence.
    a) True
    b) False

25. When people make _____ attributions for successes and _____ attributions for failures, they are making self-serving attributions.
    a) external; dispositional
    b) internal; dispositional
    c) internal; external
    d) external; internal

26. All of the following are reasons why people make self-serving attributions EXCEPT which one?
    a) to maintain self-esteem
    b) because we want to present ourselves to others in a positive way
    c) because of the information we have available to us
    d) because we are motivated to be accurate

27. Which of the following is a type of defensive attribution?
    a) realistic hopefulness
    b) unrealistic hopefulness
    c) belief in a just world
    d) illusion of vulnerability

28. Which of the following is true about the correspondence bias?
    a) It is the tendency to believe that people's behavior matches their personalities.
    b) It occurs across cultures.
    c) People in collectivist cultures are more likely to adjust it to take into account situational information compared to people from individualist cultures.
    d) All the above are true about the correspondence bias.

29. Taylor and Fiske's (1975) study on perceptual salience demonstrated that:
   a) when participants were facing a speaker in a conversation, they judged that speaker as having more impact on the conversation.
   b) hearing a conversation made the issues in that conversation particularly accessible.
   c) the fundamental attribution error is less likely to be made when an issue is not particularly salient to an individual.
   d) the spotlight effect is especially strong when we have been primed to think about our positive qualities, but not our negative attributes.

30. When they looked at how Japanese media described the performance of Japanese gold medalists in the 2000 and 2002 Olympics, Markus et al. (2006) found that the medalists were described
   a) only in terms of the athlete's abilities.
   b) only in terms of how their coaches, teammates, and family had contributed to their success.
   c) in broad terms, including the individual's ability but also discussing past successes and failures, and the role other people (such as coaches) had played in the success.
   d) mostly in terms of how they had overcome past failures.

31. Hare & Tomasello (2005) have conducted research on the ability of other species to read nonverbal cues. They have found that
   a) only humans can read nonverbal cues.
   b) dogs are adept at reading "dog nonverbals" and human nonverbals.
   c) dogs are adept at reading "dog nonverbals" but not human nonverbals.
   d) dogs are completely incapable of reading any nonverbal cues.

32. Children as young as _____ months to a year express the six basic emotions with the facial expressions we associate with adults.
   a) 3
   b) 6
   c) 7
   d) 9

33. According to research by Justin Kruger and his colleagues (2005), e-mail writers do not realize, to a sufficient extent, the problem caused by loss of nonverbal cues.
   a) True
   b) False

34. In America, we presume that if someone is kind the person is also
   a) full of pride.
   b) funny.
   c) unintelligent (especially if the person is blond).
   d) generous.

35. The covariation model assumes that people make causal attributions in a(n) _____ way.
   a) unrealistic
   b) calculating
   c) rational, logical
   d) irrational, illogical

36. On December 1, 2005, the American Public Transportation Association had a "Tribute to Rosa Parks Day." In her honor passengers were asked, via a posted sign on the adjacent window, to leave the seat behind the driver empty. A journalist questioned individuals who sat in the seat in spite of the sign and found that these people
    a) had not seen the sign.
    b) were too tired to care.
    c) were racist.
    d) had medical conditions and needed to sit down, but there were no other seats available.

37. In the two-step process of making attributions, we will engage in the second step if we
    a) consciously slow down and think carefully before reaching a judgment.
    b) are motivated to reach as accurate a judgment as possible.
    c) are suspicious about the behavior of the target person.
    d) all of the above

38. Research has indicated that differing cultural values affect the kind of information that people notice and pay attention to.
    a) True
    b) False

39. Amy assumes that her poor grade on an exam is due to the fact that she is working too many hours at her job, but she assumes that the poor grade received by the student sitting next to her is due to laziness and a lack of motivation. Amy's behavior best illustrates the
    a) differential attribution bias.
    b) actor/observer difference.
    c) fundamental attribution error.
    d) perceptual salience error.

40. Preliminary research suggests that in cultures with extremes of wealth and poverty, just world attributions are
    a) nonexistent.
    b) uncommon.
    c) more common than in cultures where wealth is more evenly distributed.
    d) less common than in cultures where wealth is more evenly distributed.

SHORT ANSWER REVIEW

Social perception is the study of how we form (1) _____ (p. 84) of other people and how we make (2) _____ (84) about them. One important source of information that we use is people's (3) _____ (p. 84) behavior, such as their facial expressions, body movements, and tone of voice. Frequently these are the most (4) _____ (p. 84) channels of nonverbal communication. Nonverbal cues serve many functions in communication. They help us express our emotions, our attitudes, and our (5) _____ (p. 85). Nonverbal cues are often considered more (6) _____ (p. 85) than words.

Darwin believed that the primary emotions conveyed by the face are universal: All humans (7) _____ (p. 86) or express these emotions in the same way, and all humans can (8) _____ (p. 86) or interpret them with equal accuracy. The six major emotional expressions are anger, happiness, surprise, fear, (9) _____ (p. 86), and sadness. These six major emotions are the first to appear in human development. This is true as well for young children who have been (10) _____ (p. 87) from birth. Decoding facial expressions accurately is complicated and can be inaccurate for two reasons. People frequently display (11) _____ (p. 88): One part of their (12) _____ (p. 88) registers one emotion while another part registers a different emotion. A second reason why decoding facial expressions can be inaccurate has to do with (13) _____ (p. 88).

Paul Ekman and his colleagues have concluded that (14) _____ (p. 88) are particular to each culture and dictate what kinds of emotional expressions people are supposed to show. Gestures of the hands and arms are a fascinating means of communication. Gestures for which there are clear, well-understood definitions are called (15) _____ (p. 89). The important point about emblems is that they are not universal.

Except for certain specific situations, such as talking on the telephone, everyday life is made up of (16) _____ (p. 89) nonverbal social interaction. Typically, many nonverbal cues are available to us when we talk to or observe other people. We should be very careful when we email because the emotion in our message can be easily (17) _____ (p. 92).

Schemas allow us to form impressions quickly, without having to spend weeks with people to figure out what they are like. An (18) _____ (p. 92) is a type of schema people use to group various kinds of personality traits together. These theories are developed over time and with (19) _____ (p. 93). They are also strongly tied to (20) _____ (p. 93).

Attribution theory is a description of the way in which people explain the (21) _____ (p. 95) of other people's behavior. Fritz Heider proposed that we make one of two attributions. An internal attribution is the inference that a person is behaving in a certain way because of something about the (22) _____ (p. 95). An external attribution is an inference that a person is behaving a certain way because of something about the (23) _____ (p. 95) he or she is in. According to Kelley's theory, called the covariation model, we use (24) _____ (p.96) information, distinctiveness information, and consistency information when making attributions.

We have a tendency to infer that people's behavior (25) _____ (p. 99) to (matches) their disposition (personality)—this is called the correspondence bias. The correspondence bias is so pervasive that many social psychologists call it the (26) _____ (p. 99). One reason we tend to fall prey to the correspondence bias is that when we try to explain someone's behavior, our focus of attention is usually on the (27) _____ (p. 100), not on the surrounding situation. People, not the situation, have perceptual salience for us. We go through a two-step process when we make attributions. First we make an internal attribution. Next we attempt to adjust this attribution by considering the (28) _____ (p. 102) the person was in. But we often don't make enough of an adjustment in this second step. We will engage in this second step if we consciously slow down and think carefully before reaching a judgment, if we are (29) _____ (p.102) to reach as accurate a judgment as possible, or if we are (30) _____ (p. 102) about the behavior of the target person. The correspondence bias is influenced by culture.

An interesting twist on the correspondence bias is that it applies unevenly. The actor/observer difference is a tendency to see other people's behavior as dispositionally caused but focusing more on the role of (31) _____ (p. 107) factors when explaining one's own behavior. One reason for this difference in attributions is perceptual salience. It also occurs because actors have more information about (32) _____ (p. 108) than observers do.

When people's (33) _____ (p. 109) is threatened, they often make self-serving attributions. These attributions refer to our tendency to take credit for our successes (by making internal attributions) but blame others or the situation (by making external attributions) for our failures. Most people try to maintain their self-esteem whenever possible, even if that means distorting reality by changing a thought or (34) _____ (p. 109). We also engage in self-serving attributions because we want people to think well of us and to admire us. People sometimes alter their attributions to deal with other kinds of threats to their self-esteem. Defensive attributions are explanations for behavior that avoid feelings of (35) _____ (p. 110) and mortality. One form of defensive attribution is the belief in a (36) _____ (p. 110)—the assumption that people get what they deserve and deserve what they get.

There is a link between culture and attributional biases. In a recent meta-analysis of 266 studies conducted all over the world, Amy Mezulis and her colleagues (2004) found that the self-serving bias is strongest in the (37) _____ (p. 111) and some other Western countries. On the other hand, some Asian cultures displayed a markedly low or even absent level of self-serving bias. In many traditional Asian cultures, the values of (38) _____ (p. 111) are highly valued. Chinese students are expected to attribute their successes to other people, such as their teachers or parents, or to other aspects of the situation, such as the (39) _____ (p. 111). In individualistic cultures like the Unites States, people tend toward the self-serving bias. In collectivistic cultures like China, the (40) _____ (p. 112) is true.

ESSAY REVIEW

1. Define social perception and nonverbal communication. Describe the functions nonverbal communication serve in social perception.

2. Discuss the potential problems and things you should keep in mind regarding communicating via electronic mail (e-mail).

3. Define attribution theory and describe the two types of attributions commonly made. Discuss the role these attributions play in marriages.

4. Define the correspondence bias and identify the other name this tendency is called by. What role does perceptual salience play in the correspondence bias? Describe the two-step process used in making attributions.

5. Discuss self-serving attributions and why we make them. Define defensive attributions and give an example of one.

EXIT TESTS

EXIT TEST 1

1. Humans have a special kind of brain cell called _____ that respond when we perform an action and when we see someone else perform the same action.
   a) mirror cells
   b) reflection cells
   c) mirror neurons
   d) reflective neurons

2. Guilt, shame, embarrassment, and pride are the first emotions to appear in human development.
   a) True
   b) False

3. Tammy is feeling surprised, angry, and disgusted, all at the same time. Tammy's face will likely display
   a) only one of these emotions.
   b) two of these emotions at most.
   c) an affect blend.
   d) a multichannel affect.

4. Tom, an American businessperson, is making a sales presentation to Chen, a Chinese businessperson. As Tom makes his presentation, Chen smiles and nods his head up and down. Tom assumes that Chen is pleased with his presentation and that he will make a sale. However, Chen has no intention of making a deal with Tom, but in the culture Chen is from, it would be rude to show his lack of interest nonverbally. Tom and Chen have different
   a) display rules.
   b) emblems.
   c) channels of communication.
   d) interpretation biases.

5. Masuda and colleagues (2008) conducted a study on decoding facial expressions in which they presented participants in the United States and Japan with cartoon drawings of people in groups. They found that the facial expressions on the group members' faces had
   a) a great effect on both the American and Japanese participants' ratings of the central figure.
   b) little effect on the Japanese participants' ratings of the central figure.
   c) a great effect on Americans' ratings of the central figure.
   d) little effect on Americans' ratings of the central figure.

6.   Implicit personality theories consist of ideas about what kinds of _____ go together.
    a)   personality disorders
    b)   personality traits
    c)   temperament types
    d)   people

7.   Nonverbal behavior and implicit personality theories are fail-safe indicators of what a person is really thinking or feeling.
    a)   True
    b)   False

8.   _____ refers to how other people behave toward the same stimulus.
    a)   Consensus
    b)   Distinctiveness
    c)   Consistency
    d)   Confirming

9.   _____ salience helps to explain why the correspondence bias is so widespread.
    a)   Visual
    b)   Actor
    c)   Perceptual
    d)   Situational

10.   The same behavior can trigger _____ attributions in people observing the behavior and _____ attributions in the person performing the behavior.
    a)   target-based; category-based
    b)   category-based; target-based
    c)   situational; dispositional
    d)   dispositional; situational

EXIT TEST 2

1.   Mirror neurons appear to be the basis of our ability to feel _____.
    a)   anger.
    b)   empathy.
    c)   sympathy.
    d)   happiness.

2.   Dogs are adept at reading not only "dog nonverbals" but human nonverbals as well, and even outperform _____ when it comes to understanding human nonverbal cues.
    a)   chimpanzees
    b)   humans
    c)   apes
    d)   cats

3.   Recent research on the facial expression of contempt suggests that it is recognized cross-culturally like the six major emotions.
    a)   True
    b)   False

4. Members of American culture become suspicious when a person doesn't "look them in the eye" while speaking however, in other parts of the world, direct eye gaze is considered
   a) to be rude unless you are speaking to someone of low status.
   b) to be a sign you have something to hide.
   c) haughty.
   d) invasive or disrespectful.

5. The Social Interpretations Task (SIT) videotape is composed of 20 scenes of naturally occurring
   a) attributional biases.
   b) affect blends.
   c) nonverbal behavior.
   d) verbal communication.

6. The eye-tracking results in the Masuda and colleagues (2008) study did not suggest that there was anything interesting going on, at a physiological level, in people who engage in analytic versus holistic thinking.
   a) True
   b) False

7. Hoffman et al. (1986) hypothesized that cultural implicit personality theories influence the way people
   a) form impressions of others.
   b) choose a mate.
   c) communicate nonverbally.
   d) develop into adults.

8. Cathy sees a mother in the grocery store shaking her child very roughly. Cathy assumes that the mother has had a very stressful day and that she normally would not treat her child this way. What type of attribution has Cathy made?
   a) sympathetic
   b) empathetic
   c) internal
   d) external

9. The pervasive, fundamental theory or schema most of us have about human behavior is that people do what they do because of the kind of people they are, not because of the situation they are in.
   a) True
   b) False

10. People in individualistic cultures prefer situational attributions, while people in collectivistic cultures prefer dispositional attributions.
    a) True
    b) False

STUDY ACTIVITIES

1. You have a friend who is a new police officer. Based on what you learned about the correspondence bias and the practice of videoing interrogations, what advice can you give your friend to increase the fairness of the impressions made from these videos?

2. Describe Kelley's covariation model of attribution including the types of information people use to make attributions about an actor's behavior.

3. Give a recent example of self-serving attributions that you have made for success and failure.

4. Describe a situation in which you made the fundamental attribution error. Why do you think you made this error in attribution?

5. What is an implicit personality theory? How can relying on schemas lead us astray?

6. What is the premise of the covariation model? What information do we examine for covariation when we form attributions? When are people most likely to make an internal attribution or an external attribution according to the covariation model?

7. What is the actor/observer difference? Why does it occur? Can you think of a time when you have fallen prey to this bias?

8. What are cultural differences in the occurrence of the correspondence bias?

9. You are a police officer and you have just interviewed two people who witnessed a bank robbery. The witnesses are both students and one is from America while the other is from Korea. They have given you very different descriptions of the scene. How can you explain these differences based on what you've learned in the chapter?

10. Your best friend is going on vacation and will be traveling to several countries outside the U.S. Knowing that your friend has a habit of using a lot of gestures during speech, what warning should you give your friend and why?

Chapter 4 Answers

Practice Test

1.   A (p. 89)
2.   C (p. 95)
3.   C (p. 107)
4.   A (p. 110)
5.   D (p. 84)
6.   A (p. 88)
7.   C (p. 89)
8.   C (p. 85)
9.   D (p. 88)
10.   B (p. 95)
11.   B (p. 84)
12.   D (pp. 96-97)
13.   B (p. 105)
14.   D (p. 102)
15.   C (p. 86)
16.   C (p. 103)
17.   D (pp. 92-94)
18.   B (p. 95)
19.   A (p. 97)
20.   B (p. 96)
21.   A (p. 87)
22.   D (p. 111)
23.   C (p. 92)
24.   B (p. 111)
25.   C (p. 109)
26.   D (pp. 109-110)
27.   C (p. 110)
28.   D (pp. 98-107)
29.   A (pp. 101-102)
30.   C (pp. 111-112)
31.   B (p. 84)
32.   B (p. 87)
33.   A (p. 91)
34.   D (p. 92)
35.   C (p. 97)
36.   A (p. 99)
37.   D (p. 102)
38.   A (p. 104)
39.   B (p. 107)
40.   C (pp. 112-113)

Short Answer Review

1. impressions (p. 84)
2. inferences (p. 84)
3. nonverbal (p. 84)
4. revealing (p. 84)
5. personality (p. 85)
6. honest (p. 85)
7. encode (p. 86)
8. decode (p. 86)
9. disgust (p. 86)
10. blind (p. 87)
11. affect blends (p. 88)
12. face (p. 88)
13. culture (p. 88)
14. display rules (p. 88)
15. emblems (p. 89)
16. multichannel (p. 89)
17. misunderstood (p. 92)
18. implicit personality theory (p. 92)
19. experience (p. 93)
20. culture (p. 93)
21. causes (p. 95)
22. person (p. 95)
23. situation (p. 95)
24. consensus (p. 96)
25. corresponds (p. 99)
26. fundamental attribution error (p. 99)
27. person (p. 100)
28. situation (p. 102)
29. motivated (p. 102)
30. suspicious (p. 102)
31. situational (p. 107)
32. themselves (p. 108)
33. self-esteem (p. 109)
34. belief (p. 109)
35. vulnerability (p. 110)
36. just world (p. 110)
37. United States (p. 111)
38. modesty and harmony with others (p. 111)
39. quality of their high school (p. 111)
40. reverse (p. 112)

Essay Review

1. Your essay should include:
    *   Social perception is the study of how we form impressions of, and make inferences about, other people. (p. 84)
    *   Nonverbal communication refers to how people communicate, intentionally or unintentionally, without words. (p. 84)
    *   Nonverbal cues help us express our emotions, our attitudes, and our personality. Nonverbal cues are often considered more "honest" than words. (p. 85)

2. Your essay on communicating via electronic mail should include:
    *   Relying on words alone always results in an impoverished medium of communication. (p. 92)
    *   Be very careful when you e-mail because you can easily be misunderstood and those misunderstandings can have serious effects on your interactions with others. (p. 92)
    *   Remember that you are very likely to think your meaning is clear in an e-mail, when in fact, it is only clear to you. (p. 92)

3. Your essay on attribution theory should include:
    *   Attribution theory is a description of the way in which people explain the causes of their own and other people's behavior. (p. 95)
    *   Internal attributions are inferences that a person is behaving in a certain way because of something about the person, such as attitude, character, or personality. (p. 95)
    *   An external attribution is an inference that a person is behaving a certain way because of something about the situation he or she is in. (p. 95)
    *   Satisfied spouses tend to make internal attributions for their partner's positive behaviors and external attributions for their partner's negative behaviors. In contrast, spouses in distressed marriages tend to display the opposite pattern. (pp. 95-96)

4. Your essay on the correspondence bias should include:
    *   The correspondence bias is the tendency to infer that people's behavior corresponds to (matches) their disposition (personality). This bias is so pervasive that many social psychologists call it the fundamental attribution error. (p. 100)
    *   One reason people fall prey to the correspondence bias is that when we try to explain someone's behavior, our focus of attention is usually on the person, not the surrounding situation. People, not the situation, have perceptual salience for us. (pp. 100-101)
    *   In the two-step process of making attributions, we first make an internal attribution. We then attempt to adjust this attribution by considering the situation the person was in. (p. 102)

5. Your essay on self-serving attributions should include:
    *   Self-serving attributions are explanations for one's successes that credit internal, dispositional factors and explanations for one's failures that blame external, situational factors. (p. 109)
    *   We make self-serving attributions to maintain our self-esteem, to present ourselves in a positive way to others, and because of the information that is available to us. (p. 109)
    *   A defensive attribution is an explanation for behavior that avoids feelings of vulnerability and mortality. (p. 110)

- The belief in a just world is one form of defensive attribution. It is an attribution wherein people assume that bad things happen to bad people and that good things happen to good people. (p. 110)

Exit Test 1

1.   C (p. 84)
2.   B (p. 87)
3.   C (p. 88)
4.   A (p. 88)
5.   D (p. 104)
6.   B (p. 92)
7.   B (p. 95)
8.   A (p. 96)
9.   C (p. 101)
10.   D (p. 107)

Exit Test 2

1.   B (p. 84)
2.   A (p. 84)
3.   A (pp. 87-88)
4.   D (p. 89)
5.   C (p. 89)
6.   B (p. 105)
7.   A (p. 93)
8.   D (p. 95)
9.   A (p. 99)
10.   B (p. 104)

Study Activities

1.   I would recommend that the video interrogations show both the suspect and the detective as this "equal-focus" camera perspective may help reduce attributional bias. 102. (pp. 102-103)

2.   Kelley focused on the information (consensus, distinctiveness, and consistency) that we use to decide whether to make an internal or an external attribution for multiple instances of behaviors. (pp. 96-97)

3.   Your example should depict an internal attribution for a recent success and an external attribution for a recent failure. (p. 109)

4.   The situation you describe should illustrate an instance in which you overestimated the extent to which others' behavior was cause by internal factors (e.g., my roommate failed the exam because he is not smart), but your behavior was caused by situational factors (e.g., I failed the exam because the test was too hard). The concept of perceptual salience may be useful in explaining this error. (p. 99)

5.   An implicit personality theory is a type of schema people use to group various kinds of personality traits together. Relying on schemas can lead us astray, because we might make the wrong assumptions about an individual; we might even resort to stereotypical thinking, where our schema, or stereotype, leads us to believe that the individual is like all the other members of his or her group. (p. 92)

6.   The covariation model is a theory that states that to form an attribution about what caused a person's behavior, we systematically note the pattern between the presence or absence of possible causal factors and whether or not the behavior occurs. The information we examine includes consensus information (the extent to which other people behave the same way toward the same stimulus as the actor does), distinctiveness information (the extent to which one particular actor behaves in the same way to different stimuli), and consistency information (the extent to which the behavior between one actor and one stimulus is the same across time and circumstances). We are likely to make an internal attribution when consensus is low, distinctiveness is low, and consistency is high. We are likely to make an external attribution when consensus is high, distinctiveness is high, and consistency is high. (pp. 96-97)

7.   The actor/observer difference is the tendency to see other people's behavior as dispositionally caused but focusing more on the role of situational factors when explaining one's own behavior. One reason it occurs is because of perceptual salience. We notice other people's behavior more than their situation; we notice our own situation more than our own behavior. Actors also have more information about themselves than observers do. (pp. 107-108)

8.   People in individualistic cultures do prefer dispositional attributions about others, relative to people in collectivistic cultures, who prefer situational attributions. (p. 103)

9.   The differences are probably due to culture. Research has indicated that differing cultural values affect the kind of information that people notice and pay attention to. The American student has been exposed to an individualistic culture and probably has an analytic thinking style which would result in the student noticing the properties of objects (people) while the Korean student probably has a holistic thinking style which leads to noticing the whole picture. (p. 104)

10.   I should warn my friend not to use gestures in other countries because they are not universal. The gesture may have a meaning very different from the intended meaning. (pp. 89-90)

CHAPTER 5

The Self: Understanding Ourselves in a Social Context

CHAPTER 5 OVERVIEW

The first part of Chapter 5 considers our self-knowledge and how definitions of the self differ according to culture and gender. **Self-concept** is the content of the self; that is, our knowledge about who we are. **Self-awareness** is the act of thinking about ourselves. These two aspects of the self combine to create a coherent sense of identity. Some research suggests that there are other species that have a rudimentary self-concept. Sense of self develops in humans at around 18 months of age.

The self serves four important functions: *Self-knowledge,* whereby we formulate and organize what we know about ourselves; *self-control,* whereby we make plans and execute decisions; *self-presentation,* whereby we try to put our best foot forward to others, *self-justification,* whereby we try to put our best foot forward to ourselves.

There are cultural differences in defining the sense of self. In many Western cultures, people have an **independent view of the self**, which is a way of defining oneself in terms of one's own internal thoughts, feelings, and actions and not in terms of the thoughts, feelings, and actions of other people. Many Asian and non-Western cultures have an **interdependent view of the self**, which is a way of defining oneself in terms of one's relationships to other people and recognizing that one's behavior is often determined by the thoughts, feelings, and actions of others. Connectedness and interdependence between people is valued, whereas independence and uniqueness are frowned upon.

There are also gender differences in defining the self. Women have more relational interdependence, meaning that they focus more on their close relationships. Men have more collective interdependence, meaning that they focus on their memberships in larger groups. These differences persist into adulthood.

The next part of this section of the chapter examines knowing ourselves. One way to gain self-knowledge is through introspection. **Introspection** is the process whereby people look inward and examine their own thoughts, feelings, and motives. **Self-awareness theory** is the idea that when people focus their attention on themselves, they evaluate and compare their behavior to their internal standards and values. Self-awareness can be aversive when it reminds people of their shortcomings.

Sometimes it can be difficult to know why we feel the way we do. **Causal theories** are theories about the causes of one's own feelings and behaviors. We learn many of these theories from the culture in which we grow up. The only problem is that our schemas and theories are not always correct and thus can lead to incorrect judgments about the causes of our actions. When people list reasons for an attitude, they often change their attitude, at least temporarily. This is referred to as **reasons-generated attitude change**.

Next, the chapter discusses how people gain self-knowledge by examining their own behaviors. This is called **self-perception theory**. The self-perception theory helps readers understand how rewards influence people's motivation to perform tasks. **Intrinsic motivation** is the desire to engage in an activity because we enjoy it or find it interesting. **Extrinsic motivation** is the desire to engage in an activity because of external rewards or pressures. If an external reward is received for a behavior that was intrinsically motivated the **overjustification effect** may occur—the tendency of people to view their behavior as caused by compelling extrinsic reasons, making them underestimate the extent to which it was caused by intrinsic reasons. Intrinsic motivation may be maintained if performance-contingent rewards are used instead of task-contingent rewards. **Performance-contingent rewards** are rewards that are based on how well we perform a task. **Task-contingent rewards** are rewards that are given for performing a task, regardless of how well the task is done.

Two theories in the chapter, the two-factor theory of emotion and the cognitive appraisal theories of emotion, help explain how people experience emotions and how they interpret the causes of their emotions. Schacter's **two-factor theory of emotion** is the idea that emotional experience is the result of a two-step self-perception process in which people first experience physiological arousal and then seek an appropriate explanation for it. Many everyday situations present more than one plausible cause for our arousal, and it is difficult to identify how much of the arousal is due to one source or another. The **misattribution of arousal** is a process whereby people make mistaken inferences about what is causing them to feel the way they do. **Appraisal theories of emotion** are theories asserting that emotions result from people's interpretations and explanations of events, even in the absence of physiological arousal.

Some people believe that their abilities are set in stone; they either have them or they do not. The psychologist Carol Dweck calls this a **fixed mindset**, the idea that we have a set amount of an ability that cannot change. Other people have what Dweck calls a **growth mindset**, which is the idea that their abilities are malleable qualities that they can cultivate and grow. Research shows that the mindset people have is a major factor in their success or failure.

The next section of the chapter discusses using other people to know ourselves. **Social comparison theory** is the idea that we learn about our own abilities and attitudes by comparing ourselves to other people. If we want to know what excellence is—the top level to which we can aspire—we engage in **upward social comparison**: We compare ourselves to people who are better than we are on a particular ability. **Downward social comparison**—comparing yourself to people who are worse than you on a particular trait or ability—is a self-protective, self-enhancing strategy. Another way we can feel better about ourselves is to compare our current performance with our own past performance. When it comes to our view of the social world often we adopt the views our friends hold. **Social tuning** is the process whereby people adopt another person's attitudes.

The next section of this chapter describes the executive function of the self. One of the functions of the self is self-control. Another important function of the self is to be the chief executive who makes choices about what to do in the present and plans for the future. Regulating our behavior and choices in optimal ways can be easier said than done. One form of self-control that does not work very well and often backfires is *thought suppression*, whereby we try to push thoughts out of our minds. Often, the more we try not to think about something, the more those very thoughts keep coming to mind. A better strategy is to go ahead and think about the forbidden topic while trying to exert will power when it comes to acting on those thoughts. According to the *self-regulatory resource model*, we are more likely to succeed when we have plenty of energy when we are trying to control our actions. According to this approach self-control requires energy, and spending this energy on one task limits the amount that can be spent on another task.

The last section in this chapter focuses on how and why people present themselves to other people. **Impression** management refers to the attempt by people to get others to see them as they want to be seen. People have different impression management strategies. One is **ingratiation**—using flattery or praise to make yourself likable to another, often higher-status person. Ingratiation can backfire if the recipient of your ingratiation senses that you're being insincere. Another strategy is **self-handicapping**. This is the strategy whereby people create obstacles and excuses for themselves so that if they do poorly on a task, they can avoid blaming themselves. People in all cultures are concerned with the impression they make on others, but the nature of this concern and the impression management strategies people use differ considerably from culture to culture.

CHAPTER 5 OUTLINE

• William James (1890) defined a basic duality of the self: it is both the known, "Me," and the knower, "I." In modern terminology, the "Me" is the **self-concept**, or content of the self—our knowledge about who we are, and the "I" is **self-awareness**, or thinking about ourselves.

• Gallup's studies examined whether animals have a sense of self by looking at their reactions when placed in front of a mirror. He found that the great apes seem to have a sense of self—they recognize that their image has changed when anesthetized and a red dye is placed on part of their face. A similar test used with human infants suggested that self-recognition develops at about two years of age.

• Studies suggest that chimps and orangutans, and possibly dolphins, have a rudimentary self-concept.

• Self-recognition in humans develops at around age two.

• Other developmental studies show that the concept of self evolves from being concrete and focused on observable characteristics to being more abstract and focused on psychological characteristics during the course of childhood and adolescence.

• The self serves four important functions: *Self-knowledge,* whereby we formulate and organize what we know about ourselves; *self-control,* whereby we make plans and execute decisions; *self-presentation,* whereby we try to put our best foot forward to others; *self-justification,* whereby we try to put our best foot forward to ourselves.

I. Self-Knowledge

A. Cultural Differences in Defining the Self

• In many Western cultures, people have an **independent view of the self**, focusing on their unique characteristics, thoughts, feelings, and actions; while in many Asian and other non-Western cultures, people have an **interdependent view of the self**, defining themselves in terms of relationships with other people.

• Singelis (1994) developed a scale to measure these two senses of the self (sample items are given on p. 120).

B. Gender Differences in Defining the Self

• Research suggests that women have more *relational* interdependence, focusing more on their close relationships, while men have more *collective* interdependence, focusing on their memberships in larger groups.

• Cross and Madson (1997) point out that this difference starts in childhood and persists into adulthood. Women focus more on intimacy and on cooperation with a small number of close others, while men focus more on their social groups. In line with this, Gabriel and Gardner (1999) found that, when asked to describe an emotional event in their lives, women described events involving personal relationships while men described events involving social groups (Figure 5.1, p. 121).

• When considering gender differences, we need to be cautious: The psychological differences between men and women are far fewer than the ways in which they are the same.

C. Knowing Ourselves Through Introspection

• Intuitively, we recognize that **introspection**, the process whereby people look inward and examine their own thoughts, feelings, and motives, is one basis of self-knowledge. However, people do not rely on this as much as we expect, and even when they do introspect, they may not recognize why they feel or act the way they do.

1. Focusing on the Self: Self-Awareness Theory

• Csikszentmihalyi and Figurski (1992) conducted a study where participants recorded their thoughts whenever a randomly-timed beeper sounded; thoughts about the self were surprisingly infrequent

(Figure 5.2, p. 123). Only eight percent of total thoughts recorded were about the self; more often, the participants thought about work, chores, and time.
• According to **self-awareness theory**, when we do focus attention on ourselves, we compare our current behavior against internal standards and values. When we become aware of a discrepancy, we attempt to reduce it by changing our behavior to match. If we cannot do this, we will find self-awareness very uncomfortable (see Figure 5.3, p. 124).
• Baumeister has postulated that, because self-awareness can be unpleasant, we will be motivated to "escape the self" by engaging in drinking, binge eating, sexual masochism, suicide attempts, or spiritual practices such as prayer or meditation.
• Self-focus is not always aversive or damaging. It can be a way of keeping you out of trouble, by reminding you of your sense of right and wrong.
• Dov Cohen and his colleagues have found that East Asians are more likely to have an *outside perspective on the self,* viewing themselves through the eyes of other people. People who grow up in Western cultures are more likely to have an *insider perspective on the self,* focusing on their own private experiences without considering how other people see them.

2. Judging Why We Feel the Way We Do: Telling More Than We Can Know
• Many of our mental processes occur outside of awareness—we are aware of the final result of our thoughts, but not of the process by which we got there. However, when asked to provide an explanation for why we have the opinions we do, we easily come up with a reason. Thus, introspection may not lead us to the true causes of our feelings and behavior, but we'll manage to convince ourselves it did (Nisbett & Wilson, 1977). Nisbett and Wilson referred to this phenomenon as "telling more than we can know" because people's explanations of their feelings and behavior often go beyond what they can reasonably know.
• Diary studies that track people's moods show that, although people have strong **causal theories** about the causes of their own feelings and behavior—for example, thinking that factors like the amount of sleep the previous night might influence their moods—these theories are generally wrong.
• Nisbett and Wilson (1977) conducted a study in which participants viewed a film. For half of the participants, a "construction worker" buzzed a power-saw outside the room during the viewing. Although the participants (and the researchers!) thought the noise would influence evaluations of the film, it didn't do so, demonstrating a faulty causal theory.
• People do not rely solely on their causal theories when introspecting about the reasons for their feelings and behaviors.
• Introspecting about our past actions and current thoughts does not always yield the right answer about why we feel the way we do.

3. The Consequences of Introspecting about Reasons
• Wilson's work has shown that there may be a downside risk to introspecting about reasons when making decisions—namely, we may come up with inaccurate reasons. We may sometimes convince ourselves that these incorrect reasons are correct. This leads to **reasons-generated attitude change**, attitude change that results from thinking about the reasons for one's attitudes. People assume that their attitudes match the reasons that are plausible and easy to verbalize. This may be problematic when the "right" reasons (e.g., for why you love someone) are hard to verbalize or inaccessible, and incorrect reasons are easy to verbalize or accessible. The attitudes expressed immediately after doing a "reasons analysis" may be temporarily altered by the results of the analysis, and thus do not predict future behavior or attitudes very well.

D. Knowing Ourselves by Observing Our Own Behavior
• Bem's **self-perception theory** states that when our attitudes and feelings are uncertain or ambiguous, we infer these states by observing our behavior and the situation in which it occurs.

• We are especially likely to infer our feelings from our behavior when (1) our initial feelings are weak or unclear, and (2) we think about why we have behaved the way we have and decide that it was our free choice.

• In other words, we are using the same attributional principles described in Chapter 4 to make inferences about our own attitudes.

1. Intrinsic versus Extrinsic Motivation

• **Intrinsic motivation** is the desire to engage in an activity because we enjoy it or find it interesting; **extrinsic motivation** is the desire to engage in an activity because of external rewards or pressures.

1. The Overjustification Effect

• According to self-perception theory, extrinsic rewards may hurt intrinsic motivation. When we are rewarded for engaging in an intrinsically motivating activity, we may now place too much importance on extrinsic reasons and assume that we are doing the behavior in order to achieve the extrinsic reward. This is known as the **overjustification effect**.

• For example, Greene, Sternberg, and Lepper (1976) rewarded 9-10 year-olds for playing math games. After the rewards were terminated, children spent significantly less time with the games than they had before they ever got rewards (Figure 5.4, p. 141).

2. Preserving Intrinsic Interest

• Recent research reveals that there are conditions under which the overjustification effect can be avoided: (1) when initial interest in the task is low, as opposed to high; and (2) when one uses **performance-contingent rewards** that are based on how well a task is done and which provide information and positive feedback rather than **task-contingent rewards** that are given for performing a task regardless of how well it is done. However, even performance-contingent rewards must be used carefully, because they can backfire by making people anxious about being evaluated.

2. Understanding Our Emotions: The Two-Factor Theory of Emotion

• Schacter (1964) proposed the **two-factor theory of emotion**: that emotion results from first perceiving physiological arousal and then finding an explanation or label for that arousal (see Figure 5.5, p. 144).

• In a study by Schacter and Singer (1962), participants were given an injection of either epinephrine (adrenaline) or a placebo upon arriving at the lab. They were told that the injection was a vitamin that affected vision and were either told the actual effects that epinephrine has or were told that they might experience some symptoms, but not those produced by epinephrine. Participants were then placed with an angry acting confederate in a waiting room (for half the participants; the other half were placed with a euphoric acting confederate). The dependent variable was the emotion felt. Those participants who (a) had been given epinephrine to induce arousal and (b) were NOT told the symptoms that the injection would make them experience felt more angry (or more euphoric) than participants in the other groups.

• An implication of this theory is that people's emotions are somewhat arbitrary, depending on the most plausible explanation for arousal. Thus in their experiment, the researchers were able to prevent people from becoming angry by proving a nonemotional explanation for why they felt aroused, and they could make people feel a very different emotion by changing the most plausible explanation for arousal.

3. Finding the Wrong Cause: Misattribution of Arousal

• **Misattribution of arousal** is the process whereby people make mistaken inferences about what is causing them to feel the way they do. Many studies have demonstrated the misattribution of arousal to emotional states that was demonstrated initially by Schacter and Singer. For example, Dutton and Aron (1974) had a woman approach men who had either just crossed over a scary bridge or who had had a chance to rest on a bench after crossing. Those men who had just crossed over the scary bridge before being approached by the woman and asked to complete a questionnaire were more likely to call her and ask her out (Figure 5.6, p.147).

4. Interpreting the Social World: Appraisal Theories of Emotion
• Attribution is not the only means by which we learn what we feel. **Appraisal theories of emotion** hold that emotions result from people's interpretations of events, even in the absence of any physiological arousal. Your view of (1) whether the event had good or bad implications for you and (b) your view of what caused the event are particularly important determinants of experienced emotion.
• These theories differ from Schacter and Singer's theory in the importance of arousal—according to these theories, arousal does not always come first; cognitive appraisals alone are a sufficient cause of emotion.
• When people are aroused and uncertain where this arousal comes from, Schacter and Singer's theory may apply, but when they are not aroused, cognitive arousal theories may apply. Both theories agree that one way people learn about themselves is by observing events, including their own behavior, and trying to explain those events.

E. Mindsets: Understanding Our Own Abilities
• One important kind of self-knowledge is how we explain our own talents and abilities to ourselves.
• A **fixed mindset** is the idea that we have a set amount of an ability that cannot change. A **growth mindset** is the idea that our abilities are malleable qualities that we can cultivate and grow.
• People withthe fixed mindset are more likely to give up after setbacks and are less likely to work on and hone their skills. People with the growth mindset view setbacks as an opportunity to improve through hard work.

F. Using Other People to Know Ourselves
• The self-concept does not develop in a solitary context but is shaped by the people around us.
• Gallup's ape studies show that social contact is critical to the very development of a self-concept—only those apes raised with others passed the "red dye" mirror test.
1. Knowing Ourselves by Comparing Ourselves to Others
• We also come to know ourselves by comparison to other people. Festinger's (1954) **social comparison theory** is the idea that, when objective criteria for self-evaluation are not present, we learn about our own abilities and attitudes by comparing ourselves to other people.
• When do people compare themselves with others? When there is little objective information available.
• With whom do we compare ourselves? Gilbert suggests that initially we compare ourselves to everyone, and then we seek an appropriate comparison. Others most similar to us provide the most appropriate comparisons.
• When our goal is to find out information about ourselves, we are likely to engage in comparison to others who are similar to us on the important dimension.
• Sometimes we engage in **upward social comparison**, comparing ourselves to people who are better than we are on a particular trait or ability, in order to assess our own abilities. We may look to experts to set the standard of excellence, but it is often more useful to compare ourselves to someone who is similar to us.
• We also use social comparison to boost our egos; in this case, we are likely to engage in **downward social comparison**, or comparing ourselves to people who are worse than we are on a particular trait or ability. For example, Wood et al. (1985) found that cancer patients used downward comparisons to make themselves feel more optimistic about the course of their own illness.
• Another way we can feel better about ourselves is to compare our current performance with our own past performance, another sort of downward comparison.

Chapter 5

2. Knowing Ourselves by Adopting Other People's Views
• When it comes to our views of the social world, we often adopt the views our friends hold.
• One explanation for people holding common views is that people who have similar views are attracted to each other and are more likely to form social bonds than people who have dissimilar views.
• Another explanation is that under some conditions people adopt the views of the people they hang out with. Charles Cooley called this the "looking glass self," by which he meant that we see ourselves and the social world through the eyes of other people and often adopt those views. According to recent research this is especially true when two people want to get along with each other.
• **Social tuning**, the process whereby people adopt another person's attitudes, can happen even when we meet someone for the first time, if we want to get along with that person.

II. Self-Control: The Executive Function of the Self
•Another important function of the self is to be the chief executive who makes choices about what to do in the present and plans for the future. Regulating our behavior and choices in optimal ways can be easier said than done, as anyone who has been on a diet or tried to quit smoking knows.
•One form of self-control that does not work very well and often backfires is *thought suppression*, whereby we try to push thoughts out of our minds. According to the *self-regulatory resource model*, we are more likely to succeed if we make sure that we have plenty of energy when we are trying to control our actions.
•Recent research suggests that this "energy" we spend when exerting self-control is in the level of glucose in the bloodstream at any given point.

III. Impression Management: All The World's A Stage
• **Impression management** occurs when we attempt to get others to see us as we want to be seen.
• As Erving Goffman pointed out, we are all like stage actors who are trying our best to convince the "audience" (the people around us) that we are a certain way, even if we really are not.
• **Ingratiation** is the process whereby people flatter, praise, and try to make themselves likable to a higher status person. Ingratiation can backfire if the other recognizes we are doing it.
• **Self-handicapping** is creating obstacles and excuses for ourselves (in advance of a poor performance) so that if we do poorly, we have a ready-made excuse. People self-handicap either by behaviorally creating obstacles (e.g., drinking the night before an exam) or by citing verbal excuses.
• One downside risk of self-handicapping is that it may actually cause the poor performance that is so feared, as we come to believe our own excuses and exert less effort on the task.
1. Culture, Impression Management, and Self-Enhancement
• People in all cultures are concerned with the impression they make on others, but the nature of this concern and the impression management strategies people use differ considerably from culture to culture.

LEARNING OBJECTIVES

After reading Chapter 5, you should be able to do the following:

1.   Define self-concept. Define self-awareness. Discuss animal and human research on the sense of self. Discuss how our self-concepts change with age. (p. 118)

2.   Identify and define the four important functions of the self. (p. 119)

3.   Describe different conceptions of the self across cultures. Contrast the independent view of the self with the interdependent view of the self. (pp. 119-120)

4.   Discuss the research findings on gender differences in the definition of the self. (pp. 121-122)

5.   Discuss introspection as a source of self-knowledge. Describe self-awareness theory and what kinds of information self-awareness reveals. Identify the emotional and behavioral consequences of self-awareness. Discuss when self-awareness is aversive and how we attempt to stop being self-aware. (pp. 122-124)

6.   Differentiate between the outside perspective on the self and the insider perspective on the self. (p. 124)

7.   Distinguish between thoughts people have about how they feel or what kind of person they are, and why they feel the way they do. Discuss the role of causal theories in telling more than we can know. (pp. 125-128)

8.   Identify the consequences of introspecting about reasons and the kinds of information that come to mind when people introspect about reasons. Define reasons-generated attitude change and discuss its consequences. Discuss why analyzing reasons may change a person's feelings. (pp. 128-129)

9.   Describe Daryl Bem's self-perception theory. Identify when and how people use observations of their own behavior as a source of self-knowledge. (p. 129)

10.   Describe the relationships among intrinsic motivation, external rewards, and the overjustification effect. Define task-contingent and performance-contingent rewards. Identify conditions under which overjustification can be avoided. (pp. 129-131)

11.   Identify the two factors or steps required to understand our own emotional states according to Schachter's two-factor theory of emotion. Discuss the implications of Schachter's theory for the idea that emotions are somewhat arbitrary. Discuss how the two-factor theory explains the misattribution of arousal. (pp. 131-135)

12.   Identify the central idea of cognitive appraisal theories of emotion. List the two kinds of appraisals that are important in determining our emotions in response to an event. Compare and contrast Schachter's two-factor theory with the cognitive appraisal theories. (p. 136)

13.   Define fixed mindset and growth mindset and explain how they impact behavior. (pp. 136-137)

14.   Identify the postulates of social comparison theory. Discuss when people engage in social comparison and with whom they choose to compare themselves when their goal is to construct an accurate self-image. Discuss the motives underlying upward and downward social comparisons and the consequences of engaging in each. (pp. 137-139)

15.   Explain what Cooley meant by the term "looking glass self." Discuss the process of social tuning. (p. 139)

16.   Discuss the executive function of the self and describe the self-regulatory resource model. (pp. 140-141)

17.   Define impression management. Identify two self-presentation strategies that people use in everyday life. Define ingratiation. (pp. 142-143)

18.   Distinguish between two ways that people self-handicap. Discuss the advantages and disadvantages of self-handicapping. (p. 143)

19.   Describe the relationship between culture, impression management, and self-enhancement. (p. 144)

KEY TERMS

1. _____   The content of the self; that is, our knowledge about who we are. (p. 118)

2. _____   The act of thinking about ourselves. (p. 118)

3. _____   A way of defining oneself in terms of one's own internal thoughts, feelings, and actions and not in terms of the thoughts, feelings, and actions of other people. (p. 119)

4. _____   A way of defining oneself in terms of one's relationships to other people; recognizing that one's behavior is often determined by the thoughts, feelings, and actions of others. (p. 119)

5. _____   The process whereby people look inward and examine their own thoughts, feelings, and motives. (p. 122)

6. _____   The idea that when people focus their attention on themselves, they evaluate and compare their behavior to their internal standards and values. (p. 123)

7. _____   Theories about the causes of one's own feelings and behaviors. (p. 127)

8. _____   Attitude change resulting from thinking about the reasons for one's attitudes; people assume their attitudes match the reasons that are plausible and easy to verbalize. (p. 128)

9. _____   The theory that when our attitudes and feelings are uncertain or ambiguous, we infer these states by observing our behavior and the situation in which it occurs. (p. 129)

10. _____   The desire to engage in an activity because we enjoy it or find it interesting, not because of external rewards or pressures. (p. 130)

11. _____   The desire to engage in an activity because of external rewards or pressures, not because we enjoy the task or find it interesting. (p. 130)

12. _____   The tendency of people to view their behavior as caused by compelling extrinsic reasons, making them underestimate the extent to which it was caused by intrinsic reasons. (p. 130)

13. _____   Rewards that are given for performing a task, regardless of how well the task is done. (p. 131)

14. _____   Rewards that are based on how well we perform a task. (p. 131)

15._____ The idea that emotional experience is the result of a two-step self-perception process in which people first experience physiological arousal and then seek an appropriate explanation for it. (p. 132)

16._____ The process whereby people make mistaken inferences about what is causing them to feel the way they do. (p. 135)

17._____ Theories holding that emotions result from people's interpretations and explanations of events, even in the absence of physiological arousal. (p. 136)

18._____ The idea that we have a set amount of an ability that cannot change. (p. 136)

19._____ The idea that our abilities are malleable qualities that we can cultivate and grow. (p. 136)

20._____ The idea that we learn about our own abilities and attitudes by comparing ourselves to other people. (p. 137)

21._____ Comparing ourselves to people who are worse than we are on a particular trait or ability. (p. 138)

22._____ Comparing ourselves to people who are better than we are on a particular trait or ability. (p. 139)

23._____ The process whereby people adopt another person's attitudes. (p. 139)

24._____ The attempt by people to get others to see them as they want to be seen. (p. 142)

25._____ The process whereby people flatter, praise, and generally try to make themselves likable to another person, often of higher status. (p. 142)

26._____ The strategy whereby people create obstacles and excuses for themselves so that if they do poorly on a task, they can avoid blaming themselves. (p. 142)

GUIDED REVIEW
PRACTICE TEST

1. When asked "Who am I?" a child is most likely to respond:
   a) "I'm a nine-year-old."
   b) "I'm a happy person."
   c) "My friends think I'm friendly."
   d) "I'm against corporal punishment."

2. What is most likely an accurate view of the self in people in Eastern cultures?
   a) the independent view
   b) the correspondent view
   c) the interdependent view
   d) the individualistic view

3. Chen is from China. He is most likely to have a/an
   a) forward-looking perspective on the self.
   b) rear-view perspective on the self.
   c) insider perspective on the self.
   d) outside perspective on the self.

4. According to Daryl Bem's (1972) self-perception theory, when internal cues about attitudes or personality are weak, ambiguous, or uninterpretable, people:
   a) cannot form accurate self-perceptions.
   b) engage in introspection to determine how they feel and so clarify the meaning of their internal cues.
   c) compare their behaviors to stronger internal cues such as values and standards for behavior.
   d) infer their own internal states by observing their own overt behavior.

5. The act of thinking about ourselves is called:
   a) self-perception.
   b) self-concept.
   c) self-schemas.
   d) self-awareness.

6. Giving teenagers extra privileges in exchange for doing household chores will probably not produce the overjustification effect because:
   a) extrinsic interest in this activity is initially high.
   b) intrinsic interest in this activity is initially low.
   c) teenagers have already learned to operate within a system of rewards and punishments.
   d) extra privileges are not extrinsic motivators for teenagers.

7. Which type of rewards are more likely to lead to the overjustification effect?
   a) performance-contingent rewards
   b) task-contingent rewards
   c) instrinsic-contingent rewards
   d) response-contingent rewards

8. The two factors in Schachter's (1964) two-factor theory of emotion are:
   a) physiological arousal and introspection.
   b) overt behavior and observing that behavior from an external perspective.
   c) physiological arousal and seeking a label that explains the arousal.
   d) overt behavior and seeking an explanation for the behavior.

9. Which of the following demonstrates the misattribution of arousal?
   a) You rarely pet cats and infer that you do not like them.
   b) You panic in the belief that you will fail an exam after taking two caffeine tablets to get you through an "all-nighter."
   c) You find your job at the bookstore less enjoyable following a substantial raise in pay.
   d) All of the above demonstrate the misattribution of arousal.

10.   What is the main difference between the two-factor theory of emotion and the appraisal theories of emotion?
   a)   The two-factor theory does not acknowledge the existence of physiological arousal.
   b)   The appraisal theories do not acknowledge the role of cognitive interpretations of events in the experience of emotion.
   c)   The appraisal theories acknowledge biological influences on emotional experience.
   d)   The appraisal theories do not acknowledge the existence of physiological arousal in the experience of emotion.

11.   Which of the following is true about self-control?
   a)   We are better at it when we are well rested.
   b)   Being under stress increases people's self-control.
   c)   People are better at self-control if they haven't been practicing it very long.
   d)   Dieters are most likely to break their diets in the middle of the afternoon.

12.   Which of the following theories begins with the supposition that people have a need to evaluate their opinions and abilities?
   a)   impression management theory
   b)   the two-factor theory of emotion
   c)   social comparison theory
   d)   self-perception theory

13.   Which of the following is an example of ingratiation?
   a)   boasting that the school's track star is your roommate
   b)   setting out to impress your psychology classmates with the knowledge you gained over the summer working at a clinic
   c)   partying rather than studying the night before a difficult exam
   d)   complimenting your professor on his choice of ties today

14.   Which of the following is true about introspection?
   a)   Males are more introspective than females.
   b)   Introspection is useful in explaining why we feel or behave the way we do.
   c)   As an internal process, it cannot be initiated by external factors.
   d)   We do not rely on this source of information as often as we think we do.

15.   Deciding that you are in a bad mood because it is Monday is an example of a(n)
   a)   availability heuristic.
   b)   causal theory.
   c)   perceptual set.
   d)   self-schema.

16.   Which of the following demonstrates the overjustification effect?
   a)   A band member enjoys her job as a guitarist in a band and decides to go solo.
   b)   Hugo loves to read and joins a book club that requires a monthly fee.
   c)   Pamela quits her job as a secretary because she finds it boring and goes back to school.
   d)   An engineer who loved to solve mechanical problems as a child now views them as dreary tasks.

17. Participants in a study by Schachter and Singer (1962) who unwittingly took epinephrine, a drug that causes arousal, felt angry when filling out an insulting questionnaire in the presence of another angry individual because:
    a) epinephrine made them angry.
    b) they experienced arousal and sought out an explanation or label for that arousal in the situation.
    c) the epinephrine heightened the feeling of annoyance produced by the questionnaire.
    d) heightened arousal enabled subjects to experience empathy for the other individual and so experience his anger.

18. According to _____ theory, when we attend to ourselves we compare our current actions to our internal values.
    a) self-perception
    b) self-awareness
    c) attribution
    d) self-evaluation maintenance

19. Writing a list of explanations for why people chose their romantic partners may decrease temporarily their love for their partners due to:
    a) cognitive dissonance.
    b) reasons-generated attitude change.
    c) self-awareness.
    d) overjustification effect.

20. Research has found that self-recognition, a rudimentary self-concept, develops at around _____ of age.
    a) two months
    b) six months
    c) one year
    d) eighteen months

21. In order to gain important self-knowledge, people choose to compare themselves to:
    a) others who are similar to them on the important attribute or dimension.
    b) individuals regarded as "typical" on the important attribute or dimension.
    c) individuals regarded as "the best" on the important attribute or dimension.
    d) others who are inferior to them on the important attribute or dimension.

22. While self-handicapping may prevent unflattering attributions for our failures, it often has the negative consequence of
    a) creating the impression that one is a pompous, arrogant braggart.
    b) creating the impression that one is "kissing up."
    c) causing the poor performance that is feared in the first place.
    d) increasing dependence on others for self-esteem.

23. Enjoyment is to _____ motivation as reward is to _____ motivation.
    a) intrinsic; extrinsic
    b) internal; external
    c) extrinsic; intrinsic
    d) external; internal

24. We use ____ social comparison when we want to better ourselves and we use ____ social comparison when we want to feel better about ourselves.
    a) downward; upward
    b) upward; downward
    c) external; internal
    d) biased; unbiased

25. When we want people to form a particular impression of ourselves we engage in:
    a) self-perception.
    b) self-appraisal.
    c) impression management.
    d) self-management.

26. According to Festinger's social comparison theory, when will people compare themselves with other people and with whom do they compare themselves?
    a) when they have an objective standard for comparison and with people who are dissimilar to them
    b) when they have an objective standard for comparison and with people who are similar to them
    c) when they DO NOT have an objective standard for comparison, when they are uncertain about themselves, and with people who are dissimilar to them
    d) when they DO NOT have an objective standard for comparison, when they are uncertain about themselves, and with people who are similar to them

27. Wilson et al. (1993) found that the decisions people make following reasons-generated attitude change:
    a) are usually accurate.
    b) are ones that people tend to regret.
    c) reveal valuable information about their self-concepts.
    d) tend to be consistent with their true attitudes.

28. Participants in Nisbett and Wilson's (1977) experiment reported that a distracting noise had affected their ratings of a film when, in fact, it had not. These results may be explained by concluding that participants:
    a) failed to use causal theories.
    b) failed to use introspection.
    c) exhibited reasons-generated attitude change.
    d) generated a faulty causal theory.

29. Rose Marie once found painting to be an enjoyable hobby. Now that she works as a commercial artist, however, she rarely paints in her spare time. Rose Marie might begin to enjoy painting again if she:
    a) focuses on the external rewards that painting offers her.
    b) learns new painting techniques.
    c) focuses on the intrinsic reasons for painting and distances herself from the external rewards she receives from her job.
    d) quits her job and becomes a self-employed artist.

30.   Csikszentmihalyi and Figurski (1982) asked participants to wear beepers, and upon being beeped several times a day, list their thoughts and activities. Their results indicated that:
   a)   more than fifty percent of thoughts were about the self.
   b)   the vast majority of individuals' daily thoughts were about mundane chores and tasks.
   c)   for the most part, people are not thinking about anything; the majority of the time they reported "no thoughts."
   d)   none of the above

31.   Studies indicate that all of the following animals may have a rudimentary self-concept EXCEPT
   a)   cats.
   b)   chimps.
   c)   orangutans.
   d)   dolphins.

32.   When it comes to the outside and insider perspectives on the self and people in East Asian and Western cultures
   a)   people in Western cultures always adopt the insider perspective and people in East Asian cultures always adopt the outside perspective.
   b)   people in Western cultures always adopt the outside perspective and people in East Asian cultures always adopt the insider perspective.
   c)   people in both cultures can adopt either perspective, but the "default" state people tend to adopt differs.
   d)   people in East Asian cultures always adopt an outside perspective but people in Western cultures usually adopt an insider perspective but also adopt an outside perspective on occasion.

33.   According to the self-regulatory resource model, self control is an unlimited resource.
   a)   True
   b)   False

34.   Women are joining the workforce in Japan in record numbers, and more women are postponing or forgoing marriage in favor of
   a)   staying with their parents to help support them.
   b)   devoting their lives to a religious order.
   c)   cohabitating (living together without marriage).
   d)   careers.

35.   According to self-awareness theory we become self-conscious, in the sense that we become objective, judgmental observers of ourselves.
   a)   True
   b)   False

36.   Dweck uses the term _____ to refer to the idea that abilities are malleable qualities that can be cultivated and grown.
   a)   malleable mindset
   b)   fixed mindset
   c)   growth mindset
   d)   changeable mindset

37. Self-awareness is particularly aversive when it reminds people of their
    a) strengths.
    b) "to do" lists.
    c) shortcomings.
    d) none of the above

38. It is impossible to praise children too much for their efforts.
    a) True
    b) False

39. Which of the following people is engaged in social tuning?
    a) Alan, who is standing up for what he believes in.
    b) Jake, who is disagreeing with his friend.
    c) Judith, who is refusing to let her friends influence her.
    d) Charlie, who is adopting the same views as his date.

40. Recent research suggests that the "energy" that we spend when exerting self-control comes from glucose.
    a) True
    b) False

SHORT ANSWER REVIEW

The content of the self; that is, our (1) _____ (p. 118) about who we are, is our self-concept. Self-awareness is the act of (2) _____ (p. 118) about ourselves. These two aspects of the self combine to create a coherent sense of identity. Self-recognition in humans develops around the age of eighteen months. A child's (3) _____ (p. 118) is concrete. As we mature, we place less emphasis on physical characteristics and more on (4) _____ (p. 118) and on considerations of how other people judge us.

The self serves four important functions: *Self-knowledge,* whereby we (5) _____ (p. 119) what we know about ourselves; (6) _____ (p. 119), whereby we make plans and execute decisions; *self-presentation,* whereby we try to put our best foot forward to (7) _____ (p. 119), *self-justification,* whereby we try to put our best foot forward to (8) _____ (p. 119).

Culture influences how we define the self. In many Western cultures, people have an (9) _____ (p. 119), which is a way of defining oneself in terms of one's own internal thoughts, feelings, and actions and not in terms of the thoughts, feelings, and actions of others. Many Asian and

Chapter 5

other non-Western cultures have an interdependent view of the self, which is a way of defining oneself in terms of one's (10) _____ (p. 119) and recognizing that one's behavior is often determined by the thoughts, feelings, and actions of others. This does not mean that every member of a Western culture has an independent view of the self and that every member of an Asian culture has an interdependent view of the self. Within cultures, there are differences in the self-concept, and as contact between cultures increases, differences between cultures may (11) _____ (p. 121).

Gender also influences how we define the self. Women have more (12) _____ (p. 121), meaning that they focus more on their close relationships. Men have more (13) _____ (p. 121), meaning that they focus on their memberships in larger groups.

One way we come to know ourselves is through introspection. Introspection is the process whereby people look (14) _____ (p. 122) and examine their own thoughts, feelings, and motives. According to self-awareness theory, when people focus their attention on themselves, they evaluate and compare their behavior to their (15) _____ (p. 123) and values. Self-awareness can be aversive when it reminds people of their shortcomings, and under these circumstances people try to (16) _____ (p. 124).

Recent research indicates that culture influences how self-aware we are. (17) _____ (p. 124) are more likely to have an *outside perspective on the self*, viewing themselves through the eyes of other people. People who grow up in Western cultures are more likely to have an *insider perspective on the self*, focusing on their own (18) _____ (p. 124) without considering how other people see them.

Even when we are self-aware and introspect to our heart's content, it can be difficult to know why we feel the way we do. Causal theories are theories about the causes of one's own (19) _____ (p. 127) and behaviors. Sometimes we try to think about the reasons for our attitudes. This can bring about a

126
Copyright © 2010 by Pearson Education, inc. All rights reserved.

change in our attitudes. Reasons-generated attitude change is attitude change resulting from (20)

_____ (p. 128) about the reasons for one's attitudes. Over time, the effects of analyzing reasons

tends to wear off, and people's original "hard to explain" attitudes return. If people base important

decisions right after analyzing reasons, they might make a decision they later (21) _____ (p. 128).

Sometimes we are unsure about how we feel about something. Self-perception theory states that

when our attitudes and feelings are uncertain or ambiguous, we infer these states by (22) _____ (p.

129) our behavior and the situation in which is occurs. Our behavior may be motivated by intrinsic or

extrinsic factors. Intrinsic motivation is the desire to engage in an activity because we (23) _____

(p. 130) it or find it interesting, not because of external rewards or pressures. Extrinsic motivation is the

desire to engage in an activity because of external rewards or (24) _____ (p. 130), not because we

enjoy the task or find it interesting. Rewards can hurt intrinsic motivation. The (25) _____ (p. 130)

effect is the tendency for people to view their behavior as caused by compelling extrinsic reasons, making

them underestimate the extent to which it was caused by intrinsic reasons. Research indicates that rewards

will undermine interest only if interest was (26) _____ (p. 131) initially. Also, the type of reward

makes a difference. A (27) _____ (p. 131) reward, in which rewards are based on how well we

perform a task is less likely to decrease interest in a task—and may even increase interest—than a task-

contingent reward, in which rewards are given for performing a task regardless of (28) _____ (p.

131) the task is done.

How do we identify and understand our own emotions? Stanley Schacter proposed a two-factory

theory of emotion. This is the idea that emotional experience is the result of a two-step (29) _____

(p. 132) process in which people first experience physiological arousal and then seek an appropriate

explanation for it. Sometimes people form mistaken emotions. Misattribution of arousal is a process

whereby people make mistaken inferences about what is (30) _____ (p. 135) them to feel the way they do. Appraisal theories of emotion hold that emotions result from people's (31) _____ (p. 136) and explanations of events, even in the absence of physiological arousal.

How we explain our own talents and abilities is another very important kind of self-knowledge. Some people believe that their abilities are set in stone; they either have them or they do not. The psychologist Carol Dweck calls this a (32) _____ (p. 136), the idea that we have a set amount of an ability that cannot change. Other people have what Dweck calls a growth mindset, which is the idea that their abilities are malleable qualities that they can cultivate and grow. Research shows that the mindset people have is crucial to their (33) _____ (p. 136).

The self-concept does not develop in a solitary context but is shaped by the (34) _____ (p. 137) around us. Social (35) _____ (p. 137) theory holds that we learn about our own abilities and attitudes by comparing ourselves to other people. The nature of our goals affects the comparisons we make. When we want an accurate assessment of our abilities and opinions, we compare ourselves to people who are similar to us. When we want information about what we can strive toward, we engage in (36) _____ (p. 139) social comparison: We compare ourselves to people who are better than we are on a particular ability. When our goal is (37) _____ (p. 139), we compare ourselves to those who are less fortunate. We may also know ourselves by adopting other people's views. (38) _____ (p. 139) is the process whereby people adopt another person's attitudes. This can happen even when we meet someone for the first time, if we want to get along with that person.

One of the functions of the self is self-control. Another important function of the self is to be the chief executive who makes (39) _____ (p. 140) about what to do in the present and plans for the future. One form of self-control that does not work very well and often backfires is *thought suppression*, whereby we try to push thoughts out of our minds. Often, the more we try not to think about something, the more those very thoughts keep coming to mind. A better strategy is to (40) _____ (p 141) the forbidden topic while trying to exert will power when it comes to acting on those thoughts. According to the (41) _____ (p. 141), we are more likely to succeed when we have plenty of energy when we are trying to control our actions. According to this approach self-control requires energy, and spending this energy on one task limits the amount that can be spent on another task.

Impression management is the attempt by people to get others to see them the way they (42) _____ (p. 142). People have different impression management strategies. One is (43) _____ (p. 142)—using flattery or praise to make yourself likable to another, often higher-status person. This can backfire if the recipient of your ingratiation senses that you're being insincere. Another strategy is self-handicapping. This is a strategy whereby people create (44) _____ (p. 142) and excuses for themselves so that if they do poorly on a task, they can avoid blaming themselves. Self-handicapping often has the adverse effect of causing the poor performance we feared to begin with. People in all cultures are concerned with the impression they make on others, but the nature of this concern and the impression management (45) _____ (p. 144) people use differ considerably from culture to culture.

Essay Review

1. Argue that self-perception theory is a variation on attribution theory discussed in Chapter 4.

2. You have been dating someone for a week now and have decided that, before the relationship goes any further, it would be a good idea to introspect about the reasons WHY you like this person. What is likely to happen as you introspect? What negative consequence might arise from your introspection?

3. What are the advantages and disadvantages of self-awareness?

4. Compare and contrast self-perception theory and the two-factor theory of emotion.

5. You have worked in the library for two years. One year ago, if someone had asked you how much you liked your job, you would have said that you liked it very much. Since then, you have received a large raise in pay. Why, if you overjustify your reason for working at the library, will you claim to like the job less following your raise?

EXIT TESTS

EXIT TEST 1

1. Knowledge about who we are is
    a) self-awareness.
    b) our self-concept.
    c) self-esteem.
    d) self-assessment.

2. When an animal has a rudimentary self-concept it will
    a) growl at its own image in a mirror.
    b) pet a mirror when it is reflecting the animal's own image.
    c) realize that the image in the mirror is itself and not another animal.
    d) ignore its own image in a mirror.

3. Steve Heine and colleagues (2008) found that self-awareness can be induced by placing people in front of mirrors or video cameras. They found this effect was
    a) more true of Westerners than East Asians.
    b) more true of East Asians than Westerners.
    c) equally true of East Asians and Westerners.
    d) more true of West Asians than East Asians.

4. Women have more _____ interdependence while men have more _____ interdependence.
    a) friendship-oriented; career-oriented
    b) familial; work-related
    c) collective; relational
    d) relational; collective

5. In the study by Steve Heine and colleagues (2008), Japanese participants acted as if they had "mirrors in their heads."
    a) True
    b) False

6. Causal theories are theories about the causes of other people's feelings and behaviors.
    a) True
    b) False

7. Which theory states that we infer our attitudes from our behavior when our attitudes are ambiguous?
    a) self-awareness
    b) self-inferential
    c) self-perception
    d) causal theory of self

8. Kay is writing a manuscript because she is being paid to and not because she enjoys it. Kay's motivation is
    a) overjustified.
    b) self-punishment.
    c) intrinsic.
    d) extrinsic.

9.   You are in charge of designing a program to encourage children at a local elementary school to read. Which of the following would be the best approach for you to take?
      a)   Offer children a reward for each book that they read and write a book report about.
      b)   Offer children a reward for each book that they read.
      c)   Tell the children that they will not get recess unless they read at least 5 pages of a book each day.
      d)   Offer children a reward for visiting the school library.

10.   An implication of Schacter's two-factor theory of emotion is that people's emotions are
      a)   easily predicted.
      b)   somewhat arbitrary.
      c)   never arbitrary.
      d)   caused solely by changes in the nervous system.

EXIT TEST 2

1.   A central idea of _____ theories of emotion is that emotions result from people's interpretations and explanations of events, even in the absence of physiological arousal.
      a)   evaluative
      b)   appraisal
      c)   interpretative
      d)   explanatory

2.   To determine how to be a better manager, Roberto compares his performance to the senior level managers at his firm. Which theory best explains Roberto's behavior?
      a)   social comparison theory
      b)   self-awareness theory
      c)   self-reference effect
      d)   self-perception theory

3.   Jessica feels badly about the C she got on her exam until she talks with several students who failed the exam. Jessica feels better because she engaged in a
      a)   peer evaluation.
      b)   social comparative situation.
      c)   downward social comparison.
      d)   upward social comparison.

4.   Social tuning is a process whereby people adjust their attitudes because their attitudes are inconsistent with their behavior.
      a)   True
      b)   False

5.   Research has shown that students who have a fixed mindset about intelligence are
      a)   more likely to suffer from depression.
      b)   less likely to drop out of school.
      c)   less likely to give up and do poorly on subsequent tests.
      d)   more likely to give up and do poorly on subsequent tests.

6.   Which person is engaging in self-handicapping?
    a)   Pam, who signed up to work a lot of extra hours the week before her midterm exams.
    b)   Steve, who refuses to get a flu shot.
    c)   Mike, who is not feeling well but refuses to see a doctor.
    d)   Josephine, whose doctor told her to use a cane until her injured ankle heals but she often forgets to use it.

7.   Cross-cultural research on impression management indicates that
    a)   only people in collectivistic cultures are concerned with impression management.
    b)   only people in individualistic cultures are concerned with impression management.
    c)   people in all cultures are concerned with the impression they make on others but the strategies they use differ.
    d)   people in all cultures are concerned with the impression they make on others and the strategies they use are pretty much the same.

8.   Asking people of different ages to answer the question "Who am I?" is a way to study changes in
    a)   self-esteem.
    b)   self-concept.
    c)   self-awareness.
    d)   self-perception.

9.   Mindsets do not change thus, someone with a fixed mindset cannot change to a growth mindset.
    a)   True
    b)   False

10. Self-focus can be a way of keeping you out of trouble.
    a)   True
    b)   False

Study Activities

1.   What is a self-concept and how does it change from childhood to adulthood? How would you describe your own self-concept?

2.   Identify and define the functions of the self.

3.   How do self-concepts differ in Western cultures compared to Eastern cultures?

4.   How do self-concepts differ according to gender? Is your own self-concept consistent with this? Explain.

5.   According to self-awareness theory, what are the strategies people use to become less self-aware?

6.   Why is self-knowledge sometimes difficult to obtain?

7.   What is the main difference between the two-factor theory of emotion and appraisal theories of emotion?

8.   Why do we engage in social comparison? Describe a time when you engaged in an upward social comparison and a time when you engaged in a downward social comparison.

9.   What is impression management? How do we manage our impressions? What have you done recently to engage in impression management?

10.   What are two ways that we self-handicap? Can you describe a time when you engaged in one of these behaviors?

Chapter 5 Answers

Practice Test

1.   A (p. 118)
2.   C (p. 119)
3.   D (p. 124)
4.   D (p. 129)
5.   D (p. 118)
6.   B (pp. 130-131)
7.   B (p. 131)
8.   C (p. 132)
9.   B (p. 135)
10. D (p. 136)
11. A (p. 141)
12. C (p. 137)
13. D (p. 142)
14. D (pp. 122-123)
15. B (p. 127)
16   D (p. 130)
17. B (p. 134)
18. B (p. 123)
19. B (p. 128)
20. D (p. 118)
21. A (p. 138)
22. C (p. 143)
23. A (p. 130)
24. B (pp. 139-140)
25. C (p. 142)
26. D (pp. 137-138)
27. B (p. 128)
28. D (p. 127)
29. C (pp. 130-131)
30. B (p. 123)
31. A (p. 118)
32. C (p. 124)
33. B (p. 141)
34. D (p. 121)
35. A (p. 123)
36. C (p. 136)
37. C (p. 124)
38. B (p. 132)
39. D (p. 139)
40. A (p. 141)

Short Answer Review

1.   knowledge (p. 118)
2.   thinking (p. 118)
3.   self-concept(p. 118)
4.   psychological states (p. 118)
5.   formulate and organize (p. 119)
6.   self-control (p. 119)
7.   others (p. 119)
8.   ourselves (p. 119)
9.   independent view of the self (p. 119)
10.   relationships to other people (p. 119)
11.   decrease (p. 121)
12.   relational interdependence (p. 121)
13.   collective interdependence (p. 121)
14.   inward (p. 122)
15.   internal standards (p. 123)
16.   avoid it (p. 124)
17.   East Asians (p. 124)
18.   private experiences (p. 124)
19.   feelings (p. 127)
20.   thinking (p. 128)
21.   regret (p. 128)
22.   observing (p. 129)
23.   enjoy (p. 130)
24.   pressures (p. 130)
25.   overjustification (p. 130)
26.   high (p. 131)
27.   performance-contingent (p. 131)
28.   how well (p. 131)
29.   self-perception (p. 132)
30.   causing (p. 135)
31.   interpretations (p. 136)
32.   fixed mindset (p. 136)
33.   success (p. 136)
34.   people (p. 137)
35.   comparison (p. 137)
36.   upward (p. 139)
37.   self-enhancement (p. 139)
38.   Social tuning (p. 139)
39.   choices (p. 140)
40.   go ahead and think about (p. 141)
41.   self-regulatory resource model (p. 141)
42.   want to be seen (p. 142)
43.   ingratiation (p. 142)
44.   obstacles (p. 142)
45.   strategies (p. 144)

Essay Review

1.   According to self-perception theory, when the causes of our behavior are ambiguous, we are in functionally the same role as an outside observer attributing our own behavior to our attitudes and traits (note that these are therefore internal attributions). (p. 129)

2.   As you introspect about the reasons why you are attracted to your recent dating partner, you are likely to bring to mind reasons that sound plausible and are available, but which may not be the actual reasons. A negative consequence of identifying the wrong reasons is that you may change your mind about how you feel to match those reasons. For instance, if you decide that you are attracted to someone because the two of you share a common hobby, you may decide that such a reason is not justification for pursuing a relationship and lose interest. (p. 128)

3.   When we're self-aware, we form more accurate judgments of ourselves and may behave in a manner more consistent with our internal values and standards. However, self-awareness is uncomfortable and may cause us to engage in deleterious behaviors such as drinking alcohol, etc., to avoid self-awareness when we cannot change our behaviors. (p. 123-124)

4.   Both theories maintain that we come to understand ourselves by observing our own behavior and finding an appropriate explanation. The theories differ in two ways. First, each explains how we come to know a different feature of ourselves. Self-perception theory explains how we know what we think and what kind of person we are. The two-factor theory explains how we know how we feel. Second, each theory claims we use a different type of behavior to achieve self-understanding. Self-perception theory says we make internal attributions from observing overt behavior. The two-factor theory states we label behavior that is associated with physiological arousal. (pp. 129, 131-134)

5.   Before your pay raise, there were no large extrinsic rewards for working at the library. When asked, therefore, you are more likely to conclude that you work there because you like it. If you overjustify your reason for working there after your pay raise, the conspicuous external reward will grab your attention, cause you to discount the role of your intrinsic interest in the job, and lead you to conclude that you like the job less.
(pp. 130-131)

Exit Test 1

1.   B (p. 118)
2.   C (p. 118)
3.   A (p. 125)
4.   D (p. 121)
5.   A (p. 125)
6.   B (p. 127)
7.   C (p. 129)
8.   D (p. 130)
9.   A (p. 131)
10.   B (p. 134)

Exit Test 2

1.   B (p. 136)
2.   A (p. 137)
3.   C (p. 138)
4.   B (p. 139)
5.   D (p. 137)
6.   A (pp. 142-143)
7.   C (p. 144)
8.   B (p. 118)
9.   B (p. 137)
10.   A (p. 124)

Study Activities

1.   Self-concept is the content of the self; that is, our knowledge about who we are. Typically a child's self-concept is concrete, with references to clear-cut, easily observable characteristics like age, sex, neighborhood, and hobbies. As we mature, we place less emphasis on physical characteristics and more on psychological states and on considerations of how other people judge us. (pp. 118-119)

2.   The self serves four important functions: Self-knowledge, whereby we formulate and organize what we know about ourselves; self-control, whereby we make plans and execute decisions; self-presentation, whereby we try to put our best foot forward to others, self-justification, whereby we try to put our best foot forward to ourselves. (p. 119)

3.   In many Western cultures, people have an independent view of the self, which is a way of defining oneself in terms of one's own internal thoughts, feelings, and actions and not in terms of the thoughts, feelings, and actions of others. Many Asian and other non-Western cultures have an interdependent view of the self, which is a way of defining oneself in terms of one's relationships to other people and recognizing that one's behavior is often determined by the thoughts, feelings, and actions of others. (p. 119)

4.   Women have more relational interdependence, meaning that they focus more on their close relationships. Men have more collective interdependence, meaning that they focus on their memberships in larger groups. (p. 121)

5.   Sometimes people attempt to escape the self by alcohol abuse, binge eating, and sexual masochism. Many forms of religious expression and spirituality are also effective means of avoiding self-focus. (pp. 123-124)

6.   Self-knowledge can be difficult to obtain because many of our basic mental processes occur outside of awareness. We are usually aware of the final result of our thought processes but often unaware of the cognitive processing that led to the result. (p. 126)

7.   The main difference between the two-factor theory of emotion and appraisal theories of emotion concerns the role of arousal. According to cognitive appraisal theories, arousal does not always come first; the cognitive appraisals alone are a sufficient cause of emotional reactions. (p. 136)

8.   We engage in social comparison to learn about our own abilities and attitudes. (p. 137)

9.   Impression management is the attempt by people to get others to see them as they want to be seen. We may manage our impressions by ingratiation or self-handicapping. (p. 142)

10.   In its most extreme form, people create obstacles that reduce the likelihood they will succeed on a task so that if they do fail, they can blame it on these obstacles rather than on their lack of ability. The second type involves devising ready-made excuses in case we fail. (p. 143)

CHAPTER 6

The Need to Justify Our Actions: The Costs and Benefits of Dissonance Reduction

CHAPTER 6 OVERVIEW

Chapter 6 focuses on the consequences of the need people have to justify their actions in order to maintain their self-esteem. The introduction to the chapter discusses the mass suicide of the cult called Heaven's Gate. Members of the group died believing that they were "ridding themselves of their earthly containers" so that a gigantic spaceship (whose arrival was signaled by the comet Hale-Bopp) could pick them up and take them to a new incarnation.

The first section of the chapter discusses maintaining a stable, positive self-image. **Cognitive dissonance** is a drive or feeling of discomfort, originally defined as being caused by holding two or more inconsistent cognitions and subsequently defined as being caused by performing an action that is discrepant from one's customary, typically positive self-conception. Cognitive dissonance is a major motivator of human thought and behavior. It always produces discomfort, and in response, we try to reduce it. We may reduce dissonance by changing our behavior, by attempting to justify our behavior through changing one of the dissonant cognitions, or by attempting to justify our behavior by adding new cognitions. People often do not anticipate how successfully they will reduce dissonance. **Impact bias** is the tendency to overestimate the intensity and duration of our emotional reactions to future negative events.

The need to maintain self-esteem leads to thinking that is not always rational; rather, it is rationalizing. People who are in the midst of reducing dissonance are so involved with convincing themselves that they are right that they frequently end up behaving irrationally and maladaptively. Humans do not always process information in an unbiased way. Rather, we distort it in a way that fits our preconceived notions.

Every time we make a decision, we experience dissonance. In any decision, the chosen alternative is seldom entirely positive, and the rejected alternative is seldom entirely negative. **Postdecision dissonance** is dissonance aroused after making a decision, typically reduced by enhancing the attractiveness of the chosen alternative and devaluating the rejected alternative. The more important the decision, the greater the dissonance. The more permanent and less revocable the decision, the greater the need to reduce dissonance. Because of this, salespeople have developed techniques for creating the illusion that irrevocability exists. **Lowballing** is a strategy whereby a salesperson induces a customer to agree to purchase a product at a very low cost, subsequently claims it was an error, and then raises the price; frequently the customer will agree to make the purchase at the inflated price. Dissonance reduction following a difficult moral decision can cause people to behave either more or less ethically in the future.

Neuroscientists have recently shown that cognitive dissonance and its reduction are reflected in the way the brain processes information. One study found that the reasoning areas of the brain virtually shut down when a person is confronted with dissonant information, and the emotion circuits of the brain light up happily when consonance is restored.

Most people are willing to work hard to get something they really want. **Justification of effort** is the tendency for individuals to increase their liking for something they have worked hard to attain. If a person agrees to go through a demanding or unpleasant experience in order to attain some goal or object, that goal or object becomes more attractive.

Sometimes we may act in a way that contradicts our attitudes. These actions may or may not cause dissonance depending on whether we have external justification for the behavior. **External justification** is a reason or an explanation for dissonant personal behavior that resides outside the individual. When you can't find external justification for your behavior, you will attempt to find **internal justification**—you will try to reduce dissonance by changing something about yourself (e.g., your attitude or behavior). If we state an opinion or attitude that runs counter to our own private belief or attitude, referred to as **counterattitudinal advocacy**, and we have no external justification for making the statement, we may change our attitude.

Counterattitudinal advocacy can be used to tackle social problems such as race relations and racial prejudice, and to prevent the spread of AIDS. **Hypocrisy induction** is the arousal of dissonance by having individuals make statements that run counter to their behaviors and then reminding them of the inconsistency between what they advocated and their behavior. The purpose is to lead individuals to more responsible behaviors. The induction of hypocrisy has also been applied to the problem of road rage.

All societies run, at least in part, on punishment or the threat of punishment. Under severe threat, people have external justification not to engage in a forbidden activity. However, when a threat is mild there is insufficient external justification not to engage in a forbidden activity. When there is **insufficient punishment,** people experience dissonance for having resisted a desired activity or object. Usually this results in the person devaluing the forbidden activity or object. The less severe the threat, the less external justification there is; the less external justification, the greater the need for internal justification. When attitudes change from attempts at self-justification, **self-persuasion** occurs and the change is long-lasting. This not only applies to tangible rewards or punishments but also to intangible ones as well.

When we act either kindly or cruelly toward a person, we never quite feel the same way about that person again. Ben Franklin demonstrated this when he asked to borrow a rare book from a fellow legislator who did not like him. After the fellow legislator loaned Franklin the book he began to speak to Franklin and even be nice to him. They became friends and the friendship continued until the death of the fellow legislator. Research has confirmed that if we have done someone a favor, we are more likely to feel more positively toward that person. Conversely, if we treat someone poorly we may come to like him or her less. If we victimize people we may come to hate and derogate them.

We can find the effects of dissonance in almost every part of the world, but it does not always take the same form. Self-justification occurs in societies that are less individualistic than the United States however, it may be triggered in more communal ways. Sakai found that in Japan, not only does a person experience dissonance after saying that a boring task is interesting and enjoyable, but in addition, if a person merely observes someone he knows and likes saying that a boring task is interesting and enjoyable, that will cause the observer to experience dissonance. Consequently, in that situation, the observers' attitudes change.

Dissonance-reducing behavior can be useful because it restores our sense of stability and allows us to maintain our self-esteem. But if we spent all of our time and energy defending our egos, we would never learn from our mistakes. We must become more aware of the human tendency toward self-justification. But this process is an unconscious one. Nevertheless, once we know that we are prone to justify our actions, we can begin to monitor our thinking and, in effect "catch ourselves in the act." We can then begin to examine our behavior critically and dispassionately. We then stand a chance of breaking out of the cycle of action followed by self-justification followed by more intense action.

The final section of the chapter revisits the story of Heaven's Gate, discussed at the beginning of the chapter. A high degree of cognitive dissonance within the minds of the participants in this group influenced their attitudes about the telescope. They had given up too much to turn back at that point, so they had to continue to believe the spaceship was coming.

CHAPTER 6 OUTLINE

• The Heaven's Gate mass suicide is described. Members of the group died believing that they were "ridding themselves of their earthly containers" so that a gigantic spaceship (whose arrival was signaled by the comet Hale-Bopp) could pick them up and take them to a new incarnation. How could intelligent and sane people believe and do such a self-destructive thing?

I. Maintaining a Stable, Positive Self-Image

• One of the most powerful motivators of human behavior is the need to preserve a stable, positive self-concept. During the course of a lifetime, we experience many challenges to our beliefs that we are reasonable, decent people. This chapter concerns how we cope with such challenges.

A. The Theory of Cognitive Dissonance

• **Cognitive dissonance** is the feeling of discomfort caused by information that is discrepant from your customary, typically positive, self-concept.

• Leon Festinger originated the concept of cognitive dissonance, defining it as inconsistency between any two cognitions; subsequent research indicated that dissonance is most powerful when we perform an action or learn something that threatens our self-image.

• Experiencing dissonance motivates an attempt to reduce it, (a) by changing our behavior to bring it in line with the dissonance cognition, or by justifying our behavior by (b) changing one of the cognitions to make it less dissonant, or (c) adding new cognitions that are consonant with the behavior (see Figure 6.1, p. 151).

1. Why We Overestimate the Pain of Disappointment

• People often do not anticipate how successfully they will reduce dissonance. **Impact bias** is the tendency to overestimate the intensity and duration of our emotional reactions to future negative events.

B. Rational Behavior versus Rationalizing Behavior

• The need to reduce dissonance and maintain self-esteem produces thinking that is rationalizing rather than rational.

• For example, Jones and Kohler (1959) found that Southerners deeply committed to either segregation or desegregation tended to remember the plausible arguments that supported their position and the implausible arguments that supported the opposing position; to do otherwise would arouse dissonance.

• Because of this, people who are deeply committed to a position will almost never be persuaded to change their minds, no matter how powerful opposing arguments may be.

C. Decisions, Decisions, Decisions

1. Distorting Our Likes and Dislikes

• **Postdecision dissonance** is aroused after we make any important decision; it is reduced by enhancing the attractiveness of the chosen alternative and devaluating the rejected alternative.

• For example, Brehm (1956) had women rate several appliances, and then gave them a choice of receiving one of two appliances she had rated equally attractive. When asked to re-rate the products 20 minutes later, the chosen appliance was rated more, and the nonchosen, less attractive than originally rated.

2. The Permanence of the Decision
• The more permanent (less irrevocable) a decision, the greater the need to reduce dissonance after making it.
• For example, Knox and Inkster (1968) showed that, at the racetrack, people who had already placed their bets were more certain their horse would win than were those who had yet to place their bets.
• Gilbert and Ebert (2002) tested the irrevocability hypothesis in a photography class. Students were asked to rate two photographs and told they would get to choose one to keep. The students were randomly assigned to one of two conditions: Condition One: students were informed that they had the option to exchange photographs within a five-day period; Condition Two: students were told that their choices were final. The results of the experiment showed that students who had the option of exchanging photographs liked the one they finally ended up with less than those who made the final choice on the first day. An interesting addition to this study was that students were asked to predict whether keeping their options open would make them more or less happy with their decision. They predicted that keeping their options open would make them happier. They were wrong.

3. Creating the Illusion of Irrevocability
• **Lowballing** is an unscrupulous strategy whereby a salesperson induces a customer to agree to purchase a product at a very low cost; subsequently claims it was an error, and then raises the price; frequently the customer will agree to make the purchase at the inflated price. This is because signing a check or contract creates the illusion of irrevocability.

4. The Decision to Behave Immorally
• Dissonance reduction following a difficult moral decision (for example, to cheat or not) can cause people to behave either more or less ethically in the future, because people's attitudes will polarize in the attempt to justify the ethical choice they made (See Figure 6.2, page 157).

5. How Dissonance Affects Personal Values
• Mills (1958) made it easy for sixth graders to cheat on a competitive exam with prizes to the winners, and surreptitiously observed who cheated. Children who cheated showed a more lenient attitude, and those who resisted the temptation, a harsher attitude, than their pre-test scores.
• Viswesvaran & Deshpande (1996) found that executives who believed that managerial success could only be achieved through unethical behavior experienced far greater dissonance in the form of job dissatisfaction than those who did not hold this belief.

D. Dissonance, the Brain, and Evolution
• Neuroscientists have recently shown that cognitive dissonance and its reduction are reflected in the way the brain processes information. The reasoning areas of the brain virtually shut down when a person is confronted with dissonant information, and the emotion circuits of the brain light up happily when consonance is restored.

E. Justifying Your Effort
• People work hard to get what they want. What happens when a person works hard and the goal doesn't seem worth it after all? People are unlikely to change their self-concept to believe that they were unskilled or lacked sense (which is what would be implied by thinking the goal was worthless); instead they may change their attitude towards the goal and see it positively—the **justification of effort**.
• Aronson and Mills (1959) performed the classic experiment demonstrating this effect. Women were put through a severe, mild, or no initiation procedure in order to join a club, which then seemed worthless; those women who went through the severe initiation to get in, however, thought it was worthwhile (Figure 6.3, p. 158).

F. The Psychology of Insufficient Justification
1. Counterattitudinal Advocacy
• **Counterattitudinal advocacy** is the process by which people are induced to state publicly an attitude that runs counter to their own attitude.

• Sometimes when this occurs there is **external justification**, or reasons that lie outside the individual, for having made the statement. In this case the person's attitude doesn't change.

• In other cases, however, there is not obvious external justification for making the counterattitudinal statement—there is only **internal justification** of the lie by changing the attitude or behavior.

• Festinger and Carlsmith (1959) demonstrated this in the classic experiment where participants were induced to lie to another student about the interest level of an experimental task, and agreed to do so for either $1 or $20. Those who lied for $20 didn't change their attitudes about how boring the task was, but those who lied for $1 did.

• A.R. Cohen demonstrated that the tendency to change one's attitude to justify public statements occurred for students writing counter-attitudinal essays about their attitudes towards the police (a salient issue at the time), for $.50 or $1 (but not for students paid more).

• Nel, Helmreich, and Aronson (1969) had college students opposed to the legalization of marijuana compose and recite a videotaped speech favoring its legalization, for either small or large incentives. In addition, they varied the ostensible audience for the videotape: high school students who had already made up their minds, whether for or against legalization, or high school students who were undecided. Attitude change occurred for those who made the videotape for a small incentive and thought it would be played to the undecided audience.

G. Advocacy and Hypocrisy Applied to Social Problems
• Leippe and Eisenstadt (1994, 1998) induced white college students to write a counter-attitudinal essay publicly endorsing a proposal to double the amount of funds for scholarships for African American students by cutting the funds available to white students. In line with dissonance theory predictions, those who wrote the essay became more favorable and supportive of African American students.

• Hing and colleagues (2002) were able to induce hypocrisy among students deemed "aversive racists" (those low in explicit prejudice but high in implicit prejudice) to reduce prejudicial behaviors.

1.The Hypocrisy Paradigm
• The **hypocrisy paradigm** refers to the arousal of dissonance by having individuals make statements that run counter to their behaviors and then reminding them of the inconsistency between what they advocated and their behavior. The purpose is to lead individuals to more responsible behavior.

• Aronson, Stone, and colleagues have tried to use the counter-attitudinal advocacy paradigm to induce college students to practice safe sex. They have been successful with a procedure that first makes students mindful of their past failures to do so, and then asks them to make a videotape for high-schoolers advocating condom use 100% of the time. To resolve the dissonance thus induced, students become more willing to buy and use condoms (Figure 6.4, p. 163).

2. Hypocrisy Induction and Road Rage
• Takaku (2006) tested the effect of induced hypocrisy on reducing road rage. He found that when people are reminded of their own fallibility, they are quicker to go from anger to forgiveness than if this reminder is not induced. The reminder reduces their felt need to retaliate.

3. The Power of Mild Punishment
• Harsh punishments teach us to try to avoid getting caught, and thus require constant vigilance to be effective. In contrast, **insufficient punishment** induces dissonance about why one is not engaging in the behavior, and inspires dissonance reduction by devaluing the forbidden activity or object.

• Aronson and Carlsmith (1963) demonstrated with preschoolers that mild, insufficient punishment was effective in changing the attitude towards a forbidden, previously very attractive, toy.

4. Does Self-Persuasion Last?

• When attitude change occurs due to insufficient reward or punishment, it becomes very enduring, because the mechanism of change is **self-persuasion** and self-justification.

• For example, Freedman (1965) replicated the Aronson and Carlsmith forbidden toy experiment and showed that the induced attitude change persisted over several weeks in a new context (see Figure 6.5, p. 165).

5. Not just Tangible Rewards or Punishments

• Enduring attitude change can occur not only due to tangible rewards and punishments, but also due to the intangible rewards or punishments of pleasing or displeasing liked others (see Figure 6.6, p. 166).

• Zimbardo et al. (1965) showed that army reservists asked to eat fried grasshoppers for either a stern, unpleasant officer or a well-liked, pleasant one. Those induced to eat them by the stern officer reported that they liked them better, since they lacked the external justification of desiring to please the officer.

H. Good and Bad Deeds

1. The Ben Franklin Effect

• Dissonance theory and folk wisdom suggest that we like people not for the favors they have done us but for the favors we have done them. Ben Franklin used this strategy to manipulate a political rival to become a friend, asking him for a favor.

• Jecker and Landy (1969) showed that research participants who did a favor of returning their experimental payment to the experimenter liked him more than those who did the favor for the department or were not asked to do the favor (see Figure 6.7).

• The Leippe and Eisenstadt (1994) race relations study described earlier is an example of this effect.

• Conversely, Williamson et al. (1996) found that the failure to offer help led to a decline in the attractiveness of the other.

2. Hating Our Victims

• If we harm someone, this induces dissonance between our action and our self-concept as a decent person; to resolve this dissonance, we may derogate our victim.

• Davis and Jones (1960) induced students to insult a confederate to his face; after doing so (but not before), they found him less attractive.

• We are more likely to derogate people we have harmed if they are innocent victims. For example, Bersheid, Boye, and Walster (1968) had participants deliver a shock to a confederate who would or would not have a chance to retaliate; only those "victims" who could not retaliate were derogated.

• Derogating victims by de-humanizing perceptions of them may lead to a continuation or escalation of violence (e.g., the Holocaust).

I. Culture and Dissonance

• Triandis (1992) has found that in less individualistic cultures than ours, dissonance-reducing behavior often takes a backseat to behavior that promotes group harmony rather than individual consistency.

• Hong (1992) suggests that dissonance-reducing behavior is less extreme in Japan because Japanese culture considers acceptance of inconsistency as a sign of maturity and open-mindedness. This suggestion is supported in work by Heine and Lehman (1997), who found that Japanese natives were less likely to self-justify following a decision than were Canadians.

• Alternatively, it may be that self-justification occurs in collectivist societies but is triggered in more communal ways. In support of this, Sakai (1998) did a replication of the Festinger and Carlsmith experiment and found that observers as well as subjects experienced dissonance when the subject said the boring task was interesting, and both reduced dissonance by seeing the task as interesting.

II. Some Final Thoughts on Dissonance: Learning from Our Mistakes
• Dissonance-reducing behavior can be useful because it restores our sense of stability and allows us to maintain our self-esteem. But if we spent all of our time and energy defending our egos, we would never learn from our mistakes.
• We must become more aware of the human tendency toward self-justification. But this process is an unconscious one. Nevertheless, once we know that we are prone to justify our actions, we can begin to monitor our thinking and, in effect "catch ourselves in the act." We can then begin to examine our behavior critically and dispassionately. We then stand a chance of breaking out of the cycle of action, followed by self-justification, followed by more intense action.
• The attempt to reduce dissonance can prevent us from learning from our mistakes and can lead us to sweep our mistakes under the rug or even turn them into virtues, perpetuating error and leading to tragedy. For example, Robert McNamara's memoirs indicate that he came to believe that the war in Vietnam was unwinnable in 1967; rather than advising withdrawal, he remained silent and 30 years later published a book attempting to justify his silence.
• More recently, President George W. Bush wanted to believe that Iraqi leader Saddam Hussein possessed weapons of mass destruction (WMD). After the invasion of Iraq, administration officials, when asked "Where are the WMD?" said that Iraq is a big country and they have them well hidden, but asserted that they would be found. As the months dragged on and still no WMD were found, they continued to assert that they would find them. Why? Because they were experiencing enormous dissonance. They had to believe they would find them. Dissonance was reduced by adding new cognitions to justify the war: Suddenly we learned that the U.S. mission was to liberate the nation from a cruel dictator and give the Iraqi people the blessings of democratic institutions.
• How can a leader avoid falling into the self-justification trap? Bringing in skilled advisors from outside the inner circle can help because they are not caught up in the need to reduce dissonance from their earlier decision making.

III. Heaven's Gate Revisited
• While many factors played a role in the Heaven's Gate mass suicide, the large sacrifices made by cult members for their beliefs led members to explain away the lack of a spaceship as due to a telescope malfunction and carry out their suicide. To have done otherwise would have created too much dissonance to bear.

LEARNING OBJECTIVES

After reading Chapter 6, you should be able to do the following:

1.   Describe the theory of cognitive dissonance. Discuss the conditions that elicit dissonance and what strategies we use to reduce dissonance. (p. 150-154)

2.   Define impact bias and identify the determining factor as to how upset we will be after a disappointment. Explain what is meant by rational behavior versus rationalizing behavior. (p. 152)

3. Identify the consequences of making important decisions. Define post-decision dissonance. Explain how changing our attitudes after a decision serves to reduce dissonance. (pp. 153-155)

4. Identify the role played by the irrevocability of decisions in producing dissonance. Define "lowballing" and explain why the technique is effective. (pp. 155-156)

5. Describe the effects of deciding to behave morally or immorally on the experience of dissonance and the reduction of dissonance. (pp. 156-157)

6. Define what is meant by justification of effort. Identify the consequences of working hard to attain something worthless and the importance of volunteering such effort. (pp. 158-159)

7. Distinguish between internal and external justification. Define counterattitudinal advocacy. Describe the effects of inducing counterattitudinal advocacy with minimum external justification. Discuss the application of counterattitudinal advocacy and/or the hypocrisy paradigm to race relations, AIDS prevention, and road rage. (pp. 159-163)

8. Explain how insufficient punishment and insufficient justification lead to self-persuasion. Describe the effects of self-persuasion on behavior. (pp. 163-166)

9. Discuss the effects of doing favors for people we don't like. Define the Ben Franklin effect. (pp. 166-168)

10. Describe the effects on the self of harming others. Identify the causes and consequences of dehumanizing victims. (pp. 168-169)

11. Discuss the effects of culture on dissonance reduction. (p. 170)

12. In regards to dissonance, explain how we can learn from our mistakes. (pp. 171-172).

13. Explain how cognitive dissonance can be used to explain the actions of the members of Heaven's Gate. (pp. 172-173)

KEY TERMS

1. _____ A drive or feeling of discomfort, originally defined as being caused by holding two or more inconsistent cognitions and subsequently defined as being caused by performing an action that is discrepant from one's customary, typically positive self-conception. (p. 150)

2. _____ The tendency to overestimate the intensity and duration of our emotional reactions to future negative events. (p. 152)

3. _____ Dissonance aroused after making a decision, typically reduced by enhancing the attractiveness of the chosen alternative and devaluating the rejected alternatives. (p. 154)

4. _____ An unscrupulous strategy whereby a salesperson induces a customer to agree to purchase a product at a very low cost, subsequently claims it was an error, and then raises the price; frequently the customer will agree to make the purchase at the inflated price. (p. 155)

5. _____ The tendency for individuals to increase their liking for something they have worked hard to attain. (p. 158)

6. _____ A reason or an explanation for dissonant personal behavior that resides outside the individual. (p. 159)

7. _____ The reduction of dissonance by changing something about oneself. (p. 160)

8. _____ Stating an opinion or attitude that runs counter to one's private belief or attitude. (p. 160)

9. _____ The arousal of dissonance by having individuals make statements that run counter to their behaviors and then reminding them of the inconsistency between what they advocated and their behavior. The purpose is to lead individuals to more responsible behavior. (p. 163)

10. _____ The dissonance aroused when individuals lack sufficient external justification for having resisted a desired activity or object, usually resulting in individuals' devaluing the forbidden activity or object. (p. 164)

11. _____ A long-lasting form of attitude change that results from attempts at self-justification. (p. 165)

GUIDED REVIEW

PRACTICE TEST

1. An individual who strongly opposes helmet laws is excited to find a study which shows that neck injuries are a more common outcome of motorcycle accidents when helmets are worn than when helmets are not worn. This individual is reducing dissonance by:
   a) changing behavior to bring it in line with the dissonant cognition.
   b) adding cognitions that justify the behavior.
   c) modifying dissonant cognitions to justify the behavior.
   d) adopting a self-concept that is consistent with the behavior.

2. If a participant in Brehm's (1956) study claimed that an iron and an electric can opener were equally desirable appliances, she was asked to choose one of these as a gift. Later she was asked to rerate the two appliances. If she chose the can opener, her second rating of the appliances were typically:
   a) lower for the can opener and higher for the iron.
   b) lower for the can opener and lower for the iron.
   c) higher for the can opener and higher for the iron.
   d) higher for the can opener and lower for the iron.

3. An insurance salesperson offers a home insurance policy to customers at a very low rate. Just before the sale, however, he claims to have realized an error in his calculations. The actual cost of the policy, he claims, is substantially greater than he originally estimated. What is the name of the unscrupulous strategy used by the insurance salesperson?
    a) lowballing
    b) hard selling
    c) counterattitudinal advocacy
    d) rationalizing

4. Mills (1958) had children compete on a difficult exam under conditions that made cheating easy and presumably undetectable. The children's attitudes toward cheating were measured the next day and revealed that:
    a) children who cheated adopted a harsher attitude toward cheating while those who resisted cheating became more lenient toward cheating.
    b) children adopted a more lenient attitude toward cheating after competing with each other.
    c) children who cheated became more lenient toward cheating while those who resisted cheating adopted a harsher attitude toward cheating.
    d) children became more lenient toward cheating after competing with each other.

5. In the Festinger and Carlsmith (1959) experiment, participants who were paid $20.00 to lie felt less dissonance than subjects paid $1.00 because receiving $20.00:
    a) put participants in a good mood that counteracted dissonance.
    b) provided self-verification cues that participants were in fact moral people.
    c) was sufficient external justification for lying.
    d) allowed subjects to affirm their worth and circumvented dissonance.

6. Dehumanizing the victim increases:
    a) dissonance caused by our cruel treatment of others.
    b) the likelihood that cruel treatment will continue or even escalate.
    c) empathy for the victim.
    d) the likelihood that hostilities will end.

7. We can find the effects of dissonance in almost every part of the world
    a) except in countries that are at war.
    b) but in some places it is only present in women and not men.
    c) and the form is usually the same.
    d) but it does not always take the same form.

8. According to the text, if we spent all our time and energy defending our egos
    a) we would never learn from our mistakes.
    b) we would run out of cognitive resources.
    c) our relationships would deteriorate.
    d) we would have a more complex self-concept.

9. Experiments by Egan and colleagues (2007) did not support the notion that cognitive dissonance developed evolutionarily.
    a) True
    b) False

10. In order to learn from our mistakes, we must be able to:
    a) circumvent dissonance by affirming our positive qualities.
    b) find both internal and external justification for our behaviors.
    c) deny the existence of inconsistent beliefs.
    d) tolerate dissonance long enough to examine the situation objectively.

11. In general, the most rational way to reduce dissonance that follows foolish or immoral behavior is to:
    a) justify the behavior by adding cognitions to support it.
    b) justify the behavior by modifying dissonant cognitions.
    c) change the behavior to bring it in line with the dissonant cognition.
    d) adopt a self-concept that is consistent with the behavior.

12. Imagine that you've agreed to buy a notoriously unreliable but attractive sports car, instead of a less attractive but dependable station wagon. Which of the following will reduce dissonance in this situation?
    a) knowing that you've purchased an unreliable car
    b) thinking that you could rely on the station wagon
    c) putting a substantial down payment on the sports car
    d) imagining how good you'll look in the sports car

13. When a counterattitudinal advocacy is accomplished with a minimum of external justification,
    a) private attitudes change in the direction of public statements.
    b) public statements change in the direction of private attitudes.
    c) private attitudes and public statements tend to spread apart.
    d) private attitudes are subtly revealed in public statements.

14. Aronson and Carlsmith (1963) told children that they were not allowed to play with a highly desirable toy and measured the children's liking for the toy after this rule was obeyed in the experimenter's absence. They found that children's liking for the toy:
    a) increased when the rule was accompanied by a mild threat.
    b) decreased when the rule was accompanied by a severe threat.
    c) decreased when the rule was accompanied by a mild threat.
    d) increased when the experimenter left the room.

15. Dissonance theory predicts that if we do a favor for someone we dislike, we will:
    a) expect a favor in return.
    b) come to like that person.
    c) feel that we are weak.
    d) expect to be taken advantage of.

16. Aronson et al. (1991) found that students who composed arguments in favor of the use of condoms, recited them on videotape, and were made aware of their own failure to use condoms were:
    a) less likely to buy condoms than the students in the other conditions.
    b) more likely to buy condoms than the students in the other conditions.
    c) less likely to report using condoms than the students in the other conditions.
    d) equally likely to buy condoms as the students in the other conditions.

17. In a study by Hing and colleagues (2002), hypocrisy was induced among students to reduce prejudicial behaviors towards
    a) Asians.
    b) Native Americans.
    c) African Americans.
    d) Hispanics.

18. Ross is afraid that he might lose Rachel. Ross believes that if this happens he will be devastated and severely depressed. However, when he and Rachel do break up he handles it much better than he thought he would. This illustrates
    a) coping skills underestimation.
    b) faulty self-prediction phenomenon.
    c) impact bias.
    d) self-affirmation theory.

19. Neuroscientists have recently shown that cognitive dissonance and its reduction are reflected in the way the brain processes information.
    a) True
    b) False

20. People may say that they like a boring task on which they spent a lot of time and expense due to:
    a) justification of effort.
    b) post-decision dissonance.
    c) lowballing.
    d) insufficient punishment.

21. The success of the lowballing technique is due to:
    a) the commitment already made to the purchase.
    b) the illusion of irrevocability.
    c) dissonance reduction techniques.
    d) all the above.

22. In a study by Gilbert and Ebert (2002) on the Harvard campus, students were asked to rate and then choose between two photographs. Which of the following is true about this study's findings?
    a) Students who had to make their final choice on the first day liked their photographs least.
    b) Students who had to make their final choice on the first day liked their photographs best.
    c) Students who had the option of exchanging their photographs within a five-day period liked their photographs best.
    d) There was no difference between the students who chose on the first day and those who had the option of exchanging their photographs on how much they liked their photographs.

23. According to the text, how can leaders avoid falling into the self-justification trap?
    a) Leaders should caution their advisors against self-justification.
    b) Research shows leaders should wait at least 72 hours before making a final decision on something.
    c) Leaders can bring in skilled advisors from outside the inner circle.
    d) Leaders should ask someone in their group to think of all the reasons why the proposed course of action may be a bad one.

24. Large rewards and severe punishments are examples of _____ justification for behavior and result in _____ attitude change.
    a) internal; great
    b) external; great
    c) internal; little
    d) external; little

25. Which of the following concepts explains why the members of Heaven's Gate did not change their beliefs even in the face of strong evidence that they were wrong?
    a) cognitive dissonance
    b) impact bias
    c) insufficient punishment
    d) self-affirmation theory

26. Charles loves to go drag racing. One day, he comes across an article indicating how dangerous the sport can be. He starts to feel tense. How might Charles get rid of this uneasy feeling, according to cognitive dissonance theory?
    a) decide that he does not want to drag race in the future
    b) convince himself that the source of the article is not credible
    c) selectively expose himself to information that says that drag racing can be safe
    d) any of the above may reduce dissonance

27. Ann Marie supports drilling in the Alaskan wilderness. Shawn wants to convince her that drilling there should be banned. According to cognitive dissonance theory, what could Shawn do to change her attitude?
    a) give her a large reward to openly endorse a ban on drilling
    b) provide her with many strong arguments and facts that support a ban on drilling
    c) create the illusion that everyone else favors a ban on drilling, so that going against them makes her feel uncomfortable
    d) offer her a small, but adequate, reward to openly endorse a ban on drilling

28. Cognitive dissonance is:
    a) the sense of well-being that arises when self-esteem needs and needs for accuracy are satisfied.
    b) the confusion that occurs when situations evoke emotions that do not seem appropriate for the given situation.
    c) the discomfort caused by engaging in a behavior that is discrepant from one's conception of oneself as a decent and sensible person.
    d) a change in attitude that follows the careful analysis of arguments relevant to an issue.

29. Aronson and Mill's (1959) study of participants' initiation before joining a discussion group about sex showed that:
    a) a severe initiation led students to like the group more.
    b) all participants liked to talk about sex.
    c) going through a demanding and unpleasant screening process will have a negative impact on evaluations of a group.
    d) a mild initiation was the most effective in causing increases in evaluations of a group.

30. Knox and Inkster's (1968) study of individuals placing bets on horses showed that:
    a) bettors began to doubt their decision after they placed their bets.
    b) bettors became more confident in their horses' odds of winning after placing their bets.
    c) the act of placing a bet causes dissonance because of the conflict between people's morals and actions.
    d) bettors selecting long-shots (i.e., horses with a low probability of winning) tended to have very high levels of self-esteem.

31. Which of the following people was the first to investigate the precise workings of cognitive dissonance?
    a) Jack Brehm
    b) Ben Franklin
    c) Elliot Aronson
    d) Leon Festinger

32. Given that people have successfully reduced dissonance in the past, why is it that they are not aware that they will do so in the future?
    a) The process of reducing dissonance occurs only rarely.
    b) The process of reducing dissonance is very difficult.
    c) The process of reducing dissonance is largely unconscious.
    d) Only people with low self-esteem believe they will not be able to reduce dissonance.

33. The reasoning areas of the brain are very active when a person is confronted with dissonant information.
    a) True
    b) False

34. When consonance is restored, the emotion circuits of the brain light up happily.
    a) True
    b) False

35. In the Gilbert and Ebert (2002) study in which Harvard students were asked to rate and then choose between two photographs, students were also asked whether keeping their options open would make them more or less happy with their decision. The researchers found that the students
    a) inaccurately predicted that keeping their options open would make them happier with their decision.
    b) accurately predicted that keeping their options open would make them happier with their decision.
    c) accurately predicted that people whose options were not kept open would be happier with their choices.
    d) none of the above

36. All other things being equal, which of the following people is most likely to believe that their job is great?
    a) Earl, who got his job without even having to apply or interview because of a networking contact.
    b) Sara, who had to fill out an application and request that her college transcript be sent to the employer.
    c) Mike, who got his job through an employment agency.
    d) Andrea, who had to fill out an application on-line, send in a resume, go through three interviews and make a presentation to her department in order to get her job.

37. To reduce her cognitive dissonance, Lori changes her attitude. Lori has engaged in
    a) attitude justification.
    b) counterattitudinal advocacy.
    c) internal justification.
    d) external justification.

38. In a study by Nel et al. (1969) students who believed that marijuana was harmful were induced to compose and recite a videotaped speech favoring its use and legalization. The researchers found that
    a) the larger the incentive, the greater the softening of the attitude toward the use and legalization of marijuana.
    b) the smaller the incentive, the greater the softening of the attitude toward the use and legalization of marijuana.
    c) none of the students changed their attitudes about marijuana.
    d) all of the students experienced a softening of their attitudes toward the use and legalization of marijuana regardless of the size of the incentive.

39. If your child is bullying her little sister and you want her to stop, research indicates you should
    a) threaten her with mild punishment.
    b) threaten her with moderate punishment.
    c) threaten her with severe punishment.
    d) none of the above, you should never threaten children.

40. Self-persuasion is a form of attitude change that does not last long.
    a) True
    b) False

SHORT ANSWER REVIEW

Most of us have a need to see ourselves as (1) _____ (p. 150), moral, and smart. When we are confronted with information implying that we may have behaved in ways that are (2) _____ (p. 150), immoral, or stupid, we experience a good deal of discomfort. This feeling of discomfort caused by performing an action that runs (3) _____ (p. 150) to one's customary (typically positive) conception of oneself is referred to as cognitive dissonance. Cognitive dissonance always produces discomfort, and in response, we try to (4) _____ (p. 150) it.

There are three basic ways to reduce dissonance. First, we can change our (5) _____ (p. 151) to bring it in line with the dissonant cognition. Another way to reduce dissonance is to (6) _____ (p. 151) our behavior through changing one of the dissonant cognitions. Finally, we can attempt to justify our behavior by adding new (7) _____ (p. 151).

People often do not anticipate how successfully they will reduce dissonance. Several studies have suggested that when people think about how they will react to future (8) _____ (p. 152) events they show an impact bias, whereby they overestimate the intensity and duration of their negative emotional reactions. This overestimation is due to the fact that the process of reducing dissonance is largely (9) _____ (p. 152). Because the dissonance reduction process is mostly unconscious, we do not anticipate that it will save us from future angst.

The need to maintain our self-esteem leads to thinking that is not always rational; rather it is (10) _____ (p. 152). People who are in the midst of reducing dissonance are so involved with convincing themselves that they are right that they frequently end up behaving irrationally and (11) _____ (p. 152).

Every time we make a decision, we experience dissonance. In any decision, the (12) _____ (p. 153) alternative is seldom entirely positive, and the rejected alternative is seldom entirely negative. The dissonance we experience after making a decision is called postdecision dissonance. To reduce dissonance we change the way we feel about the chosen and unchosen alternatives, (13) _____ (p. 153) them apart in our minds in order to feel better about the choice we made. The more important the decision is, the (14) _____ (p. 154) the dissonance. Decisions also vary in terms of how (15) _____ (p. 154) they are—that is, how difficult they are to revoke. The more permanent and less revocable the decision, the greater the need to reduce dissonance. Sometimes salespeople will create the illusion of irrevocability. Lowballing is a strategy whereby a salesperson induces a customer to agree to purchase a product at a very low cost, subsequently claims it was an (16) _____ (p. 155), and then raises the price; frequently the customer will agree to make the purchase at the inflated price.

Dissonance reduction following a difficult (17) _____ (p. 156) decision can cause people to behave either more or less ethically in the future. What happens is not merely a rationalization of your own behavior but an actual change in your system of (18) _____ (p. 156). Neuroscientists have

recently shown that cognitive dissonance and its reduction are reflected in the way the (19) _____

(p. 157) processes information. The (20) _____ (p. 157) areas of the brain virtually shut down when

a person is confronted with dissonance information, and the emotion circuits of the brain light up happily

when consonance is restored.

Most people are willing to work hard to get something they really want. If we work hard for

something that turns out not to be worthwhile, we may experience dissonance. Justification of effort is the

tendency for individuals to (21) _____ (p. 158) their liking for something they have worked hard to

attain. If a person agrees to go through a (22) _____ (p. 159) or an unpleasant experience in order to

attain some goal or object, that goal or object becomes more (23) _____ (p. 159).

Sometimes we may act in a way that contradicts our attitudes. These actions may or may not

cause dissonance depending on whether we have (24) _____ (p. 159) for the behavior. External

justification is a reason or an explanation for dissonant personal behavior that resides (25) _____ (p.

159) the individual. When you can't find external justification for your behavior, you will attempt to find

internal justification—you will try to reduce dissonance by changing something about (26) _____

(p. 160). If we state an attitude or opinion that runs counter to our private belief or attitude—

counterattitudinal advocacy—and we have little external justification, we begin to believe what we said.

Counterattitudinal advocacy has been used to address social (27) _____ (p. 161).

All societies run, in part, on punishment or the threat of punishment. Insufficient punishment

refers to the dissonance aroused when individuals lack (28) _____ (p. 164) external justification for

having resisted a desired activity or object, usually resulting in an individual's devaluing the forbidden

object or activity. The less (29) _____ (p. 164) you make the threat, the less external justification

there is; the less external justification, the greater the need for internal justification. (30) _____ (p.

Chapter 6

165) is a long-lasting form of attitude change that results from attempts at self-justification. Self-

persuasion is more permanent than direct attempts at persuasion precisely because, with self-persuasion,

the persuasion takes place internally and not because of external coaxing or (31) _____ (p. 165).

Large rewards and severe punishments, because they are strong external justifications, encourage

compliance but prevent real attitude change.

Dissonance theory predicts that we will like a person more after doing the person a favor. Ben

Franklin used this to win over a fellow legislator who did not like him and it is now referred to as the (32)

_____ (p. 166-167). Likewise, if you treat someone badly, it can affect your opinion in a negative

way and you may hate your victim. Research suggests that during a war, military personnel have a greater

need to derogate (33) _____ (p. 169) victims than military victims.

We can find the effects of dissonance in almost every part of the world, but it does not always

take the same (34) _____ (p. 170). It may be that self-justification occurs in less individualistic

societies but is triggered in more (35) _____ (p. 170) ways.

Cognitive dissonance-reducing behavior can allow us to maintain our self-esteem but it can also

prevent us from learning from our mistakes. To prevent this, we must become more (36) _____ (p.

171) of the human tendency toward self-justification. Sometimes leaders fall into the self-justification

trap. Leaders can avoid this trap by brining in skilled advisors from (37) _____ (p. 172) the inner

circle because they are not caught up in the need to reduce dissonance from earlier decision making.

ESSAY REVIEW

1.   What is cognitive dissonance and how can it be reduced?

2.   Define postdecision dissonance and identify how it is typically reduced and two things that can
         increase it.

3. Describe what is meant by justification of effort. Differentiate between external and internal justification. What is counterattitudinal advocacy and how can it change an attitude?

4. Describe insufficient punishment and explain how it can lead to self-persuasion.

5. Explain how the Ben Franklin effect works. How might treating someone poorly influence our behavior?

EXIT TESTS

EXIT TEST 1

1. Ken thinks of himself as a generous person, but he passes by a Salvation Army volunteer collecting donations without contributing. Later Ken feels uncomfortable about not giving since he thinks of himself as generous. Ken is experiencing
   a) self-justification.
   b) identity confusion.
   c) cognitive dissonance.
   d) conflictive cognitions.

2. Cognitive dissonance can be reduced by
   a) changing our behavior to bring it in line with the dissonant cognition.
   b) attempting to justify our behavior through changing one of the dissonant cognitions.
   c) attempting to justify our behavior by adding new cognitions.
   d) all of the above.

3. The hypocrisy paradigm was first used during the 1990s by Elliot Aronson and his students to induce students to buy condoms.
   a) True
   b) False

4. Karen is convinced that she will be devastated if she does not get into the school of her first choice for graduate school. However, when Karen gets a rejection letter from her first choice school she takes it pretty well. This illustrates the
   a) affect underestimation tendency.
   b) impact bias.
   c) false prophecy effect.
   d) easy coping phenomenon.

5. Jones & Kohler found that participants who heard arguments regarding racial segregation remembered the _____ arguments agreeing with their own position and the _____ arguments agreeing with the opposing position.
   a) plausible; implausible
   b) implausible; plausible
   c) factual; fictional
   d) fictional; factual

6. Larry and Kim have purchased the exact same plasma televisions, but at different stores. The store Larry purchased his television at has a 90-day return policy in which he can get a full refund if he keeps his receipt. Kim purchased her television at a store where all sales are final. Which of the following is most likely to be true?
    a) Larry will like his television better than Kim will because he will engage in self-persuasion.
    b) Larry will like his television better than Kim will because he doesn't have to worry about being able to return it if he wants to.
    c) Kim will like her television more than Larry will because her decision to purchase it is irrevocable.
    d) Larry and Kim will like their televisions equally well because they bought the exact same televisions.

7. Dan wants to buy a new vehicle. The salesperson offers Dan a really low price on a vehicle that Dan likes so Dan agrees to purchase the vehicle. After writing up the deal the salesperson says to Dan, "I have to get this approved by my manager." The salesperson returns 20 minutes later and tells Dan that the manager would not approve the deal because the dealership would lose money on the vehicle. Dan is told that if he wants the vehicle he will have to pay $1500 more. Dan has just experienced
    a) door-in-the-face technique.
    b) the impact bias.
    c) the bait-and-switch technique.
    d) lowballing.

8. In a study on attitudes about cheating in an elementary school conducted by Judson Mills (1958), students who cheated later adopted a harsher attitude toward cheating.
    a) True
    b) False

9. If a person goes through a demanding or unpleasant experience in order to attain some goal or object, that goal or object becomes
    a) more attractive.
    b) less attractive.
    c) self-affirming.
    d) self-satisfying.

10. Kaitlin is in favor of the death penalty, however, she has written a 3-page paper for a class describing reasons why the death penalty should be abolished. Which of the following conditions would most likely lead to an attitude change in Kaitlin in which she would feel more favorable about abolishing the death penalty?
    a) If the paper was worth 30% of her course grade.
    b) If the paper was worth 20% of her course grade.
    c) If the paper was worth only 5 points of extra credit.
    d) If the paper was worth 50 points of extra credit.

EXIT TEST 2

1. The members of Heaven's Gate bought an expensive high-powered telescope to see the spaceship that they believed was following the Hale-Bopp Comet. When they could not see the spaceship, dissonance led them to
   a) become depressed.
   b) buy an even more expensive and high-powered telescope.
   c) return the telescope and believe that it was broken.
   d) leave the cult and return to their families.

2. Reducing dissonance is done consciously.
   a) True
   b) False

3. We experience dissonance
   a) every time we make a decision.
   b) only when we make irrevocable decisions.
   c) only when we make important decisions.
   d) only rarely after making a decision, provided we have good self-esteem.

4. Liz has just reduced cognitive dissonance by changing her attitude. Liz has engaged in
   a) attitudinal dissonance reduction.
   b) counterattitudinal advocacy.
   c) external justification.
   d) internal justification.

5. In the Festinger & Carlsmith (1959) experiment participants were asked to lie and say that a boring task was interesting. Which participants rated the task as somewhat enjoyable?
   a) those paid $1
   b) those paid $20
   c) all the participants rated it as somewhat enjoyable
   d) all the participants rated it as totally boring

6. Nel et al. (1969) approached college students who initially believed that marijuana was harmful and induced them to compose and recite a videotaped speech favoring its use and legalization. Some were offered large incentives; others were offered small incentives. What were the findings?
   a) All of the students continued to be against the legalization of marijuana.
   b) All of the students felt more favorably about marijuana after making the speech.
   c) The smaller the incentive, the greater the softening of the attitude toward the use and legalization of marijuana.
   d) The greater the incentive, the greater the softening of the attitude toward the use and legalization of marijuana.

7.   Leippe and Eisenstadt (1994, 1998) induced white college students to write a counterattitudinal essay publicly endorsing a controversial proposal at their university to double the amount of funds available for academic scholarships for African American students by cutting the amount of scholarship funds available to white students by 50%. The results indicated that
   a)   none of the white students changed their attitudes toward the policy.
   b)   not only did the white students feel more favorably about the policy, but they also adopted a more favorable attitude toward African Americans.
   c)   the white students felt more favorably about the policy, but their attitudes toward African Americans did not change.
   d)   the white students felt more negatively about the policy after being induced to write the counterattitudinal essay.

8.   Dr. McCoy does not want students to write on her exams. Which of the following should she do to keep most students from writing on the exam?
   a)   telling her students that if they are caught writing on the exam they will be given a zero on the exam and will not be allowed to retake the exam
   b)   announcing to the class that under no circumstances are they to write on the exam
   c)   telling her students that if they write on the exam she will take 10 points off their grade
   d)   writing "Please do not write on this exam. Thank you." on the exam

9.   Which of the following brings about long-lasting attitude change?
   a)   self-persuasion
   b)   external justification
   c)   cognitive dissonance
   d)   impact bias

10.   Zimbardo et al. (1965) had either a stern, unpleasant officer or a well-liked, pleasant officer ask army reservists to eat fried grasshoppers. They found that
   a)   all of the recruits reported hating eating the grasshoppers.
   b)   all of the recruits reported more positive attitudes toward eating grasshoppers.
   c)   those recruits who ate the grasshoppers for the unpleasant officer adopted more positive attitudes toward eating grasshoppers.
   d)   those recruits who ate the grasshoppers for the pleasant officer adopted more positive attitudes toward eating grasshoppers.

STUDY ACTIVITIES

1.   How do groups ensure the loyalty of their members by requiring them to endure severe initiation procedures before joining?

2.   Suppose you are a parent, and you would like to instill good study skills and a love of education in your children. How should you reward them when they do well in their studies?

3.   The announcer on the radio congratulates caller number ten. She's just won a prize and is asked what her favorite radio station is. Ecstatically, she states the station's call letters. Why is her subsequent opinion of the station likely to be higher if her prize was a T-shirt than if her prize was $100?

4.   Argue that humans are very flexible in maintaining their self-esteem by discussing the various strategies we may use to reduce dissonance according to the theory of cognitive dissonance.

5.   What is lowballing and why is it an effective persuasion technique? Have you ever been the victim of this strategy? If so, describe your experience.

6.   What are the effects of insufficient punishment on the judgments of an object or entity? What are the effects of mild versus severe threats on the level of dissonance experienced?

7.   Why is self-persuasion a long-lasting form of attitude change?

8.   What are the consequences of doing something unpleasant for a friend, compared to doing something unpleasant for someone who is disliked?

9.   Describe what happens in the brain when a person is confronted with dissonant information. How does the brain react when consonance is restored?

10.   How can a leader avoid falling into the self-justification trap?

Chapter 6 Answers

Practice Test
1.   B (p. 151)
2.   D (p. 154)
3.   A (p. 155)
4.   C (p. 157)
5.   C (p. 160)
6.   B (p. 169)
7.   D (p. 170)
8.   A (p. 171)
9.   B (p. 157)
10.   D (p. 171)
11.   B (p. 156)
12.   D (pp. 153-154)
13.   A (pp. 160-161)
14.   C (pp. 164-165)
15.   B (pp. 166-167)
16.   B (p. 162)
17.   A (pp. 161-162)
18.   C (p. 152)
19.   A (p. 157)
20.   A (p. 158)
21.   D (pp. 155-156)
22.   B (pp. 154-155)
23.   C (p. 172)
24.   D (pp. 159-160)
25.   A (pp. 172-173)
26.   D (p. 151)
27.   D (pp. 159-161)
28.   C (p. 150)
29.   A (p. 158)
30.   B (p. 154-155)
31.   D (p. 150)
32.   C (p. 152)
33.   B (p. 157)
34.   A (p. 157)
35.   A (pp. 154-155)
36.   D (p. 158)
37.   C (p. 160)
38.   B (p. 161)
39.   A (pp. 163-164)
40.   B (p. 165)

Short Answer Review

1. reasonable (p. 150)
2. irrational (p. 150)
3. counter (p. 150)
4. reduce (p. 150)
5. behavior (p. 151)
6. justify (p. 151)
7. cognitions (p. 151)
8. negative (p. 152)
9. unconscious (p. 152)
10. rationalizing (p. 152)
11. maladaptively (p. 152)
12. chosen (p. 153)
13. cognitively spreading (p. 153)
14. greater (p. 154)
15. permanent (p. 154)
16. error (p. 155)
17. moral (p. 156)
18. values (p. 156)
19. brain (p. 157)
20. reasoning (p. 157)
21. increase (p. 158)
22. demanding (p. 159)
23. attractive (p. 159)
24. external justification (p. 159)
25. outside (p.159)
26. yourself (p. 160)
27. problems (p. 161)
28. sufficient (p. 164)
29. severe (p. 164)
30. Self-persuasion (p. 165)
31. pressure (p. 165)
32. Ben Franklin effect (pp. 166-167)
33. civilian (p. 169)
34. form (p. 170)
35. communal (p. 170)
36. aware (p. 171)
37. outside (p. 172)

Essay Review

1. Your essay on cognitive dissonance should include:
    - Cognitive dissonance is a feeling of discomfort, originally defined as being caused by holding two or more inconsistent cognitions and subsequently defined as being caused by performing an action that is discrepant from one's customary, typically positive self-conception. (p. 150)
    - Cognitive dissonance can be reduced by changing our behavior to bring it in line with the dissonant cognition; by attempting to justify our behavior through changing one of the dissonant cognitions; or by attempting to justify our behavior by adding new cognitions. (p. 151)

2.   Your essay on postdecision dissonance should include:
- Postdecision dissonance is dissonance aroused after making a decision. (p. 153)
- Postdecision dissonance is typically reduced by enhancing the attractiveness of the chosen alternative and devaluating the rejected alternatives (p. 153)
- The more important the decision, the greater the dissonance. The more permanent and less revocable the decision, the greater the need to reduce dissonance. (p. 154)

3.   Your essay on justification of effort should include:
- Justification of effort is the tendency for individuals to increase their liking for something they have worked hard to attain. (p. 158)
- External justification is a reason or an explanation for dissonant personal behavior that resides outside the individual. Internal justification refers to the reduction of dissonance by changing something about oneself. (p. 159)
- Counterattitudinal advocacy refers to stating an opinion or attitude that runs counter to one's private belief or attitude. When we do this with little external justification, what we believe begins to look more and more like the lie we told. (p. 160)

4.   Your essay should include:
- Insufficient punishment is the dissonance aroused when individuals lack sufficient external justification for having resisted a desired activity or object. (p. 164)
- The less severe the threat, the less external justification there is; the less external justification, the greater the need for internal justification. (p. 164)
- Internal justification leads to self-persuasion, a long-lasting form of attitude change that results from attempts at self-justification. (p. 165)

5.   Your essay should include:
- The Ben Franklin effect is a phenomenon that involves dissonance. When we like people, we show it by treating them well. The reverse is also true. When we are subtly induced to do a favor for someone we do not like, doing the favor can create dissonance and a change in attitude. Ben Franklin was disliked by a fellow legislator so he asked the person if he could borrow a book from him. Franklin borrowed the book for a week and then returned it with a note expressing his gratitude. Afterwards Franklin and the legislator became friends and their friendship lasted until the legislator died. (p. 167)
- If we treat someone poorly, we may come to hate and/or derogate our victim. (pp. 168-169)

Exit Test 1

1.   C (p. 150)
2.   D (p. 151)
3.   A (p. 162)
4.   B (p. 152)
5.   A (p. 153)
6.   C (pp. 154-155)
7.   D (pp. 155-156)
8.   B (p. 157)
9.   A (pp. 158-159)
10.   C (pp. 159-160)

Exit Test 2

1. C (p. 148)
2. B (p. 152)
3. A (p. 153)
4. D (p. 160)
5. A (pp. 160-161)
6. C (p. 161)
7. B (p. 161)
8. D (p. 164)
9. A (p. 165)
10. C (p. 166)

Study Activities

1. Members will justify their efforts to join the group and will find the group attractive even if the group turns out to have little to offer. (pp. 158-159)

2. Based on Festinger and Carlsmith's (1959) study on demonstrating the effects of insufficient justification, you should describe the fact that providing children with large rewards for their good performance at school is likely to provide them with an external justification for their studies, and that their motivation to study will likely decrease when the possibility of the reward is removed. Instead, a strategy using small rewards for studying would serve as an insufficient justification for studying, and it is likely that they would develop an internal justification for their behavior (i.e., they study because they like doing so, not to achieve rewards). (pp. 159-160)

3. A prize of $100 is sufficient external justification for claiming loyalty to any radio station. A T-shirt is insufficient justification that will motivate a search for internal justification and will result in a more favorable evaluation of the radio station. (pp. 159-160)

4. Cognitive dissonance theory maintains that we reduce dissonance by changing behaviors or by adding or changing cognitions to justify behaviors. (pp. 150-151)

5. Lowballing is a strategy whereby a salesperson induces a customer to agree to purchase a product at a very low cost, subsequently claims it was an error, and then raises the price. There are at least three reasons why lowballing works. First, although the customer's decision to buy is certainly reversible, a commitment of sorts does exist and there is an illusion of irrevocability. Second, the feeling of commitment triggered the anticipation of an exciting event—acquiring the item the person intended to purchase. To not get the item would produce dissonance and disappointment. Third, although the final price is substantially higher than the customer thought it would be, it is probably only slightly higher than buying the item somewhere else. The person feels that since they are there they might as well go ahead and get the item. (pp. 155-156)

6. When there is insufficient punishment for not performing a behavior, dissonance is produced because there is insufficient justification for performing the behavior. Thus, the person devalues the forbidden activity in order to reduce the dissonance caused by not engaging in it. This is what occurs when a person is only threatened with mild punishment. When a person is threatened with severe punishment, no dissonance occurs and no attitude change occurs because the person has sufficient external justification for not engaging in the forbidden activity. (pp. 163-165)

7.   Self-persuasion is more permanent than direct attempts at persuasion because, with self-persuasion, the persuasion takes place internally and not because of external coaxing or pressure. (p. 165)

8.   If we do something unpleasant for a friend, our negative attitude toward the activity will not change because we have external justification for performing the behavior—we wanted to help our friend. However, if we do something unpleasant for someone we do not like, our attitude toward the activity will improve somewhat in order to reduce the dissonance we experience since we have no external justification for the behavior. (p. 167)

9.   The reasoning areas of the brain virtually shut down when a person is confronted with dissonant information, and the emotion circuits of the brain light up happily when consonance is restored. (p. 157)

10.   A leader can avoid falling into the self-justification trap by bringing in skilled advisors from outside the inner circle, because they are not caught up in the need to reduce dissonance from their earlier decision making. (p. 172)

CHAPTER 7

Attitudes and Attitude Change: Influencing Thoughts and Feelings

CHAPTER 7 OVERVIEW

In Chapter 7, the topics of attitudes and attitude change are examined. **Attitudes** are evaluations of people, objects, and ideas. Researchers have addressed the question of where attitudes come from. Some attitudes are linked to our genes. Even if there is a genetic component, our social experiences clearly play a major role in shaping our attitudes.

Attitudes can be cognitively, affectively, or behaviorally based. A **cognitively based attitude** is based primarily on people's beliefs about the properties of an attitude object. An **affectively based attitude** is based more on people's feelings and values than on their beliefs about the nature of an attitude object. The function of attitudes based on values and feelings is not so much to paint an accurate picture of the world as to express and validate one's basic value system. Affectively based attitudes can also result from a sensory reaction, aesthetic reaction, or they can be the result of conditioning. **Classical conditioning** is the phenomenon whereby a stimulus that elicits an emotional response is repeatedly paired with a neutral stimulus that does not, until the neutral stimulus takes on the emotional properties of the first stimulus. In **operant conditioning**, behaviors that we freely choose to perform become more or less frequent, depending on whether they are followed by a reward or punishment.

A **behaviorally based attitude** stems from people's observations of how they behave toward an object. According to Daryl Bem's self-perception theory, under certain circumstances, people don't know how they feel until they see how they behave. People infer their attitudes from their behavior only when there are no other plausible explanations for their behavior.

Once an attitude develops, it can exist at two levels. **Explicit attitudes** are ones we consciously endorse and can easily report. People also have **implicit attitudes**, which are involuntary, uncontrollable, and at times unconscious evaluations.

Attitudes do sometimes change. When attitudes change, they often do so in response to social influence. Attitude change can come from cognitive dissonance—when people behave inconsistently with their attitudes and cannot find external justification for their behavior. Although dissonance techniques are powerful, they are very difficult to carry out on a mass scale. To change as many people's attitudes as possible, you would have to resort to other techniques of attitude change. You would probably use some sort of **persuasive communication**, which is a communication such as a speech or television advertisement that advocates a particular side of an issue.

Social psychologists have conducted many studies over the years on what makes a persuasive communication effective. The **Yale Attitude Change Approach** refers to the study of the conditions under which people are most likely to change their attitudes in response to persuasive messages, focusing on "who said what to whom"—the source of the communication, the nature of the communication, and the nature of the audience.

The **elaboration likelihood model** of persuasion specifies when people will be influenced by what the speech says and when they will be influenced by more superficial characteristics. The theory states that under certain conditions, people are motivated to pay attention to the facts in a communication, and so they listen carefully to and think about the arguments. This is the **central route to persuasion**. The **peripheral route to persuasion** is the case whereby people do not elaborate on the arguments in a persuasive communication but are instead swayed by peripheral cues. People are more likely to take the central route if they are motivated and have the ability to pay attention to the facts. Motivation is higher when the communication is personally relevant. People's motivation to pay attention to a speech depends on their personality. Some people enjoy thinking things through more than others do; they are said to be high in the **need for cognition**. People high in need for cognition are more likely to pay close attention to relevant arguments, whereas people low in need for cognition are more likely to rely on peripheral cues. It is more difficult to pay attention to a communication if we are tired, distracted, or if the issue is too complex and hard to evaluate. People who base their attitudes on a careful analysis of the arguments will be more likely to maintain this attitude over time, more likely to behave consistently with this attitude, and more resistant to counterpersuasion than people who base their attitudes on peripheral cues.

To get people to consider carefully constructed arguments you have to get their attention. One way to get people's attention is to scare them. A **fear-arousing communication** is a persuasive message that attempts to change people's attitudes by arousing their fears. The effectiveness of fear-arousing communication depends on whether the fear influences people's ability to pay attention to and process the arguments in a message. If a moderate amount of fear is created and people believe that listening to the message will teach them how to reduce this fear, they will be motivated to analyze the message carefully and will likely change their attitudes via the central route.

Another way in which emotions can cause attitude change is by acting as a signal for how we feel about something. According to the **heuristic-systematic model of persuasion**, when people take the peripheral route to persuasion, they often use heuristics. Our emotions and moods can themselves act as heuristics to determine our attitudes. The only problem is that sometimes it is difficult to tell where our feelings come from. We may misattribute feelings created by one source to another source.

The success of various attitude change techniques depends on the type of attitude we are trying to change. Several studies have shown that if an attitude is cognitively based, try to change it with rational arguments; if it is affectively based, try to change it with emotional appeals. Advertisements are more effective when they emphasize the attitudes of the culture they are trying to influence. Anything you can do to increase people's confidence in their thoughts about your message will make it more effective, as long as your arguments are strong and convincing.

The next section of the chapter discusses resisting persuasive messages. **Attitude inoculation** refers to making people immune to attempts to change their attitudes by initially exposing them to small doses of the arguments against their positions. Being alert to product placement can also aid in resisting persuasive messages. Products are often shown in television shows and movies. They seem to be simply part of the show but they are really placed in these programs as advertisements. One reason that product placement may be so successful is that people do not realize that someone is trying to influence their attitudes and behavior. Warning people about an upcoming attempt to change their attitudes makes them less susceptible to that attempt. Attitude inoculation has been used to help adolescents to resist pressure from peers to smoke.

It is important not to use too heavy a hand when trying to immunize people against assaults on their attitudes. There is harm to administering strong prohibitions—the stronger they are, the more likely they will boomerang, causing an increase in interest in the prohibited activity. According to **reactance theory**, people do not like to feel that their freedom to do or think whatever they want is being threatened. When they feel that their freedom is threatened, an unpleasant state of reactance is aroused, and people can reduce this reactance by performing the threatened behavior.

The next section of the chapter addresses the question "When will attitudes predict behavior?" The relationship between attitudes and behavior is not simple. Attitudes will predict spontaneous behaviors only when they are highly accessible to people. **Attitude accessibility** refers to the strength of the association between an object and an evaluation of it, which is typically measured by the speed with which people can report how they feel about an issue or object. The best-known theory of how attitudes predict deliberate behaviors is the **theory of planned behavior**. According to this theory, when people have time to contemplate how they are going to behave, the best predictor of their behavior is their intention, which is determined by three things: their attitudes toward the specific behavior, their subjective norms, and their perceived behavioral control.

The final section of the chapter discusses the power of advertising. Most people think that advertising works on everyone but themselves. People are influenced by advertisements more than they think. If advertisers are trying to change an affectively based attitude, then it is best to fight emotions with emotions. If people's attitudes are more cognitively based, we need to ask an additional question: How personally relevant is the issue? If you are dealing with a cognitively based attitude that is not of direct personal relevance, you might succeed in changing their attitudes via the peripheral route, but this type of attitude change tends not to be long-lasting. The trick here is to make your product personally relevant. Many advertisements also try to make people's attitudes more affectively based by associating the product with important emotions and values.

Subliminal messages are words or pictures that are not consciously perceived but may nevertheless influence people's judgments, attitudes, and behaviors. Subliminal messages can be auditory as well. There is no evidence that the types of subliminal messages encountered in everyday life have any influence on people's behavior. There is evidence for subliminal effects in carefully controlled laboratory studies. To get subliminal effects, researchers have to make sure that the illumination of the room is just right, that people are seated just the right distance from a viewing screen, and that nothing else is occurring to distract them as the subliminal stimuli are flashed. Even in the laboratory, there is no evidence that subliminal messages can get people to act counter to their wishes, values, or personalities.

Ads are more powerful when people consciously perceive them. Advertising influences more than just our consumer attitudes. Advertisements transmit cultural stereotypes in their words and images, subtly linking products with desired images. Gender stereotypes are particularly pervasive in advertising imagery. The stereotypes conveyed in advertisements are far from harmless. The media can have powerful effects on people's attitudes, both directly and indirectly.

CHAPTER 7 OUTLINE

I. The Nature and Origin of Attitudes
• Social psychologists define an **attitude** as an enduring evaluation, positive or negative, of people, objects, or ideas.

A. Where Do Attitudes Come From?
• Tesser (1993) suggests that some attitudes are linked to our genes. Evidence for this is based on the finding that identical twins raised apart (and not knowing of each other) have more similar attitudes to each other than do fraternal twins. Attitude similarity is probably mediated indirectly by similarity of temperament and personality.
• Even if there is a genetic component, social experience clearly plays a large role in shaping attitudes.
• Although all attitudes have the three components, any given attitude can be based more on one component than another.

1. Cognitively Based Attitudes
• **Cognitively based attitudes** are based primarily on a person's beliefs about the properties of the attitude object; their function is "object appraisal," meaning that people classify objects according to the rewards or punishments they provide.

2. Affectively Based Attitudes
• **Affectively based attitudes** are based more on people's feelings and values than on their beliefs. Their function may be value-expressive. Thus, attitudes towards political candidates are generally more affectively than cognitively based.
• Other affectively based attitudes can be the result of a sensory reaction or of conditioning.
• **Classical conditioning** is learning by association (a stimulus that elicits an emotional response is repeatedly experienced along with a neutral stimulus that does not, until the neutral stimulus takes on the emotional properties of the first stimulus). **Operant conditioning** is the case whereby behaviors that people freely choose to perform increase or decrease in frequency, depending on whether they are followed by positive reinforcement or punishment (see Figure 7.1, p. 193).
• Affectively based attitudes have these features in common: they do not result from rational examination of the issues; they are not governed by logic; and they are often linked to people's values.

3. Behaviorally Based Attitudes
• **Behaviorally based attitudes** are based on self-perception of one's own behavior when the initial attitude is weak or ambiguous.

B. Explicit versus Implicit Attitudes
• Once an attitude develops, it can exist at two levels. **Explicit attitudes** are ones we consciously endorse and can easily report. **Implicit attitudes** on the other hand, are involuntary, uncontrollable, and at times, unconscious evaluations.
• One of the most popular methods to measure implicit attitudes is the Implicit Association Test or IAT, in which people categorize words or pictures on a computer. You can find out more about this test at https://implicit.harvard.edu/implicit.

C. How Do Attitudes Change?
• Attitudes may be very changeable; changes are frequently due to social influence.

D. Changing Attitudes by Changing Behavior: Cognitive Dissonance Theory Revisited
• Attitudes may change due to the *cognitive dissonance* resulting from behavior that appears to have insufficient internal justification; changing the attitude to correspond with the behavior provides an internal justification.
• *Counterattitudinal advocacy* is hard to induce on a mass scale, so people usually attempt to change the attitudes of the masses through persuasive communication.
• **Persuasive communication** is communication advocating a particular side of an issue.

E. Persuasive Communications and Attitude Change
• The study of persuasive communication by social psychologists began under Hovland with the **Yale Attitude Change approach**, which examines the conditions under which people are most likely to change their attitude in response to a persuasive message and which focuses on who (*the source of the communication*) said what (*the communication itself*) to whom (*the audience*) (Figure 7.2, p. 185).
• A problem with the Yale Attitude Change approach is that it does not define the conditions under which one aspect of a communication should be emphasized over others.

1. The Central and Peripheral Routes to Persuasion
• Two influential theories, Chaiken's *heuristic-systematic persuasion model* and Petty and Cacioppo's *elaboration likelihood model* have tried to specify when people will be more

influenced by message content and when they will be more influenced by superficial characteristics of the message.

• Both theories state that under certain conditions, people are motivated to pay attention to and think about (elaborate on) the facts in a message. Under other conditions, people are not motivated to pay attention to the facts a message presents and only attend to superficial characteristics.

• More specifically, the **elaboration likelihood model** states that there are two ways in which persuasive communications can cause attitude change. The **central route to persuasion** is the case whereby people elaborate on a persuasive communication, listening carefully to and thinking about the arguments; this occurs when people have both the ability and the motivation to listen carefully to a communication. The **peripheral route to persuasion** is the case whereby people do not elaborate on the arguments in a persuasive communication but are instead swayed by peripheral cues or surface characteristics (e.g., who gave the speech).

• The audience's motivation to listen and ability to listen determine which route they will take (Figure 7.3, p. 186).

2. The Motivation to Pay Attention to the Arguments

• The personal relevance of a message influences motivation; thus, when a message is relevant, the amount of persuasion depends on argument quality.

• Petty, Cacioppo, & Goldman (1981) had students listen to a persuasive message advocating a senior comprehensive exam. Personal relevance was manipulated by saying that the exam was considered for next year or for ten years hence. Also, the message contained either strong or weak arguments and was presented by either a high or low prestige source. They found that under high relevance, people were more influenced by strong than by weak arguments, regardless of source prestige; while under low relevance, people were influenced by the prestige of the speaker more than by the quality of the arguments (Figure 7.4, p. 187).

• People's motivation to listen carefully to message content may also depend on their level of **need for cognition**, the extent to which they seek out and think about information in their social worlds.

3. The Ability to Pay Attention to the Arguments

• People's ability to attend to message content may be influenced by tiredness, outside distracters, or by the complexity of the message.

4. How to Achieve Long-Lasting Attitude Change

• Attitude change will be more long-lasting if it occurs through the central route; thus develop strong arguments and get people to think about them by making the issue personally relevant.

F. Emotion and Attitude Change

• In order to get people to use the central processing route, you need to get their attention. This can be done by playing to their emotions.

1. Fear-Arousing Communications

• **Fear-arousing communications** are persuasive messages that attempt to change people's attitudes by arousing their fears. They are most effective if they induce a moderate amount of fear and if people believe that listening to the message will provide them with actions they can take to reduce this fear. If the message is too scary or not scary enough, it will fail (Figure 7.5, p. 190).

2. Emotion as a Heuristic

• Chaiken's **heuristic-systematic model of persuasion** states that there are two ways in which persuasive communications can cause attitude change; people either systematically process the merits of the arguments, or they use mental shortcuts (heuristics). Thus when people take the peripheral route to persuasion they often use heuristics, e.g., "(Message) length equals strength" or "Experts are always right."

• Emotions and moods themselves can be used as a heuristic; we ask ourselves "How do I feel about it?" and if we feel good, we infer we have a positive attitude. This can get us into trouble if the good feelings are due to something other than the attitude object and we make a misattribution that the attitude object is the source.

3. Emotion and Different Types of Attitudes
• Studies suggest that it is most effective to try to change cognitively based attitudes by using the central route to persuasion, but to change affectively based attitudes by using emotional persuasion.
• Shavitt (1990) found that people were most persuaded by informational, utilitarian ads for products (e.g., air conditioners) towards which they had cognitively based attitudes and by value or social-identity laden ads for products (e.g., perfume) towards which they have affectively based attitudes (Figure 7.6, p. 192).

4. Culture and Different Types of Attitudes
• Han and Shavitt (1994) found that Americans were most influenced by ads that stressed independence and self-improvement while Koreans were most influenced by ads (for the same product) that stressed interdependence and social standing.
• In general, advertisements work best if they are tailored to the kind of attitude they are trying to change.

G. Confidence in One's Thoughts and Attitude Change
• Anything you can do to increase people's confidence in their thoughts about your message will make it more effective, as long as your arguments are strong and convincing.

III. Resisting Persuasive Messages

A. Attitude Inoculation
• One way to bolster people against persuasion attempts is to have them consider the arguments for and against their attitude before somebody attacks it.
• The **attitude inoculation** procedure does this by exposing people to a small dose of the argument against their position; this induced them to counterargue and provides a "vaccination" that helps people ward off later, stronger influence attempts.

B. Be Alert to Product Placement
Companies pay the makers of a TV show to incorporate their product into the script, which is called product placement. Several studies have found that warning people about an upcoming product placement makes them less susceptible to that persuasive attempt.

C. Resisting Peer Pressure
• Several programs have tried to prevent smoking in adolescents by exposing them to mild versions of attempts to get them to smoke and having them role play counteracting these pressures. These programs appear successful in reducing teen smoking.

D. When Persuasion Attempts Boomerang: Reactance Theory
• It is important not to use too heavy a hand when trying to immunize people against assaults on their attitudes. If you administer too strong a prohibition, the prohibition may boomerang and lead to an increase in the prohibited activity. **Reactance theory** explains this by saying that strong prohibitions threaten a person's feeling of freedom, and the boomerang is an attempt to restore that feeling of freedom.
• Pennebaker and Sanders (1976) found that graffiti was reduced more by a sign with a mild prohibition than by a sign with a strong one.

IV. When Will Attitudes Predict Behavior?
• People's behavior does not always correspond to their attitude.
• LaPiere did a classic field study in the 1930s, where he found that hotel and restaurants served a Chinese couple despite their written statements that they would not do so.
• Later research reveals that attitudes do predict behavior, but only under certain conditions.

A. Predicting Spontaneous Behaviors
• People's attitudes will predict/be consistent with their spontaneous behaviors when the attitudes are highly accessible. **Attitude accessibility** refers to the strength of the association between an attitude object and a person's evaluation of that object, measured by the speed with which people can report how they feel about the object. If the attitudes are not highly accessible, arbitrary aspects of the situation will tend to determine behavior.

B. Predicting Deliberative Behaviors
• Ajzen and Fishbein's **theory of planned behavior** is a theory of how attitudes predict planned, deliberative behavior; according to this theory the best predictors of these behaviors are the person's specific attitudes, his or her subjective norms, and their perceived behavioral control (Figure 7.7, p. 213).
1. Specific Attitudes
• The attitude that is important is not a general attitude but their attitude towards the specific behavior in question. For example, Davidson and Jaccard (1979) showed that married women's use of birth control pills was much better predicted by their attitude towards using the pills during the next two years than it was by their attitudes towards the pills or towards birth control (Table 7.1, p. 213).
2. Subjective norms
• People's beliefs about how those they care about will view the behavior in question. Asking people about their subjective norms increases the ability to predict planned, deliberative behaviors.
3. Perceived behavioral control
• The ease with which people believe they can perform the behavior. If people think it is easy to perform the behavior, they are more likely to form a strong intention to do it.
• Considerable research supports the idea that asking people about these three determinants of their intentions increases the ability to predict their planned, deliberative behaviors.

V. The Power of Advertising
• Wilson and Brekke (1994) found that most people think advertising works on everybody but themselves.
• Contrary to such beliefs, the evidence indicates that advertising works, in the sense that sales increase.
• The best evidence that advertising works comes from studies using split cable market tests, where advertisers work in conjunction with cable companies and stores to show ads to a randomly selected group of people and see whether these people are more likely to buy the product.
• Ads work particularly well for new products.

A. How Advertising Works
• Advertisers should consider the kind of attitude they are trying to change. If they are trying to change an affectively based attitude, it is best to take an emotional approach (e.g., associate feelings of excitement, energy, and sexual attractiveness with the brand). If they are trying to change a cognitively based attitude, they also need to consider the personal relevance of the attitude.
• If a product is personally relevant, the best way to change it is through strong arguments; if a product is not personally relevant, advertising may attempt to make it seem so (e.g., Gerald Lambert created the term "halitosis" to increase sales for Listerine).

B. Subliminal Advertising: A Form of Mind Control?

• **Subliminal messages** are words or pictures that are not consciously perceived but that supposedly influence people's judgments, attitudes, and behaviors.

• In the 1950s, J. Vicary convinced a movie theater to flash the subliminal messages "Drink Coca-Cola" and "Eat popcorn" during a movie, and he claimed large increases in sales from this manipulation, provoking a large public outcry. Since then, audiotapes with subliminal messages to help people make personal changes have developed a large market.

1. Debunking the Claims about Subliminal Advertising

• Although most people believe that subliminal messages work, and there have been many popular attempts to indicate that they do, controlled studies do not indicate that they are effective when used in everyday life.

2. Laboratory Evidence for Subliminal Influence

• There is some evidence that subliminal messages may be effective in controlled, laboratory studies. Karremans and colleagues (2006) exposed students to subliminal flashes of the words "Lipton Ice" or a nonsense word made of the same letters. All students were asked whether they would prefer Lipton Ice or a brand of Dutch mineral water if they were offered a drink at that moment. If students were not thirsty at the time, the subliminal flashes had no effect on their drink preference. But if students were thirsty, those who had seen the subliminal flashes of "Lipton Ice" were significantly more likely to choose that drink than were students who had seen subliminal flashes of nonsense words.

• Subliminal effects only occur under very carefully controlled conditions and do not override people's wishes and desires.

C. Advertising, Cultural Stereotypes, and Social Behavior

• Ads are more powerful when people consciously perceive them.

• Advertisements transmit cultural stereotypes in their words and images, subtly linking products with desired images (e.g., Marlboro ads linking cigarettes with the rugged macho Marlboro Man).

• Gender stereotypes are particularly pervasive in advertising imagery. Men are portrayed as doers and women as observers.

• Stereotypes conveyed in advertisements are far from harmless. The media can have powerful effects on people's attitudes, both directly and indirectly.

LEARNING OBJECTIVES

After reading Chapter 7, you should be able to do the following:

1.   Define an attitude and identify its components. Discuss the differences between cognitively based attitudes and affectively based attitudes. (pp. 178-181)

2.   Explain how affectively based attitudes are formed via classical conditioning and operant conditioning. (pp. 180-181)

3.   Define a behaviorally based attitude and discuss how it is formed. (pp. 181-182)

4.   Distinguish between explicit and implicit attitudes. (p. 182)

5.   Discuss the role of cognitive dissonance in attitude change. Explain what is meant by internal justification. Identify what you would need to do if you wanted to change attitudes on a mass scale. (pp. 183-184)

6. Describe the Yale Attitude Change approach. Identify and define the three factors in an influence setting emphasized by this approach. Provide examples of each factor. Identify a problem with the Yale Attitude Change Approach. (p. 184)

7. Describe the aim of attitude change models like Petty and Cacioppo's elaboration likelihood model and Chaiken's heuristic-systematic model of persuasion. (p. 185 & 191)

8. Identify the two routes to persuasion described in the elaboration likelihood model. Identify the factors that determine the route people take. Identify factors that increase people's motivation and ability to pay attention to the arguments. Discuss how attitudes changed by the central route to persuasion differ from attitudes changed by the peripheral route. (pp. 184-185 & 189)

9. Discuss the influence of emotion on persuasion. Identify the role of fear-arousing communications in persuasion. Describe the conditions under which fear appeals foster or inhibit attitude change. (pp. 189-191)

10. Describe the process whereby emotions act as heuristics to persuasion according to the heuristic-systematic model of persuasion. Identify the problem with using emotions as a guide to attitude formation. (p. 191)

11. Identify the most effective means of changing affectively and cognitively based attitudes. (p. 192)

12. Discuss cross-cultural differences in the kinds of attitudes people have and how these attitudes are changed. (p. 193)

13. Identify the purpose of attitude inoculation. Describe product placement and what makes it effective. Discuss how attitude inoculation is used to help teens resist peer pressure. Discuss the role of reactance when persuasion attempts "boomerang." (pp. 194-197)

14. Describe the conditions under which attitudes predict spontaneous and deliberative behaviors. Discuss the role of attitude accessibility in predicting spontaneous behaviors. (pp. 197-198)

15. Discuss the role of people's intentions and other variables outlined in the theory of planned behavior in predicting deliberative behaviors. Define and explain the relationship between attitudes toward behaviors, subjective norms, and perceived behavioral control that is outlined in the theory of planned behavior. (pp. 198-199)

16. Identify the most effective advertising strategies for changing affectively and cognitively based attitudes when personal relevance is high, for changing cognitively based attitudes when personal relevance is low, and for selling bland products that evoke few emotions. (pp. 200-202)

17. Discuss the controversial topic of subliminal advertising and evaluate the claim that subliminal messages are effective. Describe evidence for subliminal influence from laboratory experiments. Identify what research has found regarding the power of advertising that is consciously perceived. (pp. 202-204)

18. Discuss how advertising transmits information regarding cultural stereotypes. (pp. 204-205)

Chapter 7

KEY TERMS

1. _____ Evaluations of people, objects, and ideas. (p. 178)

2. _____ An attitude based primarily on people's beliefs about the properties of an attitude object. (p. 179)

3. _____ An attitude based more on people's feelings and values than on their beliefs about the nature of an attitude object. (p. 179)

4. _____ The phenomenon whereby a stimulus that elicits an emotional response is repeatedly paired with a neutral stimulus that does not, until the neutral stimulus takes on the emotional properties of the first stimulus. (p. 180)

5. _____ The phenomenon whereby behaviors that people freely choose to perform increase or decrease in frequency, depending on whether they are followed by positive reinforcement or punishment. (p. 180)

6. _____ An attitude based on observations of how one behaves toward an attitude object. (p. 181)

7. _____ Attitudes that we consciously endorse and can easily report. (p. 182)

8. _____ Attitudes that are involuntary, uncontrollable, and at times unconscious. (p. 182)

9. _____ Communication advocating a particular side of an issue. (p. 184)

10. _____ The study of the conditions under which people are most likely to change their attitudes in response to persuasive messages, focusing on "who said what to whom"—the source of the communication, the nature of the communication, and the nature of the audience. (p. 184)

11. _____ A model explaining two ways in which persuasive communications can cause attitude change: *centrally*, when people are motivated and have the ability to pay attention to the arguments in the communication, and *peripherally*, when people do not pay attention to the arguments, but are instead swayed by surface characteristics. (p. 185)

12. _____ The case whereby people elaborate on a persuasive communication, listening carefully to and thinking about the arguments. (p. 185)

13. _____ The case whereby people do not elaborate on the arguments in a persuasive communication but are instead swayed by peripheral cues. (p. 187)

14. _____ A personality variable reflecting the extent to which people engage in and enjoy effortful cognitive activities. (p. 188)

15. _____ Persuasive messages that attempt to change people's attitudes by arousing their fears. (p. 190)

16. _____ An explanation of the two ways in which persuasive communications can cause attitude change: either systematically processing the merits of the arguments or using mental shortcuts (heuristics). (p. 191)

17. _____ Making people immune to attempts to change their attitudes by initially exposing them to small doses of the arguments against their position. (p. 194)

18. _____ The idea that when people feel their freedom to perform a certain behavior is threatened, an unpleasant state of reactance is aroused, which they can reduce by performing the threatened behavior. (p. 196)

19. _____ The strength of the association between an attitude object and a person's evaluation of that object, measured by the speed with which people can report how they feel about the object. (p. 198)

20. _____ The idea that the best predictors of a person's planned, deliberate behaviors are the person's attitudes toward specific behaviors, subjective norms, and perceived behavioral control. (p. 198)

21. _____ Words or pictures that are not consciously perceived but may nevertheless influence people's judgments, attitudes, and behaviors. (p. 202)

GUIDED REVIEW

PRACTICE TEST

1. Responding to a "puppies for sale" ad, you arrive at the seller's home and immediately fall in love with the first puppy you see. The component of your attitude toward the puppy that is exemplified by such a reaction is called the ____ component.
   a) behavioral
   b) cognitive
   c) affective
   d) heuristic

2. While studying the conditions under which people are most likely to be influenced by persuasive communications, Hovland and colleagues at Yale repeatedly asked:
   a) who says what to whom?
   b) when will logical arguments persuade people and when will more superficial characteristics do so?
   c) why are communications persuasive?
   d) what condition produces the most influence?

3. Distraction during a persuasive message and message complexity prevent the careful consideration of relevant arguments by decreasing the:
   a) motivation to attend to relevant arguments.
   b) ability to attend to relevant arguments.
   c) personal relevance of the message.
   d) degree of association between message characteristics and internal response cues.

4.   Though fear-arousing communications are threatening, people will reduce this threat by changing their attitudes and behaviors only when:
     a)   the communication produces an extremely high level of fear.
     b)   the fear-arousing message can be easily ignored.
     c)   the fear-arousing communication is directed at individuals with high levels of self-esteem.
     d)   the fear-arousing communication offers suggestions about how to avoid the threat.

5.   Children may adopt prejudiced attitudes through operant conditioning if their parents:
     a)   associate such attitudes with emotionally positive stimuli.
     b)   punish them for expressing such attitudes.
     c)   reward them for expressing such attitudes.
     d)   present arguments favoring such attitudes.

6.   Which of the following is true regarding when attitudes will predict spontaneous or deliberative behaviors?
     a)   Attitudes will predict spontaneous behaviors when they are very accessible.
     b)   Attitude-behavioral consistency is high among people with accessible attitudes.
     c)   Deliberate behaviors are predicted by people's intentions.
     d)   All the above are true.

7.   A personality variable that has been linked to the use of the central route to persuasion is:
     a)   need for emotion.
     b)   need for reason.
     c)   need for explanation.
     d)   need for cognition.

8.   Words or pictures that are not consciously perceived but may be influential are:
     a)   exceptional messages.
     b)   subliminal messages.
     c)   reactance messages.
     d)   unconscious messages.

9.   The theory of planned behavior states that all of the following are predictors of people's planned, deliberative behaviors EXCEPT:
     a)   subjective norms.
     b)   perceived behavioral control.
     c)   attitudes toward the specific behavior.
     d)   social norms.

10. According to Petty and Cacioppo's (1986) elaboration likelihood model, when people are persuaded by surface characteristics of a message, such as how long the message is, they have taken the _____ route to persuasion.
     a)   central
     b)   peripheral
     c)   heuristic
     d)   subjective

11. Attitudes changed by the central route to persuasion are:
    a) maintained over time.
    b) consistent with behaviors.
    c) resistant to counterpersuasion.
    d) all the above.

12. Shavitt (1990) presented participants with cognitively or affectively oriented ads for products about which people had either cognitively or affectively based attitudes. Results indicated that participants were most influenced by:
    a) cognitively based ads.
    b) affectively based ads.
    c) ads that "matched" the type of attitude they had.
    d) cognitively based ads that were self-relevant and affectively based ads that were not relevant.

13. When you encounter an object and your attitude toward that object comes immediately to mind, your attitude is said to be highly:
    a) resistant.
    b) accessible.
    c) deliberative.
    d) intentional.

14. After strongly prohibiting the reading of banned books, Professor Jones has noticed an increased interest by her students in the books. Which of the following theories best explains this outcome?
    a) theory of reasoned action
    b) elaboration likelihood model
    c) reactance theory
    d) classical conditioning theory

15. Responses to which of the following questions will best predict whether someone donates clothes to the Salvation Army next Sunday at noon?
    a) "How much are you willing to help others?"
    b) "How do you feel about making donations to charities?"
    c) "How do you feel about donating clothes to the Salvation Army?"
    d) "How do you feel about donating clothes to the Salvation Army next Sunday at noon?"

16. Rudman and colleagues (2007) found evidence that implicit attitudes are rooted more in people's _____ experiences whereas explicit attitudes are rooted more in their _____ experiences.
    a) pleasant; unpleasant
    b) unpleasant; pleasant
    c) childhood; recent
    d) recent; childhood

17. An attitude change theory that states that we can satisfy our need to justify engaging in attitude-discrepant behaviors by changing our attitudes is:
    a) self-evaluation maintenance theory.
    b) cognitive dissonance theory.
    c) elaboration likelihood theory.
    d) self-affirmation theory.

18.   Fear-evoking persuasive appeals fail if they are too strong and threatening because:
        a)   people become defensive.
        b)   people deny the threat.
        c)   people will not think rationally about the issue.
        d)   all the above are reasons.

19.   Heuristic processing is to the _____ route to persuasion as systematic processing is to the _____ route to persuasion.
        a)   primary; secondary
        b)   secondary; primary
        c)   peripheral; central
        d)   central; peripheral

20.   Making people immune to persuasion attempts by exposing them to small doses of arguments against their position is called:
        a)   attitude inoculation.
        b)   attitude vaccination.
        c)   attitude reactance.
        d)   attitude prevention.

21.   Regarding attitude-behavior consistency, it is important to measure people's beliefs about how others will view the given behavior. These beliefs are called:
        a)   subjective norms.
        b)   objective norms.
        c)   injunctive norms.
        d)   social norms.

22.   Which of the following is FALSE regarding subliminal messages?
        a)   There is no evidence that subliminal messages, both those used in everyday life and those manipulated in the lab, influence people's behavior.
        b)   Subliminal tapes, for example to boost self-esteem or improve memory, are ineffective.
        c)   Ads that are consciously perceived exert more influence on people's attitudes than do those that are not consciously perceived.
        d)   All the above are false.

23.   If someone asks you "how much do you like pizza?" you will likely report a(n) _____ towards pizza.
        a)   implicit attitude
        b)   explicit attitude
        c)   central attitude
        d)   peripheral attitude

24.   According to the Yale Attitude Change approach, which of the following is true?
        a)   Distracted audiences are persuaded less often than are audiences not distracted.
        b)   People with moderate self-esteem are less persuadable than are people with low or high self-esteem.
        c)   It is best to present a one-sided persuasive communication.
        d)   People are more susceptible to attitude change when they are between the ages of 18 and 25.

25.   An attitude is a(n):
   a)   behavior following from complex social stimuli.
   b)   evaluation of people, objects, and ideas.
   c)   influence to the real or imagined presence of others.
   d)   belief about how other people will view one's behavior.

26.   Participants in a study by Petty et al. (1981) were told that their university was thinking about requiring senior comprehensive exams either immediately or in 10 years. Participants paid greater attention to arguments favoring the exams when they believed that the exam policy might take effect immediately because:
   a)   the issue was personally relevant.
   b)   a decision had to be made very soon.
   c)   the participants knew friends who were seniors.
   d)   the participants were opposed to the exam policy.

27.   When we can find little external justification for behavior that is inconsistent with an attitude, changing the attitude so that it is consistent with the behavior is one way to reduce:
   a)   reactance.
   b)   personal relevance.
   c)   attitude accessibility.
   d)   cognitive dissonance.

28.   Techniques such as the IAT are useful in assessing:
   a)   implicit attitudes.
   b)   explicit attitudes.
   c)   attitude change following a persuasive appeal.
   d)   need for cognition.

29.   According to the elaboration likelihood model of persuasion, the _____ of persuasive arguments has more impact when people's personal involvement in the issue is _____.
   a)   strength; low
   b)   strength; high
   c)   quantity; high
   d)   both a and c

30.   Which was NOT an independent variable in Petty, Ciacioppo, and Goldman's (1981) study of attitudes toward comprehensive exams?
   a)   source expertise
   b)   quality of argument
   c)   personal relevance
   d)   participants' attitudes toward comprehensive exams

31.   Linda believes that spinach is good for you. This belief represents the _____ component of Linda's attitude.
   a)   affective
   b)   behavioral
   c)   cognitive
   d)   componential

32. People's attitudes about appliances such as vacuum cleaners and refrigerators are most likely _____ based.
    a) cognitively
    b) affectively
    c) behavioral
    d) dissonance

33. Joe believes he is not prejudiced toward homosexuals, yet he does not want gay couples living in his neighborhood, or gays or lesbians working in his office building. Joe's attitude toward homosexuals is
    a) explicit.
    b) implicit.
    c) central.
    d) peripheral.

34. According to the Yale Attitude Change Approach, speakers are more persuasive if they are only moderately attractive because we assume they are more intelligent.
    a) True
    b) False

35. According to the Yale Attitude Change Approach it is best to give your speech before another person presenting an opposing viewpoint when
    a) your argument is weaker than the other person's argument.
    b) you are giving the speech in the evening when people are beginning to feel tired.
    c) there will be a delay between the speeches and people will make up their minds right after hearing the second one.
    d) the speeches are to be given back to back and there will be a delay before people have to make up their minds.

36. Who is most likely to pay close attention to an advertisement for children's aspirin?
    a) Mary, who is 50 and has never had children
    b) Mark and Jeanette who are 58 and have two grown children
    c) Tammy, who has a 4-year-old daughter
    d) Tabitha, who is 26-years old and just found out she is pregnant for the first time

37. Ron is listening to a speech about a topic that is only slightly relevant to him. Which of the following is most likely to influence Ron?
    a) who the speaker is
    b) the strength of the arguments
    c) how interesting the speech is
    d) how informative the speech is

38. One way in which emotions can cause attitude change is by acting as a signal for how we feel about something.
    a) True
    b) False

39. In a study by Han & Shavitt (1994) Americans were more persuaded by ads stressing interdependence.
    a) True
    b) False

40. A movie contains a scene in which a character is shown drinking a can of Coke. This is an example of
   a) a subliminal message.
   b) an implicit advertisement.
   c) an implicit argument.
   d) product placement.

SHORT ANSWER REVIEW .

Attitudes are (1) _____ (p. 178) of people, objects, and ideas. Attitudes are made up of three parts that together form our evaluation of the "attitude object." A cognitively based attitude is based primarily on people's (2) _____ (p. 179) about the properties of an attitude object. An affectively based attitude is based more on people's (3) _____ (p. 179) and values than on their beliefs about the nature of an attitude object. Affectively based attitudes can result from a (4) _____ (p. 180) reaction, or an aesthetic reason. Still others can be the result of (5) _____ (p. 180) or operant conditioning. A behaviorally based attitude stems from people's (6) _____ (p. 181) of how they behave toward an object.

Once an attitude develops, it can exist at two levels. Explicit attitudes are ones we (7) _____ (p. 182) endorse and can easily report. Implicit attitudes are involuntary, uncontrollable, and at times (8) _____ (p. 182). When attitudes change, they often do so in response to (9) _____ (p. 183). One way that attitudes can change is when people behave inconsistently with their (10) _____ (p. 183) and cannot find external justification for their behavior—cognitive dissonance. Although dissonance techniques are powerful, they are very difficult to carry out on a (11) _____ (p. 184). To change as many people's attitudes as possible, you would probably construct some sort of (12) _____ (p. 184), which is a communication that advocates a particular side of an issue.

The Yale Attitude Change approach is the study of the (13) _____ (p. 184) under which people are most likely to change their attitudes in response to persuasive messages. It focuses on "who said what to whom"—the (14) _____ (p. 184) of the communication, the nature of the communication, and the nature of the audience.

According to the (15) _____ (p. 185) model there are two ways in which persuasive communications can cause attitude change. The central route to persuasion is the case whereby people elaborate on a persuasive communication, listening (16) _____ (p. 185) to and thinking about the arguments. The peripheral route to persuasion is the case whereby people do not elaborate on the (17) _____ (p. 186) in a persuasive communication, but are instead swayed by peripheral cues. If people are truly (18) _____ (p. 187) in the topic and thus (19) _____ (p. 187) to pay close attention to the arguments, and if they have the ability to pay attention, they are more likely to take the central route. One thing that determines whether people are motivated to pay attention to a communication is the personal (20) _____ (p. 187) of the topic. It can be difficult to pay attention to a message if we're (21) _____ (p. 189), distracted, or if the issue is too complex and hard to evaluate.

If we want to create long-lasting attitude change, we should try to get people to use the (22) _____ (p. 189) route. People who base their attitudes on a careful analysis of the arguments will be more likely to maintain this attitude over time, more likely to behave (23) _____ (p. 189) with this attitude, and more resistant to counterpersuasion than people who base their attitudes on peripheral cues.

Before people will consider your carefully constructed arguments, you have to get their (24) _____ (p. 189). One way we can get people's attention is to scare them. Fear-arousing communications are persuasive messages that attempt to change people's attitudes by (25) _____ (p. 190) their fears. If a (26) _____ (p. 190) amount of fear is created and people believe that listening to the message will teach them how to (27) _____ (p. 190) this fear, they will be motivated to analyze the message carefully and will likely change their attitudes via the central route.

Another way in which emotions can cause attitude change is by acting as a (28) _____ (p. 191) for how we feel about something. According to the heuristic-systematic model of persuasion, when people take the (29) _____ (p. 191) route to persuasion, they often focus on heuristics. Our emotions and moods can themselves act as (30) _____ (p. 191) to determine our attitudes. The only problem is that sometimes it is difficult to tell where our feelings (31) _____ (p. 191). We can make mistakes about what is causing our mood, misattributing feelings created by one source to another.

The success of various attitude change techniques depends on the type of attitude we are trying to change. Several studies have shown that if an attitude is cognitively based, try to change it with (32) _____ (p. 192) arguments; if it is affectively based, try to change it with emotional appeals. Advertisements work best if they are tailored to the kind of attitude they are trying to change. Anything you can do to increase people's (33) _____ (p. 194) in their thoughts about your message will make it more effective, as long as your arguments are (34) _____ (p. 194).

There are ways to resist persuasive messages. One thing you can do is consider the arguments against your attitude before someone attacks it. The more people have thought about pro and con arguments beforehand using the technique known as (35) _____ (p. 194), the better they can ward off attempts to change their minds using logical arguments. It is also helpful to be alert to product (36) _____ (p. 195). Attitude inoculation has been used to help adolescents resist (37) _____ (p. 195-196).

It is important not to use too heavy a hand when trying to (38) _____ (p. 196) people against assaults on their attitudes. There is harm to administering strong (39) _____ (p. 196)—the stronger they are, the more likely they will (40) _____ (p. 196), causing an increase in interest in the prohibited activity. According to reactance theory, people do not like to feel that their (41) _____ (p. 196) to do or think whatever they want is being threatened. When their freedom is threatened, an unpleasant state of reactance is aroused, and people can reduce this reactance by performing the threatened behavior.

Predicting behavior from attitudes is not simple. There are many times when behavior and attitudes are consistent, but attitudes predict behavior only under specific conditions. Attitudes will predict spontaneous behaviors only when they are highly (42) _____ (p. 198) to people. The best-known theory of how attitudes predict deliberative behaviors is the (43) _____ (p. 198). According to this theory, when people have time to contemplate how they are going to behave, the best predictor of their behavior is their (44) _____ (p. 198), which is determined by three things: their attitudes toward the specific behavior, their subjective norms, and their perceived behavioral control.

Most people think advertising works on everyone but (45) _____ (p. 200) however, most people are influenced by advertisements more than they think. If advertisers are trying to change an affectively based attitude, it is best to fight emotions with (46) _____ (p. 200). If people's attitudes are more cognitively based we need to ask how (47) _____ (p. 200) the issue is.

Subliminal messages are words or (48) _____ (p. 202) that are not consciously perceived but may nevertheless influence people's judgments, attitudes, and behaviors. There is no evidence that the types of subliminal messages encountered in everyday life have any influence on people's (49) _____ (p. 203). Ads are more influential when people consciously perceive them.

Advertisements transmit cultural (50) _____ (p. 205) in their words and images. (51) _____ (p. 205) stereotypes are particularly pervasive in advertising imagery. Men are doers; women are observers. The images conveyed in advertisements are far from harmless.

ESSAY REVIEW

1. What is an attitude and where do attitudes come from? What is the difference between an explicit and implicit attitude?

2. When do people infer their attitudes from their behavior? Explain Bem's self-perception theory.

3. According to the Yale Attitude Change Approach, what are the three main elements in a persuasive situation? Explain the characteristics that make each element more persuasive.

4. Describe the factors that make a person more likely to take a central route when exposed to a persuasive communication.

5. Explain the heuristic-systematic model of persuasion. What is the problem with using our emotions and moods as heuristics?

EXIT TESTS

EXIT TEST 1

1. Attitudes can be based in all of the following **EXCEPT**
   a) the ego.
   b) cognitions.
   c) affect.
   d) behavior.

2. Brian was listening to a song on the radio when he got a telephone call informing him that his best friend had been killed in a car accident. Now Brian dislikes that song and changes the station any time the song comes on the radio. Brian's attitude about the song was formed through
   a) cognitive dissonance.
   b) stimulus association bias.
   c) classical conditioning.
   d) operant conditioning.

3. Sue was not sure what her favorite flower was. However, after landscaping the garden at her new home, she realized that she planted more roses than any other flower. Sue concluded that roses must be her favorite flower. Sue's attitude toward roses is _____ based.
   a) affectively
   b) behaviorally
   c) cognitively
   d) dissonance

4. Which of the following is a personality factor influencing people's motivation to pay attention to a speech?
   a) whether the person is distracted
   b) how tired the person is
   c) personal relevance
   d) need for cognition

5. In a 1967 study by Leventhal et al., which participants reduced their smoking the most?
   a) participants who saw the film about lung cancer and read a pamphlet with instructions on how to quit smoking
   b) participants who did not see the film but received the pamphlet
   c) participants who saw the film but did not receive the pamphlet
   d) none of the participants reduced their smoking

6. Which of the following do we ask when using emotions as heuristics?
   a) What will my friends think?
   b) What will the neighbors think?
   c) How do I feel about it?
   d) Will my parents approve?

7. Our attitudes toward perfumes and colognes tend to be _____ based.
   a) cognitively
   b) affectively
   c) behaviorally
   d) dissonance

8. Children can be especially vulnerable to product placement.
   a) True
   b) False

9. Alicia's parents told her that she is forbidden to date Sean. Now Alicia feels even more strongly about Sean and she sneaks out of the house to be with him. Alicia has experienced
   a) subjective conflict.
   b) attitudinal conflict.
   c) dissonance.
   d) reactance.

10. Attitude accessibility is typically measured by how strongly a person feels about an issue.
    a) True
    b) False

EXIT TEST 2

1. Anytime Joshua's mom asks him to help with the dishes he replies "No, that's woman's work." When Joshua says this his dad smiles, pats him on the back, and says "That's my boy!" Joshua's attitude about helping with the dishes has been shaped by
   a) cognitive dissonance.
   b) stimulus association bias.
   c) classical conditioning.
   d) operant conditioning.

2. When asked what his favorite cuisine is Dave replies, "Well, it must be Mexican, because I am always going to Mexican restaurants." Dave's attitude is _____ based.
   a) cognitively
   b) affectively
   c) behaviorally
   d) dissonance

3. When attitudes change, they rarely do so in response to social influence.
    a) True
    b) False

4. Counterattitudinal advocacy is a powerful way to change people's attitudes on a mass scale.
    a) True
    b) False

5. Which of the following states that people take either a central or a peripheral route to persuasion?
    a) elaboration likelihood model
    b) Yale Attitude Change approach
    c) heuristic-systematic model of persuasion
    d) all of the above

6. Kendra decided to purchase a new perfume because she saw her favorite actress advertising it on television. Kendra's decision to purchase the perfume was
    a) cognitively based.
    b) behaviorally based.
    c) made through the peripheral route.
    d) made through the central route.

7. April has a good relationship with her parents and she respects their opinion. April is out with a group of friends who all suddenly decide to get tattoos. April's friends want her to go along and get a tattoo as well. Although she has never discussed tattoos with her parents, April suspects that her parents would not approve of them. According to the theory of planned behavior, is April likely to get a tattoo?
    a) Yes, because of reactance.
    b) Yes, because of subjective norms.
    c) No, because of perceived behavioral control.
    d) No, because of subjective norms.

8. A 2002 meta-analysis of studies that tested the effects of a media message on substance abuse in youths was encouraging in that kids became more negative toward the use of substances.
    a) True
    b) False

9. How did Gerald Lambert make mouthwash personally relevant?
    a) He said in his advertisement, "All your friends are using it."
    b) He invented a problem, halitosis.
    c) He marketed it as a way to prevent throat infections.
    d) all of the above

10. Rudman and colleagues (2007) found that people whose mother was overweight, and were close to their mothers, had positive implicit attitudes toward overweight people, even if they held negative explicit attitudes.
    a) True
    b) False

STUDY ACTIVITIES

1.	Give examples of cognitively, affectively, and behaviorally based attitudes.

2.	When do persuasive attempts "boomerang" and why?

3.	As a marketing specialist, what advertising approach would you recommend to the maker of greeting cards?

4.	Describe Petty and Cacioppo's (1986) elaboration likelihood model. What are the two routes to persuasion that people may take? What determines the route taken? What are the effects of persuasion by each route?

5.	Describe the "attitude inoculation" technique used to help people resist attempts to persuade them. How has this technique been adapted in order to make individuals resistant to peer pressure?

6.	When does counterattitudinal advocacy lead to private attitude change? What is the process underlying this change?

7.	What are some examples of peripheral cues? What route to persuasion leads to lasting attitude change?

8.	What level of fear is most effective in a persuasive communication? What is the best strategy if you are hoping to arouse fear in your persuasive communication? Why?

9.	Under what conditions do attitudes predict spontaneous and deliberative behaviors? How does the theory of planned behavior predict deliberative behaviors?

10.	Discuss the evidence concerning whether subliminal messages in a persuasive communication influence our behavior in a laboratory setting or in everyday life.

Chapter 7 Answers

Practice Test

1. C (p. 179)
2. A (p. 184)
3. B (p. 189)
4. D (p. 190)
5. C (p. 180)
6. D (pp. 197-199)
7. D (p. 188)
8. B (p. 202)
9. D (pp. 198-199)
10. B (p. 186)
11. D (p. 189)
12. C (p. 192)
13. B (p. 198)
14. C (pp. 196-197)
15. D (pp. 198-199)
16. C (pp. 182-183)
17. B (pp. 183-184)
18. D (pp. 190-191)
19. C (pp. 186, 191)
20. A (p. 194)
21. A (p. 199)
22. A (pp. 202-204)
23. B (p. 182)
24. D (p. 185)
25. B (pp. 178-179)
26. A (pp. 187-188)
27. D (p. 183-184)
28. A (p. 182)
29. B (pp. 184-188)
30. D (p. 187)
31. C (p. 179)
32. A (p. 179)
33. B (p. 182)
34. B (p. 184)
35. D (p. 185)
36. C (p. 187)
37. A (p. 187)
38. A (p. 191)
39. B (p. 193)
40. D (p. 195)

Short Answer Review

1. evaluations (p. 178)
2. beliefs (p. 179)
3. feelings (p. 179)
4. sensory (p. 180)
5. classical (p. 180)
6. observations (p. 181)
7. consciously (p. 182)
8. unconscious (p. 182)
9. social influence (p. 183)
10. attitudes (p. 183)
11. mass scale (p. 184)
12. persuasive communication (p. 184)
13. conditions (p. 184)
14. source (p. 184)
15. elaboration likelihood (p. 185)
16. carefully (p. 185)
17. arguments (p. 186)
18. interested (p. 187)
19. motivated (p. 187)
20. relevance (p. 187)
21. tired (p. 189)
22. central (p. 189)
23. consistently (p. 189)
24. attention (p. 189)
25. arousing (p. 190)
26. moderate (p. 190)
27. reduce (p. 190)
28. signal (p. 191)
29. peripheral (p. 191)
30. heuristics (p. 191)
31. come from (p. 191)
32. rational (p. 192)
33. confidence (p. 194)
34. strong and convincing (p. 194)
35. attitude inoculation (p. 194)
36. placement (p. 195)
37. peer pressure (pp. 195-196)
38. immunize (p. 196)
39. prohibitions (p. 196)
40. boomerang (p. 196)
41. freedom (p. 196)
42. accessible (p. 198)
43. theory of planned behavior (p. 198)
44. intention (p. 198)
45. themselves (p. 200)
46. emotions (p. 200)
47. relevant (p. 200)
48. pictures (p. 202)
49. behavior (p. 203)

50.   stereotypes (p. 205)
51.   Gender (p. 205)

Essay Review

1.   Your essay on attitudes should include:
- Attitudes are evaluations of people, objects, and ideas. (p. 178)
- Some attitudes are linked to our genes. Sometimes our attitudes are based primarily on the relevant facts. To the extent that people's evaluation is based primarily on their beliefs about the properties of an attitude object, we say it is a cognitively based attitude. An attitude based more on emotions and values than on an object appraisal of pluses and minuses is called an affectively based attitude. These can come from classical or operant conditioning. A behaviorally based attitude stems from people's observations of how they behave toward an object. (p. 179-181)
- An explicit attitude is one that we consciously endorse and can easily report. Implicit attitudes are involuntary, uncontrollable, and at times, unconscious. (p. 182)

2.   Your essay on behaviorally based attitudes should include:
- People infer their attitudes from their behavior when their initial attitude is weak or ambiguous. (pp. 181-182)
- According to Bem's self-perception theory, under certain circumstances, people don't know how they feel until they see how they behave. People infer their attitudes from their behavior only when there are no other plausible explanations for their behavior. (pp. 181-182)

3.   Your essay on the Yale Attitude Change approach should include:
- The three main elements of the Yale Attitude Change approach are: who (the source of the communication), what (the nature of the communication), and to whom (the nature of the audience). (p. 184)
- The source is more persuasive if it is credible and if the speaker is attractive. (Figure 7.2, p. 184)
- The message is more persuasive if people do not perceive it as an influence attempt. In general, two-sided messages are more effective. If two speeches are being given, it is best to go first if the speeches are given back to back and there will be a delay before people have to make up their minds. If there is a delay between the speeches and people will make up their minds right after hearing the second one, it is best to go last. (Figure 7.2, p. 184)

4.   Your essay should include:
- People have to be motivated to take the central route and have the ability to pay attention to the facts. (pp. 185-188)
- One thing that determines whether people are motivated to pay attention to a communication is the personal relevance of the topic. The more personally relevant an issue is, the more willing people are to pay attention to the arguments in a speech, and therefore the more likely people are to take the central route to persuasion. (pp. 187-189)

5.   Your essay on the heuristic-systematic model of persuasion should include:
- The heuristic-systematic model of persuasion is an explanation of the two ways in which persuasive communication can cause attitude change: either systematically processing the merits of the arguments or using mental shortcuts (heuristics), such as "Experts are always right." (p. 191)
- The only problem with using our emotions and moods as heuristics is that sometimes it is difficult to tell where our feelings come from. We can make mistakes about what is causing our mood and misattribute our feelings created by one source to another source. (p. 191)

Exit Test 1

1.   A (pp. 179-181)
2.   C (p. 180)
3.   B (p. 181)
4.   D (p. 188)
5.   A (p. 190)
6.   C (p. 191)
7.   B (p. 192)
8.   A (p. 195)
9.   D (pp. 196-197)
10.   B (p. 198)

Exit Test 2

1.   D (p. 180)
2.   C (p. 181)
3.   B (p. 183)
4.   B (p. 184)
5.   A (p. 185)
6.   C (p. 186)
7.   D (p. 199)
8.   A (p. 201)
9.   B (p. 202)
10.   A (pp. 182-183)

Study Activities

1.   Your example should indicate that a cognitively based attitude is founded on people's beliefs about the properties of the attitude object, that an affectively based attitude is founded on people's emotions and values that are evoked by the attitude object, and that a behaviorally based attitude is derived from people's observations of how they behave toward the attitude object. (pp. 179-181)

2.   Persuasive attempts "boomerang," or cause an increased interest in the activity your persuasive attempt is aimed at discouraging, when strong prohibitions for engaging in the activity are used. In part, this occurs because, according to reactance theory, we are motivated to restore a sense of freedom when we perceive that we are not free to engage in the activity. One means of restoring a sense of freedom is to perform the behavior. The boomerang effect also occurs because strong prohibitions provide ample and conspicuous external justification for not engaging in the behavior. Under such conditions, overjustification is likely to occur. That is, people will

underestimate the intrinsic reasons for avoiding the behavior and come to believe that they enjoy the activity more. (pp. 196-197)

3.   People's attitudes toward greeting cards are clearly affectively based. Your approach should therefore be to play on these emotions. You would recommend presenting ads that depict joyous birthdays and weddings, proud moments like graduation, etc. (pp. 179 & 200)

4.   According to the Elaboration Likelihood Model, people take the central route to persuasion when they are both motivated and able to attend to arguments presented. Subsequent attitude change will persist, be consistent with behaviors, and resist counterpersuasion. If people are either unmotivated or unable to attend to the arguments, they will attend to cues, which are peripheral to the message, and take the peripheral route to persuasion. Subsequent attitude change will be short-lived, be inconsistent with behaviors, and will change again in the face of counterpersuasion.
(pp. 185-189)

5.   Attitude inoculation makes people immune to attempts to change cognitively based attitudes by initially exposing them to small doses of the arguments against their position. Peer pressure is likely to play on adolescents' feelings of autonomy and social rejection. That is, it is directed at changing affectively, rather than cognitively based attitudes. The attitude inoculation technique can be modified by exposing adolescents to small doses of peer pressure during role-playing interventions. (pp. 194-196)

6.   Counterattitudinal advocacy can lead to private attitude change when the person does not have sufficient external justification for their behavior. Cognitive dissonance is the process underlying this change. (pp. 183-184)

7.   Peripheral cues are surface characteristics of the message such as the length of the message, who delivers the message (e.g. expert, celebrity), or the attractiveness of the communicator. The central route to persuasion leads to lasting attitude change. (pp. 186 & 189)

8.   A moderate level of fear is best. The moderate amount of fear should be combined with a message that will teach people how to reduce the fear because then the audience will be motivated to analyze the message carefully and will likely change their attitudes via the central route. (pp. 190-191)

9.   Attitudes predict spontaneous behaviors only when they are highly accessible to people. Attitudes can predict deliberate behaviors when you know about the person's intentions. According to the theory of planned behavior, intention is determined by three things: the person's attitude toward the specific behavior, the person's subjective norms, and the person's perceived behavioral control. (pp. 197-199)

10.   Many studies of subliminal perception have been conducted and there is no evidence that the types of subliminal messages encountered in everyday life have any influence on people's behavior. There is evidence for subliminal effects in carefully controlled laboratory studies. However, to get subliminal effects, researchers have to make sure that the illumination of the room is just right, that people are seated just the right distance from a viewing screen, and that nothing else is occurring to distract them as the subliminal stimuli are flashed. These messages might have subtle influences on people's liking for an ambiguous stimulus, but they cannot override their wishes and desires.
(pp. 203-204)

CHAPTER 8

Conformity: Influencing Behavior

CHAPTER 8 OVERVIEW

This chapter deals with the powerful influence that people have to get others to conform or to influence their actions and decisions. The first section of the chapter discusses conformity. American mythology has celebrated the rugged individualist in many ways, however sometimes people choose to conform. **Conformity** refers to a change in one's behavior due to the real or imagined influence of other people.

The next section of this chapter addresses informational social influence. **Informational social influence** is the influence of other people that leads us to conform because we see others as a source of information to guide our behavior; we conform because we believe that others' interpretation of an ambiguous situation is more correct than ours and adopting their interpretation will help us choose an appropriate course of action. Informational social influence usually results in **private acceptance**, wherein people genuinely believe in what other people are doing or saying rather than **public compliance**, in which people conform to other people's behavior publicly without necessarily believing in what they are doing or saying. In situations where it is important to be accurate, the tendency to conform to other people through informational social influence increases.

Using other people as a source of information can backfire when they are wrong about what is going on. **Contagion** occurs when emotions and behaviors spread rapidly throughout a group; one example is mass psychogenic illness. **Mass psychogenic illness** is the occurrence, in a group of people, of similar physical symptoms with no known physical cause. People are more likely to conform to informational social influence when the situation is ambiguous, a crisis, or if experts are present.

The next section of the chapter addresses normative social influence. **Normative social influence** occurs when we change our behavior to match that of others in order to be liked and accepted by them. We conform to the group's **social norms**, implicit or explicit rules for acceptable behaviors, values, and attitudes. Normative social influence usually results in public compliance, but not private acceptance of other people's ideas and behaviors. In a series of classic studies, Solomon Asch found that people would conform, at least some of the time, to the obviously wrong answer of the group. However, when it is important to be accurate, people are more likely to resist normative social influence and go against the group, giving the right answer. Resisting normative social influence can lead to ridicule, ostracism, and even rejection by the group. Normative social influence operates on many levels in social life: It influences our eating habits, hobbies, fashion, body image, and so on, and it promotes correct (polite) behavior in society.

Social impact theory specifies when normative social influence is most likely to occur by referring to the strength, immediacy, and number of people in the group. We are more likely to conform when the group is one we care about, when the group members are unanimous in their thoughts or behaviors, when the group has three or more members, and when we are members of collectivist cultures. The very act of conforming normatively to important groups *most* of the time can earn you the right to deviate occasionally without serious consequences. **Idiosyncrasy credits** refer to the tolerance a person earns, over time, by conforming to group norms. Under certain conditions **minority influence** can occur in which an individual (or small number of people) can influence the majority. The key is consistency in the presentation of the minority viewpoint.

The next section of this chapter discusses using social influence to promote beneficial behavior. There is a way that we can use the tendency to conform to affect people's behavior for the common good. Social norms can be used to subtly induce people to conform to correct, socially approved behavior. A culture's social norms are of two types. **Injunctive norms** have to do with what we think other people approve or disapprove of. **Descriptive norms** concern our perceptions of the way people actually behave in a given situation, regardless of whether the behavior is approved or disapproved of by others. Communicating injunctive norms is a more powerful way to create change than communicating descriptive norms. The social norms technique, providing information about social norms, has been used to decrease alcohol binge drinking on college campuses. However, researchers have noted a major problem with this approach: Sometimes, it "boomerangs."A "descriptive norm plus injunctive norm" message has been found to be more successful in studies designed to reduce electricity use.

The final section of this chapter examines obedience to authority. In the most famous series of studies in social psychology, Stanley Milgram examined obedience to authority figures. He found chilling levels of obedience, to the point where a majority of participants administered what they thought were near-lethal shocks to a fellow human being. Normative pressures make it difficult for people to stop obeying authority figures. They wish to please the authority figure by doing a good job. The obedience experiment was a confusing situation for participants, with competing, ambiguous demands. Unclear about how to define what was going on, they followed the orders of the expert. Participants conformed to the wrong norm: they continued to follow the "obey authority" norm when it was no longer appropriate. It was difficult for them to abandon this norm for three reasons: the fast-paced nature of the experiment, the fact that the shock levels increased in small increments, and their loss of a feeling of personal responsibility.

Stanley Milgram's study of obedience is widely considered to be one of the most important contributions to the field of psychology. However, his studies were criticized as unethical for several reasons including deception, a lack of true informed consent, the psychological distress caused, the fact that participants were not told they had the right to withdraw, and inflicted insight. Burger's (2009) replication of Milgram's experiment found no significant difference in obedience rates between his participants and Milgram's. Burger's ethically necessary changes in methodology make a direct comparison to Milgram's results difficult.

CHAPTER 8 OUTLINE

I. Conformity: When and Why
• **Conformity** is a change in behavior due to the real or imagined influence of others.
• American culture celebrates the rugged individualist, but even in our own culture extremes of conformity, such as Jonestown, Heaven's Gate, and the My Lai massacre occur. Social psychologists suggest that these events occurred not because the people involved were crazy but because they were subjected to very strong situational influences.

II. Informational Social Influence: The Need to Know What's "Right"
• In many situations, we are uncertain how to think or to act. We use the behavior of others to help us figure out what is going on in the situation and what to do about it. **Informational social influence** occurs when we conform because we see other people as a source of information. We conform because we believe that others' interpretation of an ambiguous situation is more correct than ours and will help us choose an appropriate course of action.
• Sherif (1936) conducted an experiment that made use of the autokinetic effect, the illusion that a still point of light in an otherwise dark visual field moves. People vary in how much motion they perceive. Thus the autokinetic effect provides an ambiguous situation. When people were put in groups to make

their estimates, over several trials, the differing estimates of the people converged (Figure 8.1). This conformity was apparently due to informational social influence, because it resulted in **private acceptance** of the group norm out of genuine belief in their correctness (rather than **public compliance**, or a change in behavior without a change in belief): subjects in variations of the study maintained their adherence to the group norm in private and up to a year later.

A. The Importance of Being Accurate
• Recent research has extended Sherif's work, employing judgment tasks that are more like real life, and demonstrating that the importance to the individual of being accurate at the task affects informational social influence.
• Baron et al. (1996) gave participants an eyewitness task, showing them a picture of a perpetrator and then having them pick that person out of a lineup. The task was made ambiguous by having the perpetrator dressed differently in the lineup than in the original photo, and by flashing the lineup for only half a second. The importance of the task was manipulated by telling some groups that this was a new test to identify accurate eyewitnesses that the local police department was adopting and they were helping develop norms for the task, and by giving them $20; and by telling other groups that the task was a test under development. Participants took part in groups with three confederates, who gave the wrong answer on seven critical trials. Baron et al. found that participants were more influenced (in this case by informational social influence) by the confederate's answers when the task was more important—an important extension of Sherif's work.

B. When Informational Conformity Backfires
• Informational influence is often involved in crisis situations. For example, the 1938 Orson Welles *War of the Worlds* radio broadcast (a teleplay, presented in broadcast news format, about an alien invasion) led to widespread panic because many people missed the beginning of the broadcast (which identified it as a play) and turned to each other to see how they should behave. Additionally people interpreted other events in their environment (e.g., no cars driving down the street) as due to the invasion, intensifying their fears and leading to a **contagion** situation (one where emotions or behaviors spread rapidly through a crowd).
• Another example of informational conformity backfiring is **mass psychogenic illness**, the occurrence, in a group of people, of similar physical symptoms with no known physical cause.
• A recent case occurred in Tennessee in 1998, when a teacher and many students experienced a variety of symptoms that led to their being hospitalized and the school evacuated. No physical cause for the incident was found. Jones et al. (2000) determined that mass psychogenic illness was the cause.
• Cases of mass psychogenic illness typically begin with just one or a few people, and typically these people are experiencing some kind of stress in their lives. As a reasonable explanation for the illness is developed, it becomes more credible and thus more widespread.
• Such occurrences can spread more rapidly today than formerly because of instantaneously available media (which can also more quickly try to squelch the panic).

C. When Will People Conform to Informational Social Influence?
1. When the Situation Is Ambiguous
• Ambiguity is the most crucial variable in determining whether people use each other as a source of information.
2. When the Situation Is a Crisis
• Crisis situations leave us limited time to act; which may make us scared and panicky. If we turn to others who are also panicked for information, our own panic and irrationality may be intensified.
3. When Other People Are Experts
• The more expertise or knowledge someone has, the more people will turn to them as a guide in an ambiguous situation. Unfortunately experts are not always reliable sources of information.

III. Normative Social Influence: The Need to Be Accepted

• Examples are presented of teenagers engaging in life-threatening behavior. This behavior occurs not because the teens are unaware of the risk, but because they want to be accepted and liked by their peers. To do so, they conform to the group's **social norms**, the implicit or explicit rules a group has for the acceptable behaviors, values, and beliefs of its members. Group members who do not conform are ridiculed, punished, or rejected by other group members. In Japan, a dozen teenage victims of bullying killed themselves in one year (Jordan, 1996).

• Humans are a social species and thus have a fundamental need for social companionship that forms the basis for **normative social influence**, conformity in order to be liked and accepted by others. Normative conformity often results in public compliance without private acceptance.

A. Conformity and Social Approval: The Asch Line Judgment Studies

• Asch (1951, 1956) conducted a series of classic experiments on normative social influence. In contrast to Sherif's work, Asch used a situation that was clearly defined rather than ambiguous. Specifically, he used a line judgment task, where participants were presented with a series of three lines of differing lengths, and were asked to match a target line to one of the three; the correct answer was obvious (Figure 8.2). Unbeknownst to the subject, the other seven participants were confederates. The real subject always answered last. In two-thirds of the trials, the confederates unanimously agreed on an incorrect answer. A surprising amount of conformity occurred: 76% conformed at least once, and on average, people conformed on about a third of the trials where the confederates gave the wrong answer (Figure 8.3). Interviews with participants indicated that they did not want to feel different or foolish. The Asch experiment is especially surprising since people were concerned about looking foolish in front of complete strangers, and there were no tangible risks or punishments for failing to conform.

• In a variation of the study, subjects wrote their answers on paper, rather than saying them aloud; in this variation, conformity dropped dramatically. This demonstrates the power of social disapproval in the original study in shaping a person's behavior.

B. The Importance of Being Accurate Revisited

• The Baron et al. (1996) study described earlier included experimental conditions designed to trigger normative social influence. In these conditions, the eyewitness identification task was made extremely easy by showing participants the lineup for five seconds and by letting them view each pair of slides twice. Control subjects got 97% correct on these conditions, demonstrating that this task was indeed unambiguous and analogous to the Asch line judgment situation. Importance of being accurate was manipulated as before. In this case, participants in the low-importance condition conformed 33% of the time, a result similar to Asch's findings. Participants in the high-importance condition conformed 16% of the time—indeed, a lesser amount of conformity, but still some. Even when the group is wrong, the right answer is obvious, and there are strong incentives to be accurate, people will find it difficult to risk social disapproval.

C. The Consequences of Resisting Normative Social Influence

• What happens when people manage to resist normative group influence? Other group members start paying attention to the deviant and trying to convince him or her to conform; if she or he does not, eventually the deviant will be rejected.

• Schacter (1951) demonstrated how groups respond to an individual who ignores the group's normative influence. Groups read a case history of "Johnny Rocco," a juvenile delinquent. The case typically led to middle-of-the-road positions about the case. An accomplice in the group was instructed to disagree with the group's recommendations. The deviant received most of the communication from other group members until near the end (when it was apparent that communication wouldn't work); at this point, other group members began to ignore the deviant, and

Chapter 8

on a subsequent task, they recommended that the deviant be eliminated from further group discussions if group size were reduced.

D. Normative Social Influence in Everyday Life
• Fashions and fads represent innocuous examples of normative conformity.

1. Social Influence and Women's Body Image
• A more sinister example of social influence is women's attempts to conform to cultural definitions of an attractive body, where the current fashion is to be extremely thin.
• Anderson et al. (1992) analyzed 54 different cultures' perception of the ideal female body. Heavy female bodies were considered the most beautiful in cultures with unreliable food supplies; and only in cultures where the food supply was very reliable was the slender body valued. In all cultures except those where the food supply was very reliable, the moderate-to-heavy body range was preferred by the majority (p. 228, Figure 8.4).
• What is attractive has changed many times over the past 100 years, as an analysis of models in women's magazines indicates (p. 229, Figure 8.5). Women learn what standard is appropriate through *informational social influence*, but *normative social influence* helps explain their attempts to create the desired body through dieting and eating disorders.
• Research shows that women tend to perceive themselves as overweight and heavier than they actually are, especially when they have just been looking at media portrayals of thin women. These pressures lead to an increase in eating disorders: recent statistics show that one-third of 12-13 year-old girls are actively trying to lose weight.
• Crandall (1988) examined normative social influences on bulimia in two college sororities. He found that each sorority had its own norm for the "right" amount of binge eating, and that popularity within the sorority was associated with adherence to this norm. Although pledge's friendships were not related to the norm at first, they were by the end of the first year.

2. Social Influence and Men's Body Image
• There is little research in this domain, but some initial studies suggest that men are beginning to come under the same pressure to achieve an ideal body that women have experienced for decades. Petrie et al. (1996) found no change in the shoulder-to-waist and chest-to-waist ratios over the decades, but pointed out that their technique could not pick up changes in musculature. Other evidence suggests that indeed the male ideal is now much more muscular. For example, Pope et al. (1999) found changes in the musculature of G.I. Joe dolls, and in the percentage of ads portraying men in some state of undress (while the percentage of such ads for women has remained fairly stable). Other research by these investigators shows that while men are accurate in perceiving their own body mass, both their ideal and what they believe women would find attractive has considerably more muscle.

E. When Will People Conform to Normative Social Influence?
• Latané's **social impact theory** suggests that conforming to normative pressures depends on the strength (personal importance), immediacy (physical proximity), and number of other people in a group. According to the theory, conformity will increase directly with the amount of strength and immediacy; but that increases in numbers will show diminishing returns (i.e., going from 3 to 4 makes more of a difference than going from 53 to 54). The theory has done a good job of predicting the actual amount of conformity that occurs.

1. When the Group Size is Three or More
• Asch's research (and subsequent investigations) show that conformity does not increase much after group size reaches 4 or 5 other people (p. 233, Figure 8.6).

2. When the Group is Important
• Normative pressures are much stronger when they come from people whose friendship, love, or respect we cherish. A consequence is that it can be dangerous to have important policy decisions

made by highly cohesive groups, who may care more about pleasing each other than about making the best decision.
• The very act of conforming normatively to important groups *most* of the time can earn you the right to deviate occasionally without serious consequences. **Idiosyncrasy credits** refer to the tolerance a person earns, over time, by conforming to group norms.

3. When One Has No Allies in the Group
• A variation of Asch's experiment demonstrated the importance of group unanimity: when only one other person gave the right answer, the level of conforming to the group dropped to only 6% (from 32%). This influence explains how members of cults or other groups can maintain beliefs that seem ridiculous to most others.

4. When the Group's Culture is Collectivistic
• Differences in cultures' individualist vs. collectivist orientation have implications for conformity. The Asch experiment has been replicated in several cultures. Some (e.g., Norway and the Bantus of Zimbabwe) find much higher levels of conformity than the U.S. In Japan, conformity was lower than in the U.S., because conformity is directed at groups to which one belongs and not groups of strangers. Berry (1967) suggested and provided some data in support of the idea that hunting cultures will favor independence while agricultural cultures will favor cooperation and conformity. Replications of the Asch experiment in the U.S. and Britain in the 1980s showed decreasing amounts of conformity within the culture.

F. Minority Influence: When the Few Influence the Many
• Moscovici argues that the individual or the minority can affect change in the majority (**minority influence**). The key to this is consistency over time and between members of the minority.
• A recent meta-analysis by Wendy Wood et al. leads to the conclusion that majorities often cause public compliance because of normative social influence, whereas minorities often cause private acceptance because of informational social influence.

IV. Using Social Influence to Promote Beneficial Behavior
• Cialdini, Reno, and Kallgren have developed a model of normative conduct, where *social norms* (the rules society has for acceptable beliefs, values, and behaviors) can be used to subtly induce people to conform to correct, socially approved behavior.
•**Injunctive norms** are people's perception of what behaviors are approved or disapproved of by others
 descriptive norms are people's perceptions of how people actually behave in given situations, regardless of whether the behavior is approved of or disapproved of by others.

A. The Role of Injunctive and Descriptive Norms
• In one study (Reno et al., 1993), participants were exposed either to a confederate walking by (the control group), a confederate walking by and dropping an empty fast-food bag (*descriptive norm* condition), or a confederate picking up a littered fast-food bag (*injunctive norm* condition). This occurred in either a heavily littered or a clean and unlittered parking lot. When participants came to their cars, they found a large handbill slipped onto the windshield. Results indicated that 37 to 38% of the control group littered, regardless of how clean the parking lot was. In the descriptive norm condition, littering was reduced in the clean lot condition, where the confederate's behavior served to remind people of the prevailing norm for cleanliness displayed by the clean lot, but it was not reduced in the littered lot condition, where the confederate's behavior reinforced the idea displayed by the dirty lot that it was okay to litter. Finally, participants in the injunctive norm condition littered least of all, regardless of the condition of the parking lot (see Figure 8.7).
• The researchers concluded that injunctive norms are more powerful than descriptive norms in producing desired behavior. They also noted that norms are always present, but not always salient; some aspect of the situation (in this case, the confederate's behavior) needs to draw people's attention to the norm so that they think about it. Thus, information that communicates injunctive social

norms—what society approves and disapproves of—needs to be present to create positive behavior change.

1. Using Norms to Change Behavior: Beware the "Boomerang Effect"
• The social norms technique, providing information about social norms, has been used to decrease alcohol binge drinking on college campuses. However, researchers have noted a major problem with this approach: Sometimes, it "boomerangs."A "descriptive norm plus injunctive norm" message has been found to be more successful in studies designed to reduce electricity use.

V. Obedience to Authority
• Philosopher Hannah Arendt (1965) argued that the atrocities of the Holocaust occurred not because the participants were psychopaths but because they were ordinary people bowing to extraordinary social pressures.
• Milgram (1964, 1974, 1976) examined the power of obedience to authority in social psychology's most famous laboratory experiment. Participants believed they were in a study on the effects of punishment on learning; they were assigned the role of the teacher and their partner (actually a confederate of the experiment) was assigned the role of the learner. The teacher was assigned to punish the learner for every mistake in a paired associate's task by delivering an electric shock. Each mistake is to receive a progressively higher level of shock. The learner protests, but the experimenter insists that the experiment must continue (Figure 8.8). Milgram found that 62.5% of the participants gave the full 450 mv "Danger XXX" shock, and that 80% continued past the learner's announcement that he had a heart condition and refused further participation.
• College students, middle-class adults, and professional scientists asked to estimate beforehand the degree of obedience estimated that only 1% of the participants would go all the way.

A. The Role of Normative Social Influence
• A variation on the Milgram experiment demonstrates the role of normative influence (Figure 8.9). Significantly less compliance was demonstrated if two other "teachers" refused to continue.

B. The Role of Informational Social Influence
• Other variations on the experiment (Figure 8.9) demonstrate the role of informational influence due to how confusing the situation was. Significantly less compliance was demonstrated if (a) the orders to continue came from another "teacher" rather than from the experimenter; or (b) two experimenters disagreed about whether the experiment should be continued.

C. Other Reasons Why We Obey
1. Conforming to the Wrong Norm
• Anther factor influencing obedience in situations such as the Milgram experiment and the My Lai massacre are mindlessness and the foot-in-the-door phenomenon: mindlessness leads to initial compliance, and initial compliance begets subsequent compliance. In the Milgram experiment, this was abetted by the quick pace of the experiment and the fact that the shock increased in very small doses.
2. Self-Justification
•Additionally, dissonance reduction played a factor: each increase in shock led to dissonance, and each rationalization of this dissonance provided the basis for escalating the shock a bit further.
3. The Loss of Personal Responsibility
• Milgram stressed the idea that the loss of a sense of personal responsibility for one's actions was a critical component explaining the results of the obedience studies.

D. The Obedience Studies, Then and Now
1. Conforming to the Wrong Norm
• Stanley Milgram's study of obedience is widely considered to be one of the most important contributions to the field of psychology. However, his studies were criticized as unethical for several reasons including deception, a lack of true informed consent, the psychological distress caused, the fact that participants were not told they had the right to withdraw, and inflicted insight.

• Burger's (2009) replication of Milgram's experiment found no significant difference in obedience rates when between his participants and Milgrams. Burger's ethically necessary changes in methodology make a direct comparison to Milgram's results difficult.

1. It's Not about Aggression
• Is a universal aggressive urge a factor in obedience to cruel authority? A variation of the Milgram experiment gave subjects permission to choose their own level of shock; they were told that information about all levels was informative, to make them feel free to choose whichever level they desired. Most participants gave very mild shocks; only 2.5% gave the highest level.

• In sum, social pressures can combine in insidious ways to make humane people act inhumane.

LEARNING OBJECTIVES

After reading Chapter 8, you should be able to do the following:

1. Define conformity. Identify the motivation underlying informational social influence. (pp. 214-215)

2. Describe Sherif's (1936) experiment. Discuss why Sherif chose to use the autokinetic effect in his experiment. Describe the results of Sherif's experiment. (pp. 215-216)

3. Distinguish between private acceptance and public compliance. Identify which of these is produced by informational social influence. (pp. 215-216)

4. Explain the relationship between conformity due to informational social influence and the importance of being accurate. (pp. 216-217)

5. Describe the conditions under which informational social influence backfires. Identify examples of contagion and mass psychogenic illnesses. Discuss the role of the mass media in the spread of modern mass psychogenic illness. (pp. 218-219)

6. Identify three situations that produce conformity to informational social influence. (pp. 219-220)

7. Identify the motivation underlying normative social influence. Define and give examples of social norms. (pp. 221-222)

8. Describe Asch's (1956) experiment. Identify how the situation in Asch's experiment differed from the situation in Sherif's experiment. Describe the basic findings of Asch's experiment. Explain why these findings were surprising. (pp. 222-224)

9. Identify whether private acceptance or public compliance usually results from normative social influence. Describe Asch's variation of his original experiment and explain how this resulted in strong evidence for normative influence. (pp. 224-225)

10. Explain the relationship between conformity due to normative social influence and the importance of being accurate. (pp. 225-226)

11. Discuss the consequences of resisting normative social influence. Describe Schachter's (1951) experiment and discuss its results. (p. 226)

12. Discuss examples of normative social influence from harmless trends and fads to more sinister forms of conformity including many women's attempts to conform to an extremely thin standard of feminine physical attractiveness. Describe the changes in cultural standards for feminine physical attractiveness in the last century. (pp. 227-230)

13. Discuss the relationship between social influence and men's body image and how cultural norms regarding men's body image have changed in the second half of the last century. (pp. 230-232)

14. Identify when people will conform to normative social influence. Describe social impact theory. Identify the relationships among the strength, immediacy, and number of influence sources, and subsequent conformity. List some predictions made by the theory when strength, immediacy, and the number of influence sources are manipulated.
(pp. 232-234)

15. Identify three characteristics of the group that increase conformity to normative social influence. Identify what size group induced maximum conformity in Asch's experiments. Discuss why it might be dangerous to have policy decisions made by highly cohesive groups. Discuss the effects of having an ally on conformity to normative social influence. Discuss the findings of cross-cultural research on conformity and the results of conformity studies replicated in the same culture after many years. (pp. 232-235)

16. Discuss the necessity of minority influence for introducing change within groups. Identify how a minority must express its views if it is to exert influence. Identify the kind of social influence minorities exert and what effect this has on the majority. (pp. 235-236)

17. Discuss how social influence can be used to promote constructive behavior. Define injunctive and descriptive norms. Describe how injunctive and descriptive norms can reduce problematic behaviors such as littering and increase beneficial social behavior. (pp. 237-240)

18. Describe Milgram's obedience studies. Identify what percentage of participants in Milgram's studies obeyed the experimenter completely. Discuss variations of the original study which demonstrate the kinds of social influence that caused obedience. Discuss the roles of normative and informational influence in explaining Milgram's findings. (pp. 240-245)

19. Explain the boomerang effect and explain how "descriptive norm plus injunctive norm" messages can be used to prevent the boomerang effect. (pp. 239-240)

20. Identify two key aspects of the situation that caused participants in Milgram's obedience studies to continue following an "obey authority" norm long after it was appropriate to do so. (pp. 243-245)

21. Identify the reasons Milgram's study has been criticized. Describe Burger's (2009) replication of Milgram's study and compare and contrast Burger's and Milgram's studies. (pp. 247-248)

22.   Discuss the evidence that suggests participants in Milgram's experiments were not expressing a universal aggressive urge. (pp. 248-249)

KEY TERMS

1. _____ A change in one's behavior due to the real or imagined influence of other people. (p. 214)

2. _____ The influence of other people that leads us to conform because we see them as a source of information to guide our behavior; we conform because we believe that others' interpretation of an ambiguous situation is more correct than ours and will help us choose an appropriate course of action. (p. 215)

3. _____ Conforming to other people's behavior out of a genuine belief that what they are doing or saying is right. (p. 215)

4. _____ Conforming to other people's behavior publicly without necessarily believing in what we are doing or saying. (p. 216)

5. _____ The rapid spread of emotions or behaviors through a crowd. (p. 218)

6. _____ The occurrence, in a group of people, of similar physical symptoms with no known physical cause. (p. 218)

7. _____ The implicit or explicit rules a group has for the acceptable behaviors, values, and beliefs of its members. (p. 221)

8. _____ The influence of other people that leads us to conform in order to be liked and accepted by them; this type of conformity results in public compliance with the group's beliefs and behaviors but not necessarily private acceptance of those beliefs and behaviors. (p. 222)

9. _____ The idea that conforming to social influence depends on the strength of the group's importance, its immediacy, and the number of people in the group. (p. 232)

10. _____ The tolerance a person earns, over time, by conforming to group norms; if enough idiosyncrasy credits are earned, the person can, on occasion, behave deviantly without retribution from the group. (p. 233)

11. _____ The case where a minority of group members influence the behavior or beliefs of the majority. (p. 236)

12. _____ People's perceptions of what behaviors are approved or disapproved of by others. (p. 238)

13. _____ People's perceptions of how people actually behave in given situations, regardless of whether the behavior is approved or disapproved of by others. (p. 238)

GUIDED REVIEW

PRACTICE TEST

1. Why did individual estimates of a light's apparent motion converge when participants in Sherif's (1951) experiment called out their estimates in a group?
    a) because participants used each other as a source of information
    b) because participants wanted to be liked by the others
    c) because participants badgered each other until everyone agreed
    d) because the mere presence of others had subtle effects on participants' visual processes

2. Nolan and colleagues (2008) gave a sample of California residents information urging them to conserve electrical energy in their homes. The household members received one of four messages. Which of the messages was successful in causing people to conserve significantly more energy?
    a) the message in which participants were told that the majority of their neighbors conserved electrical energy
    b) the message urging them to conserve electrical energy in order to protect the environment
    c) the message urging them to conserve electrical energy in order to benefit society
    d) the message urging them to conserve electrical energy in order to save money

3. How was Asch's conformity study different from Sherif's?
    a) Asch created an ambiguous situation while Sherif created an unambiguous one.
    b) Asch created an unambiguous situation while Sherif created an ambiguous one.
    c) The subjects in Asch's study were better problem solvers than those in Sherif's study.
    d) Accomplices in Asch's study imposed greater pressure on participants than did accomplices in Sherif's study.

4. When participants in Asch's (1956) study indicated which of three comparison lines matched a standard line by writing their responses on a piece of paper rather than by saying them out loud, conformity:
    a) increased somewhat.
    b) remained the same.
    c) dropped dramatically.
    d) dropped slightly.

5. According to Latané's (1981) social impact theory, the amount of influence that people whose opinions differ from your own will exert will be greatest if they are in a group that is:
    a) comprised of three people.
    b) important.
    c) unanimous.
    d) b and c.

6. Replications of Asch's (1956) conformity research across many cultures and different time periods indicate that amounts of conformity:
    a) are constant culture to culture and over time in a given culture.
    b) vary from culture to culture but are constant over time in a given culture.
    c) vary from culture to culture and over time in a given culture.
    d) are constant culture to culture but vary over time in a given culture.

7. Which of the following is true about people's susceptibility to conforming due to informational social influence?
   a)   People are more likely to conform due to informational social influence when the situation is straightforward than when it is not straightforward.
   b)   People are more likely to conform due to informational social influence when it is important to be accurate than when it is unimportant.
   c)   People are more likely to conform due to informational social influence when accuracy is unimportant than when it is important.
   d)   People are less likely to conform due to informational social influence when the situation is unclear than when it is straightforward.

8. In a study by Goldstein and colleagues (2008), which message was successful in getting hotel guests to reuse their towels?
   a)   the message asking guests to reuse their towels to save the environment
   b)   the message asking guests to reuse their towels to save water
   c)   the message asking guests to reuse their towels to save energy
   d)   the message stating that the majority of guests in this room reuse their towels

9. In Milgram's obedience studies participants played the role of "teacher" in what they believed was an experiment on the effects of punishment on learning. Throughout the experiment they feared they might kill a "learner" with increasingly strong electrical shocks. Mild prods by an authority to "please continue" were nonetheless enough to get ___ percent of Milgram's participants to obey completely.
   a)   1.0
   b)   12.5
   c)   36.0
   d)   62.5

10. Which of the following forms of social influence induced the participants in Milgram's obedience studies to administer the maximum level of shock possible to a helpless learner?
    a)   normative social influence
    b)   informational social influence
    c)   both normative and informational social influence
    d)   neither normative nor informational social influence

11. Whereas normative social influence leads to _____, informational social influence produces _____.
    a)   private acceptance; public compliance
    b)   public compliance; private acceptance
    c)   conformity; minority influence
    d)   minority influence; conformity

12. A teacher at a high school in Tennessee reported the smell of gasoline in her classroom; soon she experienced headache, nausea, shortness of breath and dizziness. Others in the school later reported similar symptoms. The school was evacuated and closed. When investigators found nothing wrong with the school and no cause for the symptoms, the symptoms were labeled

    _____.
    a)   hypochondriasis
    b)   mass psychogenic illness
    c)   schizophrenia
    d)   conversion

Chapter 8

13.   Asch (1956) presented participants with three comparison lines and a standard line that clearly
        matched one of the comparison lines. When participants were asked to publicly identify the
        matching line they went along with a rigged majority and made incorrect judgments:
        a)   almost every time.
        b)   about half of the time.
        c)   about a third of the time.
        d)   almost never.

14.   Bibb Latané's social impact (1981) theory describes:
        a)   characteristics that make a group influential.
        b)   the type of people who are most likely to conform.
        c)   when conformity is foolish and when it is wise.
        d)   cognitive processes involved in "mindless" conformity.

15.   Two Asch-type studies conducted in Japan found that when the group unanimously gave the
        incorrect answer, Japanese students were less conformist in general than North Americans.
        a)   True
        b)   False

16.   Results of a national survey by Puhl and colleagues (2008) indicated that weight discrimination
        against women is _____ in American society and is
        a)   decreasing; not nearly as common as other forms of discrimination.
        b)   increasing; almost as common as discrimination based on sexual orientation.
        c)   decreasing; almost nonexistent.
        d)   increasing; almost as common as racial discrimination.

17.   After hearing a minority opinion, majority members may come to realize that there are different
        perspectives from their own and consider the issue more carefully. Subsequent change in the
        majority's opinion will be the result of _____ social influence.
        a)   consensual
        b)   informational
        c)   responsive
        d)   normative

18.   Why did obedience by participants in Milgram's studies drop drastically when two accomplices,
        acting as fellow teachers, refused to obey the experimenter?
        a)   because the participant could not continue without the help of the accomplice
                teachers
        b)   because similar peers exert more normative social influence than do dissimilar authority
                figures
        c)   because the accomplices served as allies which enabled participants to resist normative
                social influence
        d)   because the two accomplices outnumbered the experimenter and formed an influential
                majority

19.   The "escalation" of shocks that subjects administered in Milgram's studies resulted because:
   a)   participants found it difficult to stop shocking the learner after justifying the administration of each previous level of shock.
   b)   participants became desensitized to shocking the learner.
   c)   participants convinced themselves that the experimenter was solely responsible and simply followed his requests.
   d)   participants became convinced that it was acceptable to shock the learner and their natural aggressive tendencies took over.

20.   Mass psychogenic illness is a form of:
   a)   normative social influence.
   b)   contagion.
   c)   informational social influence.
   d)   both b and c.

21.   What did researchers discover was wrong with the message "Students at your school, on average, drink only X number of drinks per week?"
   a)   It had no impact on drinking behavior.
   b)   Most students did not read the message.
   c)   Most of the students did not believe the message.
   d)   Students who drank very little increased their drinking after reading the message.

22.   Normative social influence involves conformity to a group's social norms. These norms are rules for acceptable:
   a)   behaviors.
   b)   values.
   c)   beliefs.
   d)   all the above.

23.   Baron et al. (1996) found that people are _____ likely to conform due to normative social influence when an unambiguous task is an _____ one.
   a)   less; important
   b)   more; important
   c)   less; unimportant
   d)   none of the above

24.   People learn what body type is considered attractive in their culture due to _____, and their attempts to create this ideal body type are an example of conformity due to _____.
   a)   contagion; normative social influence
   b)   informational social influence; normative social influence
   c)   informational social influence; mass psychogenic illness
   d)   normative social influence; informational social influence

25.   Resisting the normative social influence of a group is easier if one has built up _____ with the group.
   a)   reciprocity credits
   b)   conformity credits
   c)   influence credits
   d)   idiosyncrasy credits

26. Knowing that lying is wrong is a(n) _____ norm, while knowing that there are situations when people lie is a(n) _____ norm.
    a) social; injunctive
    b) descriptive; social
    c) injunctive; descriptive
    d) descriptive; injunctive

27. According to Kallgren et al. (2000), injunctive norms are:
    a) more likely to produce desirable behaviors than are descriptive norms.
    b) less likely to produce desirable behaviors than are descriptive norms.
    c) equally effective as descriptive norms in producing desirable behaviors.
    d) equally ineffective as descriptive norms in producing desirable behaviors.

28. Ramona held a relatively anti-environmental view in high school. Last year, she began attending a college where pro-environmental attitudes and people are the norm. Gradually, Ramona starts to express more pro-environmental views than in the past. Her new attitudes are likely due to:
    a) her authoritarian personality.
    b) the psychology of inevitability.
    c) having to compete with other women for dates.
    d) conformity processes.

29. According to research on informational social influence, which of the following would be the best way to help a child overcome his fear of escalators?
    a) carefully explain the safety features of escalators
    b) offer him a small reward for riding the escalator
    c) make him ride an escalator repeatedly until he no longer fears it
    d) have him watch as some of his classmates ride up and down the escalator.

30. Schachter's (1951) "Johnny Rocco" study demonstrated that:
    a) an individual disagreeing with the group consensus is generally ignored throughout the group discussion and decision-making process.
    b) groups greatly respect and value the contributions of those dissenting from the majority opinion.
    c) attitudes toward members of our groups are largely a function of their physical attractiveness.
    d) none of the above.

31. Ambiguity is the most crucial variable for determining how much people use each other as a source of information.
    a) True
    b) False

32. A social phenomenon in Japan is the *hikikomori*, in which teenagers (mostly male)
    a) withdraw from all social interaction and stay alone in their bedrooms in their parents' homes.
    b) conform to group norms and commit illegal acts.
    c) engage in dangerous behaviors because of normative social influence.
    d) engage in dangerous behaviors because of informational social influence.

33. Brain imaging research supports the idea that normative social influence occurs because people feel positive emotions when they stand up for their beliefs.
    a) True
    b) False

34. A heavy body type is considered the ideal female body in cultures with
    a) developing economies.
    b) food supplies that are infrequently scarce.
    c) food supplies that are frequently scarce.
    d) food supplies that are plentiful.

35. According to your text, Japanese women experience strong normative pressures to be
    a) intelligent.
    b) thin.
    c) generous.
    d) family-oriented.

36. Compared to the 1960s, the ideal male body is now much
    a) heavier.
    b) hairier.
    c) less muscular.
    d) more muscular.

37. In social impact theory, the strength of the group refers to
    a) how important the group is to us.
    b) how many people are in the group.
    c) whether or not we have any allies.
    d) how close the group is to us in space and time.

38. "In America, the squeaky wheel gets the grease. In Japan,
    a) the squeaky wheel gets oil."
    b) he who stands out, stands alone."
    c) the nail that stands out gets pounded down."
    d) the nail that stands out gets pulled out."

39. Replications of the Asch study conducted 25 to 40 years after the original in the Western countries like the United States and Britain, have found that conformity percentages have
    a) not changed.
    b) increased slightly.
    c) greatly increased.
    d) decreased.

40. Why was Milgram's study of obedience criticized?
    a) his sample size was too small
    b) for being unethical
    c) only men participated in the study
    d) the sample was not diverse enough

Chapter 8

SHORT ANSWER REVIEW

American mythology has celebrated the rugged (1) _____ (p. 213) in many ways, however sometimes people are conforming. Conformity refers to a change in one's behavior due to the real or imagined (2) _____ (p. 214) of other people.

Informational social influence is the influence of other people that leads us to conform because we see them as a source of (3) _____ (p. 215) to guide our behavior; we conform because we believe that others' interpretation of an (4) _____ (p. 215) situation is more correct than ours and will help us choose an appropriate course of action. An important feature of informational social influence is that it can lead to (5) _____ (p. 215), when people conform to the behavior of others because they genuinely believe that these other people are right rather than public compliance, when people conform to other people's behavior publicly without necessarily (6) _____ (p.216) in what they are doing or saying. In situations where it is important to be (7) _____ (p. 217), the tendency to conform to other people through informational social influence increases.

Using other people as a source of information can backfire when they are wrong about what is going on. Contagion occurs when emotions and behaviors spread (8) _____ (p. 218) throughout a group; one example is mass psychogenic illness. Mass psychogenic illness is the occurrence, in a group of people, of similar (9) _____ (p. 218) with no known physical cause. People are more likely to conform to informational social influence when the situation is ambiguous, a (10) _____ (p. 220), or if experts are present.

Normative social influence occurs when we change our behavior to match that of others in order to be (11) _____ (p. 222) and accepted by them. We conform to the group's social norms, implicit or explicit rules for acceptable behaviors, values, and attitudes. Normative social influence usually results in (12) _____ (p. 222) but not (13) _____ (p. 222) of other people's ideas and behaviors. In a series of classic studies, Solomon Asch found that people would conform, at least some of the time, to the obviously (14) _____ (p. 223) answer of the group. However, when it is important to be (15) _____ (p. 225), people are more likely to resist normative social influence and go against the group, giving the right answer. Resisting normative social influence can lead to ridicule, ostracism, and even rejection by the group. Normative social influence operates on many levels in social life: It influences our eating habits, hobbies, fashion, body image, and so on, and it promotes correct (polite) behavior in society.

Social impact theory specifies when normative social influence is most likely to occur by referring to the strength, immediacy, and (16) _____ (p. 232) of people in the group. We are more likely to conform when the group is one we care about, when the group members are unanimous in their thoughts or behaviors, when the group has three or more members, and when we are members of (17) _____ (p. 235) cultures. The very act of conforming (18) _____ (p. 233) to important groups most of the time can earn you the right to deviate occasionally without serious consequences. Conforming to a group over time earns you (19) _____ (p. 233), much like putting money in the bank. Under certain conditions (20) _____ (p. 236) can occur in which an individual (or small number of people) can influence the majority. The key is (21) _____ (p. 236) in the presentation of the minority viewpoint.

There is a way that we can use the tendency to conform to affect people's behavior for the common good. Social norms can be used to subtly induce people to conform to correct, socially approved behavior. A culture's social norms are of two types. (22) _____ (p. 238) have to do with what we think other people approve or disapprove of. Descriptive norms concern our perceptions of the way people (23) _____ (p. 238) in a given situation, regardless of whether the behavior is approved or disapproved of by others. Researchers have concluded that injunctive norms are (24) _____ (p. 239) than communicating descriptive norms in producing desirable behavior. The social norms technique has

213

been used for decreasing alcohol binge drinking on college campuses. Researchers have noted a major

problem with this approach: Sometimes, it (25) _____ (p. 239).

Obedience is a social norm that is valued in (26) _____ (p. 240) culture. You simply can't

have people doing whatever they want all the time—it would result in (27) _____

(p. 240). Obedience can have extremely serious and even tragic consequences. People will obey the

orders of an authority figure to hurt or even (28) _____ (p. 240) other human beings. In the most

famous series of studies in social psychology, (29) _____ (p. 241) examined obedience to authority

figures. He found chilling levels of obedience, to the point where a majority of participants administered

what they thought were near-lethal shocks to a fellow human being. Normative pressures make it difficult

for people to stop obeying authority figures. They wish to please the authority figure by doing a good job.

The obedience experiment was a confusing situation for participants, with competing, ambiguous

demands. Unclear about how to define what was going on, they followed the orders of the expert.

Participants conformed to the wrong norm: they continued to follow the (30) _____ (p. 245) norm

when it was no longer appropriate. It was difficult for them to abandon this norm for three reasons: the

fast-paced nature of the experiment; the fact that the shock levels increased in small increments; and their

loss of a feeling of personal (31) _____ (p. 246).

Milgram's studies were criticized as (32) _____ (p. 247) for several reasons. First, the study

involved (33) _____ (p. 247). Second, there was no true (34) _____ (p. 247) on the part of

the participants. Third, their role as Teacher caused them (35) _____ (p. 247); for many

participants, this occurred at a high level. Fourth, the participants were not told that they had the (36)

_____ (p. 247); in fact, the Experimenter told them the exact opposite. Fifth, the participants

experienced (37) _____ (p. 247). When the study ended, some of them had learned things about

themselves that they had not agreed to beforehand.

In 2006, Jerry M. Burger (2009) conducted the first obedience experiment in the United States in 30 years. In order to conduct this study under modern ethical guidelines, Burger had to make a number of changes to the procedures. Burger found (38) _____ (p. 248) in obedience rates between his participants and Milgram's.

ESSAY REVIEW

1. Give three reasons why participants obeyed the experimenter in Milgram's studies.

2. Compare and contrast informational and normative social influence. Why are they called "social" influences? What motives underlie each type of influence and what effects does each type have on our behavior?

3. Why is Asch's conformity study "one of the most dramatic illustrations of blindly going along with the group, even when the individual realizes that by doing so he turns his back on reality and truth?" (Moscovici, 1985, p. 349)

4. Describe Bibb Latané's (1981) social impact theory. What are the sources of social impact and what characteristics of these sources determine the amount of impact a group will have?

5. Discuss the reasons why Milgram's study on obedience has been criticized for being unethical.

EXIT TESTS

EXIT TEST 1

1. In America, we think of ourselves as a nation of rugged individualists. This cultural self-image has been shaped by
   a) the manner in which our nation was founded.
   b) our system of government.
   c) our society's historical experience with western expansion.
   d) all of the above.

2. A change in one's behavior due to the real or imagined influence of other people is the definition of
   a) social psychology.
   b) conformity.
   c) informational social influence.
   d) normative social influence.

3.   Earl goes to a local high school to see a play. He has never been to the high school before and
      does not know where the auditorium is, so he parks in the area of the parking lot where he sees a
      lot of other cars and enters the building through the same doors he sees other people entering.
      This is an example of
      a)   compliance.
      b)   obedience.
      c)   informational social influence.
      d)   normative social influence.

4.   In Sherif's experiment on conformity using the autokinetic effect, conformity lead to
      a)   private acceptance.
      b)   public compliance.
      c)   no change in true attitudes.
      d)   private disbelief.

5.   A variable that affects informational social influence is how important it is to the individual to be
      _____.
      a)   liked
      b)   accepted
      c)   perceived as intelligent
      d)   accurate

6.   _____ refers to the rapid spread of emotions or behaviors through a crowd.
      a)   Infectious affect
      b)   Contagion
      c)   Mass psychogenic illness
      d)   Infectious behavior

7.   Japanese psychologists state that many *hikikomori* were the victims of _____ before their
      withdrawal.
      a)   child abuse
      b)   sexual abuse
      c)   severe bullying
      d)   violent crimes

8.   Research on individuals who have been isolated for long periods of time indicates that being
      deprived of human contact is stressful and traumatic.
      a)   True
      b)   False

9.   Berns et al. (2005) conducted research using functional magnetic resonance imaging (fMRI) to
      examine the alterations in brain activity of research participants as they either normatively
      conformed to a group's judgment, or maintained their independence and disagreed with the
      group. When participants disagreed with the group and refused to give the wrong answer the
      _____ in the brain was activated.
      a)   visual/perceptual area
      b)   amygdala
      c)   right caudate nucleus
      d)   both b and c

10. In the study by Baron et al. (1996) in which normative social influence was triggered during an eyewitness identification task, conformity was _____ percent in the low-importance condition and _____ percent in the high-importance condition.
    a) 33; 16
    b) 76; 33
    c) 16; 33
    d) 33; 76

EXIT TEST 2

1. Schacter's (1951) "Johnny Rocco" study found that group members tried to convince the deviant to agree with them throughout the discussion until near the end, when communication with him dropped sharply.
   a) True
   b) False

2. Societal pressure to be very thin is associated with an increase in
   a) depression.
   b) suicide.
   c) eating disorders.
   d) personality disorders.

3. Research by Pope et al. (2000) showed that like women, men tend to have distorted body images (in other words, they do not see their bodies accurately).
   a) True
   b) False

4. A meta-analysis from eight of Milgram's studies indicated that when disobedience occurred, it was most likely to happen at the point when
   a) the Learner first says "ouch."
   b) the Learner screams that he has a heart condition.
   c) the Learner is completely silent.
   d) they got to 150 volts and the Learner is first heard yelling that he wants out and refuses to go on.

5. Social impact theory predicts that conformity will increase as
   a) strength and immediacy increase.
   b) strength and immediacy decrease.
   c) the number of people in the group decreases.
   d) desire to be correct increases.

6. In Asch's (1955) study on conformity, conformity was _____ percent when all the confederates gave the wrong answer and _____ percent when one confederate gave the right answer.
   a) 76; 33
   b) 33; 76
   c) 32; 6
   d) 6; 32

7. Conformity is most highly valued by which of the following groups?
    a) people in Lebanon
    b) the Bantu tribe of Zimbabwe
    c) people in Hong Kong
    d) people in Brazil

8. J. W. Berry compared the Inuit people of Baffin Island in Canada, a hunting and fishing society, to the Temne of Sierra Leone in Africa, a farming society, on an Asch-type conformity task. Berry found
    a) no differences between the two groups.
    b) the Temne showed a significant tendency to accept the suggestions of the group, while the Inuit almost completely disregarded them.
    c) the Inuit showed a significant tendency to accept the suggestions of the group, while the Temne almost completely disregarded them.
    d) the Temne only slightly more likely to conform than the Inuit.

9. Majorities often obtain public compliance because of _____, whereas, minorities often achieve private acceptance because of _____.
    a) normative social influence; informational social influence
    b) informational social influence; normative social influence
    c) idiosyncrasy credits; normative social influence
    d) normative social influence; idiosyncrasy credits

10. Descriptive norms motivate behavior by informing people about what is effective or adaptive behavior.
    a) True
    b) False

STUDY ACTIVITIES

1. Define conformity and identify two main reasons why we conform. Describe a time when you conformed to group behavior.

2. Describe when we are likely to conform to informational social influence. Differentiate between private acceptance and public compliance. Which one is more likely when we conform due to informational social influence? Describe a time when you conformed due to informational social influence.

3. Describe the relationship between conformity due to informational social influence and the importance of being accurate. Discuss what happens to rates of conformity when the situation is ambiguous and the importance of the task is high.

4. Define contagion and mass psychogenic illness. How do the mass media influence the likelihood of mass psychogenic illness?

5. What is the relationship between normative social influence and the importance of being accurate? What happens to rates of conformity when the situation is unambiguous and the importance of the task is high?

6. Describe how deviant group members are treated. Describe a personal experience in which you deviated from the group or someone else in your group deviated. How did the group treat the deviant?

7. Discuss the role social influence plays in women and men's body image. What do women and men in America learn that their bodies are supposed to be like? Describe how social influence has affected your own body image.

8. Discuss cross-cultural differences in conformity. Has conformity increased or decreased since the 1950s?

9. You are the Director of Alcohol Education for Saint Louis University. The goal for your department this year is to devise a campaign to decrease the amount of drinking done by your student population. How would you avoid the boomerang effect and devise a message that can successfully meet your goal?

10. What are important conditions for the occurrence of minority influence? How do minorities tend to influence majorities? What is more likely a result of minority influence, public compliance or private acceptance?

Chapter 8 Answers

Practice Test

1. A (pp. 215-216)
2. A (p. 216)
3. B (p. 222)
4. C (p. 224)
5. D (p. 233)
6. C (p. 235)
7. B (pp. 219-220)
8. D (p. 216)
9. D (p. 242)
10. C (pp. 243-245)
11. B (pp. 222; 215)
12. B (p. 219)
13. C (p. 223)
14. A (p. 232)
15. A (p. 235)
16. D (p. 230)
17. B (p. 236)
18. C (p. 244)
19. A (p. 246)
20. D (p. 218)
21. D (p. 239)
22. D (p. 221)
23. A (pp. 225-226)
24. B (p. 230)
25. D (p. 233)
26. C (p. 238)
27. A (p. 238)
28. D (p. 214)
29. D (p. 215)
30. D (p. 226)
31. A (p. 219)
32. A (p. 221)
33. B (pp. 224-225)
34. C (p. 228)
35. B (pp. 228-229)
36. D (p. 231)
37. A (p. 233)
38. C (p. 234)
39. D (p. 235)
40. B (p. 247)

Short Answer Review

1. individualist (p. 213)
2. influence (p. 214)
3. information (p. 215)
4. ambiguous (p. 215)
5. private acceptance (p. 215)
6. believing (p. 216)
7. accurate (p. 217)
8. rapidly (p. 218)
9. physical symptoms (p. 218)
10. crisis (p. 220)
11. liked (p. 222)
12. public compliance (p. 222)
13. private acceptance (p. 222)
14. wrong (p. 223)
15. accurate (p. 225)
16. number (p. 232)
17. collectivist (p. 235)
18. normatively (p. 233)
19. idiosyncrasy credits (p. 233)
20. minority influence (p. 236)
21. consistency (p. 236)
22. Injunctive norms (p. 238)
23. actually behave (p. 238)
24. more powerful (p. 239)
25. boomerangs (p. 239)
26. every (p. 240)
27. chaos (p. 240)
28. kill (p. 240)
29. Stanley Milgram (p. 241)
30. "obey authority" (p. 245)
31. responsibility (p. 246)
32. unethical (p. 247)
33. deception (p. 247)
34. informed consent (p. 247)
35. psychological distress (p. 247)
36. right to withdraw (p. 247)
37. inflicted insight (p. 247)
38. no significant difference (p. 248)

Essay Review

1. Your essay should include the following:
   - Participants complied with normative pressures to please the experimenter, used the experimenter as an expert source of information in an ambiguous situation, and got caught in a web of conflicting social norms that led them to follow an inappropriate "obey authority" norm. (pp. 243-246)
   - Self-justification also played a role. The participants' initial agreement to administer the first shock created internal pressure on them to continue to obey. As the participants

administered each successive level of shock, they had to justify it in their own minds. After they had justified a particular shock level, it became very difficult for them to decide on a place where they should draw the line and stop. (p. 246)
- The participants also experienced a loss of personal responsibility. (p. 246)

2. Your essay should include the following:
- Both forms of influence produce conformity to the behaviors of others. (pp. 215 & 222)
- Informational social influence, which produces private acceptance, is motivated by the need to be right. (p. 215)
- Normative social influence, which produces public compliance, is motivated by the need to be liked. (pp. 221-222)

3. Your essay should include the following:
- The unambiguous nature of Asch's line matching task required that participants blindly conform in order to go along. (pp.222-224)
- The demonstration is all the more dramatic because participants conformed in order to be liked by a group of strangers. (pp. 222-224)

4. Your essay on social impact theory should include the following:
- According to social impact theory, the impact that a group will have on an individual is a function of the group's strength, immediacy, and number. (p. 232)
- Strength refers to how important the group is to the individual. Normative pressures are stronger when they come from people whose friendship, love, and respect we cherish because there is a large cost to losing this love and respect. (p. 232)
- Immediacy refers to how close the group is to the individual in space and time during the influence attempt. Social impact theory predicts that conformity will increase as strength and immediacy increase. (p. 232)
- Number refers to how many people are in the group. Conformity increases as the number of people in the group increases up to four or five people, beyond that conformity does not increase much. (p. 232)

5. Your essay should include:
- First, the study involved deception. (p. 247)
- Second, there was no true informed consent on the part of participants. (p. 247)
- Third, their role as Teacher caused them psychological distress; for many participants, this occurred at a high level. (p. 247)
- Fourth, the participants were not told that they had the right to withdraw; in fact, the Experimenter told them the exact opposite. (p. 247)
- Fifth, the participants experienced inflicted insight. When the study ended, some of them had learned things about themselves that they had not agreed to beforehand. (p. 247)

Exit Test 1

1. D (p. 213)
2. B (p. 214)
3. C (p. 215)
4. A (p. 215)
5. D (p. 217)

6.   B (p. 218)
7.   C (p. 221)
8.   A (p. 221)
9.   D (p. 225)
10.   A (p. 225)

Exit Test 2

1.   A (p. 226)
2.   C (p. 230)
3.   B (p. 231)
4.   D (p. 247)
5.   A (p. 232)
6.   C (p. 233)
7.   B (p. 234)
8.   B (p. 235)
9.   A (p. 236)
10.   A (p. 238)

Study Activities

1.   Conformity is a change in one's behavior due to the real or imagined influence of other people. We conform because we believe that others' interpretation of an ambiguous situation is more accurate than ours and will help us choose an appropriate course of action. This is called informational social influence. We also conform to be liked and accepted. This is called normative social influence. (pp. 214-215 & 221-222)

2.   We are more likely to conform to informational social influence when the situation is ambiguous, when the situation is a crisis, and when other people are experts. Private acceptance is conforming to other people's behavior out of a genuine belief that what they are doing or saying is right. Public compliance is conforming to other people's behavior publicly without necessarily believing in what we are doing or saying. Informational social influence is more likely to result in private acceptance. (pp. 219-220, 215-216)

3.   When a situation is ambiguous and choosing the right answer is difficult, we look to others to give us the additional information we need. In such situations, the more important the decision is to us, the more we will rely on other people for information and guidance. Baron and his colleagues found that in a low-importance condition, participants conformed on 35% of critical trials and in the high-importance condition participants conformed on 51% of the critical trials. (pp. 216-217)

4.   Contagion refers to the rapid spread of emotions or behaviors through a crowd. Mass psychogenic illness is an occurrence, in a group of people, of similar physical symptoms with no known physical cause. The mass media play a powerful role in the dissemination of mass psychogenic illness because they allow information to spread quickly and efficiently to all segments of the population. (pp. 218-219)

5.   In situations of normative social influence, people are less likely to conform to an incorrect answer in a condition of high importance. Baron and colleagues found that in a low-importance condition participants conformed to the group's incorrect answer on 33% of the critical trials and in a high-importance condition conformity was 16%. (pp. 225-226)

6.   Deviant members can be ridiculed, punished, or even rejected by other group members. (p. 221)

7.   Informational social influence is the mechanism by which people learn what kind of body is considered attractive at a given time in their culture. Normative social influence describes attempts to create the ideal body through things like dieting and eating disorders. American society tells women they should be thin and men they should be muscular. (p. 230)

8.   Milgram found Norwegian participants conformed to a greater degree than French participants did. In another cross-cultural study, people in Lebanon, Hong Kong, and Brazil conformed to a similar extent (both to each other and to the American sample), whereas participants from the Bantu tribe of Zimbabwe conformed to a much greater degree. Although Japanese culture is more highly conforming than American culture, Japanese students are less likely to conform to complete strangers. In general however, participants in collectivistic cultures show higher rates of conformity on the line task than participants in individualistic cultures. In the last 25 to 40 years, conformity has been decreasing. (pp. 224-235)

9.   To avoid the boomerang effect, I would not use the statement that "Students at your school, on average, drink only X number of drinks a week" because students who already drink less than this may increase their drinking. Instead, I might use a message like, "Most students at your school have been decreasing the amount that they drink." (pp. 239-240)

10.   People with minority views must express the same view over time, and different members of the minority must agree with one another. Minorities exert their influence on the group via informational social influence. Minorities often achieve private acceptance because of informational social influence. (pp. 235-236)

CHAPTER 9

Group Processes: Influence in Social Groups

CHAPTER 9 OVERVIEW

This chapter discusses group processes and how individuals are influenced by the group. The first section of the chapter addresses the question "What is a group?" A **group** consists of three or more people who interact with each other and are interdependent in the sense that their needs and goals cause them to influence each other. The need to belong to groups may be innate. Groups also serve as a source of information about the social world and are an important part of our social identities. Groups can also help establish social norms, the explicit or implicit rules defining what is acceptable behavior.

Most groups have three to six members. If groups become too large, you cannot interact with all the members. Groups tend to consist of homogeneous members, in part because groups have social norms that people are expected to obey. Groups also have well-defined **social roles**, shared expectations about how people are supposed to behave. People can get so far into a social role that their personal identities and personalities get lost. Roles can be problematic when they are arbitrary or unfair. All societies, for example, have expectations about how people who occupy the roles of women and men should behave. These gender roles have changed over time. Changing roles cause conflict and they can actually affect our personalities. **Group cohesiveness**, qualities of a group that bind members together and promote liking between members, is another important property of groups that influences the group's performance.

The next section of this chapter examines the behavior of groups and individuals.. Research has compared the performance of people who are by themselves versus those in groups. When people's individual performance on a task can be evaluated, the mere presence of others leads to **social facilitation**: Their performance is enhanced on simple tasks, but impaired on complex tasks. When people's individual efforts cannot be evaluated, the mere presence of others leads to **social loafing**: Performance is impaired on simple tasks, but enhanced on complex tasks.

The next section of the chapter describes gender and cultural differences in social loafing. Social loafing is more prevalent among men than women, and more prevalent in Western than Asian cultures.

The mere presence of others can also lead to **deindividuation**, which is the loosening of normal constraints on behavior when people are in crowds, leading to an increase in impulsive and deviant acts. Deindividuation makes people feel less accountable for their actions, because it reduces the likelihood that any individual will be singled out and blamed. Deindividuation also increases obedience to group norms.

The next part of the chapter examines the process and quality of group decisions. Behavior research has compared how people make decisions when they are by themselves versus in groups. Groups make better decisions than individuals if they are good at pooling ideas and listening to the expert members of the group. Often, however, **process loss** occurs, whereby any aspect of group interaction inhibits good decision making. For example, groups often focus on the information they have in common and fail to share unique information. Unshared information is more likely to be brought up later in a discussion, suggesting that group discussions should last long enough to get beyond what everyone already knows. Groups can have **transactive memory**, a combined memory of two people that is more efficient than the memory of either individual. Tightly knit, cohesive groups are also prone to **groupthink**, which occurs when maintaining group cohesiveness and solidarity becomes more important than considering the facts in a realistic manner. Groupthink causes people to implement an inferior decision-making process. A wise leader can avoid the groupthink trap by remaining impartial, seeking outside opinions, creating subgroups, and seeking anonymous opinions.

Group polarization is the tendency for groups to make more decisions that are more extreme than the initial inclinations of its members; these group decisions can be more risky or more cautious, depending on which attitude is valued in the group. This occurs for two main reasons. According to the persuasive arguments interpretation, all individuals bring to the group a set of arguments, some of which other individuals have not considered, supporting their initial recommendation. Another person might not have considered this possibility; thus he or she becomes more conservative as well. According to the social comparison interpretation, when people discuss an issue in a group, they first check out how everyone else feels. To be liked, many people then take a position that is similar to everyone else's but a little more extreme.

A critical question is the role of the leader in group decision making. There is little support for the **great person theory**, which argues that good leadership is a matter of having the right personality traits. Leaders do adopt specific kinds of leadership styles, such as transactional or transformational. **Transactional leaders** set clear, short-term goals and reward people who meet them. **Transformational leaders** inspire followers to focus on common, long-term goals. Leadership effectiveness is a function of both the kind of person a leader is and the nature of the work situation. The **contingency theory of leadership** states that leadership effectiveness depends both on how task-oriented or relationship-oriented the leader is and on the amount of control and influence the leader has over the group. A **task-oriented leader** is concerned more with getting the job done than with workers' feelings and relationships. A **relationship-oriented leader** is concerned primarily with workers' feelings and relationships.

There is a double bind for women leaders: If they conform to societal expectations about how they ought to behave, by being warm and communal, they are often perceived as having low leadership potential. If they succeed in attaining a leadership position and act in ways that leaders are expected to act—namely, in agentic, forceful ways—they are often perceived negatively for not "acting like a woman should."

The final section of the chapter discusses conflict and cooperation. Research has examined how people resolve conflicts when they have incompatible goals. **Social dilemmas** occur when the most beneficial action for an individual will, if chosen by most people, have harmful effects on everyone. A commonly studied social dilemma is the *prisoner's dilemma*, in which two people must decide whether to look out for only their own interests or for their partner's interests as well. Creating trust is crucial in solving this kind of conflict. To increase cooperation, you can try the **tit-for-tat strategy**, which is a way of encouraging cooperation by at first acting cooperatively but then always responding the way your opponent did (cooperatively or competitively) on the previous trial. One type of social dilemma that has been studied is a **public goods dilemma**—this occurs when individuals must contribute to a common pool to maintain the public good, such as paying taxes for public schools. It is to each individual's advantage to pay as little as possible, but if everyone adopts this strategy, everyone suffers. The **commons dilemma** is a situation in which everyone takes from a common pool of goods that will replenish itself if used in moderation but will disappear if overused. Examples of this include the use of limited resources such as water and energy.

Research has found that using threats tends to escalate rather than resolve conflicts. Communication resolves conflict only when it promotes trust. **Negotiation** is a form of communication between opposing sides in a conflict in which offers and counteroffers are made and a solution occurs only when both parties agree. When two sides are negotiating and bargaining it is important to look for an **integrative solution**, whereby each side concedes the most on issues that are unimportant to it, but very important to its adversary.

CHAPTER 9 OUTLINE

I. What Is a Group?
• A **group** is three or more people who are interacting with each other and are interdependent, in the sense that to fulfill their needs and goals, they must rely on each other.

A. Why Do People Join Groups?
• Baumeister and Leary (1995) argue that people join groups because in our evolutionary past, there was a substantial survival advantage to establishing bonds with other people. Consequently, the need to belong may be innate and is present in all societies.
• Groups have many benefits, including providing information, helping us define our identity, and establishing social norms for behavior.

B. The Composition and Functions of Groups
• Most social groups range in size from three to six members.
• Members of a group tend to be alike in terms of age, sex, beliefs, and opinions. This is both because people are attracted to similar others and because groups operate in ways that encourage similarity among members.
1. Social Norms
• Groups have social norms and the consequences of violating these are pressure to conform and ultimately, rejection.
2. Social Roles
• Groups also often have well-defined **roles**, or shared expectations in a group about how particular people are supposed to behave. Roles facilitate social interaction.
• Roles also may have a cost. First, adopting a role can lead people to temporarily lose their personal identities. For example, Zimbardo and his colleagues set up a mock prison in the basement of the Stanford psychology department. They selected normal, healthy young men and randomly assigned them to be prisoners or guards. Many of the guards became aggressive and the prisoners passive and even severely anxious and depressed, even though all knew the prison was only make-believe.
3. Prison Abuse at Abu Gharib
• Phillip Zimbardo has analyzed the similarities between the abuse at Abu Ghraib prison and the prison study he conducted 30 years earlier. The military guards at Abu Ghraib were under tremendous stress, had received little supervision, and were asked to set their own rules for interrogation.
4. Gender Roles
• In many cultures, women's roles are constrained to that of wife and mother. In cultures where women's status has improved, women may experience conflict between their new job roles and the traditional roles of wife and mother that they are still expected to perform, often without assistance from their husband. A study by Twenge, (2001) has shown how women's ratings of their own assertiveness seem to mirror societal trends. From the results of the study, Twenge concluded that society at large appears to be a powerful determinant of how women view themselves (see Figure 9.1).
5. Group Cohesiveness
• **Group cohesiveness** is the qualities of a group that bind members together and promote liking between group members.
• The more cohesive a group is, the more its members are likely to stay in the group, participate in group activities, and recruit new members.
• Cohesiveness, however, can sometimes interfere with task performance (see section on decision making).

Chapter 9

II. Group and Individuals' Behaviors

A. Social Facilitation: When the Presence of Others Energizes Us
• Zajonc (1969) did a study with cockroaches that demonstrated that the roaches ran a simple maze faster when they were in the presence of an audience of other roaches than when they were alone (Figure 9.2).
• The mere presence of others improves performance on simple, well-learned tasks. For example, Triplett (1898), in one of the first social psychology experiments, showed that children wound up a fishing reel more quickly when in the presence of others than alone.

1. Simple versus Difficult Tasks
• In Zajonc's roach experiment, the roaches ran a complex maze more slowly in the presence of others than alone.
• Many other studies show that simple tasks are performed more quickly in the presence of others, but complex tasks are performed more slowly.

2. Arousal and Dominant Response
• Zajonc developed a theory of social facilitation to explain the mere presence effect: he hypothesized that the presence of others increases physiological arousal which facilitates dominant, well-learned responses, but inhibits performance on more difficult tasks.
• **Social facilitation** is the tendency for people to do better on simple tasks and worse on complex ones in the presence of others when their individual performance can be evaluated (see Figure 9.3).

3. Why the Presence of Others Causes Arousal
• Three theories try to explain why the presence of others leads to arousal.
• The first theory suggests that the presence of others makes us more alert; this theory explains both human and cockroach behavior.
• The second theory suggests that the presence of others makes us concerned for what others think of us (evaluation apprehension); according to this theory it is only others who evaluate us who should elicit the effect.
• The third theory suggests that others distract us; according to this theory, any distraction (e.g., lights or noise) should lead to social facilitation. Baron (1986) finds some support for this proposition.

B. Social Loafing: When the Presence of Others Relaxes Us
• In other social situations, being around others means that our individual efforts are less easily observed and merge to be part of the group. In these situations, the presence of others relaxes us, and **social loafing** occurs, in which performance is impaired on simple tasks but enhanced on complex ones when individual performance cannot be evaluated.
• Ringelmann (1913) found that when a group of men pulled on a rope, each individual exerted less effort than when he did it alone; Latané et al. (1979) replicated the effect and named it social loafing.

III. Gender and Cultural Differences in Social Loafing: Who Slacks Off the Most?
• Karau & Williams (1993), in a review of social loafing studies, found that the tendency to loaf is stronger in men than in women. This may be because women are more collectivist and men more individualist in orientation. Similarly, the tendency to loaf is stronger in Western than in Asian cultures.
• To summarize, if performance can be individually evaluated, the presence of others will be arousing, and will improve performance on simple tasks, but interfere with performance on complex tasks (social facilitation). If performance cannot be individually evaluated, the presence of others will be relaxing and will decrease performance on simple tasks and improve it on complex ones (social loafing) (see Figure 9.3). These findings suggest how managers should organize workers.

A. Deindividuation: Getting Lost in the Crowd

• **Deindividuation** is the feeling of anonymity and reduced sense of ourselves as individuals that can occur when people are in groups and/or anonymous; it leads to a loosening of normal constraints on behavior and an increase in impulsive and deviant acts.

• Mullen (1986) content analyzed news reports of lynchings in the U.S. from 1899-1946 and found that the larger the mob, the greater the savagery with which they killed their victims. Similarly, Watson (1973) found that cultures in which warriors hid their identities before going to fight were significantly more likely to kill, torture, or mutilate captives than cultures in which warriors did not hide their identities.

1. Deindividuation Makes People Feel Less Accountable

• One cause of this increase in impulsive, deviant behavior is making people feel less accountable for their actions, because it is less likely that any individual will be singled out and blamed.

2. Deindividuation Increases Obedience to Group Norms

• Another explanation of deindividuation is that it increases obedience to group norms. Whether or not deindividuation leads to positive or negative behavior depends on what the situation encourages. If a person has been angered, deindividuation will increase aggression; if a person is at a party with lots of good food, deindividuation will increase the amount the person eats (i.e., deindividuation leads to disinhibition of behavior).

3. Deindividuation in Cyberspace

• Before blogs and Internet chat rooms became popular, angry readers could have written letters to the editor or vented their feelings to their coworkers at the water cooler. The Internet has provided new ways in which people can communicate with each other anonymously and just as research on deindividuation predicts, in these settings people often feel free to say things that they would never dream of saying if they could be identified.

IV. Group Decisions: Are Two (or More) Heads Better Than One?

• Most important decisions in the world are made by groups, because it is assumed that groups make better decisions than individuals (e.g., juries, government and corporate decisions).

• In general, groups do better than individuals do if they rely on the person with the most expertise and are stimulated by each other's comments; however, groups can sometimes make worse decisions than individuals can.

A. Process Loss: When Group Interactions Inhibit Good Problem Solving

• **Process loss** is any aspect of group interaction that inhibits good problem solving. It can occur because groups do not try hard enough to find out who is the most competent member, because the most competent member has low status, or because the most competent member cannot break from normative conformity (in other words, cannot stand against the pressures that discourage disagreement with the group). It can also occur because of communication problems within the group.

1. Failure to Share Unique Information

• Another reason groups can fail to outperform individuals is that group members sometimes fail to share unique information (that only they know) with each other.

• Stasser and Titus (1985) gave group members either the same information about political candidates (8 positive and 4 negative attributes), or different packets of information (each person received only 2 of the 8 positive attributes, along with the same 4 negative attributes); groups who received unshared information focused on the shared information, leading them to be less likely to choose the candidate with the greater number of positive attributes (Figure 9.4).

• Kelly and Karau (1999) found that groups focus more on unshared information if it is especially diagnostic. However, facts that don't seem relevant at first can seem diagnostic when combined with other unshared facts.

• Unshared information is more likely to be brought up later in time, suggesting that group

discussions need to last long enough to get beyond what everyone already knows.
• Alternatively, individuals in a group could be given different assignments, so that they know that they alone are responsible for a particular type of information.
• **Transactive memory** occurs when the combined memory of two people is greater than each of their individual memories (Wegner, 1995).

2. Groupthink: Many Heads, One Mind
• **Groupthink** is a kind of thinking in which maintaining group cohesiveness and solidarity is more important than considering the facts in a realistic manner (see Figure 9.5).
• According to Janis's theory of groupthink, it is most likely to occur when a group is highly cohesive, isolated from contrary opinions, ruled by a directive leader who makes his or her wishes known, and using poor decision-making procedures in a high stress situation.
• The symptoms of groupthink include (a) an illusion of invulnerability; (b) a belief in the moral correctness of the group; (c) stereotyped views of the outgroup; (d) self-censorship; (e) direct pressure on dissenters to conform; often by (f) mindguards, appointed to protect the leader from contrary viewpoints, leading to (g) an illusion of unanimity
• The consequence of groupthink is defective decision making, characterized by poor information search, particularly an incomplete survey of alternative solutions and failure to examine the risks of the favored alternative, and a failure to develop contingency plans.
• Janis applied his theory to many real life situations, including the Bay of Pigs fiasco (described at the beginning of the chapter) and the Challenger explosion.

3. Avoiding the Groupthink Trap
• Groupthink can be avoided by (a) leaders that strive to remain impartial; (b) soliciting outside opinion; (c) breaking the group into subgroups that meet separately and then convene; and (d) the use of secret ballots.

B. Group Polarization: Going to Extremes
• The Choice Dilemmas Questionnaire (CDQ; Kogan & Wallach, 1964) is used to study group decision making. Many of the original studies found that groups made riskier decisions than individuals, a phenomenon known as the *risky shift*. Later research found that the risky shift occurs only if individuals' initial predispositions were to take risks; if the initial predisposition was conservative, the groups made even more conservative decisions than individuals. The finding that groups make more extreme decisions, in the direction of people's initial judgments, is known as **group polarization**.
• The *persuasive arguments interpretation* says that the phenomenon occurs because individuals present their most persuasive arguments favoring their initial judgments, and that individuals will thereby be confronted with arguments they had not previously considered.
• The *social comparison interpretation* for group polarization says that, in order to be liked, people first check out how everyone else feels and then take a position similar to everyone else's but a little more extreme.
• Both explanations have received research support.

C. Leadership in Groups
• Much research has focused on what makes a good group leader. The **great person theory** states that certain key personality traits make a person a good leader, regardless of the situation facing the leader.

1. Leadership and Personality
• Research indicates that personality traits are surprisingly unrelated to leadership. However, certain attributes do display a modest association with leadership success. These attributes are: intelligence, motivation for power, charisma and social skills, adaptability, and confidence in leadership abilities.

- Simonton (1987, 1992) found that only height, family size, and number of books published before taking office correlated with presidential effectiveness as rated by historians.

2. Leadership Styles

- Rather than deeming personality traits unimportant, social psychologists suggest that good leadership depends on a person's having the right personality characteristics for the situation.

3. The Right Person in the Right Situation

- Fiedler's **contingency theory of leadership** states that leadership effectiveness depends both on how task-oriented or relationship-oriented the leader is and on the amount of control and influence the leader has over the group. A **task-oriented leader** is concerned primarily with getting the job done and less so with the feelings of and relationships between the workers; these leaders are most effective in situations that are either "high-control" (good relations with subordinates and clearly defined work) or "low-control" (poor relations with subordinates and work that is not clearly defined). A **relationship-oriented leader** is concerned primarily with the feelings of and relationships between the workers; these leaders are most effective in situations where situational control is moderate (Figure 9.6). Tests of the theory have generally been supportive.

4. Gender and Leadership

- Eagly and her colleagues examined hundreds of studies and found that, consistent with the stereotype, women do tend to lead more democratically than men, possibly because they have better interpersonal skills. Women thus tend to be better leaders in jobs that require interpersonal skills and men tend to be better leaders in jobs that require the ability to direct and control people. However, the gender differences reported are small.

V. Conflict and Cooperation

- Often people in groups have incompatible goals, leading to conflict.
- Conflicts can be resolved peaceably, but often erupt into open hostilities.

A. Social Dilemmas

- Social **dilemmas** are conflicts in which the most beneficial action for an individual will, if chosen by most people, have harmful effects on everyone.
- Many disciplines study mixed motive conflicts; social psychology is unique in trying to study conflict experimentally. The most common technique is a game called the Prisoner's Dilemma Game (PDG) (see the Try-It! box). Each person must independently decide whether to cooperate or compete; both persons' outcomes depend on the pattern of choice. The joint pattern of choice, particularly in situations where the participants don't trust each other, leads to a mutual choice to compete and poor outcomes for both. The lack of trust and the subsequent poor outcomes often lead to an escalation of conflict. This laboratory model fits real life conflicts between countries in an arms race and couples who are divorcing.

1. Increasing Cooperation in the Prisoner's Dilemma

- Under certain conditions, both partners will make the cooperative choice, ensuring that both sides end up with a positive outcome, if: people are playing the game with a friend, expect to interact with the person in the future, or are part of a collectivist culture.
- The **tit-for-tat strategy** is a way of encouraging cooperation by first acting cooperatively, but then always responding the way the opponent did on the previous trial; it is usually effective in encouraging cooperation.
- Schopler and Insko (1999) found that two individuals who play the Prisoner's Dilemma are more cooperative than two groups who play the same game.

2. Other Kinds of Social Dilemmas

- A **public goods dilemma** is a social dilemma in which individuals must contribute to a common pool in order to maintain the public good (e.g., taxes or the blood supply).
- The **commons dilemma** (Hardin, 1968) is a social dilemma in which everyone takes from a

common pool of goods that will replenish itself if used in moderation but which will disappear if overused (e.g., resources such as water and energy).

B. Using Threats to Resolve Conflict
• Many people are tempted to use threats to get the other person to comply with their wishes.
• A classic series of studies by Deutsch and Krauss (1960, 1962) indicate that threats are not an effective way to reduce conflict. The studies used a "trucking game" (Figure 9.7). Participants play the head of a trucking company. In order to earn money, they have to drive their truck from the starting point to their destination as quickly as possible. The quickest route is a one-lane road, but both trucks cannot travel on this road at the same time. In some versions, participants were given gates they could use to block their opponent's progress on this road. When one side had a gate, the total amount of money earned was less than when there were no gates, and when both sides had gates, the amount of money earned was even less.(Figure 9.8)

C. Effects of Communication
• Variations of the Deutsch and Krauss study allowed the participants to communicate over an intercom. When communicating was participants' choice, few chose to and outcomes were poor. When the researchers required the participants to communicate on every trial, losses were reduced somewhat in the unilateral threat condition but not the bilateral threat condition; the other two conditions were unaffected. Overall, requiring people to communicate did not raise profits much, because people tended to use the intercom to convey threats.
• In a final series of studies, Krauss and Deutsch specifically instructed people how to communicate fairly; under these conditions, communication increased the amount of money both sides won, because it fostered trust.

D. Negotiation and Bargaining
• The laboratory studies discussed so far limit people's options, compared to those they have in real-life conflicts. **Negotiation** is a form of communication between opposing sides in a conflict in which offers and counteroffers are made, and a solution occurs only when both parties agree. One limit to successful negotiations is that people often assume they are locked in a conflict in which only one person can come out ahead, and they don't realize that solutions favorable to both sides may be available. **Integrative solutions** to conflict have the parties make trade-offs on issues according to their different interests; each side concedes the most on issues that are unimportant to it, but important to the other side.
• Communication is only helpful if it allows parties to develop trust. It appears that this is easier in face-to-face negotiations than in electronic communication such as email, instant messaging, text messaging, and video-conferencing.

LEARNING OBJECTIVES

After reading Chapter 9, you should be able to do the following:

1. Provide a definition of groups and state reasons why people join groups. Define social norms and social roles, including gender roles, and the function they serve in groups. Identify two possible costs to social roles and discuss their implications. Discuss the influence of group cohesiveness on group processes. (pp. 254-258)
2. Describe the relationship between social facilitation and the mere presence of others. Explain why the presence of others causes arousal. Discuss the effects of social facilitation on the performance of simple and complex tasks. (pp. 258-261)

3.   Describe social loafing and discuss why it occurs. Identify how the setting in which social loafing occurs is different from the setting in which social facilitation occurs. Identify factors that increase and decrease social loafing. (p. 262)

4.   Identify gender and cultural differences in the occurrence of social loafing. Explain these differences. (p. 263)

5.   Identify the two factors important for predicting the effects of the presence of others on performance. (p. 263)

6.   Define deindividuation and describe the effects of deindividuation on behavior. Identify conditions that increase deindividuation. Describe the conditions that determine whether deindividuation will lead to positive or negative behaviors. (pp. 263-265)

7.   Identify sources of process loss in groups. Describe how group members handle unique information during discussion. Identify how groups could improve the sharing of information. Define transactive memory. (pp. 265-267)

8.   Identify the antecedents, symptoms, and consequences of groupthink. Discuss historical examples of groupthink. Identify measures that can be taken to avoid groupthink. (pp. 267-270)

9.   Describe the effects of group discussion on attitudes that are initially risky or initially cautious. Define group polarization. Describe the cognitive and motivational explanations of group polarization. Describe Brown's culture-value theory and discuss support for this theory. (pp. 271-273)

10.   Describe the relationship between the great person theory and great leadership. Identify the personality traits and variables that are related to leadership. Explain why a social psychologist would claim that personality is not a good predictor of leadership. (pp. 273-274)

11.   Contrast the great person theory with the contingency theory of leadership. Identify the two types of leaders according to the contingency theory. Discuss the situational conditions that lead to leadership effectiveness of each type of leader. (p. 274)

12.   Discuss the relationship between gender and leadership. Discuss research findings on this topic. (pp. 275-276)

13.   Discuss the history of conflict among humans and why it is important to study ways to foster peaceful conflict resolution. Define a social dilemma. Describe the prisoner's dilemma. Define the tit-for-tat strategy. Identify the most effective strategies when playing with a cooperative opponent versus a competitive one. (pp. 276-279)

14.   Define both a public goods dilemma and the commons dilemma. Give examples of public goods dilemmas and commons dilemmas. (p. 279)

15.   Discuss the effects of using threats to resolve conflicts. Define negotiation. Identify effective negotiation strategies. Describe an integrative solution. Identify obstacles to finding integrative solutions. (pp. 279-282)

KEY TERMS

1. _____ Three or more people who interact and are interdependent in the sense that their needs and goals cause them to influence each other. (p. 254)

2. _____ Shared expectations in a group about how particular people are supposed to behave. (p. 255)

3. _____ Qualities of a group that bind members together and promote liking between members. (p. 258)

4. _____ The tendency for people to do better on simple tasks and worse on complex tasks when they are in the presence of others and their individual performance can be evaluated. (p. 260)

5. _____ The tendency for people to relax when they are in the presence of others and their individual performance cannot be evaluated, such that they do worse on simple tasks but better on complex tasks. (p. 262)

6. _____ The loosening of normal constraints on behavior when people can't be identified (such as when they are in a crowd). (p. 263)

7. _____ Any aspect of group interaction that inhibits good problem solving. (p. 266)

8. _____ The combined memory of two people that is more efficient than the memory of either individual. (p. 267)

9. _____ A kind of thinking in which maintaining group cohesiveness and solidarity is more important than considering the facts in a realistic manner. (p. 267)

10. _____ The tendency for groups to make decisions that are more extreme than the initial inclinations of its members. (p. 273)

11. _____ The idea that certain key personality traits make a person a good leader, regardless of the situation. (p. 273)

12. _____ Leaders who set clear, short-term goals and reward people who meet them. (p. 274)

13. _____ Leaders who inspire followers to focus on common, long-term goals. (p. 274)

14. _____ The idea that leadership effectiveness depends both on how task- oriented or relationship-oriented the leader is and on the amount of control and influence the leader has over the group. (p. 274)

15. _____ A leader who is concerned more with getting the job done than with workers' feelings and relationships. (p. 274)

16. _____ A leader who is concerned primarily with workers' feelings and relationships. (p. 274)

17. _____ A conflict in which the most beneficial action for an individual will, if chosen by most people, have harmful effects on everyone. (p. 277)

18. _____ A means of encouraging cooperation by at first acting cooperatively but then always responding the way your opponent did (cooperatively or competitively) on the previous trial. (p. 278)

19. _____ A social dilemma in which individuals must contribute to a common pool in order to maintain the public good. (p. 279)

20. _____ A social dilemma in which everyone takes from a common pool of goods that will replenish itself if used in moderation but will disappear if overused. (p. 279)

21. _____ A form of communication between opposing sides in a conflict in which offers and counteroffers are made and a solution occurs only when both parties agree. (p. 281)

22. _____ A solution to a conflict whereby the parties make trade-offs on issues according to their different interests; each side concedes the most on issues that are unimportant to it but important to the other side. (p. 282)

GUIDED REVIEW

PRACTICE TEST

1. A group can be defined as _____ or more people who are _____, that is their needs and goals lead them to influence one another.
   a) one; dependent
   b) two; interdependent
   c) one; interdependent
   d) three; interdependent

2. If you are asked to perform in the presence of others, you are likely to feel aroused as a result of:
   a) anticipatory arousal.
   b) increased interpersonal conflict.
   c) increased alertness and evaluation apprehension.
   d) disinhibition.

3. Compared to individuals, members of social loafing groups perform _____ on simple tasks and _____ on complex tasks.
   a) better; worse
   b) worse; better
   c) worse; worse
   d) better; better

4. To maximize the performance of seasoned workers performing familiar tasks at your production plant, you should create groups that foster:
   a) social loafing.
   b) social facilitation.
   c) deindividuation.
   d) conflict.

5. What determines whether deindividuation will lead to positive or negative behaviors?
    a) whether deindividuation is caused by decreased accountability or decreased self-awareness
    b) whether we have committed more prosocial or antisocial acts in the past
    c) whether our inhibitions prevent us from performing positive or negative behaviors outside the group
    d) whether the situation encourages positive or negative behaviors

6. Shared expectations that a group has about how people are supposed to act are called social ____, while shared expectations about how certain people in a group should behave are called social

    ____.
    a) groups; norms
    b) norms; rules
    c) rules; norms
    d) norms; roles

7. Groups that strengthen the initial inclinations of their members, pushing their members' decisions to the extreme, exhibit:
    a) the risky shift.
    b) social facilitation.
    c) process loss.
    d) group polarization.

8. A type of social dilemma whereby individuals must contribute to a common pool of resources to ensure the benefit of all is a:
    a) process dilemma.
    b) public goods dilemma.
    c) common goods dilemma.
    d) commons dilemma.

9. Integrative solutions to conflicts are most likely to be reached if:
    a) opponents find out which issues being negotiated are most important to each party.
    b) opponents compromise on all issues being negotiated.
    c) negotiations are arbitrated by a neutral third party.
    d) communication between opponents is limited to a structured exchange of ideas.

10. Zajonc et al. (1969) observed that cockroaches took longer to reach a dark box at the end of a maze when other cockroaches were present if:
    a) the maze was a simple one.
    b) the maze was a complex one.
    c) the other cockroaches first modeled the escape behavior.
    d) the other cockroaches served as a source of evaluation.

11. In order to know whether the presence of others will improve a group member's performance or hinder it, you need to know:
   a) whether the individual can be evaluated and whether the task is simple or complex.
   b) whether group members interact and whether the goals of group members conflict.
   c) whether the members of the group are disposed to be lazy and whether the group will be tightly organized.
   d) how much communication among members is possible and how well members of the group get along.

12. A social dilemma is a situation that may result in a conflict because:
   a) people work harder in groups than they do when working alone.
   b) individuals may seek to maximize personal gain at the expense of others.
   c) process loss results when individuals are in a social situation.
   d) individuals make better decisions than groups do.

13. European soccer fans attacking each other and hysterical fans at rock concerts trampling one another to death demonstrate the horrendous consequences of:
   a) social facilitation.
   b) group polarization.
   c) deindividuation.
   d) interpersonal conflict.

14. Parnell is a member of a group of people who feel very connected to each other. The characteristics of a group that tie members together and foster liking are high in his group. Parnell's group is most likely high in:
   a) group cohesiveness.
   b) social cohesion.
   c) group coercion.
   d) social facilitation.

15. Having members of a group perform an interesting and complex task and making their outputs identifiable are ways to decrease:
   a) social facilitation.
   b) social loafing.
   c) deindividuation.
   d) group polarization.

16. Which of the following proposes that leadership effectiveness can be predicted by traits that people may or may not possess?
   a) the contingency theory of leadership
   b) the integrative theory of leadership
   c) the great person theory of leadership
   d) the process theory of leadership

17. In which situations are task-oriented leaders more effective than relationship-oriented leaders?
   a) when situational control is moderate
   b) when workers get along fairly well
   c) when the task is somewhat structured
   d) when situational control is high

18.   By making it clear that he favored the Bay of Pigs invasion and by asking his advisors to consider only how the invasion should be executed, Kennedy contributed to which of the following antecedents of groupthink?
    a)   group cohesiveness
    b)   directive leadership
    c)   group isolation
    d)   high stress

19.   According to Burnstein and Vinokur's (1977) persuasive arguments interpretation, group polarization results because:
    a)   individuals bring to the group strong and novel arguments supporting their initial inclinations.
    b)   group discussion reveals the position that the group values and individuals adopt this position in order to be liked.
    c)   individuals recognize that Western culture values risk over caution.
    d)   groups actively censor opinions that deviate from those valued by our culture.

20.   Initially choosing a cooperative response, and then matching your opponent's response on subsequent trials is an effective strategy in mixed-motive games called:
    a)   dog-eat-dog.
    b)   acquiescence.
    c)   integrative solutions.
    d)   tit-for-tat.

21.   When groups don't try hard enough to discover who their most competent member is, when the most competent member finds it hard to voice disagreement, or when a group suffers from communication problems, the result may be:
    a)   social facilitation.
    b)   social dilemma.
    c)   deindividuation.
    d)   process loss.

22.   Ellen is in charge of remembering when to make doctor and dentist appointments for the family. Her partner is responsible for coordinating the family's social schedule. Each partner is obligated to remember certain information thereby increasing the total amount of information remembered. This is referred to as:
    a)   process gain.
    b)   relational memory.
    c)   transactive memory.
    d)   constructive memory.

23.   How effective a leader is depends on being the right person in the appropriate situation according to the _____ theory of leadership.
    a)   contingency
    b)   great person
    c)   relationship
    d)   task

24. Eagly and her colleagues have found that _____ tend to be autocratic leaders and _____ tend to be democratic leaders.
    a) male leaders; female leaders
    b) female leaders; male leaders
    c) older leaders; younger leaders
    d) none of the above

25. According to research discussed in the text, when you study for an exam and learn new material, you should do so
    a) while listening to your MP3 player.
    b) in a room in which the temperature is slightly cool so you will not become sleepy.
    c) by yourself.
    d) with other students who are studying for the same exam.

26. Contemporary examples of the use of water and energy resources are _____ dilemmas.
    a) public goods
    b) commons
    c) ration
    d) societal

27. A form of communication between opposing sides in a conflict in which offers and counteroffers are made and a solution is not reached until both parties agree is called:
    a) collective bargaining.
    b) tit-for-tat strategy.
    c) bartering.
    d) negotiation.

28. Mrs. Perez, the owner of a small business, needs her employees to devise a plan to beat their competitors. Since she is aware of the groupthink phenomenon, she would most likely do which of the following to avoid groupthink?
    a) keep the members of the group the same and not introduce anyone new into the group
    b) clearly express her views to the group at the beginning of the discussion
    c) have the group consider as many options as they can
    d) have the group discuss the problem quickly since last year was so successful

29. Marcy studied a very long time for the final exam in her psychology class. She knows the material extremely well and can recall it easily. The final is a departmental exam and Marcy can choose in which classroom she takes the test. When she enters one classroom on the day of the test she finds it crowded. Another classroom across the hall has only a few students in it and is not crowded. Marcy should _____ to improve her performance on the test.
    a) take her test in a classroom where a noisy study group is practicing for an exam
    b) take her test in an empty classroom
    c) take her test in the crowded classroom
    d) take her test in the classroom that is not crowded

30.   Zimbardo and colleagues (Haney, Banks, & Zimbardo, 1973) "Stanford Prison study" demonstrated:
        a)   the power that social roles have on individuals' behavior.
        b)   that personality factors are the most significant predictors of cruel and abusive behavior among prison guards.
        c)   that personality factors are the most significant predictors of anxiety and depression among inmates.
        d)   groups, such as juries and parole boards, typically are subject to groupthink and other types of process loss.

31.   Which of the following meets the definition of a group given in your text?
        a)   three people waiting at a bus stop
        b)   four students working together on a required group presentation for their social psychology class
        c)   five people waiting in line at a bank
        d)   six people who all work in the same office building

32.   Zimbardo attributes the abuse of prisoners in the Abu Ghraib prison in Iraq to
        a)   social facilitation.
        b)   social loafing.
        c)   groupthink.
        d)   secrecy and no accountability.

33.   Social roles can be problematic when they are
        a)   arbitrary
        b)   unfair
        c)   both a and b
        d)   neither a nor b

34.   According to Michelle Ryan, even when women have broken through the "glass ceiling" into top leadership positions, they are more likely than men to encounter a "glass cliff;" to be put in charge of units that are in crisis and in which the risk of failure is high.
        a)   True
        b)   False

35.   Brian Mullen content-analyzed newspaper accounts of sixty lynchings committed in the United States between 1899 and 1946 and discovered an interesting fact: The _____ in the mob, the greater the savagery and viciousness with which they killed their victims.
        a)   fewer people there were
        b)   more people there were
        c)   older the people were
        d)   younger the people were

36.   According to your text, why are people more likely to use profanity in blogs and Internet chat rooms than they are in face-to-face communications?
        a)   because they can't be identified
        b)   because it is mostly young people using blogs and chat rooms and younger people are more comfortable using profanity
        c)   because of social facilitation
        d)   because of groupthink

37. A recent review concluded that defective decision making may be less common than the original groupthink theory assumed.
    a) True
    b) False

38. Leadership styles are not closely linked with personality traits.
    a) True
    b) False

39. In a 2002 poll, _____ percent of the people surveyed preferred a man as a boss, _____ percent preferred a woman.
    a) 22; 45
    b) 45; 22
    c) 19; 32
    d) 32; 19

40. Liberman et al. (2004) found that changing the name of a game from the "Wall Street Game" to the "Community Game" increased the percentage of people who cooperated from _____ percent to _____ percent.
    a) 39; 75
    b) 56; 84
    c) 33; 71
    d) 18; 47

SHORT ANSWER REVIEW

"What is a group?" A group consists of three or more people who interact with each other and are

(1) _____ (p. 254) in the sense that their needs and goals cause them to influence each other. The

need to belong to groups may be (2) _____ (p. 254). Groups also serve as a source of (3)

_____ (p. 254) about the social world and are an important part of our social identities. Groups can

also help establish (4) _____ (p. 254), the explicit or implicit rules defining what is acceptable

behavior.

Most groups have three to (5) _____ (p. 254) members. If groups become too large, you

cannot interact with all the members. Groups tend to consist of homogeneous members, in part because

groups have social norms that people are expected to obey. Groups also have well-defined social roles,

shared (6) _____ (p. 255) about how people are supposed to behave. People can get so far into a

social role that their personal identities and personalities get lost. Roles can be problematic when they are

(7) _____ (p. 257) or unfair. All societies, for example, have expectations about how people who occupy the roles of women and men should behave. These gender roles have changed over time. Changing roles cause conflict and they can actually affect our (8) _____ (p. 257). Group cohesiveness, qualities of a group that bind members together and promote (9) _____ (p. 258) between members, is another important property of groups that influences the group's performance.

Being in the presence of other people can have a variety of interesting effects on our behavior. Research has compared the performance of people who are by themselves versus in groups. When people's individual performance on a task can be (10) _____ (p. 260), the mere presence of others leads to social facilitation: Their performance is enhanced on (11) _____ (p. 260) tasks but impaired on complex tasks. When people's individual efforts cannot be evaluated, the mere presence of others leads to (12) _____ (p. 262): Performance is impaired on simple tasks but enhanced on complex tasks. There are gender and cultural differences in social loafing. Social loafing is (13) _____ (p. 263) prevalent among men than women, and more prevalent in Western than Asian cultures.

The mere presence of others can also lead to deindividuation, which is the loosening of normal (14) _____ (p. 263) on behavior when people are in crowds, leading to an increase in impulsive and deviant acts. Deindividuation makes people feel less (15) _____ (p. 263) for their actions because it reduces the likelihood that any individual will be singled out and blamed. Deindividuation also (16) _____ (p. 264) obedience to group norms.

Most important decisions in the world today are made by (17) _____ (p. 265) because it is assumed that groups make better decisions than individuals. Behavior research has compared how people make decisions when they are by themselves versus in groups. Groups make better decisions than individuals if they are good at pooling ideas and listening to the expert members of the group. Often, however, (18) _____ (p. 266) occurs, which is any aspect of group interaction that inhibits good

decision making. For example, groups often focus on the information they have in common and fail to

share unique information. Unshared information is more likely to be brought up later in a discussion,

suggesting that group discussions should last long enough to get beyond what everyone already knows.

Groups can have transactive memory, a combined memory of two people that is more (19) _____

(p. 267) than the memory of either individual. Tightly knit, cohesive groups are also prone to groupthink,

which occurs when maintaining group (20) _____ (p. 267) and solidarity becomes more important

than considering the facts in a realistic manner. Groupthink causes people to implement an inferior

decision-making process. A wise leader can avoid the groupthink trap by remaining impartial, seeking

outside opinions, creating subgroups, and seeking anonymous opinions.

Group polarization is the tendency for groups to make more decisions that are more (21)

_____ (p. 273) than the initial inclinations of its members; these group decisions can be more risky

or more cautious, depending on which attitude is valued in the group. This occurs for two main reasons.

According to the (22) _____ (p. 273) interpretation, all individuals bring to the group a set of

arguments, some of which other individuals have not considered, supporting their initial recommendation.

Another person might not have considered this possibility; thus he or she becomes more conservative as

well. According to the (23) _____ (p. 273) interpretation, when people discuss an issue in a group,

they first check out how everyone else feels. To be liked, many people then take a position that is similar

to everyone else's but a little more extreme.

A critical question is the role of the leader in group decision making. There is little support for the

great person theory, which argues that good leadership is a matter of having the right personality traits.

Leaders do adopt specific kinds of leadership styles, such as transactional or transformational. (24)

_____ (p. 274) leaders set clear, short-term goals and reward people who meet them.

Transformational leaders inspire followers to focus on common, long-term goals. Leadership effectiveness is a function of both the kind of person a leader is and the nature of the work situation. The contingency theory of leadership states that leadership effectiveness depends both on how task-oriented or relationship-oriented the leader is and on the amount of (25) _____ (p. 274) and influence the leader has over the group. A task-oriented leader is concerned more with getting the job done than with workers' feelings and relationships. A relationship-oriented leader is concerned primarily with workers' (26) _____ (p. 274) and relationships.

There is a double bind for women leaders: If they conform to societal expectations about how they ought to behave, by being warm and communal, they are often perceived as having (27) _____ (p. 276) leadership potential. If they succeed in attaining a leadership position and act in ways that leaders are expected to act—namely, in agentic, forceful ways—they are often perceived negatively for not "acting like a woman should."

Often, people have (28) _____ (p. 276) goals, placing them in conflict with one another. Research has examined how people resolve conflicts when they have incompatible goals. Social dilemmas occur when the most beneficial action for an individual will, if chosen by most people, have (29) _____ (p. 277) effects on everyone. A commonly studied social dilemma is the prisoner's dilemma, in which two people must decide whether to look out for only their own interests or for their partner's interests as well. Creating trust is crucial in solving this kind of conflict. To increase cooperation, you can try the tit-for-tat strategy, which is a way of encouraging cooperation by at first acting (30) _____ (p. 278) but then always responding the way your opponent did (cooperatively or competitively) on the previous trial. One type of social dilemma that has been studied is a public goods dilemma—this occurs when individuals must contribute to a common pool to maintain the (31) _____ (p. 279), such as paying taxes for public schools. It is to each individual's advantage to pay as little as possible, but if everyone adopts this strategy, everyone suffers. The commons dilemma is a situation in which everyone takes from a common pool of goods that will (32) _____ (p. 279) itself if used in moderation but will disappear if overused. Examples of this include the use of limited resources such as water and energy.

Research has found that using threats tends to escalate rather than resolve conflicts. Communication resolves conflict only when it promotes trust. Negotiation is a form of communication between opposing sides in a conflict in which offers and counteroffers are made and a solution occurs only when (33) _____ (p. 281) agree. When two sides are negotiating and bargaining it is important to look for an integrative solution, whereby each side (34) _____ (p. 282) the most on issues that are unimportant to it but very important to its adversary.

ESSAY REVIEW

1. Discuss social norms and social roles as they apply to groups. When does the power of norms to shape behavior become clear and how does a group treat members who violate norms?

2. Describe how social roles can become problematic. How does this apply to the abuse at Abu Ghraib prison?

3. Define group cohesiveness. Explain how group cohesiveness influences group behavior.

4. Identify the three theories that explain why the presence of others leads to arousal.

5. Define social loafing. Describe the influence of gender and culture on social loafing.

EXIT TESTS
EXIT TEST 1

1. Group members tend to be alike in
    a)   age.
    b)   Sex.
    c)   beliefs and opinions.
    d)   all of the above.

2. Shared expectations that a group has about how people are supposed to _____ are called social norms, while shared expectations about how certain people in a group should _____ are called social roles.
    a)   behave; act
    b)   act; behave
    c)   act; believe
    d)   believe; act

245

3.   By the early 1990s, women were earning more college degrees than men.
        a)   True
        b)   False

4.   Concern about being judged is referred to as
        a)   social defacilitation.
        b)   fear of judgment tendency.
        c)   evaluation apprehension.
        d)   evaluation fear phenomenon.

5.   Which of the following people is most likely to engage in social loafing?
        a)   Mr. Ross, who is from Texas
        b)   Ms. Smith, who is from Arkansas
        c)   Mr. Ogata, who is from Japan
        d)   Ms. Kim, who is from China

6.   Deindividuation leads to
        a)   a decrease in impulsive and deviant acts.
        b)   an increase in impulsive and deviant acts.
        c)   an increase in selfish behavior.
        d)   an increase in charitable behavior.

7.   Robert Watson (1973) studied 24 cultures and found that warriors who _____ before going into battle were significantly more likely to kill, torture, or mutilate captive prisoners than warriors who _____.
        a)   spent a lot of time choosing their weapons; did not spend a lot of time choosing   their weapons.
        b)   did not spend a lot of time choosing their weapons; spent a lot of time choosing   their weapons.
        c)   did not hide their identities; hid their identities
        d)   hid their identities; did not hide their identities

8.   Deindividuation always leads to aggressive or antisocial behavior.
        a)   True
        b)   False

9.   Which of the following is a cause of process loss?
        a)   Groups might not try hard enough to find out who the most competent member is.
        b)   The most competent member might find it difficult to disagree with everyone else in the group.
        c)   Communication problems within the group.
        d)   All of the above can cause process loss.

10.   During group discussions, unshared information is usually brought up
        a)   later in the discussion.
        b)   at the very beginning of the discussion.
        c)   early in the discussion.
        d)   informally, after the group discussion is over.

EXIT TEST 2

1. When a group makes a decision that is more extreme than the initial inclination of its members it is called
    a) groupthink.
    b) risky shift.
    c) group polarization.
    d) social facilitation.

2. Which of the following states that certain key personality traits make a person a good leader, regardless of the situation?
    a) great person theory
    b) transactional theory of leadership
    c) transformational theory of leadership
    d) contingency theory of leadership

3. Which of the following states that leadership effectiveness depends both on how task-oriented or relationship-oriented the leader is and on the amount of control and influence the leader has over the group?
    a) great person theory
    b) transactional theory of leadership
    c) transformational theory of leadership
    d) contingency theory of leadership

4. Which of the following is likely to think outside the box?
    a) a transactional leader
    b) a transformational leader
    c) a contingency leader
    d) a relationship-oriented leader

5. Sigmund Freud argued that conflict is an inevitable byproduct of civilization because
    a) the goals and needs of individuals often clash with the goals and needs of their fellow human beings.
    b) of the influence of peoples' Ids.
    c) of the scarcity of certain resources.
    d) of the Thanatos.

6. Which country has been called "the murder capital of the civilized world?"
    a) Germany
    b) Iraq
    c) Mexico
    d) the United States

7. What happened when Stephen King devised a social dilemma by posting portions of a novel on the Internet and agreeing to continue to post new installments as long as at least 75% of the people who downloaded it paid a $1 fee?
    a) No one ever paid the fee.
    b) Everyone paid the fee.
    c) At first more than 75% of the people paid the fee but later less than 75% paid.
    d) At first barely 75% of the people paid but later 98% of the people paid.

8. Subtly changing the norms about what kind of behavior is expected can have large effects on how cooperative people are.
    a)   True
    b)   False

9. _____ is a social dilemma in which individuals must contribute to a common pool in order to maintain the public good.
    a)   A public pool dilemma
    b)   A public goods dilemma
    c)   A commons dilemma
    d)   The "all-for-one and one-for-all" dilemma

10. A classic series of studies by Morton Deutsch and Robert Krauss indicated that threats are an effective means of reducing conflict.
    a)   True
    b)   False

STUDY ACTIVITIES

1. What is group polarization? Discuss the role of cognitive and social factors in producing group polarization.

2. Riots and other instances of unruly mob behavior are the result of what group process? What characteristics of the group and situation combine to produce such negative behaviors?

3. Describe several causes, symptoms, and consequences of groupthink.

4. What is negotiation? Identify a limit to successful negotiation. What is an integrative solution?

5. What is the definition of a group? Why do people join groups? Identify a group to which you belong. Which of the reasons for joining groups applies to you for this group?

6. Discuss the implications that social facilitation and social loafing have for organizing groups in work situations.

7. What is process loss in groups? How does it occur? Imagine that you are coordinating a problem solving group at work. Describe the steps you would take to avoid process loss.

8. According to the contingency theory of leadership, what are two types of leaders? If you were in a leadership position, which type of leader do you think you would be and why do you think you would be that type?

9. What is a social dilemma? Differentiate between a public goods dilemma and a commons dilemma and give an example of each.

10. Are threats an effective means to reduce conflict? When can communication alleviate conflict?

Chapter 9 Answers

Practice Test

1.   D (p. 254)
2.   C (pp. 260-261)
3.   B (p. 262)
4.   B (p. 260)
5.   D (p. 264)
6.   B (p. 255)
7.   D (p. 273)
8.   B (p. 279)
9.   A (pp. 281-282)
10. B (pp. 259)
11. A (pp. 258-262)
12. B (p. 277)
13. C (p. 263)
14. A (p. 258)
15. B (p. 262)
16. C (p. 273)
17. D (p. 274)
18. B (pp. 268-269)
19. A (p. 273)
20. D (p. 278)
21. D (p. 266)
22. C (p. 267)
23. A (p. 274)
24. A (p. 275)
25. C (p. 262)
26. B (p. 279)
27. D (p. 281)
28. C (p. 270)
29. C (pp. 259-260)
30. A (pp. 255-256)
31. B (p. 254)
32. D (p. 256)
33. C (p. 257)
34. A (p. 275)
35. B (p. 264)
36. A (p. 265)
37. B (p. 269)
38. A (p. 274)
39. D (p. 276)
40. C (p. 278)

Short Answer Review

1. interdependent (p. 254)
2. innate (p. 254)
3. information (p. 254)
4. social norms (p. 254)
5. six (p. 254)
6. expectations (p. 255)
7. arbitrary (p. 257)
8. personalities (p. 257)
9. liking (p. 258)
10. evaluated (p. 260)
11. simple (p. 260)
12. social loafing (p. 262)
13. more (p. 263)
14. constraints (p. 263)
15. accountable (p. 264)
16. increases (p. 264)
17. groups (p. 265)
18. process loss (p. 266)
19. efficient (p. 267)
20. cohesiveness (p. 267)
21. extreme (p. 273)
22. persuasive arguments (p. 273)
23. social comparison (p. 273)
24. Transactional (p. 274)
25. control (p. 274)
26. feelings (p. 274)
27. less (p. 276)
28. incompatible (p. 276)
29. harmful (p. 277)
30. cooperatively (p. 278)
31. public good (p. 279)
32. replenish (p. 279)
33. both parties p. 281)
34. concedes (p. 282)

Essay Review

1. Your essay should include:
   - All societies have norms about which behaviors are acceptable, some of which all members are expected to obey and some of which vary from group to group. Social norms govern the behavior of people in groups. (p. 255)
   - Social roles are shared expectations in a group about how particular people are supposed to behave. Whereas norms specify how all group members should act, roles specify how people who occupy certain positions in the group should behave. (p. 255)
   - The power of norms to shape behavior becomes clear when we violate them too often: We are shunned by other group members and, in extreme cases, pressured to leave the group. (p. 255)

2.   Your essay should include the following:
- People can get so far into a role that their personal identities and personalities get lost. The social role can be so powerful that it takes over our personal identities to the point that we become the role we are playing. (p. 256)
- The prison environment with secrecy and no accountability gave people permission to do things they ordinarily would not. The military guards were under tremendous stress, had received little supervision, and were asked to set their own rules for interrogation. (p. 256)

3.   Your essay on group cohesiveness should include:
- Group cohesiveness refers to qualities of a group that bind members together and promote liking between members. (p. 258)
- The more cohesive a group is, the more its members are likely to stay in the group, take part in group activities, and try to recruit new like-minded members. (p. 258)
- If the function of the group is to work together to solve problems, the relationship between performance and cohesiveness is complex. Cohesiveness can cause a group to perform well if a task requires close cooperation between the group members. Cohesiveness can get in the way of optimal performance if maintaining good relations among group members becomes more important than finding good solutions to the problem. (p. 258)

4.   Your essay should include the following:
- The first explanation suggests that the presence of other people makes us more alert and that causes arousal. (p. 260)
- The second explanation focuses on the fact that people are often concerned about how other people are evaluating them. The concern about being judged, called evaluation apprehension, can cause mild arousal. (p. 261)
- The third explanation centers on how distracting other people can be. Divided attention produces arousal. (p. 261)

5.   Your essay on social loafing should include the following:
- The tendency for people to do worse on simple tasks but better on complex tasks when they are in the presence of others and their individual performance cannot be evaluated. (p. 262)
- The tendency to loaf is stronger in men than in women. (p. 263)
- The tendency to loaf is stronger in Western cultures than Asian cultures. (p. 263)

Exit Test 1

1.   D (p. 255)
2.   B (p. 255)
3.   A (p. 257)
4.   C (p. 261)
5.   A (p. 263)
6.   B (p. 263)
7.   D (p. 264)
8.   B (p. 264)
9.   D (p. 266)
10.   A (p. 266)

Chapter 9

Exit Test 2

1. C (p. 273)
2. A (p. 273)
3. D (p. 274)
4. B (p. 274)
5. A (p. 276)
6. D (p. 276)
7. C (p. 277)
8. A (p. 278)
9. B (p. 279)
10. B (pp. 279-280)

Study Activities

1. Group polarization is the tendency for a group to make decisions that are more extreme than the initial inclinations of its members. According to a persuasive arguments interpretation of group polarization, the phenomenon results because members present strong and novel arguments in support of their initial recommendation to the group during discussion. According to a social comparison interpretation, discussion serves to reveal the recommendation that is favored by the group. In order to be liked by the group, members then adopt a recommendation similar to everyone else's but a little more extreme. (p. 273)

2. Deindividuation loosens constraints on behaviors when crowds make members less accountable for their actions and foster anonymity. Add to this a situation that presents negative cues and inhibitions against negative behaviors will be decreased. Negative behavior will ensue. (pp. 263-264)

3. Groupthink occurs when certain preconditions are met, such as when the group is highly cohesive, is isolated from contrary opinion, and is ruled by a directive leader. Symptoms of groupthink include feelings of invulnerability, self-censorship, direct pressures on dissenters to conform, and an illusion of unanimity. Groupthink prevents groups from considering the full range of alternatives available to them, from developing contingency plans, and from considering the risks of the preferred choice. (pp. 267-270)

4. Negotiation is a form of communication between opposing sides in a conflict in which the parties make offers and counteroffers, and where a solution occurs only when both parties agree. One limit to successful negotiation is that people often assume that they are locked in a conflict in which only one party can come out ahead. An integrative solution is a solution to a conflict whereby the parties make trade-offs on issues according to their different interests; each side concedes the most on issues that are unimportant to it but important to the other side. (pp. 281-282)

5. A group consists of three or more people who interact and are interdependent in the sense that their needs and goals cause them to influence each other. Forming relationships with people is a basic human need and may be innate. Groups can also be an important source of information about our social world, become an important part of our identity, and help us establish social norms. (pp. 254-255)

6.   In a work group, people will do better on simple tasks and worse on complex tasks than they would if they were working alone. However, people in work groups are likely to do worse on simple tasks and better on complex tasks if their individual performance cannot be evaluated. (pp. 260 & 262)

7.   Process loss refers to any aspect of group interaction that inhibits good problem solving. Process loss can occur when groups do not try hard enough to find out who the most competent member is and instead rely on someone who really doesn't know what he or she is talking about. It can also occur because the most competent member might find it difficult to disagree with everyone else in the group. Other causes of process loss involve communication problems within the group—in some groups, people don't listen to each other; in others, one person is allowed to dominate the discussion while the others tune out. Process loss can also occur because of a tendency for groups to focus on what its members already know in common, failing to discuss information that only some members have. To avoid process loss you should try to discover who the most competent member is; make sure everyone in the group gets an opportunity to speak; and make sure discussions last long enough for unshared information to be brought up. (pp. 265-266)

8.   According to contingency theory, there are task-oriented leaders and relationship-oriented leaders. (p. 274)

9.   A social dilemma is a conflict in which the most beneficial action for an individual will, if chosen by most people, have harmful effects on everyone. A public goods dilemma is a social dilemma in which individuals must contribute to a common pool in order to maintain the public good. Taxes are an example of a public goods dilemma. A commons dilemma is a social dilemma in which everyone takes from a common pool of goods that will replenish itself if used in moderation, but will disappear if overused. Limited resources such as water and energy are examples of commons dilemmas. (pp. 277-279)

10.   No, threats are not an effective means for reducing conflict. Communication can reduce conflict if it fosters trust. (pp. 279-280)

CHAPTER 10

Interpersonal Attraction: From First Impressions to Close Relationships

CHAPTER 10 OVERVIEW

This chapter addresses factors involved in interpersonal attraction. The first section of the chapter addresses the question, "What Causes Attraction?" One of the variables that cause initial attraction between two people is physical proximity, or the **propinquity effect**: People who you come into contact with the most are the most likely to become your friends and lovers. This occurs because of the **mere exposure effect**: Exposure to any stimulus produces liking for it. Similarity between people, whether in attitudes, values, personality traits, or demographic characteristics, is also a powerful cause of attraction and liking. Similarity is a more powerful predictor of attraction than complementarity, the idea that opposites attract.

In general, we like others who behave as if they like us—reciprocal liking. Physical attractiveness also plays an important role in liking. Research finds that men and women rank physical attractiveness as equally important. The powerful role that physical appearance plays in attraction is not limited to heterosexual relationships. People from different cultures perceive facial attractiveness quite similarly. The crucial variable that explains interpersonal attraction may actually be familiarity. Averaging many faces together produces one face that looks typical, familiar, and physically attractive. Research has also found that when participants rate the attractiveness of faces, they prefer the faces that most resemble their own. The "what is beautiful is good" stereotype indicates that people assume that physical attractiveness is associated with other desirable traits.

One theory of interpersonal attraction is social exchange theory. **Social exchange theory** states that how people feel about their relationships depends on their perception of the rewards they receive and the costs they incur. In order to determine whether people will stay in a relationship, we also need to know their **comparison level**—their expectations about the outcomes of their relationship—and their **comparison level for alternatives**—their expectations about how happy they would be in other relationships. **Equity theory** states that the most important determinant of satisfaction is the amount of equity in the relationship, wherein the rewards and costs they experience and the contributions they make to the relationship are roughly equal to those of the other person.

The next section of the chapter examines close relationships. Love can be defined in different ways. One definition of love makes a distinction between **companionate love**—feelings of intimacy that are not accompanied by intense longing and arousal—and **passionate love**—feelings of intimacy that are accompanied by intense longing and arousal. Although love is a universal emotion, cultural variations in the definition of love do occur. Love has a somewhat different emphasis in collectivistic and individualistic cultures.

The next section of the chapter focuses on love and relationships. **Evolutionary psychology** explains social behavior in terms of genetic factors that have evolved over time according to principles of natural selection. The **evolutionary approach to love** is derived from evolutionary biology and holds that men and women are attracted to different characteristics in each other because this maximizes their reproductive success.

According to the theory of **attachment styles**, the kinds of bonds we form early in life influence the kinds of relationships we form as adults. The **secure attachment style** is characterized by trust, a lack of concern with being abandoned, and the view that one is worthy and well liked. The **avoidant attachment style** is characterized by a suppression of attachment needs, because attempts to be intimate have been rebuffed; people with this style find it difficult to develop intimate relationships. The **anxious/ambivalent attachment style** is characterized by a concern that others will not reciprocate one's desire for intimacy, thus resulting in higher-than-average levels of anxiety. The key assumption of attachment theory is that the particular attachment style we learn as infants and young children becomes our working model or schema for what relationships are like.

Research has shown ample support for social exchange theory in intimate relationships in cultures as different as Taiwan and the Netherlands. Of course, we know that many people do not leave their partners, even when they are dissatisfied and their other alternatives look bright. Research indicates that we need to consider at least one additional factor to understand close relationships—a person's level of investment in the relationship. According to the **investment model** of close relationships, people's commitment to a relationship depends not only on their satisfaction with the relationship in terms of rewards, costs, and comparison level and their comparison level for alternatives, but also on how much they have invested in the relationship that would be lost by leaving it.

The equity of rewards and costs is different in long-term relationships than in short-term relationships. Interactions between new acqaintances are governed by equity concerns that are called exchange relationships. In **exchange relationships**, people keep track of who is contributing what and feel taken advantage of when they feel they are putting more into the relationship than they are getting out of it. In comparison, interactions between close friends, family members, and romantic partners are governed less by an equity norm and more by a desire to help each other in times of need. In these **communal relationships**, people give in response to the other's needs, regardless of whether they are paid back.

The final section of this chapter discusses ending intimate relationships. The breaking-up process is composed of stages. In the intrapersonal stage the individual thinks a lot about his or her dissatisfaction with the relationship. In the dyadic stage the individual discusses the breakup with the partner. In the social stage the breakup is announced to other people. Then the process goes back to the intrapersonal stage again when the individual recovers from the breakup and forms an account, or version, of how and why it happened.

Strategies for responding to problems in a romantic relationship include both constructive and destructive behaviors. Destructive behaviors include actively harming the relationship and passively allowing the relationship to deteriorate. Constructive behaviors include actively trying to improve the relationship and passively remaining loyal to the relationship. Fatal attractions occur when the qualities in a person that once were attractive become the very qualities that repel. A powerful variable that predicts how a person will weather the breakup is the role he or she plays in the decision to terminate the relationship.

CHAPTER 10 OUTLINE

I. What Causes Attraction?
• When social psychologist Ellen Berscheid asked people of various ages what made them happy, at or near the top of their lists were making and maintaining friendships and having positive, warm relationships.
• The absence of meaningful relationships with other people makes people feel lonely, worthless, hopeless, helpless, powerless, and alienated.
• This chapter explores the antecedents of attraction, from initial liking of two people meeting for the first time to the love that develops in close relationships.

Chapter 10

A. The Person Next Door: The Propinquity Effect
• One of the simplest determinants of interpersonal attraction is proximity (sometimes called propinquity).
• The people who, by chance, are the ones you see and interact with the most often are the most likely to become your friends and lovers; this is known as the **propinquity effect**.
• Festinger, Schacter, and Back (1950) tracked friendship formation among couples in graduate housing; the closer together people lived, even within a building, the more likely they were to become close friends (Figure 10.1).
• The propinquity effect works because of the **mere exposure effect**, the finding that the more exposure we have to a stimulus, the more apt we are to like it (provided the stimulus is not noxious, in which case exposure leads to greater disliking).
• Moreland and Beach (1992) had confederates attend a class either 0, 5, 10, or 15 times during the term; the more visits, the more they were liked, even though the confederates did not interact with the other students.
• In a computer-mediated world we can get to know people who are very far away physically but very close in cyberspace.

B. Similarity
• Propinquity increases familiarity, which leads to liking, but something more is needed to fuel a growing friendship or a romantic relationship.
• That "fuel" is similarity, a match between our interests, attitudes, values, backgrounds, or personality and those of another person.
• Although folk wisdom suggests that *complementarity,* or attraction to opposites, prevails, but the research evidence shows that similarity, not complementarity, draws people together.
1. Opinions and Personality
• Newcomb (1961) found in a college housing study that similarity in background, attitudes, and values predicted friendship formation. People who are similar are attractive because (a) they validate our own self-worth; and (b) we assume that people who disagree with us have negative personality traits.
• Boyden et al. (1984) found strong support for personality similarity in gay men's relationships; other researchers find support for similarity in heterosexual relationships and friendships.
2. Interpersonal Style
• Similarity of communication skills and interpersonal style has also been found   (Burleson & Samfer, 1996).
3. Interests and Experiences
• Similarity also fuels proximity by leading similar people to choose similar situations, which leads to the development of further common bonds.
4. Some Final Comments about Similarity
• While similarity is a very important variable in close relationships, it is important to make a distinction between "actual" (or real) similarity and "perceived" similarity, that is, the degree to which one believes oneself is similar to another.
• A lack of similarity does appear to play an important role in one type of relationship. When we begin a romantic relationship, we typically want a serious, committed relationship; but sometimes we just want a "fling."
• David Amodio and Carolin Showers (2005) found that whether it was similarity or complementarity that was important depended on the level of commitment that research participants felt toward their romantic partner and their relationship. If participants wanted a committed relationship, they chose a similar partner; however, if they felt a low level of commitment to the relationship, they favored dissimilar partners.

C. Reciprocal Liking

• One of the most potent determinants of our liking someone is if we believe that that person likes us (reciprocal liking). Gold et al. (1984) showed that men greatly liked a woman who nonverbally displayed liking, even though she disagreed with them on important issues.

• If we believe somebody else likes us, we will be a more likable person in their presence; this will lead them to actually like us more—a self-fulfilling prophecy (Curtis & Miller, 1986).

• A person's level of self-esteem moderates how we are affected by other people's liking us. Swann and his colleagues have shown that people with high or moderate self-esteem like, and want to interact with, those who like them, but people with low self-esteem preferred to interact with somebody who earlier criticized them than somebody who earlier praised them.

• This pattern of reaction sets up a self-fulfilling prophecy.

D. Physical Attractiveness and Liking

• Physical attractiveness is a major determinant of liking in studies of first impressions.

• Hatfield et al. (1966) conducted a classic computer dating study that randomly matched students for a blind date at a dance at freshman orientation. Of all the characteristics that could determine liking and a desire to date the person again, the major determinant was physical attractiveness.

• Debate has existed on sex differences in the importance of physical attractiveness. A meta-analysis by Feingold (1990) finds that both sexes value attractiveness, although men value it somewhat more than women; however, this difference is larger for stated attitudes and values than for actual behavior.

• Regan and Berscheid (1995, 1997) find that both sexes rate physical attractiveness as the most important characteristic determining desire of a sexual partner.

• Physical attractiveness plays a powerful role in homosexual as well as heterosexual relationships (at least among gay men).

1. What Is Attractive?

• The media bombards us with a standard of beauty; and also associates beautiful characters with morally good ones; because of the media we develop shared standards of beauty.

• For both sexes, this standard includes large eyes, prominent cheekbones, and a big smile. For women, a small nose and chin, narrow cheeks, and high eyebrows are considered attractive; for men, a large chin is considered attractive (Cunningham et al., 1990).

2. Cultural Standards of Beauty

• Surprisingly, there is a large agreement across cultures in what is considered physically attractive in the human face.

• Langlois and Roggman hypothesize that this agreement may be due to evolutionary mechanisms, and suggested that the attractive faces are those whose features are those that are statistically average. A test using computer composites of 16 different faces supports the hypothesis.

• Average faces are not the *most* attractive; they are just more attractive than the individual faces that are averaged in the composite. Perrett et al. (1994) showed this distinction in a study in which Caucasian and Asian participants rated "highly attractive" composites of both races higher than "average attractive" composites.

3. The Power of Familiarity

• This statistically average face is typical or familiar. Berscheid and Reis (1998) suggest that it is this familiarity that is the crucial variable that explains attraction; we prefer the familiar and safe to the unfamiliar and potentially dangerous.

• Familiarity also underlies propinquity, similarity, and reciprocal liking.

4. Assumptions about Attractive People
• People assume that physical attractiveness is highly correlated with other desirable traits; this is known as the "what is beautiful is good" stereotype (Table 10.1). The beautiful are thought to be more sociable, extraverted and socially competent than the less attractive; and are also seen as more sexual, happier, and more assertive.
• The "what is beautiful is good" stereotype appears to operate across cultures; Korean students, like North Americans, agree that physically attractive people are more socially skilled, friendly, and better adjusted. However, while North American individualists believed that beautiful people were independent and self-reliant, Korean collectivists believed they had integrity and concern for others. Thus the attractive characteristics include those perceived to be attractive in the culture.
• There is a kernel of truth to the association between physical attractiveness and sociability; this may be due to a self-fulfilling prophecy. In support of this idea, Snyder, Tanke, and Berscheid (1977) showed that, when men thought that the woman they were talking with over the phone was physically attractive, they acted more warmly towards her; this led her, in turn, to act warmer, more confident, and more animated. Anderson and Bem (1981) replicated the study showing the same effect for women's beliefs about men's attractiveness.
• Three meta-analyses examining the effect of attractiveness found no gender difference, indicating that physical attractiveness is as important to women as it is to men.

E. Theories of Interpersonal Attraction: Social Exchange and Equity
1. Social Exchange Theory
• **Social exchange theory** states that how people feel about a relationship depends on their perceptions of the *rewards* and *costs* of the relationship, the kind of relationship they believe they deserve or expect to have (their **comparison level**) and their chances for having a better relationship with someone else (their **comparison level for alternatives**).
• The outcome of a relationship is its rewards minus its costs. How satisfied one is with this outcome depends on one's comparison level, and how likely one is to stay in an unsatisfactory relationship is determined by the comparison level for alternatives.
• Generally the research evidence supports the theory.
2. Equity Theory
• **Equity theory** argues that people are happiest with relationships in which the rewards and costs a person experiences and the contributions he or she makes to the relationship are roughly equal to the rewards, costs, and contributions of the other person. According to the theory, both under- and over-benefited partners should be motivated to restore equity, although research finds that this is truer for the under-benefited.

II. Close Relationships
• Until recently, there was little research in social psychology on enduring relationships, because they are more difficult to study scientifically: random assignment is impossible, and feelings can be hard to measure.

A. Defining Love
• There seem to be multiple kinds of love, and different scales to measure these have been developed in the past decade.
1. Companionate versus Passionate Love
• **Companionate love** is the feelings of intimacy and affection we feel for another person when we care deeply for the person, but do not necessarily experience passion or arousal in his or her presence.

• **Passionate love** is the feelings of intense longing, accompanied by physiological arousal, we feel for another person; when our love is reciprocated, we feel great fulfillment and ecstasy, but when it is not, we feel sadness and despair.

• Cross-cultural research indicates that Americans value passionate over companionate love, while Chinese do the reverse; while the Taita of Kenya, East Africa, value both equally. Jankowiak and Fisher (1992) found evidence for passionate love in 147 societies (see Table 10.2).

B. Culture and Love

• Although love is a universal emotion, how we experience it (and what we expect from close relationships) is linked to culture.

• For example the Japanese concept of *amae* (a very positive emotional state in which one is a totally passive love object cared for by the romantic partner) has no equivalent in English; the Chinese concept of *gan qing* includes practical love and help as romantic; and the Korean concept of *jung* expresses the tie developed over time and experience that binds two people together in either positive or negative relationships.

• Shaver et al. (1992) found both similarities and differences in concepts of love cross-culturally in a concept-sorting task; for example, Chinese have many love concepts that are also sad.

• Similarly, Rothbaum and Tsang (1998) examined the lyrics of popular love songs in the U.S. and China and found that Chinese love songs had significantly more references to suffering, based on Chinese culture's belief in predestination of interpersonal relationships (*yuan*); however, Chinese love songs were as passionate and erotic as American ones.

• How romantic love is defined and experienced can vary across individualistic and collectivistic cultures. Dion and Dion (1988, 1993) suggest that romantic love is an important basis for marriage in individualistic societies but is less valued in collectivist ones, where the wishes of family and other group members count more.

• In support of this hypothesis, Dion and Dion (1993) found that students from Asian cultures were more likely to endorse storgic, friendship-based love; Simmons et al. (1986) found that Japanese students had the least passionately romantic view of love in a cross-cultural comparison; and Levine et al. (1995) found that marrying for love was most important to respondents in Westernized countries and least important to participants in underdeveloped Eastern countries.

• Thus, while romantic love may be nearly universal across cultures, different rules alter how that state is experienced and expressed.

III. Love and Relationships

• This section examines how the factors examined in relationship formation play out over time.

A. Evolution and Love: Choosing a Mate

• Evolutionary biology judges an animal's "fitness" in terms of its reproductive success; the **evolutionary approach to love** states that men and women are attracted to different characteristics in each other: men are attracted by women's appearance; women are attracted by men's resources—because these foster reproductive success. Reproductive success is not just part of the game; it *is* the game. This biological concept has been applied to social behavior by psychologists, who define **evolutionary psychology** as the attempt to explain social behavior in terms of genetic factors that evolved over time according to the principles of natural selection.

• Buss and his colleagues suggest that this approach explains the different strategies of men and women in romantic relationships. Data that is supportive comes from cross-cultural studies of preferences in relationships and from findings that men are more upset by sexual infidelity and women by emotional infidelity. Gangestead and Buss (1993) show that physical attractiveness (possibly associated with health) is especially valued in regions of the world where disease is common. However, this preference existed for both sexes, supporting the evolutionary perspective in general but questioning the proposed gender differences.

•The evolutionary approach to love has attracted its share of debate. For example, an alternative explanation is that there were evolutionary advantages for females to have multiple sexual partners too, not just for males. It has also been argued that men may value physical attractiveness in a partner simply because they have been taught to value it. Similarly, research has found that women value physical attractiveness as much as men when they are considering a potential sexual partner as opposed to a potential marriage partner. Finally, some researchers note that the preference for different qualities in a mate can be explained without resorting to evolutionary principles: Around the world, women have less power, status, wealth, and other resources than men do. In support of this latter interpretation, Gangestead (1993) found an association between women's economic resources and their preference for a physically attractive man.

B. Attachment Styles in Intimate Relationships
• The **attachment styles** approach (based on the work of Bowlsby and Ainsworth) to close relationships focuses on the expectations people develop about relationships based on the relationship they had with their primary caregiver when they were infants. The theory suggests that these influence the kinds of relationships we have as adults.
• The **secure attachment style** develops in those who have responsive caregivers as infants and is characterized by trust, a lack of concern with being abandoned, and the view that one is worthy and well liked. The **avoidant attachment style** develops in those who have aloof and distant caregivers as infants and is characterized by a suppression of attachment needs, because attempts to be intimate have been rebuffed; people with this style find it difficult to develop intimate relationships; the **anxious/ambivalent attachment style** develops in those who had inconsistent and overbearing caregivers as infants and is characterized by a concern that others will not reciprocate one's desire for intimacy, resulting in higher than average levels of anxiety.
• The key assumption of the theory is that the attachment style we learn as infants becomes our schema for relationships and generalizes to all of our relationships with others.
• Hazen and Shaver (1987) asked people to select one of three overall descriptors of attachment style (presented in Table 10.3); their selection was related to the quality of their romantic relationships. This and other data connecting people's reports of relationships with their parents to reports of romantic relationships are consistent with attachment theory.
• Collins et al. (2006) and Simpson et al. (1992) brought heterosexual couples into the lab and measured their attachment styles; then they told the woman that the next part of the procedure would be upsetting but that they couldn't say more, and left her to wait with her boyfriend. Secure women turned to their boyfriends for support while avoidant women withdrew; secure boyfriends were supportive but avoidant boyfriends were less so.

1. **Attachment Style Combinations**
•Attachment style affects communication in a relationship and the attributions partners make about each other.
• Kirkpatrick and Davis (1994) studied couples in which one member was avoidant and one was anxious/ambivalent; while the expectations of these two types are complementary, these relationships are low in satisfaction and high in communication problems. Despite this, anxious women paired with avoidant men had very stable relationships, because they attribute relationship problems to their partner's gender. In contrast, couples in which the man is anxious and the woman is avoidant do not last long because each person's behavior is seen as especially troubling because it deviates from the stereotype.
• Attachment styles can change over time and in the context of different relationships.

2. **The Genetic Contribution to Attachment Styles**
•A person's genotype may predispose him or her to a specific attachment style, which will then be further affected, one way or the other, by influences in the environment.
•Research indicates that attachment styles can be fluid and are capable of change over the course of a lifetime.

C. Social Exchange in Long-Term Relationships
• Research has shown ample support for social exchange theory in intimate relationships. Rusbult (1983) finds that rewards are always important in determining the outcome of relationships, while costs become increasingly important over time. Her **investment model** of relationships defines investments as anything people have put into relationships that would be lost if they left it. The greater the investment, the less likely people are to leave a relationship, even if satisfaction is low and other alternatives look promising (Figures 10.2 and 10.3). Thus, people's commitment to a relationship depends on their satisfaction with the relationship, their view of alternatives, and how much they have invested in the relationship.
•Van Lange et al. (1997) found that the investment model predicts couples' willingness to make sacrifices for their relationship.
•Rusbult and Martz (1995) surveyed women at a battered women's shelter and found that those who had stayed in an abusive relationship were less dissatisfied, had fewer alternatives, and had higher investments in their marriages.

D. Equity in Long-Term Relationships
• In new or casual relationships, people trade benefits "in kind." In intimate relationships, people trade very different resources and are looser about it.
• **Exchange relationships** are relationships governed by the need for equity; while **communal relationships** are relationships in which people's primary concern is being responsive to the other person's needs(Figure 10.4).
• People in communal relationships are not completely unconcerned with equity—if the relationship is inequitable, they will be dissatisfied. However, the accounting is looser and occurs over time.

IV. Ending Intimate Relationships
• The American divorce rate is still nearly 50%, and some demographers estimate that nearly two-thirds of all current first marriages will end. In addition, romantic relationships outside of marriage end every day.

A. The Process of Breaking Up
• Accounts of breakups by participants reveal five basic categories: positive tone, verbal de-escalation, behavioral de-escalation, negative identity management, and justification.
• Duck (1982) theorizes that there are four stages of dissolution of a relationship: intrapersonal (focusing on dissatisfaction), dyadic (revealing these to the partner), social (announcing the breakup to others), and back to intrapersonal (devising accounts of the breakup as we recover from it) (Figure 10.5).
• Strategies for responding to problems in a romantic relationship include both constructive and destructive behaviors. Destructive behaviors include actively harming the relationship and passively allowing the relationship to deteriorate. Constructive behaviors include actively trying to improve the relationship and passively remaining loyal to the relationship. Rusbult's research suggests that destructive behaviors harm relationships more than constructive behavior helps, and that if both partners act destructively, the relationship typically ends.
• Femlee (1995) found that 30% of breakups in college were "fatal attractions": the qualities that were initially attractive later became the reasons for a breakup.
• Recent research shows no sex difference in who ends romantic relationships.

B. The Experience of Breaking Up
• Akert and others find that the role people play in a breakup is a key determinant of how they feel about it: breakees were most upset, breakers least, and mutuals in the middle. Women experienced somewhat more negative emotions than men. And whether people wanted to remain friends depended on gender: men only were interested if the breakup had been mutual; women were more interested overall, especially if they had been the breakee (Figure 10.6).

261

Chapter 10

LEARNING OBJECTIVES

After reading Chapter 10, you should be able to do the following:

1.   Describe the role of propinquity in attraction. Define the mere exposure effect. Distinguish between physical and functional distance. Explain why the propinquity effect works. (pp. 289-290)

2.   Discuss the importance of similarity in attraction. Explain why we like people whose characteristics, including interpersonal style and communication skill, and beliefs are similar to our own. (pp. 291-292)

3.   Discuss the importance of reciprocal liking in attraction and close relationships. Discuss the role of self-esteem in reciprocal liking. (pp. 292-293)

4.   Discuss the consequences of physical attractiveness for liking strangers and for maintaining relationships. Identify the facial features associated with high attractiveness in females and in males. Discuss cross-cultural findings on cultural standards of beauty. Explain how familiarity may play a role in the perception of attractiveness. (pp. 293-297)

5.   Describe the "what is beautiful is good" stereotype and explain how this stereotype might produce a self-fulfilling prophecy. Discuss cross-cultural research on this stereotype. (pp. 297-299)

6.   Describe social exchange theory. Identify the basic concepts of social exchange theory. Distinguish between comparison level and comparison level for alternatives. (pp. 299-300)

7.   Describe equity theory and indicate how partners in a relationship respond when they are over- or underbenefited in an inequitable relationship. Identify how equity theory differs from social exchange theory. (p. 300)

8.   Identify obstacles to the study of long-term, close relationships. (p. 301)

9.   Distinguish between passionate and companionate types of love proposed by Hatfield and Walster. Describe cultural differences in the experience of companionate and passionate types of love. Discuss cultural differences in how people label the experiences of romantic love, in the emotions associated with romantic love, and in how people make decisions to marry. Identify cultural differences in love styles. (pp. 301-304)

10.   Describe the evolutionary approach to romantic love. Identify the differences between men and women in the characteristics involved in mate selection and the different strategies of men and women in romantic relationships. Discuss support for evolutionary theory and discuss alternative explanations for the research findings. (pp. 304-307)

11.   Identify the key assumption of attachment theory and distinguish between the three attachment styles. Discuss support for attachment theory as it relates to intimate relationships. Describe attachment style combinations. (pp. 307-311)

12.   Describe the research findings on the relationship between genes and attachment style. (pp. 311-312)

13. Discuss support for social exchange theory in long-term relationships. Describe the relationship between social exchange theory and Rusbult's investment model. Identify the three things we need to know in order to predict relationship commitment. (pp. 312-314)

14. Describe how partners' concerns with equity differ depending on whether the partners are involved in an exchange or in a communal relationship. Identify the types of relationships that are likely to be communal. (pp. 314-315)

15. Describe Duck's four-step process of relationship dissolution. (p. 316)

16. Identify and describe the four types of destructive and constructive behaviors that occur in a troubled relationship. (p. 317)

17. Discuss research on "fatal attractions." (p. 317)

18. Identify the relationship between gender and who will end a relationship. Identify the most important determinant of how people feel after a romantic relationship is terminated. Identify individual and situational factors that determine whether ex-loved ones will want to remain friends. (pp. 317-318)

KEY TERMS

1. _____ The finding that the more we see and interact with people, the more likely they are to become our friends. (p. 289)

2. _____ The finding that the more exposure we have to a stimulus, the more apt we are to like it. (p. 290)

3. _____ The idea that people's feelings about a relationship depend on their perceptions of the rewards and costs of the relationship, the kind of relationship they deserve, and their chances for having a better relationship with someone else. (p. 299)

4. _____ People's expectations about the level of rewards and punishments they are likely to receive in a particular relationship. (p. 300)

5. _____ People's expectations about the level of rewards and punishments they would receive in an alternative relationship. (p. 300)

6. _____ The idea that people are happiest with relationships in which the rewards and costs experienced and the contributions made by both parties are roughly equal. (p. 300)

7. _____ The intimacy and affection we feel when we care deeply for a person but do not experience passion or arousal in the person's presence. (p. 301)

8. _____ An intense longing we feel for a person, accompanied by physiological arousal; when our love is reciprocated, we feel great fulfillment and ecstasy, but when it is not, we feel sadness and despair. (p. 301)

9. _____ A theory derived from evolutionary biology that holds that men and women are attracted to different characteristics in each other (men are attracted by women's appearance; women are attracted by men's resources) because this maximizes their chances of reproductive success. (p. 304)

10. _____ The attempt to explain social behavior in terms of genetic factors that evolved over time according to the principles of natural selection. (p. 304)

11. _____ The expectations people develop about relationships with others, based on the relationship they had with their primary caregiver when they were infants. (p. 307)

12. _____ An attachment style characterized by trust, a lack of concern with being abandoned, and the view that one is worthy and well liked. (p. 307)

13. _____ An attachment style characterized by a suppression of attachment needs, because attempts to be intimate have been rebuffed; people with this style find it difficult to develop intimate relationships. (p. 308)

14. _____ An attachment style characterized by a concern that others will not reciprocate one's desire for intimacy, resulting in higher-than-average levels of anxiety. (p. 308)

15. _____ The theory that people's commitment to a relationship depends not only on their satisfaction with the relationship in terms of rewards, costs, and comparison level and their comparison level for alternatives but also on how much they have invested in the relationship that would be lost by leaving it. (p. 312)

16. _____ Relationships governed by the need for equity (i.e., for an equal ratio of rewards and costs). (p. 315)

17. _____ Relationships in which people's primary concern is being responsive to the other person's needs. (p. 315)

GUIDED REVIEW

PRACTICE TEST

1. When you were eight years old, chances are you were best friends with someone who lived on your block. Social psychologists would attribute this to:
   a) the effects of attitude similarity.
   b) your uniquely similar interests.
   c) matched levels of physical attractiveness.
   d) the propinquity effect.

2. In their study of "blind dates," Elaine Hatfield and her colleagues (1966) found that an individual's desire to date his or her partner again was best predicted by the partner's:
   a) physical attractiveness.
   b) dominance and sensitivity.
   c) complementary personality traits.
   d) intelligence.

3. Research has found all of the following facial features to be considered physically attractive EXCEPT:
   a) large eyes.
   b) wide cheeks.
   c) big smile.
   d) small nose.

4. Social exchange theory maintains that people are happiest with relationships when:
   a) the perceived rewards of the relationship are equal to the perceived costs of the relationship.
   b) the rewards and costs a person experiences are roughly equal to the rewards and costs of the other person in a relationship.
   c) the actual rewards and costs of the relationship exceed the expected rewards and costs.
   d) the perceived rewards of the relationship outweigh the perceived costs of the relationship.

5. When the rewards and costs a person experiences and the contributions he/she makes to the relationship are roughly equal to the rewards, costs, and contributions of the other person, the relationship is:
   a) equitable.
   b) communal.
   c) intimate.
   d) passionate.

6. Mindy broke up with her boyfriend Mark because she believed she could have a better relationship with Ken. This illustrates
   a) equity theory.
   b) comparison level for alternatives.
   c) the investment model.
   d) a communal relationship.

7. People are likely to remain committed to an intimate relationship even if they are dissatisfied with it and even if alternative relationships look promising if:
   a) they suffer from low self-esteem.
   b) they have a high comparison level.
   c) they have benefited from the relationship in the past.
   d) they have invested heavily in the relationship.

8. In a happy communal relationship, partners believe that equity:
   a) is of no importance.
   b) should exist at any given time.
   c) will be maintained in the long run.
   d) requires close monitoring at all times.

9. At the end of a romantic relationship, who is most likely to want to remain friends with his/her ex-lover?
   a) a female who has taken responsibility for the breakup
   b) a male who has taken responsibility for the breakup
   c) a male whose partner has taken responsibility for the breakup
   d) a female whose partner has taken responsibility for the breakup

10. The desire to be validated and the conclusions we draw about people's characters based on their attitudes lead us to prefer people whose attitudes:
   a) complement our own.
   b) are similar to our own.
   c) are generally positive.
   d) are well informed.

11. The comparison level for alternatives is based on:
   a) perceptions of the level of rewards and punishments received from your primary caregiver during infancy.
   b) perceptions of the level of rewards and punishments others are receiving in their present relationships.
   c) expectations about the level of rewards and punishments others would receive if they were sharing a relationship with your partner.
   d) expectations about the level of rewards and punishments you would receive if you were in a different relationship.

12. A tit-for-tat equity norm governs _____ relationships.
   a) exchange
   b) communal
   c) familial
   d) romantic

13. Attachment styles are the expectations people develop about:
   a) the level of rewards and punishments they are likely to receive in a particular relationship.
   b) the level of rewards and punishments they would receive in an alternative relationship.
   c) the kinds of actions by their partners that constitute a threat to their self-worth and produce feelings of jealousy.
   d) relationships with others based on the relationship they had with their primary caregiver when they were infants.

14. An individual who has an anxious/ambivalent attachment style:
   a) finds it difficult to trust others and to develop close intimate relationships.
   b) is able to develop a mature, lasting relationship.
   c) wants to become very close to his/her partner but worries that his/her affections will not be returned.
   d) is not interested in developing a close relationship.

15. Which of the following is the final step in Duck's (1982) process of relationship dissolution?
   a) discussing the breakup with one's partner
   b) telling one's friends of the breakup
   c) forming an account of how and why the breakup occurred
   d) withdrawing emotionally from others

16. An approach which states that men are attracted by women's appearance and that women are attracted by men's resources is the:
   a) communal exchange theory.
   b) investment model.
   c) propinquity effect.
   d) evolutionary approach to love.

17. The more times we see someone, the more inclined we are to like the person. This is called the _____ effect.
    a) propinquity
    b) familiarity
    c) mere exposure
    d) social facilitation

18. According to a 2006 study by Leskovec and Horvitz, _____ degrees of separation appear to explain quite well how interconnected people are in this media age.
    a) 8 (or 9)
    b) 5 (or 6)
    c) 6 to 10
    d) 6 (or 7)

19. Which of the following is true regarding cultural standards that dictate which facial characteristics are considered beautiful?
    a) No cross-cultural agreement exists in what makes up a beautiful or a handsome face.
    b) Some cross-cultural agreement exists in what makes up a beautiful or a handsome face.
    c) Standards of beauty may reflect people's preferences for the familiar over the unfamiliar.
    d) Both b and c are true.

20. Which of the following is FALSE regarding assumptions people have about attractive people?
    a) The concern for physical attractiveness affects men's lives more than it does women's lives.
    b) The "what is beautiful is good" stereotype operates across cultures.
    c) Attractive people are higher in social competence than unattractive people.
    d) Attractive people are thought to be more popular and assertive than unattractive people.

21. Relationship satisfaction depends on people's comparison level or what they expect the outcome of their relationship to be in terms of:
    a) whether they can replace it with a better one.
    b) rewards and benefits.
    c) rewards and costs.
    d) time and money.

22. Intense longing and physiological arousal are to _____ love as intimacy and affection are to _____ love.
    a) fatuous; romantic
    b) companionate; romantic
    c) passionate; companionate
    d) romantic; empty

23. Chinese couples tend to value _____ love more than American couples do.
    a) passionate
    b) companionate
    c) *amae*
    d) *jung*

24. The Taita of Kenya, in East Africa, conceptualize romantic love as a combination of companionate love and passionate love.
    a) True
    b) False

25. Which of the following is true regarding the role of culture in defining love?
    a) The Japanese have a term for love (*amae*) for which there is no equivalent word in the English language.
    b) Fixing someone's bicycle could be considered a romantic act in China.
    c) Research has found that love in Chinese songs is less erotic than love expressed in American songs.
    d) Both a and b are true.

26. Which of the following is FALSE regarding love in individualist versus collectivist societies?
    a) Romantic love is a more important basis for marriage in individualist compared to collectivist societies.
    b) Families often arrange the marriages of their children in collectivist societies.
    c) Marrying for love is most important to participants in Eastern cultures.
    d) Culture determines how romantic love is experienced and expressed.

27. Individuals having which of the following attachment styles have the most short-lived romantic relationships?
    a) anxious/ambivalent
    b) avoidant
    c) secure
    d) detached

28. Individuals having which of the following attachment styles are the most likely to report never having been in love?
    a) anxious/ambivalent
    b) avoidant
    c) secure
    d) sincere

29. According to the study of attachment styles and relationship success (Kirkpatrick & Davis, 1994), which of the following relationship pairs had very stable relationships?
    a) anxious/ambivalent men involved with secure women
    b) anxious/ambivalent men involved with avoidant women
    c) secure women involved with avoidant men
    d) anxious/ambivalent women involved with avoidant men

30. According to Rusbult's (1983) investment model of commitment, which of the following is NOT a predictor of relationship commitment?
    a) satisfaction with the relationship
    b) love felt towards a partner
    c) level of investment in the relationship
    d) quality of alternatives to the relationship

31.   In Festinger, Schacter, and Back's study on relationships among couples in apartment buildings, they found that _____ percent of the next-door neighbors indicated they were close friends.
a)   69
b)   41
c)   22
d)   10

32.   In Festinger, Schacter, and Back's study on relationships among couples in apartment buildings, they found that _____ percent of couples who lived on opposite ends of the hall indicated they were close friends.
a)   69
b)   41
c)   22
d)   10

33.   Randy did not like the new theme song for his favorite show the first time he heard it, but as the season went on, he realized he liked the song better and better. Randy's increased liking of the theme song is due to
a)   operant conditioning.
b)   classical conditioning.
c)   the mere exposure effect.
d)   the repetitive auditory stimulus effect.

34.   Montoya and his colleagues found that in long-term relationships, actual similarity predicted liking and attraction better than perceived similarity did.
a)   True
b)   False

35.   Johnston and colleagues found that women unconsciously respond to a more masculinized face than an average male face when their ability to conceive is high, but not when it is low.
a)   True
b)   False

36.   Research on attachment styles indicates that one's genes account for _____ percent of the anxious and avoidant styles, with one's environment accounting for the rest.
a)   15 to 25
b)   25 to 45
c)   20 to 45
d)   20 to 50

37.   Infants prefer photographs of attractive faces to unattractive ones.
a)   True
b)   False

38.   We stereotype beautiful people as gifted in the area of social competence. Research
a)   disconfirms this belief.
b)   is unclear on this issue.
c)   has overwhelmingly supported this belief.
d)   has supported this belief somewhat.

Chapter 10

39.   In many areas of West Africa, happily married couples do not live together in the same house, nor
       do they expect to sleep together every night.
       a)   True
       b)   False

40.   Gangestad and Buss found a stronger preference for physically attractive mates in areas of the
       world where there is a
       a)   low prevalence of disease-transmitting parasites.
       b)   high prevalence of disease-transmitting parasites.
       c)   strong economy.
       d)   weak economy.

SHORT ANSWER REVIEW

One of the variables that cause initial attraction between two people is physical proximity, or the

propinquity effect: The people who, by chance, are the ones you (1) _____ (p. 289) with the most

often are the most likely to become your friends and lovers. This occurs because of the mere exposure

effect: exposure to any (2) _____ (p. 290) produces liking for it. (3) _____ (p. 291) between

people, whether in attitudes, values, personality traits, or demographic characteristics, is also a powerful

cause of attraction and liking. Similarity is a more powerful predictor of attraction than (4) _____

(p. 291), the idea that opposites attract.

In general, we like others who behave as if they like us. The term for this is (5) _____ (p.

292). Physical attractiveness also plays an important role in liking. Research finds that men and women

rank physical attractiveness as equally important. The powerful role that physical appearance plays in

attraction is not limited to (6) _____ (p. 294) relationships. People from different cultures perceive

facial attractiveness quite similarly. The crucial variable that explains interpersonal attraction may

actually be (7) _____ (p. 296). Averaging many faces together produces one face that looks typical,

familiar, and physically attractive. Research has also found that when participants rate the attractiveness

of faces, they prefer the faces that most resemble (8) _____ (p. 296). The "what is (9) _____

(p. 297) is good" stereotype indicates that people assume that physical attractiveness is associated with

other desirable traits.

One theory of interpersonal attraction is social exchange theory. Social exchange theory states that how people feel about their relationships depends on their (10) _____ (p. 299) of the rewards they receive and the costs they incur. In order to determine whether people will stay in a relationship, we also need to know their comparison level—their expectations about the (11) _____ (p. 300) of their relationship—and their comparison level for alternatives—their expectations about how happy they would be in (12) _____ (p. 300). Equity theory states that the most important determinant of satisfaction is the amount of equity in the relationship, wherein the (13) _____ (p. 300) they experience and the contributions they make to the relationship are roughly equal to those of the other person.

Love can be defined in different ways. One definition of love makes a distinction between (14) _____ (p. 301)—feelings of intimacy that are not accompanied by intense longing and arousal— and passionate love—feelings of intimacy that are accompanied by intense longing and arousal. Although love is a universal emotion, cultural variations in the definition of love do occur. Love has a somewhat different emphasis in collectivistic and individualistic cultures.

Evolutionary psychology explains social behavior in terms of genetic factors that have evolved over time according to principles of (15) _____ (p. 304). The evolutionary approach to love is derived from evolutionary biology and holds that men and women are attracted to different characteristics in each other because this maximizes their (16) _____ (p. 304).

According to the theory of attachment styles, the kinds of bonds we form (17) _____ (p. 307) influence the kinds of relationships we form as adults. The secure attachment style is characterized by (18) _____ (p. 307), a lack of concern with being abandoned, and the view that one is worthy and well liked. The avoidant attachment style is characterized by a (19) _____ (p. 308) of attachment needs, because attempts to be intimate have been rebuffed; people with this style find it

271

difficult to develop intimate relationships. The anxious/ambivalent attachment style is characterized by a concern that others will not reciprocate one's desire for intimacy, thus resulting in higher-than-average levels of (20) _____ (p. 308). The key assumption of attachment theory is that the particular attachment style we learn as infants and young children becomes our working model or schema for what relationships are like. A person's genotype may predispose him or her to a specific attachment style, which will then be further affected, one way or another, by influences in the environment.

Research has shown ample support for social exchange theory in intimate relationships in cultures as different as Taiwan and the Netherlands. Of course, we know that many people do not leave their partners, even when they are dissatisfied and their other alternatives look bright. Research indicates that we need to consider at least one additional factor to understand close relationships—a person's level of investment in the relationship. According to the (21) _____ (p. 312) of close relationships, people's commitment to a relationship depends not only on their satisfaction with the relationhship in terms of rewards, costs, and comparison level and their comparison level for alternatives, but also on how much they have invested in the relationship that would be lost by leaving it.

The equity of rewards and costs is different in long-term relationships than in short-term relationships. Interactions between new acqaintances are governed by equity concerns that are called (22) _____ (p. 315) relationships. In exchange relationships, people keep track of who is contributing what and feel taken advantage of when they feel they are putting more into the relationship than they are getting out of it. In comparison, interactions between close friends, family members, and romantic partners are governed less by an equity norm and more by a desire to help each other in times of need. In these communal relationships, people give in response to the other's (23) _____ (p. 315), regardless of whether they are paid back.

The breaking-up process is composed of stages. In the (24) _____ (p. 316) stage the individual thinks a lot about his or her dissatisfaction with the relationship. In the (25) _____ (p. 316) stage the individual discusses the breakup with the partner. In the social stage the breakup is (26) _____ (p. 316) to other people. Then the process goes back to the intrapersonal stage again when the individual recovers from the breakup and forms an (27) _____ (p. 316), or version, of how and why it happened.

Strategies for responding to problems in a romantic relationship include both constructive and destructive behaviors. Destructive behaviors include (28) _____ (p. 317) harming the relationship and passively allowing the relationship to deteriorate. Constructive behaviors include actively trying to (29) _____ (p. 317) the relationship and passively remaining loyal to the relationship. (30) _____ (p. 317) occur when the qualities in a person that once were attractive become the very qualities that repel. A powerful variable that predicts how a person will weather the breakup is the role he or she plays in the decision to terminate the relationship. Whether people want to stay friends when they break up depends on the role they played in the breakup, as well as their gender.

ESSAY REVIEW

1. Discuss the factors that have been demonstrated to increase interpersonal attraction among casual acquaintances.

2. Identify facial features associated with attractiveness in men and in women. Describe the assumptions we make about attractive people and a consequence of making such assumptions.

3. Identify the key assumption of attachment theory. Describe the formation of each of the attachment styles in infancy and the consequences of each of these for adult relationships.

4. Describe the effects of rewards, costs, and two kinds of comparison levels on the outcome of a relationship according to social exchange theory.

5. Compare and contrast social exchange theory with equity theory.

EXIT TESTS

EXIT TEST 1

1. In Festinger, Schacter, and Back's study on relationships among couples in apartment buildings, they found that _____ percent of those who lived two doors apart indicated they were close friends.
    a) 69
    b) 41
    c) 22
    d) 10

2. The propinquity effect works because of
    a) similarity.
    b) familiarity.
    c) complementary.
    d) reciprocity.

3. Chan and Cheng compared online and offline friendships that had existed for longer than a year were very similar.
    a) True
    b) False

4. Evolutionarily speaking, a woman should be most interested in a man with "good genes" when she is
    a) thinking about getting married.
    b) dating.
    c) in love.
    d) ovulating.

5. We are attracted to people whose _____ are similar to our own.
    a) attitudes
    b) interests
    c) interpersonal style
    d) all of the above

6. We do not tend to think that people who are similar to us will also like us.
    a) True
    b) False

7. Knowing that someone likes us is so powerful that it can make up for the absence of similarity.
    a) True
    b) False

8. Recent research on how men and women rank physical attractiveness indicates that
    a) neither men and women rank it as very important compared to other characteristics such as intelligence.
    b) men rank it as important, but women do not.
    c) men and women rank it as equally important.
    d) women now rank it as very important, but men only rank it as slightly important.

9. A "regular" person can be made to act like a "beautiful" one through the self-fulfilling prophecy.
    a) True
    b) False

10. Some researchers have criticized social exchange theory for ignoring _____.
    a) physical attractiveness.
    b) similarity.
    c) cultural influences.
    d) equity.

EXIT TEST 2

1. Lynn and Denise have been friends for a year. Denise buys Lynn expensive gifts for her birthday and holidays and usually insists on buying lunch or coffee when she and Lynn go out. Sometimes when Lynn and Denise go shopping, Denise will buy things for Lynn that she notices Lynn likes. Lynn does not have the money to do all these things for Denise. According to equity theory, Lynn is going to feel
    a) great because her costs are low and her rewards are high.
    b) underbenefited.
    c) overbenefited.
    d) okay with the situation because she does not have much money.

2. _____ is a Japanese term for a passive love object, indulged and taken care of by one's romantic partner.
    a) *Amae*
    b) *Gan qing*
    c) *Jung*
    d) *Yuan*

3. According to David Buss and the evolutionary approach to love, finding (and keeping) a mate requires one to
    a) hide one's resources until you determine whether the other person is a suitable match.
    b) display one's resources.
    c) show his or herself to be trustworthy.
    d) show that he or she is industrious.

4. Gillath and colleagues found that genes account for about _____ percent of the variability in attachment anxiety and avoidance.
    a) 2
    b) 10
    c) 15
    d) 20

5. Liz trusts other people and does not worry that her husband, Mike, will leave her. She feels worthy of love and believes that she is liked by many people. According to the theory of attachment styles, Liz's attachment can be described as
    a) secure.
    b) communal.
    c) avoidant.
    d) anxious/ambivalent.

6.   Yolanda is always worried that other people will not reciprocate her desire for a close, intimate relationship so even when she is in a relationship she experiences high levels of anxiety. According to the theory of attachment styles, Yolanda's attachment can be described as
    a)   secure.
    b)   communal.
    c)   avoidant.
    d)   anxious/ambivalent.

7.   Attachment styles affect communication in a relationship, but they do not affect the attributions that partners make about each other.
    a)   True
    b)   False

8.   Vicki is 58 years old and very unhappy with her marriage. She and her husband are more like roommates than spouses. Vicki is thinking about leaving her husband. If she does leave her husband, it will greatly reduce her style of living and she will not have any health insurance. She will no longer be able to live in an expensive home or buy expensive clothes. According to Rusbult's investment model, what is Vicki likely to do?
    a)   get a good lawyer
    b)   she will leave the relationship no matter what the material costs are because money cannot buy happiness
    c)   stay in the marriage
    d)   she will try to convince her husband to see a marriage counselor

9.   According to Margaret Clark and Judson Mills, interactions between new acquaintances are governed by equity concerns and are called
    a)   exchange relationships.
    b)   equity relationships.
    c)   communal relationships.
    d)   tit-for-tat relationships.

10.   Which of the following represents the correct order of the phases of relationship dissolution proposed by Duck?
    a)   dyadic, intrapersonal, social, intrapersonal
    b)   social, intrapersonal, dyadic, intrapersonal
    c)   intrapersonal, social, dyadic, intrapersonal
    d)   intrapersonal, dyadic, social, intrapersonal

STUDY ACTIVITIES

1.   Identify which two areas deep within the brain are activated when people look at a photographs of their romantic partners.

2.   Why is reciprocal liking important in attraction? What role does self-esteem play in reciprocal liking?

3.   When it comes to attractive people, we assume that "what is beautiful is good. " What role does the self-fulfilling prophecy play in the perpetuation of these assumptions? Can you think of a time when you made assumptions about someone based on his or her personal appearance?

4. What accounts for happy relationships according to equity theory? Analyze one of your own relationships using equity theory.

5. Differentiate between companionate love and passionate love.

6. How does culture influence the definition of romantic love, the emotions associated with romantic love, and the behaviors that correspond with being in love?

7. What are the major arguments of evolutionary theory as it relates to love? How does evolutionary theory explain people's choices regarding with whom they fall in love?

8. How do exchange relationships differ from communal relationships?

9. What are the four stages of relationship dissolution according to Duck?

10. Rather than terminating a romance outright, people wanting to dissolve a relationship have been known to annoy their partners and deliberately cause problems in the relationship. Is this simply the act of a coward or could there be other motives underlying the use of such a strategy?

Chapter 10 Answers

Practice Test

1. D (p. 289)
2. A (p. 293)
3. B (p. 394)
4. D (p. 399)
5. A (p. 300)
6. B (p. 300)
7. D (pp. 312-313)
8. C (p. 315)
9. D (p. 318)
10. B (p. 291)
11. D (p. 300)
12. A (p. 315)
13. D (pp. 307-308)
14. C (p. 308)
15. C (p. 316)
16. D (pp. 304-305)
17. C (p. 290)
18. D (p. 291)
19. D (pp. 294-296)
20. A (pp. 297-299)
21. C (p. 300)
22. C (p. 301)
23. B (p. 301)
24. A (pp. 301-302)
25. D (p. 303)
26. C (pp. 303-304)
27. A (p. 310)
28. B (p. 310)
29. D (p. 311)
30. B (pp. 312-313)
31. B (p. 289)
32. D (p. 289)
33. C (p. 290)
34. B (p. 292)
35. A (p. 306)
36. C (p. 312)
37. A (p. 295)
38. D (p. 298)
39. A (p. 304)
40. B (p. 305)

Short Answer Review

1. see and interact (p. 289)
2. stimulus (p. 290)
3. Similarity (p. 291)
4. complementarity (p. 291)

5. reciprocal liking (p. 292)
6. heterosexual (p. 294)
7. familiarity (p. 296)
8. their own (p. 296)
9. beautiful (p. 297)
10. perceptions (p. 299)
11. outcomes (p. 300)
12. other relationships (p. 300)
13. rewards and costs (p. 300)
14. companionate love (p. 301)
15. natural selection (p. 304)
16. reproductive success (p. 304)
17. early in life (p. 307)
18. trust (p. 307)
19. suppression (p. 308)
20. anxiety (p. 308)
21. investment model (p. 312)
22. exchange (p. 315)
23. needs (p. 315)
24. intrapersonal (p. 316)
25. dyadic (p. 316)
26. announced (p. 316)
27. account (p. 316)
28. actively (p. 317)
29. improve (p. 317)
30. Fatal attractions (p. 317)

Essay Review

1. Your essay should include the following:
    *   We develop favorable impressions of individuals when repeated exposure owing to propinquity makes the person familiar. (pp. 289-290)
    *   We like individuals whose characteristics and beliefs, interpersonal style, and interests and experiences are similar to our own. (pp. 291-292)
    *   We like people who like us, especially if we have gained in their positive estimation of us. (pp. 292-293)
    *   Finally, good looks can increase interpersonal attraction. (pp. 293-294)

2. Your essay should include the following:
    *   The facial features associated with the attractiveness of females include large eyes, a small nose, a small chin, prominent cheekbones and narrow cheeks, high eyebrows, large pupils, and a big smile. (p. 294)
    *   The features associated with attractiveness in males include large eyes, prominent cheekbones, a large chin, and a big smile. (p. 294)
    *   Assumptions people make about attractive versus less attractive people include attractive people being more sociable, extraverted, popular, sexual, happier, and more assertive than less attractive people. (p. 294)
    *   A consequence of making such assumptions is that due to the self-fulfilling prophecy, we may behave in ways that confirm our expectations about attractive people. (p. 298)

Chapter 10

3.   Your essay on attachment theory should include:
- Attachment theory assumes that attachment styles that we learn as infants and young children generalize to all of our relationships with others. (pp. 307-311)
- Infants with responsive caregivers develop a secure attachment style and are able to develop mature, stable relationships later in life. (pp. 307-311)
- Infants with aloof and distant caregivers develop an avoidant style, are untrusting, and find it difficult to develop intimacy. (pp. 307-311)
- Infants whose caregivers are inconsistent and overbearing in their affections develop an anxious/ambivalent style. These individuals desire intimacy, but fear that their affections will not be returned. (pp. 307-311)

4.   Your essay on exchange theory should include the following:
- The outcome is defined as rewards minus costs. The greater the rewards relative to the costs, the better the individual will feel about the relationship and remain in it. (pp. 299-300)
- The expectations one has about the level of rewards and punishments that one is likely to receive in a particular relationship, and in an alternative relationship, define the comparison level and comparison level of alternatives, respectively. These affect one's subjective interpretation of rewards and costs and so affect the outcome as well. (pp. 299-300)

5.   Your essay should include the following:
- Both theories claim that perceived rewards and punishments in a relationship determine relationship satisfaction. (pp. 299-300)
- Equity theory claims that the notion of fairness or equity is additionally important. According to equity theory, even if the rewards of both partners outweigh the costs, the relationship will be unsatisfying if it is inequitable. (pp. 299-300)

Exit Test 1

1.   C (p. 289)
2.   B (p. 289)
3.   A (p. 290)
4.   D (p. 306)
5.   D (pp. 291-292)
6.   B (p. 293)
7.   A (p. 293)
8.   C (pp. 293-294)
9.   A (p. 298)
10.   D (p. 300)

Exit Test 2

1.   C (p. 300)
2.   A (p. 303)
3.   B (p. 305)
4.   D (p. 312)
5.   A (p. 307)

6. D (p. 308)
7. B (p. 310)
8. C (p. 314)
9. A (p. 315)
10. D (p. 316)

Study Activities

1. The ventral tegmental area (VTA) and the caudate nucleus. (p. 309)

2. Reciprocal liking is important because we all like to be liked by others. Just knowing that someone likes us fuels our attraction to the person. Liking is so powerful that it can even make up for the absence of similarity. Reciprocal liking can also be a self-fulfilling prophecy. If we believe someone likes us, we will treat that person well and the person will respond in kind. (pp. 292-293)

3. The truth in the stereotype occurs because the beautiful receive a great deal of social attention that in turn helps them develop good social skills. This treatment turns into a self-fulfilling prophecy when the beautiful person responds in a positive way to the way he or she is treated. (pp. 298-299)

4. According to equity theory, people are happiest with relationships in which the rewards and costs experienced and the contributions made by both parties are roughly equal. (p. 300)

5. Companionate love is the intimacy and affection we feel when we care deeply for a person, but do not experience passion or arousal in the person's presence. Passionate love is an intense longing we feel for a person, accompanied by physiological arousal; when our love is reciprocated, we feel great fulfillment and ecstasy, but when it is not, we feel sadness and despair. (p. 301)

6. Although love is a universal emotion, how we experience it (and what we expect from close relationships) is linked to culture. The Japanese describe *amae* as an extremely positive emotional state in which one is a totally passive love object. The Chinese concept of *gan qing* is achieved by helping and working for another person. In Korea, *jung* is what ties two people together, it takes time and many mutual experiences. In West African settings, relationships with one's parents, siblings and other relatives are seen as more important and consequential than the more recent relationship one has formed with one's spouse. (pp. 303-304)

7. According to the evolutionary approach to love, men and women are attracted to different characteristics in each other (men are attracted by women's appearance; women are attracted by men's resources) because this maximized their chances of reproductive success. Men are attracted by women's appearance because they associate it with reproductive fitness and they are looking for women who are capable of reproducing successfully. Women are attracted by men's resources because they face high reproductive costs and want men who will be capable of supplying the resources and support needed to bear children. (pp. 304-305)

8. Exchange relationships are governed by the need for equity. In exchange relationships, people keep track of who is contributing what and feel taken advantage of when they feel they are putting more into the relationship than they are getting out of it. In communal relationships,

people's primary concern is being responsive to the other person's needs regardless of whether they are paid back. (p. 315)

9.   The stages of relationship dissolution identified by Duck include the intrapersonal (the person thinks a lot about his or her dissatisfaction with the relationship); the dyadic (the individual discusses the breakup with the partner); the social (the breakup is announced to other people); and back to the intrapersonal (the individual recovers from the breakup and forms an account, or version, of how and why it happened). (p. 316)

10.   Research suggests that the less responsible an individual is for the breakup, the worse that person is likely to feel after the romantic relationship is terminated. By causing problems in a relationship and by annoying one's partner, an individual who desires to terminate the relationship may be allowing his/her partner to take some responsibility for the breakup in order to relieve some of the pain his/her ex-lover will experience.
(pp. 317-318)

CHAPTER 11

Prosocial Behavior: Why Do People Help?

CHAPTER 11 OVERVIEW

This chapter examines the causes of **prosocial behavior**, acts performed with the goal of benefiting another person. The first section of the chapter examines the basic motives underlying prosocial behavior. This chapter is particularly concerned with prosocial behavior that is motivated by **altruism**, which is the desire to help another person even if it involves a cost to the helper. Evolutionary theory explains prosocial behavior in three ways. The first is **kin selection**, the idea that behaviors that help a genetic relative are favored by natural selection. The second is the **norm of reciprocity**, which is the expectation that helping others will increase the likelihood that they will help us in the future. The third is that it is adaptive for people to learn social norms of all kinds, and one of these norms is the value of helping others. Some evolutionary theorists argue that natural selection operates at the level of the group as well as at the individual level.

Social exchange theory argues that prosocial behavior is not necessarily rooted in our genes. Instead, people help others in order to maximize social rewards and minimize social costs. The difference from evolutionary approaches is that social exchange theory doesn't trace this desire back to our evolutionary roots; nor does it assume that the desire is genetically based. Helping behavior can be rewarding in a number of ways. It can increase the likelihood that someone will help us in return. Helping people can also relieve the personal distress of a bystander. By helping others, we can also gain such rewards as social approval from others and increased feelings of self-worth. The other side of the coin, of course, is that helping can be costly. Helping decreases when the costs are high, such as when it would put us in physical danger, result in pain or embarrassment, or simply take too much time. Social exchange theory argues that true altruism, in which people help even when it is costly to themselves, does not exist.

Pure altruism is likely to come into play when we feel empathy for the person in need of help. **Empathy** is the ability to put oneself in the shoes of another person and to experience events and emotions the way that person experiences them. According to the **empathy-altruism hypothesis**, when people feel empathy toward another person, they attempt to help that person purely for altruistic reasons.

The next section of the chapter examines personal qualities and prosocial behavior and addresses the question "Why do some people help more than others?" Basic motives are not all there is to understanding prosocial behavior. We need to understand why some people are more helpful than others are. Psychologists have been interested in the nature of the **altruistic personality**, the qualities that cause an individual to help others in a wide variety of situations. Although some people have personality qualities that make them more likely to help than others, personality factors have not been shown to be strong predictors of who will help across a variety of social situations.

There are gender differences in prosocial behavior. In virtually all cultures, norms prescribe different traits and behaviors for males and females. In Western cultures, the male sex role includes helping in chivalrous and heroic ways, whereas the female sex role includes being nurturing and helping in close, long-term relationships. Cultural differences in prosocial behavior also exist. People in all cultures are more likely to help someone they define as a member of their **in-group**, the group with which an individual identifies. People everywhere are less likely to help someone they perceive to be a member of an **out-group**, a group with which they do not identify. Cultural factors come into play in determining how strongly people draw the line between in-groups and out-groups. In addition, religion fosters prosocial behavior on some, but not all, measures. People who attend religious services report on surveys that they give more money to charity, and engage in more volunteer work, than do people who do not attend religious services.

People are more likely to help if they are in especially good moods, but also if they are in especially bad moods. Researchers have found a "feel good, do good" effect in diverse situations. When people are in a good mood they are more helpful in many ways. Being in a good mood can increase helping for three reasons. First, good moods make us look on the bright side of life. Helping other people is also an excellent way of prolonging our good mood. Finally, good moods increase self-attention. People are also more likely to help if they are in a bad mood. People often act on the idea that good deeds cancel out bad deeds. When they have done something that has made them feel guilty, helping another person balances things out, reducing their guilty feelings.

In the next section of the chapter, situational determinants of prosocial behavior are discussed. Personality, gender, culture, and mood all contribute a piece to the puzzle of why people help others. To understand why people help others, we also need to consider the nature of the social situation. People are less likely to help in dense, urban settings because of the **urban overload hypothesis** – the idea that people living in cities are constantly bombarded with stimulation and that they keep to themselves in order to avoid being overwhelmed by it. People who have lived for a long time in one place are more likely to engage in prosocial behaviors than people who have recently moved to an area.

In order to help in an emergency, people must meet five conditions: They must notice the event, interpret it as an emergency, assume responsibility, know the appropriate form of assistance, and implement their decision to help. As the number of bystanders who witness an emergency increases, the more difficult it is to meet two of these conditions – interpreting the event as an emergency and assuming responsibility. This produces the **bystander effect**: the larger the number of bystanders, the less likely any one of them is to help. In an emergency, bystanders tend to freeze, watching and listening with blank expressions as they try to figure out what is going on. When they glance at each other, they see an apparent lack of concern on the part of everyone else. This results in **pluralistic ignorance**. Bystanders assume nothing is wrong in an emergency because no one else looks concerned. Sometimes it is obvious that an emergency is occurring. In these cases, diffusion of responsibility may occur. **Diffusion of responsibility** is the phenomenon whereby each bystander's sense of responsibility to help decreases as the number of witnesses increases. Because other people are present, no single bystander feels a strong personal responsibility to act.

The nature of a relationship influences helping behavior. People in *exchange relationships* –those governed by concerns about equity – are concerned primarily with the benefits they will receive by helping others. People in *communal relationships*--those in which the primary concern is the welfare of the other person –are less concerned with the benefits they will receive and more with simply satisfying the needs of the other person.

The final section of the chapter addresses the question "How can helping be increased?" Research shows that teaching people about the barriers to bystander intervention increases the likelihood that they will help in emergencies. A new field called positive psychology has emerged that focuses on people's strengths and virtues, instead of mental disease. The social psychological approach is to investigate the conditions under which people act in positive (e.g., helpful) and negative (e.g., unhelpful) ways. Many of these conditions were discussed in this chapter. For example, people will help at a cost to themselves when they feel empathy toward a person in need. When they do not feel empathy, they will help only when it is in their self-interest.

CHAPTER 11 OUTLINE

I. Basic Motives Underlying Prosocial Behavior: Why Do People Help?
• **Prosocial behavior** is any act performed with the goal of benefiting another person.
• **Altruism** is any act that benefits another person, but does not benefit the helper and often involves some personal cost to the helper.
• Two basic questions that people have asked are whether helping is an inborn tendency or one that must be taught, and whether people ever help without receiving some benefit in return.

    A. Evolutionary Psychology: Instincts and Genes
    • *Evolutionary psychology* is the attempt to explain social behavior in terms of genetic factors that evolved over time according to the principles of natural selection.
    • Darwin recognized that altruistic behavior posed a problem for his theory: if an organism acts altruistically, it may decrease its own likelihood of surviving to pass on its genes.
       1. Kin Selection
       • **Kin selection** is the idea that behaviors that help a genetic relative are favored by natural selection. Helping a kin member may decrease one's own probability for survival/passing on one's genes, but kin share the same genes, so saving a kin member may pass on one's own genes. Self-reports from people (Burnstein, Crandall, & Kitayama, 1994), and anecdotal evidence from real emergencies show that organisms help closely related kin more than less closely related individuals.
       2. The Reciprocity Norm
       • The **norm of reciprocity** is the expectation that helping others will increase the likelihood that they will help us in the future. The idea is that as human beings were evolving, those who were the most likely to survive would be those who developed an understanding with the neighbors based on this norm; they would have been more likely to survive than either completely competitive or completely cooperative people would.
       3. Learning Social Norms
       • Simon (1990) suggests that those who are the best learners of societal norms have a survival advantage. Thus people are genetically programmed to learn social norms and one of these norms is altruism.
       • The claims of evolutionary psychologists are still being debated. For example, the theory has difficulty explaining why complete strangers sometimes help each other.
       3. Group Selection
       • Some evolutionary theorists argue that natural selection operates at the level of the group as well as at the individual level.
       • Though the idea of group selection is controversial and not supported by all biologists, it has prominent proponents.

    B. Social Exchange: The Costs and Rewards of Helping
    • *Social exchange theory* argues that much of what we do stems from the desire to maximize our outcomes and minimize our costs. Like evolutionary psychology, it is a theory based on self-interest; unlike it, it assumes that self-interest has no genetic basis.
    • Helping can be rewarding in three ways: it can increase the probability that someone will help us in return in the future; it can relieve the personal distress of the bystander; and it can gain us social approval and increased self-worth.
    • Helping can also be costly; thus it decreases when costs are high. Social exchange theory presumes that people help only when the rewards outweigh the costs. Thus social exchange theory presumes that there is no pure altruism.

Chapter 11

C. Empathy and Altruism: The Pure Motive for Helping
• Batson is the strongest proponent of the idea that people often help purely out of the goodness of their hearts. He argues that pure altruism is most likely to come into play when we experience **empathy** for the person in need; that is, when we are able to experience events and emotions the way that that person experiences them. Batson's **empathy-altruism hypothesis** states that when we feel empathy for a person, we will attempt to help purely for altruistic reasons, that is, regardless of what we have to gain. If we do not feel empathy, then social exchange concerns will come into play (see Figure 11.1).
• In a study by Toi and Batson (1982), students listened to a taped interview with a student who had ostensibly broken both legs in an accident and was behind in classes. Two factors were manipulated: empathetic vs. non-empathetic set, manipulated by instructions given to Ss; and the costs of helping, manipulated by whether or not the injured student was expected to be seen every day once she returned to class. The dependent variable was whether Ss responded to a request to help the injured student catch up in class. As the empathy-altruism hypothesis predicted, people in the high empathy condition helped regardless of cost, while those in the low empathy condition helped only if the cost of not helping was high (Figure 11.2).
• The empathy-altruism hypothesis has been much debated, with some researchers arguing that empathy increases the cost of not helping and thus increases the likelihood of helping because it lowers people's distress at seeing someone they care about suffer. However, the theory has thus far withstood these challenges.

II. Personal Qualities and Prosocial Behavior: Why Do Some People Help More than Others?

A. Individual Differences: The Altruistic Personality
• An **altruistic personality** is those aspects of a person's makeup that are said to make him or her likely to help others in a wide variety of situations.
• It turns out that there is little evidence of consistency in altruism; for example, Hartshorne and May (1929) found only a .23 correlation between different kinds of helping behaviors in children, and others have found that those who scored high on a personality test of altruism were not more likely to help than those who scored low. People's personality is clearly not the only determinant of helping. We need to consider several other critical factors as well, such as the situational pressures that are affecting people, their gender, the culture in which they grew up, and even their current mood.

B. Gender Differences in Prosocial Behavior
• Men are more likely to help in chivalrous, heroic ways, and women are more likely to help in nurturing ways involving long-term commitment. In virtually all cultures, norms prescribe different traits and behaviors for males and females. In Western cultures, the male sex role includes helping in chivalrous and heroic ways, whereas the female sex role includes being nurturing and helping in close, long-term relationships.

C. Cultural Differences in Prosocial Behavior
• It might seem as though people with an *interdependent view of the self,* who come from collectivist cultures, would be more likely to help a person in need. However, people everywhere are less likely to help a member of an **out-group**, a group with which the person does not identify, than a member of an **in-group**, the group with which the person identifies and feels he or she is a member. Cultural factors come into play in determining how strongly people draw the line between in-groups and out-groups. People in collectivist cultures may draw a firmer line between in-groups and out-groups and be more likely to help in-group members and less likely to help out-group members, than people from individualistic cultures, who have an *independent view of the self.*

• *Simpatia* in Latino and Hispanic cultures refers to a range of friendly social and emotional traits. Levine et al. (2001) found that people in cultures that value *simpatia* were more likely to help in a variety of nonemergency helping situations (Table 11.1).

D. Religion and Prosocial Behavior
• Religion fosters prosocial behavior on some, but not all, measures. People who attend religious services report on surveys that they give more money to charity, and engage in more volunteer work, than do people who do not attend religious services.

E. The Effects of Mood on Prosocial Behavior
• One reason that personality alone cannot determine helping is that helping depends on a person's current mood.
1. Effects of Positive Moods: Feel Good, Do Good
• People who are in a good mood are more likely to help. For example, Isen and Levin (1972) did a study in a shopping mall where Ss either found or did not find a dime in a phone booth. As the person emerged from the booth, a confederate walked by and dropped a sheaf of papers; 84% of those who found the dime helped compared with 4% of those who did not find the dime.
• Good moods can increase helping for three reasons: (1) good moods make us look on the bright side of life; (2) helping another prolongs the good mood, whereas not helping deflates it; (3) good moods increase self-attention, and this in turn leads us to be more likely to behave according to our values and beliefs (which tend to favor altruism).
2. Feel Bad, Do Good
• One kind of bad mood clearly leads to an increase in helping—feeling guilty.
• When people feel guilty, they are more likely to help. For example, Harris et al. (1975) found that churchgoers were more likely to donate money before, rather than after, confession (while still feeling guilty as opposed to after feeling their guilt absolved).

III. Situational Determinants of Prosocial Behavior: When Will People Help?
A. Environment: Rural versus Urban
• People in rural areas are more helpful. This effect holds over a wide variety of ways of helping and in many countries. One explanation is that people from rural settings are brought up to be more neighborly and more likely to trust strangers. An alternative hypothesis, posted by Milgram, is the **urban-overload hypothesis**, the idea that people living in cities are likely to keep to themselves in order to avoid being overloaded by all the stimulation they receive. The evidence supports the latter hypothesis, finding that where an accident occurs matters more in influencing helping than where potential helpers were born, and that population density is a more potent determinant of helping than is population size.

B. Residential Mobility
• It is not only where you live that matters, but also how often you have moved from one place to another. People who have lived for a long time in one place are more likely to engage in prosocial behaviors that help the community.
• People who have lived in one place for awhile feel more of a stake in their community.

C. The Number of Bystanders: The Bystander Effect
• Latané and Darley are two social psychologists who were working in New York at the time of the Kitty Genovese murder (described in Chapter 2). They hypothesized that, paradoxically, it might have been the large number of bystanders (38) that witnessed the murder that led to a failure to help.
• In a laboratory study, participants sat in separate booths and communicated over an intercom. As they listened, one of the other participants ostensibly had a seizure. The experimenters manipulated

how many other participants the subject believed there were. The more other people the S believed were present, the less likely they were to help and the slower they were to do so (Figure 11–3) (Darley & Latané, 1968). The **bystander effect** is the finding that the greater the number of bystanders who witness an emergency, the less likely any one of them is to help.

• Latané and Darley (1970) developed a step-by-step description of how people decide whether to help in an emergency (Figure 11.4). The five steps are:

1. Noticing an Event

• In order for people to help, they must notice that an emergency has occurred.

• Sometimes very trivial things, such as how much of a hurry a person is in, can prevent them from noticing someone else in trouble. Darley and Batson (1973) showed that seminary students who were in a hurry to give a sermon on campus were much less likely to help an ostensibly injured confederate groaning in a doorway than were those who were not in a hurry. They also found that helping was not predicted by personality scores or by the topic of the sermon (half were about to lecture on the parable of the Good Samaritan).

2. Interpreting the Event as an Emergency

• The next determinant of helping is whether the bystander interprets the event as an emergency. Ironically, when other bystanders are present, people are more likely to assume an emergency is something innocuous. This **pluralistic ignorance** occurs because people look to see others' reactions (informational influence); when they see that everyone else has a blank expression, they assume there must be no danger. This was demonstrated in a study by Latané and Darley (1970) where participants were sitting in a room when white smoke began pouring out of a vent. The more other participants there were in the room, the less likely anyone was to seek help and the longer they took to do so. For ambiguous events, then, people in groups will gain false reassurance from each other and convince each other that nothing is wrong.

3. Assuming Responsibility

• The next step that must occur if helping is to take place is for someone to take responsibility. When there are many witnesses, there is a **diffusion of responsibility**, the phenomenon whereby each bystander's sense of responsibility to help decreases as the number of witnesses increases. Everyone assumes that someone else will help, and as a result, no one does, as happened with the Kitty Genovese murder.

4. Knowing How to Help

• Even if all the previous conditions are met, a person must know what form of assistance to give. If they don't, they will be unable to help.

5. Deciding to Implement the Help

• Finally, even if you know what kind of help to give, you might decide not to intervene because you feel unqualified to help or you are too afraid of the costs to yourself.

• Markey (2000) examined helping in an Internet chat room situation; when the chat room group as a whole was asked to provide some information about finding profiles, the larger the group, the longer it took for anyone to help. However, when a specific person was addressed by name, that person helped quickly, regardless of group size.

D. The Nature of the Relationship: Communal versus Exchange Relationships

• A great deal of research on prosocial behavior has looked at helping between strangers. Although this research is very important, most helping in everyday life occurs between people who know each other well.

• *Communal relationships* (see Chapter 10) are those in which people's primary concern is with the welfare of the other, whereas *exchange relationships* are governed by equity concerns. Clark and Mills (1993), argue that the nature of the relationship is fundamentally different, such that those in communal relationships are less concerned with rewards.

• Generally we are more helpful towards friends than strangers, and we are more likely to help a partner in a communal relationship than a partner in an exchange relationship; the exception occurs when the other is beating us in a domain that is personally important and thus threatens our self-esteem; in this case, we are more likely to help strangers than friends for the purpose of self-esteem maintenance.

IV. How Can Helping Be Increased?
• An important note is that people do not always want to be helped—if being helped means that they appear incompetent, they will often suffer in silence, even at the cost of failing at the task.

A. Increasing the Likelihood that Bystanders Will Intervene
• Simply being aware of the barriers to helping can increase people's chances of overcoming those barriers. Two recent incidents on college campuses are cited as examples. Also, Beaman et al. (1978) had students listen either to a lecture about Latané and Darley's work or to one about an unrelated topic; two weeks later, in a different context, they encountered a student lying on the floor, while a confederate lounged by, apparently unconcerned. Those who had heard the bystander intervention lecture were more likely to help.

B. Positive Psychology and Prosocial Behavior
• A new field called positive psychology has emerged that focuses on people's strengths and virtues, instead of mental disease. The social psychological approach is to investigate the conditions under which people act in positive (e.g., helpful) and negative (e.g., unhelpful) ways. Many of these conditions were discussed in this chapter. For example, people will help at a cost to themselves when they feel empathy toward a person in need. When they do not feel empathy, they will help only when it is in their self-interest.

LEARNING OBJECTIVES

After reading Chapter 11, you should be able to do the following:

1. Define prosocial behavior. Define altruism. (p. 324)

2. Describe the approach of evolutionary psychology. Discuss the three factors that explain altruism according to evolutionary theory. (pp. 324-326)

3. Describe social exchange theory. Indicate how this theory is different from evolutionary theory in its explanation of altruism. Provide examples of rewards and costs associated with helping behaviors. (p. 327)

4. Define empathy. Describe the empathy-altruism hypothesis. Describe the relationship between the empathy-altruism hypothesis and social exchange theory. Describe the debate that has arisen over whether empathy-driven helping is altruistic or egoistic. Describe research that attempts to provide evidence in support of the empathy-altruism hypothesis. (pp. 328-331)

5. Indicate the limits to predicting helpfulness on the basis of personality and indicate what else we need to know in order to predict how helpful someone will be. Define altruistic personality. (p. 332)

6. Describe the relationship between gender and forms of prosocial behavior. Discuss reasons why males are more likely to help in some situations while females are more likely to help in others. (p. 332)

Chapter 11

7. Discuss cultural differences in prosocial behavior. Define in-group and out-group. Discuss the importance of in-group membership in individualistic cultures compared to interdependent ones. Describe cultural differences in helping. (pp. 332-333)

8. Discuss the relationship between religion and prosocial behavior. (p. 333)

9. Describe the effects of mood on helping. Identify why a good mood and a bad mood can result in helping behavior. (pp. 334-335)

10. Explain why, according to the urban-overload hypothesis, people in rural environments are more helpful than people in urban environments. What effect does residential mobility have on prosocial behavior? (pp. 336-337)

11. Describe the bystander effect. Identify and describe the step-by-step process by which people decide whether to intervene in an emergency. Describe the processes that may lead to nonintervention at each step in the decision tree. Define pluralistic ignorance. Define diffusion of responsibility. Discuss how bystanders influence pluralistic ignorance and the diffusion of responsibility and why these factors decrease helping behavior. (pp. 337-342)

12. Describe the relationship between helping and type of relationship. Discuss the importance of rewards in an exchange versus a communal relationship. Identify when helping a friend can threaten one's self-esteem and reduce helping. (pp. 342-343)

13. Describe how helping others can make them feel. Discuss ways to increase prosocial behavior by applying lessons learned about what increases and decreases prosocial behavior. (pp. 344-345)

14. Discuss the role of positive psychology in understanding prosocial behavior. (p. 345)

KEY TERMS

1. _____ Any act performed with the goal of benefiting another person. (p. 324)

2. _____ The desire to help another person even if it involves a cost to the helper. (p. 324)

3. _____ The idea that behaviors that help a genetic relative are favored by natural selection. (p. 324)

4. _____ The expectation that helping others will increase the likelihood that they will help us in the future. (p. 325)

5. _____ The ability to put oneself in the shoes of another person and to experience events and emotions (e.g., joy and sadness) the way that person experiences them. (p. 328)

6. _____ The idea that when we feel empathy for a person, we will attempt to help that person purely for altruistic reasons, regardless of what we have to gain. (p. 328)

7. _____ The qualities that cause an individual to help others in a wide variety of situations. (p. 332)

8. _____ The group with which an individual identifies as a member. (p. 333)

9. _____ Any group with which an individual does not identify. (p. 333)

10. _____ The theory that people living in cities are constantly being bombarded with stimulation and that they keep to themselves to avoid being overwhelmed by it. (p. 336)

11. _____ The finding that the greater the number of bystanders who witness an emergency, the less likely any one of them is to help. (p. 339)

12. _____ The case in which people mistakenly think that everyone else is interpreting a situation in a certain way, when in fact they are not. (p. 340)

13. _____ The phenomenon whereby each bystander's sense of responsibility to help decreases as the number of witnesses increases. (p. 341)

GUIDED REVIEW

PRACTICE TEST

1. Prosocial behavior is:
   a) performed without any regard to self-interests.
   b) appreciated by everyone we help.
   c) performed with the goal of benefiting another person.
   d) all the above.

2. The notion of kin selection dictates that you are most likely to help someone who is:
   a) genetically similar to you.
   b) a potential mate.
   c) physically attractive.
   d) likely to return the favor.

3. According to social exchange theory, relationships are best understood by:
   a) assuming that others will treat us the way we treat them.
   b) realizing that people desire to maximize their benefits and minimize their costs.
   c) applying evolutionary theory to social behavior.
   d) examining people's use of information gleaned by observing others in the situation.

4. Batson's empathy-altruism hypothesis states that we will help a victim of misfortune regardless of whether helping is in our best interests if:
   a) we perceive that the victim is dissimilar to us.
   b) the costs of helping are minimal.
   c) the victim is unable to control his or her performance.
   d) we experience the victim's pain and suffering.

5.   Maria is more likely than John to help a(n):
    a)   child in a burning building.
    b)   pilot struggling from the wreckage of an airplane.
    c)   man drowning in a lake.
    d)   elderly neighbor do his weekly shopping.

6.   People in interdependent cultures are _____ likely to help members of the _____ than are people in individualistic cultures.
    a)   less; in-group
    b)   more; out-group
    c)   less; out-group
    d)   there are no cultural differences in prosocial behavior

7.   Which of the following best characterizes the effects of mood on helping behavior?
    a)   Good moods increase helping.
    b)   Bad moods increase helping.
    c)   Either good or bad moods can increase helping.
    d)   Neither good nor bad moods can increase helping.

8.   Some researchers suggest that the emotion of _____ evolved in order to regulate reciprocity.
    a)   shame
    b)   gratitude
    c)   fear
    d)   love

9.   The bystander effect can be defined as:
    a)   the attempt to help people regardless of what we have to gain.
    b)   the likelihood that any one person will help decreases as the number of witnesses to an emergency increases.
    c)   the assumption that others will treat us the way we treat them.
    d)   the likelihood that people will perform impulsive and deviant acts increases as group size increases.

10.   Having identified a situation as a clear emergency requiring help, helping may still be inhibited by:
    a)   pluralistic ignorance.
    b)   diffusion of responsibility.
    c)   distraction.
    d)   overjustification.

11.   Some evolutionary theorists argue that natural selection also operates at the level of the
    a)   triad.
    b)   family.
    c)   group.
    d)   dyad.

12. Which of the following concepts have evolutionary psychologists used to explain prosocial behavior?
    a) kin selection and norms of reciprocity
    b) empathy and altruism
    c) immediate rewards and punishments
    d) urban overload and diffusion of responsibility

13. How does social exchange theory differ from the evolutionary approach to prosocial behavior?
    a) Only social exchange theory maintains that prosocial behavior is motivated by self-interest.
    b) Only social exchange theory maintains that prosocial behavior is truly altruistic.
    c) Only the evolutionary approach traces prosocial behavior back to evolutionary roots.
    d) Only the evolutionary approach maintains that people desire to maximize their rewards.

14. People who attend religious services report on surveys that they give more money to charity, and engage in more volunteer work, than do people who do not attend religious services.
    a) True
    b) False

15. Why do researchers typically find that people who score high on personality tests of altruism are no more likely to help than those who score low?
    a) because personality tests of altruism are invalid
    b) because situational influences also determine helping behavior
    c) because people's personalities change greatly over time
    d) because altruism can be instilled in children who might otherwise not score high on personality tests of altruism

16. People experiencing guilt tend to be helpful because:
    a) they often act on the idea that good deeds cancel out bad deeds.
    b) they are more likely to interpret situations as emergencies.
    c) they are more likely to notice situations in which emergencies occur.
    d) gratitude from the victim will reassure them that they are still likable.

17. Milgram's (1970) urban-overload hypothesis states that people in cities are less likely to help than people in rural areas because city dwellers:
    a) are more aware of the negative consequences of helping.
    b) are less likely to know what form of assistance they should give.
    c) keep to themselves in order to avoid excess stimulation.
    d) are more likely to use confused bystanders as a source of misinformation.

18. Latané and Darley (1970) attributed the murder of Kitty Genovese in New York City to the:
    a) large number of bystanders who witnessed the emergency.
    b) small number of bystanders who witnessed the emergency.
    c) lessons that city dwellers learn about keeping to themselves.
    d) insufficient amount of stimulation experienced by the witnesses.

19. When may we be LESS helpful toward friends than toward strangers?
    a) when the task is not important to us
    b) when helping is not costly
    c) when the rewards are great
    d) when the task is very important to our self-esteem

20. In which type of relationship are people concerned less with equity and more with how much help is needed by the other person?
    a) exchange relationships
    b) social relationships
    c) romantic relationships
    d) communal relationships

21. Which of the following best illustrates the kind of thinking influenced by diffusion of responsibility throughout a group?
    a) "Everyone seems to be reacting calmly. Maybe there's no real problem."
    b) "I hope I don't make things worse than they already are by trying to help."
    c) "Why should I risk helping when others could as easily help?"
    d) "If no one else is offering help, I guess it's up to me."

22. Altruism is:
    a) the desire to help another person even if it involves a cost to the helper.
    b) performed without any regard to self-interests.
    c) helping another with hopes of getting something in return.
    d) both a and b.

23. If people help others with the expectation that the people they help will help them in the future, they are being guided by:
    a) kin selection.
    b) norm of reciprocity.
    c) bystander effect.
    d) empathy-altruism hypothesis.

24. Which of the following is true regarding individual differences in helping behavior?
    a) Characteristics of an altruistic personality have been identified and predict helping behavior.
    b) Mood and situational pressures do not impact helping behavior.
    c) People who score high on tests of altruism are much more likely to help others than are people who score low.
    d) None of the above are true.

25. The group with which an individual identifies and of which an individual feels a part is called a(n):
    a) kin group.
    b) social group.
    c) in-group.
    d) common group.

26. All of the following are situational determinants of prosocial behavior EXCEPT which one?
    a) type of environment
    b) the number of people who are around
    c) how much empathy people feel
    d) being in a hurry

27. Latané and Darley's (1970) study of the smoke-filled room experiment demonstrated which of the following?
    a) pluralistic ignorance
    b) negative-state relief hypothesis
    c) bystander effect
    d) both a and c

28. To increase volunteerism, organizations should:
    a) mandate volunteerism.
    b) encourage volunteerism.
    c) provide people with a sense they freely chose to volunteer.
    d) do both b and c.

29. Suppose a group of individuals witness a painter fall off a ladder and groan. Because it is not clear whether the painter is seriously hurt or not, they all look to each other to see what everyone else is doing. Because no one is offering to help, each individual fails to do anything at all. This is an example of failure to help due to:
    a) shock.
    b) informational social influence.
    c) normative social influence.
    d) reciprocity.

30. According to Latané and Darley's (1970) step-by-step description of how people decide whether to help in an emergency, noticing the event is followed by:
    a) assuming responsibility.
    b) interpreting the event as an emergency.
    c) implementing a decision.
    d) knowing how to help.

31. Social exchange theory argues that true altruism does not exist.
    a) True
    b) False

32. According to the empathy-altruism hypothesis, we will help people
    a) only if we have something to gain.
    b) only if we feel empathy for them.
    c) when we feel empathy for them, regardless of what we have to gain.
    d) only if we have an altruistic personality.

33. Of the 7,000 people who received medals from the Carnegie Hero Fund Commission for risking their lives to save a stranger, _____ percent have been _____.
    a) 87; women
    b) 87; men
    c) 91; women
    d) 91; men

34.   _____ factors come into play in determining how strongly people draw the line between in-groups and out-groups.
    a)   Gender
    b)   Cultural
    c)   Mood
    d)   Residential mobility

35.   In a study by Isen and Levin (1972) on mood and helping behavior, _____ percent of the people who did not find a dime helped a man pick up his papers, whereas _____ percent of the people who found a dime stopped to help.
    a)   4; 84
    b)   1; 98
    c)   7; 78
    d)   3; 67

36.   According to the urban overload hypothesis, what would make urban dwellers just as likely to reach out to others as anyone else would?
    a)   educating them about diffusion of responsibility
    b)   educating them about the bystander effect
    c)   putting them in a calmer, less stimulating environment
    d)   putting them in a less polluted environment

37.   Who is most likely to help her community?
    a)   Joan, who has lived in St. Louis, Missouri for 20 years
    b)   Emily, who has lived in Belleville, Illinois for 21 years
    c)   Linda, who has lived in South Bend, Indiana for 45 years
    d)   Jill, who has lived in Fort Worth, Texas for 2 years

38.   Who is most likely to receive help?
    a)   Samantha, whose car has gotten a flat tire in a large downtown area during rush hour
    b)   Sandra, whose car needs a jump while she is parked in a busy grocery store parking lot
    c)   Rebecca, whose car has broken down on a busy highway
    d)   Cathy, whose car has broken down on a quiet country road

39.   Who is most likely to stop to help injured people involved in a car accident?
    a)   Rick, who is a marriage counselor
    b)   Dawn, who is a nurse
    c)   Melissa, who is a mother
    d)   Stan, who is a plumber

40.   Which of the following relationships is most likely to be based on exchange?
    a)   Laura and Tina, who recently developed a friendship at work
    b)   Rod and his wife Judy
    c)   Lisa and her daughter Sarah
    d)   Kim and her sister Pam

SHORT ANSWER REVIEW

Prosocial behavior refers to acts performed with the goal of (1) _____ (p. 324) another person. Some prosocial behavior is motivated by altruism, which is the desire to help another person even if it involves a (2) _____ (p. 324) to the helper. Evolutionary theory explains prosocial behavior in three ways. The first is kin selection, the idea that behaviors that help a (3) _____ (p. 324) relative are favored by natural selection. The second is the norm of (4) _____ (p. 325), which is the expectation that helping others will increase the likelihood that they will help us in the future. The third is that it is (5) _____ (p. 325) for people to learn social norms of all kinds, and one of these norms is the value of helping others.

Although some social psychologists disagree with evolutionary approaches to prosocial behavior, the share the view that altruistic behavior can be based on (6) _____ (p. 327). *Social exchange theory* argues that much of what we do stems from the desire to maximize our (7) _____ (p. 327) and minimize our costs. The difference from evolutionary approaches is that social exchange theory doesn't trace this desire back to our evolutionary roots; nor does it assume that the desire is (8) _____ (p. 327) based. Helping behavior can be rewarding in a number of ways. It can increase the likelihood that someone will (9) _____ (p. 327) in return. Helping people can also relieve the personal (10) _____ (p. 327) of a bystander. By helping others, we can also gain such rewards as social approval from others and increased feelings of (11) _____ (p. 327). The other side of the coin, of course, is that helping can be costly. Helping decreases when the costs are high, such as when it would put us in physical danger, result in pain or embarrassment, or simply take too much time.

People can be motivated by altruism, the desire to help another person even if it involves a cost to the helper. Pure altruism is likely to come into play when we feel (12) _____ (p. 328) for the person in need of help. Empathy is the ability to put oneself in the shoes of another person and to experience events and (13) _____ (p. 328) the way that person experiences them. According

297

to the empathy-altruism hypothesis, when people feel empathy toward another person, they attempt to help that person purely for (14) _____ (p. 328) reasons.

Some people help more than others do. Basic motives are not all there is to understanding prosocial behavior. We need to understand why some people are more helpful than others are. Psychologists have been interested in the nature of the (15) _____ (p. 332), the qualities that cause an individual to help others in a wide variety of situations. Although some people have personality qualities that make them more likely to help than others, personality factors have not been shown to be strong predictors of who will help across a variety of social situations.

There are gender differences in prosocial behavior. In virtually all cultures, norms prescribe different traits and behaviors for (16) _____ (p. 332). In Western cultures, the male sex role includes helping in (17) _____ (p. 332) and heroic ways, whereas the female sex role includes being nurturing and helping in close, (18) _____ (p. 332) relationships.

Cultural differences in prosocial behavior also exist. People in all cultures are more likely to help someone they define as a member of their in-group, the group with which an individual (19) _____ (p. 333). People everywhere are less likely to help someone they perceive to be a member of an (20) _____ (p. 333), a group with which they do not identify. Cultural factors come into play in determining how strongly people draw the line between in-groups and out-groups.

People are more likely to help if they are in especially good (21) _____ (p. 335), but also if they are in especially bad moods. Researchers have found a "feel good, do good" effect in diverse situations. When people are in a good mood they are more helpful in many ways. Being in a good mood can increase helping for three reasons. First, good moods make us look on the (22) _____ (p. 335) of life. Helping other people is also an excellent way of (23) _____ (p. 335) our good mood.

Finally, good moods increase the amount of (24) _____ (p. 335) we pay to ourselves, and this factor in turn makes us more likely to behave according to our (25) _____ (p. 335). People are also more likely to help if they are in a bad mood.

There are numerous situational determinants of prosocial behavior. (26) _____ (p. 336), gender, culture, and mood all contribute a piece to the puzzle of why people help others. To understand why people help others, we also need to consider the nature of the (27) _____ (p. 336). People are less likely to help in dense, urban settings because of the urban overload hypothesis – the idea that people living in cities are constantly bombarded with (28) _____ (p. 336) and that they keep to themselves in order to avoid being overwhelmed by it. People who have lived for a (29) _____ (p. 337) in one place are more likely to engage in prosocial behaviors than people who have recently moved to an area.

In order to help in an emergency, people must meet five conditions: They must notice the event, (30) _____ (p. 340) it as an emergency, assume responsibility, know the appropriate form of assistance, and implement their decision to help. As the number of (31) _____ (p. 339) who witness an emergency increases, the more difficult it is to meet two of these conditions – interpreting the event as an emergency and assuming responsibility. This produces the bystander effect: the larger the number of bystanders, the less likely any one of them is to help. In an emergency, bystanders tend to freeze, watching and listening with blank expression as they try to figure out what is going on. When they glance at each other, they see an apparent lack of concern on the part of everyone else. This results in pluralistic ignorance. Bystanders assume nothing is wrong in an emergency because no one else looks (32) _____ (p. 340). Sometimes it is obvious that an emergency is occurring. In these cases, diffusion of responsibility may occur. (33) _____ (p. 341) is the phenomenon whereby each bystander's sense of responsibility to help decreases as the number of witnesses increases. Because other people are present, no single bystander feels a strong personal responsibility to act.

The nature of a relationship influences helping behavior. People in (34) _____ (p. 342) – those governed by concerns about equity--are concerned primarily with the benefits they will receive by helping others. People in *communal relationships* – those in which the primary concern is the (35) _____ (p. 342) of the other person – are less concerned with the benefits they will receive and more with simply satisfying the needs of the other person.

There are ways that helping can be increased. Research shows that teaching people about the barriers to bystander intervention increases the likelihood that they will help in emergencies. A new field called (36) _____ (p. 345) psychology has emerged that focuses on people's strengths and virtues, instead of mental disease. The social psychological approach is to investigate the conditions under which people act in positive (e.g., helpful) and negative (e.g., unhelpful) ways. Many of these conditions were discussed in this chapter. For example, people will help at a cost to themselves when they feel empathy toward a person in need. When they do not feel empathy, they will help only when it is in their self-interest.

ESSAY REVIEW

1. Discuss the difference between prosocial behavior and altruism.

2. Define what is meant by an altruistic personality and discuss whether this characteristic can be used to predict prosocial behavior.

3. Describe gender differences in prosocial behavior. What have cross-cultural studies found?

4. Discuss the relationship between residential mobility and helping behavior.

5. Describe how motives to help differ in exchange versus communal relationships.

EXIT TESTS

EXIT TEST 1

1.   Which of the following is an example of prosocial behavior?
    a)   loaning a friend $20 for groceries
    b)   running into a burning building to save a child
    c)   moving the neighbor's lawn for him after his heart attack
    d)   all of the above

2.   According to social exchange theory, much of what we do stems from the desire to maximize our _____ and minimize our _____.
    a)   rewards; costs
    b)   self-esteem; self-loathing
    c)   both of the above
    d)   none of the above

3.   According to the empathy-altruism hypothesis, when we feel empathy for another person, we will attempt to help the person for purely selfish reasons.
    a)   True
    b)   False

4.   Which of the following factors need to be considered when trying to understand prosocial behavior?
    a)   personality
    b)   situational pressures
    c)   gender
    d)   all of the above

5.   People of all cultures are more likely to help someone
    a)   who is a stranger.
    b)   who can pay them back one day.
    c)   they define as a member of their in-group.
    d)   they define as a member of their out-group.

6.   Simpatia is a cultural value that refers to a range of social and emotional traits, including being friendly, polite, good-natured, pleasant, and helpful toward others.
    a)   True
    b)   False

7.   A review of dozens of studies found that when an opportunity for helping arises, it matters more whether the incident occurs in a rural or urban area than
    a)   the personality of the witnesses.
    b)   where the witnesses happened to grow up.
    e)   the mood of the witnesses.
    f)   gender of the witnesses.

8.   Pluralistic ignorance refers to bystanders' assuming that nothing is wrong in an emergency because no one else looks concerned.
    a)   True
    b)   False

9.   People in communal relationships pay less attention to _____ than people in exchange relationships.
    a)   costs
    b)   prosocial behavior
    c)   who is getting what
    d)   all of the above

10.   There is evidence that simply being aware of the barriers to helping in an emergency can increase people's chances of overcoming those barriers.
    a)   True
    b)   False

EXIT TEST 2

1.   Which of the following is an example of altruism?
    a)   helping your brother wash the dishes
    b)   helping another student pick up papers she dropped in the hallway
    c)   pulling someone out of a burning car
    d)   all the above

2.   According to the notion of kin selection, which of the following people are you most likely to help?
    a)   your daughter
    b)   your best friend
    c)   your third cousin
    d)   your boss

3.   According to social exchange theory, helping decreases when
    a)   the person is not a relative.
    b)   we are in a bad mood.
    c)   we do not anticipate an immediate reward.
    d)   the costs are high.

4.   According to Batson's empathy-altruism hypothesis which of the following thoughts is likely to lead to helping behavior?
    a)   "I think I will get a reward for this."
    b)   "I feel his pain."
    c)   "I'm sure this person will pay me back for helping."
    d)   "I'm in a great mood."

5.   If we know someone has an altruistic personality we can accurately predict that the person will help most of the time.
    a)   True
    b)   False

6. Dr. Hatfield's social psychology class is sitting in the classroom waiting for the lecture to begin. A few minutes before class time a student who is not in the class walks in and takes a seat. Unbeknownst to the rest of the class, this student is in one of Dr. Hatfield's other social psychology classes and has been given permission by Dr. Hatfield to sit in on this lecture to make up for one she missed. The students in the class look at the other student strangely, and one even confronts the student by saying "You're not in this class." The students normally in that class perceive the student from the other class as a
    a) member of their out-group.
    b) member of their in-group.
    c) problem.
    d) anomaly.

7. Who is most likely to contribute a dollar to charity?
    a) Wendy, who is on her way to biology class.
    b) Paul, who just finished his shift at work.
    c) Carl, who just found out he got a perfect score on his English exam.
    d) Professor Davis who is on his way to give a physics lecture.

8. Who is most likely to help others?
    a) Ben, who lives in the Dallas, Texas metropolitan area
    b) Don, who lives in the Chicago, Illinois metropolitan area
    c) Tom, who lives in the New York, New York metropolitan area
    d) Beth, who lives in the small town of Mishawaka, Indiana

9. Latané and Darley were convinced that Kitty Genoves's neighbors failed to help because of the stresses and stimulation of urban life.
    a) True
    b) False

10. In an experiment by Latané and Darley (1970) a participant is filling out a questionnaire while presumably waiting to take part in an experiment. Smoke begins to trickle into the room through a vent in the wall. When participants were alone in the room, _____ percent went for help within two minutes and _____ percent within 6 minutes.
    a) 30; 70
    b) 40; 60
    c) 50; 75
    d) 60; 80

STUDY ACTIVITIES

1. At a concert you see a person lying on the ground moaning and assume that this person is ill. Even though you are not a doctor, you decide to go and help this person. Describe this prosocial act from the perspective of social exchange theory.

2. Having just slipped on a busy sidewalk, you feel a searing pain in your leg and fear that it is broken. Because you are familiar with Latané and Darley's bystander intervention decision tree, you realize that people may not help for a variety of reasons. What might you do to facilitate people's decision to help you at each stage in the decision tree?

Chapter 11

3.   By considering the situational determinants of prosocial behavior, describe the steps you can take to increase helping among others.

4.   Describe the basic motives underlying prosocial behavior according to the evolutionary approach, social exchange theory, and the empathy-altruism hypothesis.

5.   Explain how attachment styles influence prosocial behavior.

6.   What are examples of cultural differences in prosocial behavior? Describe some of your own in-groups and out-groups.

7.   When and why do people in a good mood help others?

8.   What aspects of the social situation are important for prosocial behavior to occur? What is the relationship between population size and prosocial behavior? How does the urban-overload hypothesis explain the greater likelihood of prosocial behavior in towns of certain population sizes?

9.   Why does the presence of others influence people's interpretation of an event as an emergency? How does informational social influence lead to the bystander effect? What are the consequences of the bystander effect?

10.   Describe a strategy for increased prosocial behavior.

Chapter 11 Answers

Practice Test

1.   C (p. 324)
2.   A (p. 324)
3.   B (p. 327)
4.   D (p. 328)
5.   D (p. 332)
6.   C (pp. 332-333)
7.   C (pp. 334-335)
8.   B (p. 325)
9.   B (p. 339)
10. B (p. 341)
11. C (pp. 325-326)
12. A (pp. 324-325)
13. C (pp. 324-325; 327)
14. A (p. 333)
15. B (p. 332)
16. A (p. 335)
17. C (p. 336)
18. A (p. 339)
19. D (p. 343)
20. D (p. 342)
21. C (p. 341)
22. D (p. 324)
23. B (p. 325)
24. D (pp. 332 & 334-335)
25   C (p. 333)
26. C (pp. 336-342)
27. D (pp. 339-340)
28. D (p. 346)
29. B (p. 340)
30. B (p. 340)
31. A (p. 327)
32. C (pp. 328-329)
33. D (p. 332)
34. B (p. 333)
35. A (pp. 334-335)
36. C (p. 336)
37. C (p. 337)
38. D (p. 338)
39. B (p. 342)
40. A (p. 342)

Short Answer Review

1.   benefiting (p. 324)
2.   cost (p. 324)
3.   genetic (p. 324)
4.   reciprocity (p. 325)

5. adaptive (p. 325)
6. self-interest (p. 327)
7. rewards (p. 327)
8. genetically (p. 327)
9. help us (p. 327)
10. distress (p. 327)
11. self-worth (p. 327)
12. empathy (p. 328)
13. emotions (p. 328)
14. altruistic (p. 328)
15. altruistic personality (p. 332)
16. males and females (p. 332)
17. chivalrous (p. 332)
18. long-term (p. 332)
19. identifies (p. 333)
20. out-group (p. 333)
21. moods (p. 335)
22. bright side (p. 335)
23. prolonging (p. 335)
24. attention (p. 335)
25. values and ideals (p. 335)
26. Personality (p. 336)
27. social situation (p. 336)
28. stimulation (p. 336)
29. long time (p. 337)
30. interpret (p. 340)
31. bystanders (p. 339)
32. concerned (p. 340)
33. Diffusion of responsibility (p. 341)
34. exchange relationships (p. 342)
35. welfare (p. 342)
36. positive (p. 345)

Essay Review

1. Your essay should include the following:
    - Prosocial behavior is any act performed with the goal of benefiting another person. (p. 324)
    - Altruism is the desire to help another person even if it involves a cost to the helper. (p. 324)
    - According to social exchange theory, there is no true altruism. People help when the benefits outweigh the costs. (p. 327)

2. Your essay on altruistic personality should include:
    - Altruistic personality refers to the qualities that cause an individual to help others in a wide variety of situations. (p. 332)
    - Personality alone does not determine behavior. Social psychologists argue that to understand human behavior, we need to consider other critical factors as well, such as the situational pressures that are affecting people, their gender, the culture in which they grew up, and even their current mood. (p. 332)

3.   Your essay on gender differences in prosocial behavior should include:
   - In virtually all cultures, norms prescribe different traits and behaviors for males and females. In Western cultures, the male sex role includes being chivalrous and heroic; females are expected to be nurturing and caring and to value close, long-term relationships. (p. 332)
   - Of the 7,000 people who received medals from the Carnegie Hero Fund Commission for risking their lives to save a stranger, 91 percent have been men. (p. 332)
   - Researchers have focused less on helping that involves more nurturance and commitment, but a few studies have found that women do help more in long-term, nurturing relationships than men do and women are somewhat more likely to engage in volunteer work than men are. (p. 332)
   - Cross-cultural evidence suggests the same pattern. (p. 332)

4.   Your essay on residential mobility and helping behavior should include:
   - People who have lived for a long time in one place are more likely to engage in prosocial behaviors that help the community. (p. 337)
   - Living for a long time in one place leads to a greater attachment to the community, more interdependence with one's neighbors, and a greater concern with one's reputation in the community. (p. 337)

5.   Your essay should include the following:
   - Communal relationships are those in which people's primary concern is with the welfare of the other person, whereas exchange relationships are governed by concerns about equity. (p. 342)
   - In exchange relationships, people are concerned with what they are getting in return from other people. (p. 343)
   - People in communal relationships are concerned less with the benefits they will receive by helping and more with simply satisfying the needs of the other person. (p. 343)

Exit Test 1

1.   D (p. 324)
2.   A (p. 327)
3.   B (p. 328)
4.   D (p. 332)
5.   C (p. 333)
6.   A (p. 333)
7.   B (p. 336)
8.   A (p. 340)
9.   C (p. 342)
10. A (p. 344)

Exit Test 2

1.   C (p. 324)
2.   A (p. 324)
3.   D (p. 327)
4.   B (p. 328)
5.   B (p. 332)
6.   A (p. 333)

Chapter 11

7.   C (p. 334)
8.   D (p. 336)
9.   B (p. 338)
10.   C (p. 341)

Study Activities

1.   According to social exchange theory, we will help others when the rewards of helping outweigh the costs. In this situation, the rewards, such as the esteem of others at the concert and self-esteem, must have outweighed the costs. Costs include the potential embarrassment of attempting to help someone who, in fact, was not ill and the possibility that you yourself might get hurt. (p. 327)

2.   1) Get people's attention so that they will notice that there is a potential problem, 2) indicate that you are indeed hurt and need assistance, 3) single someone out by making eye contact and addressing the person so that he or she feels that the responsibility is his or hers alone, 4) suggest an appropriate form of assistance, and 5) ensure that the person implements the assistance by reassuring the person that you would be greatly appreciative of his or her help. (pp. 339-342)

3.   By reducing the stimulation people encounter, helping can be increased. You may not be able to reduce the population of a city, but as an architect you might be able to design buildings that limit the amount of unwanted contact people experience. Likewise, though you might not be able to reduce the number of bystanders present in emergency situations, you can instruct people on the causes of bystander intervention. Research has shown that such instruction increases prosocial behavior. (pp. 336-337, 344-345)

4.   According to evolutionary psychology, we are motivated to help others when helping increases the likelihood that our genes will live on in subsequent generations. Social exchange theory maintains that we help when the rewards of doing so outweigh the costs. The empathy-altruism hypothesis states that when we feel empathy for another person, altruistic concerns for that person motivate helping without any concern for ourselves. (pp. 324-331)

5.   How secure people feel has been shown to influence how much empathy they feel toward someone in need and how likely they are to help that person. When people are feeling particularly secure about their own attachment, they have a greater capacity to feel empathy toward others. (pp. 330-331)

6.   People in all cultures are more likely to help someone they define as a member of their in-group and less likely to help someone they perceive to be a member of an out-group. Cultural factors come into play in determining how strongly people draw the line between in-groups and out-groups. In many interdependent cultures, the needs of in-group members are considered more important than those of out-groups, and consequently, people in these cultures are more likely to help in-group members than members of individualistic cultures are. However, because the line between "us" and "them" is more firmly drawn in interdependent cultures, people in these cultures are less likely to help members of out-groups than people in individualistic cultures are. A particular value that strongly relates to prosocial behavior is *simpatia*. Prominent in Spanish-speaking countries, simpatia refers to a range of social and emotional traits, including being friendly, polite, good-natured, pleasant, and helpful toward others. (pp. 332-333)

7. When people are in a good mood, they are more helpful in many ways, including contributing money to charity, helping someone find a lost contact lens, tutoring another student, donating blood, and helping coworkers on the job. People are more likely to help others when they are in a good mood for a number of reasons, including doing well on a test, receiving a gift, thinking happy thoughts, and listening to pleasant music.
    (pp. 334-335)

8. Situational determinants of prosocial behavior include the environment (rural versus urban—rural more likely to help), residential mobility (long-term residents are more likely to help), and the number of bystanders (the greater the number of bystanders the less likely it is that anyone will help). People in larger towns are less likely to help than people in smaller towns. According to the urban overload hypothesis, people living in cities are constantly being bombarded with stimulation and they keep to themselves to avoid being overwhelmed by it. (pp. 336-342)

9. The presence of others influences people's interpretation of an event as an emergency because we look to others for information (informational social influence) in emergency situations. The danger is that sometimes no one is sure what is happening. Since an emergency is sudden and confusing, bystanders tend to freeze, watching and listening with blank expressions as they try to figure out what is going on. When they glance at each other, they see an apparent lack of concern on the part of everyone else. This results in a state of pluralistic ignorance. Bystanders assume that nothing is wrong in an emergency because no one else looks concerned. (pp. 340-341)

10. We can educate people about the barriers to helping in an emergency. Just being aware of these barriers can increase people's chances of overcoming these barriers. (p. 344)

CHAPTER 12

Aggression: Why Do We Hurt Other People? Can We Prevent It?

CHAPTER 12 OVERVIEW

This chapter begins with a discussion of how aggression is defined. **Aggression** is intentional behavior aimed at doing harm or causing pain to another person. **Hostile aggression** is defined as having as one's goal the harming of another; **instrumental aggression** uses inflicting harm as a means to some other end.

Next, the chapter addresses the question "Is aggression inborn or learned?" Over the centuries philosophers and psychologists have argued about whether or not humans are aggressive by nature. Some argued that it is in human nature to be aggressive, whereas others argued that humans learn aggressive behavior. Sigmund Freud theorized that humans are born with an instinct toward life, which he called **Eros**, and an equally powerful instinct toward death, which he called **Thanatos**. According to Freud, the Thanatos leads to aggressive actions.

The question of whether aggression is instinctual or situational is addressed next in this chapter. Evolutionary psychologists have argued that aggression is genetically programmed into men because it enables them to perpetuate their genes. Observations of other species suggest that animals are naturally aggressive. However, there is substantial variation in the degree of aggressiveness of our two closest animal relatives—chimpanzees and bonobos. Social psychologists argue that although aggressive behavior may be hardwired into humans, it is influenced by situational and cultural factors. Aggression is an optional strategy.

There is a great deal of variation in the levels of aggression of individuals living in different cultures. It is also the case that within a given society, for example the Iroquois, the degree of aggressiveness can change across time due to changes in the situation faced by the tribe. In our own society, there are some striking regional differences in aggressive behavior. For example, there is a "culture of honor" in the South. Multiple factors shape whether or not a culture tends to nurture aggressive behavior.

The next section of the chapter discusses neural and chemical influences on aggression. There is an area in the brain called the **amygdala**; it is thought to control aggression. Evidence suggests that the chemical **serotonin** serves to inhibit aggressive behavior and that the hormone **testosterone** is positively correlated with aggressive behavior.

Men are much more likely than women to behave aggressively in provocative situations. Men are also more likely to interpret a given situation as provocative. However, gender differences are reduced when women are actually provoked. Crime statistics show that males commit violent crimes at much higher rates then females. Sex differences in aggressive behaviors tend to hold up across cultures. Within heterosexual couples husbands are far more likely to murder their wives than vice versa.

Alcohol can increase aggressive behavior because it serves as a disinhibitor—it reduces one's social inhibitions. Research suggests that alcohol disrupts the way people usually process information so that they may respond to the most obvious aspects of a social situation and fail to pick up the more subtle elements of the situation.

When people experience pain they are far more likely to act aggressively. Discomfort, such as heat, humidity, air pollution, and offensive odors increase the likelihood of hostile and violent behavior. It has been predicted that global warming is almost certain to produce a major increase in the rate of violent crime.

The next section of the chapter discusses social situations and aggression. Many social situations lead to aggression including situations that cause frustration, such as traffic jams. The **frustration-aggression theory** states that frustration – the perception that you are being prevented from attaining a goal – increases the probability of an aggressive response. Frustration is more likely to produce aggression if one is thwarted on the way to a goal. Aggression also increases when the frustration is unexpected. Also, *relative deprivation* – the feeling that you have less than what you deserve or less than people similar to you have – can lead to frustration and aggressive behavior.

Individuals frequently aggress to reciprocate for the aggressive behavior of others. This response is reduced if there are mitigating circumstances. When convinced a provocation was unintentional, most of us will not reciprocate.

Research suggests that the mere presence of an aggressive stimulus in a situation increases the degree of aggressive behavior. An **aggressive stimulus** is an object that is associated with aggressive responses (e.g. a gun) and whose mere presence can increase the probability of aggression. In a classic study, participants angered in the presence of a gun administered more intense electric shocks to their "victim" than those angered in the same setting in which a tennis racket was substituted for the gun.

If a respected person or institution endorses aggression, it will have an impact on the attitudes and behavior of a great many people. This is especially true for children. Children frequently learn to solve conflicts aggressively by imitating adults and their peers, especially when they see that the aggression is rewarded. The people that children imitate the most are their parents. **Social learning theory** holds that we learn social behavior (e.g., aggression) by observing others and imitating them. People, especially children, learn to respond to conflict aggressively by observing aggressive behavior in adults and peers.

Most children are exposed to a great deal of violence through watching TV, movies, and playing violent video games. Long term studies show that the more TV violence observed by a child the greater the amount of violence they exhibit as teenagers and young adults. Watching TV violence has the greatest impact on youngsters who are somewhat prone to violence to begin with. Even children who are not inclined toward aggression, however, will become more aggressive if exposed to a steady diet of violent films over a long period. Exposure to violent media has also been shown to increase violent behavior in adults. Studies have found that viewing television violence can subsequently numb people's reactions when they face real-life aggression. Watching media violence can also affect our view of the world. Heavy TV viewers have an exaggerated view of the degree of violence taking place outside their own home and have a much greater fear of being personally assaulted. Research shows that viewing violence impairs the memory of viewers and, therefore, people are less likely to remember a product advertised on a violent TV program.

Almost half of all rapes or attempted rapes during the last three decades have not involved assaults by a stranger but are instances of "date rape," in which the victim is acquainted with or even dating the assailant. Scripts may contribute to this. **Scripts** are ways of behaving socially that we learn implicitly from our culture. The sexual scripts adolescents are exposed to suggest that the traditional female role is to resist the male's sexual advances and the male's role is to be persistent.

Over the past 25 years, a team of researchers has conducted careful studies, in both naturalistic and laboratory settings, to determine the effects of violent pornography. Exposure to violent pornography increases acceptance of sexual violence toward women and is almost certainly a factor associated with actual aggressive behavior toward women.

The next section of this chapter addresses the issue of how to reduce aggression. One question that has been investigated is "Does punishing aggression reduce aggressive behavior?" If the punishment is itself aggressive, it actually models such behavior to children and may engender greater aggressiveness in the child. Further, severe punishment may actually enhance the attractiveness of the transgression to the child. However, mild punishment, because it triggers cognitive dissonance in the child, has been shown to be more effective in changing behaviors. For punishment to serve as a deterrent to crime it must be both prompt and certain.

The theory of **catharsis** would predict that venting one's anger or watching others behave aggressively would serve to make one less likely to engage in subsequent acts of aggression. Research shows the contrary: acting aggressively, or observing aggressive events (such as a football game), actually increases the likelihood of future aggressive behavior. Committing an overt act of aggression against a person changes your feelings about that person, increasing your negative feelings toward the target and making future aggression against that person more likely. At a national level, violent acts against another nation lead to increasingly negative attitudes towards that nation and greater willingness to inflict further violence because it triggers the tendency to justify that action. When a nation is at war, even one that is far away, its people are more likely to commit aggressive acts against one another.

Typically, venting anger causes more harm than good. It is more effective to become aware of the anger and then to deal with it in ways that are more constructive. It is often the case that a cycle of anger and aggression can be diffused through apology. Children are less likely to act aggressively if they have been exposed to nonaggressive models. There is also some evidence that formal training on how to communicate anger or criticism in constructive ways, how to negotiate and compromise when conflicts arise, and how to be more sensitive to the needs and desires of others can be an effective means of reducing aggression. We are also less likely to aggress toward someone if we feel empathy for them. Most people find it difficult to inflict pain on a stranger unless they can find a way to dehumanize their victim. Understanding the process of dehumanization is the first step toward reversing it.

The final section of this chapter addresses the question "Could the Columbine massacre have been prevented?" A negative, exclusionary social atmosphere prevalent in high schools was one of the major root causes of the Columbine massacre. Changing the atmosphere of schools is an effective way to reduce the frequency of such occurrences.

CHAPTER 12 OUTLINE

I. What Is Aggression?
• **Aggressive action** is intentional behavior aimed at causing either physical or psychological pain. It is distinct from "assertiveness." **Hostile aggression** is an act of aggression stemming from feelings of anger and aimed at inflicting pain or injury; **instrumental aggression** involves an intention to hurt another as a means to some goal other than causing pain.

A. Is Aggression Inborn or Learned?
• Scientists do not agree on whether aggression is innate or learned. The debate has been raging for centuries. For example, Hobbes postulated that humans in our natural states are brutes and only the rules of society tame us; while Rousseau postulated that we are gentle "noble savages" who become aggressive in a restrictive society.

• Freud postulated that humans have innate instincts towards life, **Eros**, and towards death and aggression, **Thanatos**. Freud's theory was *a hydraulic theory*, making the analogy to water pressure; according to this idea, unexpected emotions build up pressure and must be expressed to relieve that pressure. Society performs the role of helping people express this instinct constructively.

B. Is Aggression Instinctual? Situational? Optional?
1. The Evolutionary Argument
• Evolutionary psychologists have argued that aggression is genetically programmed into men because it enables them to perpetuate their genes. Males are theorized to aggress for two reasons: First, males behave aggressively to establish dominance over other males. Second, males aggress "jealously" to ensure that their mate(s) are not copulating with others.
• The research supporting the evolutionary perspective is provocative but inconclusive because it is impossible to conduct a definitive experiment. Accordingly, scientists have turned to experiments with nonhuman species to gain additional insight into the extent to which aggression may be hardwired.
2. Aggression among the Lower Animals
• Kuo (1961) showed that a kitten raised with a rat would not attack it, showing that aggressive behavior can be inhibited by early experience.
• Eibl-Eibesfeldt (1963) showed that rats raised in isolation attack fellow rats using the same patterns that experienced rats do, showing that aggression does not need to be learned.
• Chimpanzees and bonobos have 98 percent of their DNA in common with human beings. The chimpanzee is known for the aggressive behavior of its male members. However, the bonobo is known for its non-aggressive behavior.
• Lore and Schultz (1993) suggest that the near universality of aggression suggests that it has survival value; however, they also note that nearly all organisms also have strong inhibitory mechanisms that enable suppression of aggression when it is in their best interests. Thus aggression is an optional strategy and is determined by previous social experiences and present social context.

C. Aggressiveness and Culture
• Berkowitz (1993) suggests that humans seem to have an inborn tendency to respond to certain provocative stimuli by striking out against the perpetrator; whether or not this aggressive action is expressed depends on the interaction of these innate propensities with learned inhibitory responses and the nature of the social situation. In humans, innate patterns of behavior are infinitely malleable; thus, cultures vary widely in the degree of aggressiveness.
• The forest Teduray, a hunter-gatherer culture in the Philippine rainforest, have established institutions and norms specifically designed to prevent intra-group violence.
1. Changes in Aggression across Time
• Changing social conditions can lead to dramatic changes in aggressive behavior. For example, the Iroquois were a peaceful people until the Europeans brought them into direct competition with the Hurons over fur; then they became fierce warriors.
2. Regionalism and Aggression
• Nisbett (1993) showed that homicide rates for white Southern males are substantially higher than for Northern white males; however, this is true only for argument-related aggression and appears due to a "culture of honor." In a follow-up study, Cohen et al. (1996) showed that southern white males bumped into and insulted by a confederate become more physiologically aroused and more likely to aggress than Northern white males.

II. Neural and Chemical Causes of Aggression

A. Serotonin and Testosterone
• The **amygdala** is an area in the core of the brain associated with aggressive behaviors. But even when the amygdala is directly stimulated, whether or not the organism will aggress depends on situational factors.
• **Serotonin** is a chemical substance occurring naturally in the midbrain that seems to have an inhibiting effect on impulsive aggression. Too little serotonin can lead to increases in aggression, as demonstrated in correlational and experimental studies with humans.
• **Testosterone** is a male sex hormone associated with aggression; too much of this substance can also lead to increases in aggression. In several correlational studies with humans, men higher in testosterone showed higher levels of impulsive or aggressive behavior.

B. Gender and Aggression
• Girls engage in covert aggression while boys' aggression is more overt. The research on gender differences in aggression shows that, while men are far more aggressive than women under ordinary circumstances are, the gender difference becomes much smaller when people are provoked (Bettencourt & Miller, 1996).
1. Does Culture Make a Difference?
• Archer and McDaniel (1995) found consistent gender differences in an 11-country study where people had to complete stories about conflict situations, with men being consistently more likely to suggest violent completions than women are. However, culture too played a major role. For example, women from Australia and New Zealand showed greater evidence of aggressiveness than men from Sweden and Korea did.
2. Violence Among Intimate Partners
• Of all the violent crimes against women in a typical year, some 22 percent were committed by their intimate male partners; for men the figure is 3 percent. Husbands are far more likely to murder their wives than vice versa. In 1998, of the 3,419 women killed in the United States, 32 percent died at the hands of a husband, boyfriend, former husband, or former boyfriend.

C. Alcohol and Aggression
• Alcohol serves as a disinhibitor and leads people to be more likely to commit actions frowned upon by society; thus alcohol can foster aggression when people are provoked, and even among those who have not been provoked and who do not behave aggressively when sober.
• The mechanism for this disinhibition appears to be a disruption in information processing, such that individuals under the effects of alcohol respond only to the earliest and most obvious aspects of a situation (e.g., having one's foot stepped on) and miss the subtleties (e.g., lack of intent). Thus, crime statistics reveal that most of the people arrested for violent crimes have been found to be legally drunk at the time of their arrest.

D. Pain, Discomfort and Aggression
• Both animal and human studies show that pain will increase the probability that an organism will aggress. For example, Berkowitz (1983, 1988) showed that students who had their arms immersed in ice water until they felt pain showed a sharp increase in their likelihood of aggressing.
• Other forms of bodily discomfort (heat, humidity, air pollution, offensive odors) may also act to lower the threshold for aggressive behaviors. For example, Carlsmith and Anderson (1979) found that between 1967 and 1971, riots were far more likely to occur on hot than on cool days (Figure 12.1). Several other correlational studies find similar results.
•An experiment to test the hypothesis that heat lowers the aggression threshold was conducted by Griffitt and Veitch (1971). They manipulated the temperature of a room while students were taking a

test; dependent variables were self-ratings of aggression and hostility towards a stranger they were asked to rate; both were higher in the hot (90°) room.
•In a recent analysis, Craig Anderson, the world's leading expert on the effects of climate and aggression, predicted that global warming is almost certain to produce a major increase in the rate of violent crime (Anderson, 2009).

III. Social Situations and Aggression

A. Frustration and Aggression
• Frustration is a major cause of aggression. Frustration occurs when a person is thwarted on the way to an expected goal or gratification. **Frustration-aggression theory** says that people's perception that they are being prevented from obtaining a goal will increase the probability of an aggressive response. Barker, Dembo, and Lewin (1941), for example, frustrated a group of children by keeping a room of very attractive toys out of their reach for a long wait; when they finally got to play with them, they played much more destructively than did the control group.
• The greater the closeness to the goal, the greater the frustration when it is thwarted and the higher the probability of aggression. Harris (1974), for example, had confederates cut into lines of people waiting; the further into line they cut, the more aggressive the reactions.
• Aggression also increases when frustration is unexpected. For example, Kulik and Brown (1979) rigged the situation so that volunteer charity solicitors failed to elicit donations; when led to expect high rates of contribution, subjects displayed more aggression (e.g., harsh voice tone).
• Frustration does not always produce aggression; rather it produces anger or annoyance and a readiness to aggress if other things about the situation are conducive to aggressive behavior (e.g., the size and nearness of the frustrating person, and that person's ability to retaliate).
• If frustration is understandable, legitimate, and unintentional, the tendency to aggress will be reduced (e.g., someone whose hearing aid has stopped working may frustrate us but we are unlikely to aggress (Burnstein & Worchel, 1962)).
• Frustration is not the same as deprivation; deprivation is a lack of a resource, whereas frustration occurs when one expects to get an outcome and doesn't; thus what causes aggression is not deprivation but *relative deprivation*, the perception that you or your group have less than you deserve, less than you have been led to expect, or less than people similar to you have. Ironically aggression is more likely to occur when social circumstances are looking up, for example, in the race riots of the 1960s or the rebellions in Eastern Europe as communism tumbled.

B. Being Provoked and Reciprocating
• People usually feel the need to reciprocate after they are provoked by aggressive behavior from another person. For example, Baron (1988) had a confederate insult another subject; when given an opportunity to aggress against the confederate, those who had been insulted were more aggressive than those who hadn't.
• We do not always reciprocate when provoked. If we think the provocation was unintentional, we are unlikely to reciprocate. And if there are mitigating circumstances, we will not aggress—so long as the circumstances are known at the time of the aggression.

C. Aggressive Objects as Cues
• The mere presence of an **aggressive stimulus**, an object that is associated with aggressive responses (e.g., a gun), can increase the probability of aggression.
• Berkowitz and LePage (1967) angered subjects in a room in which either a gun or a badminton racket was visible; those individuals who had been made angry in the presence of the gun administered more intense shocks to another student than those made angry in the presence of the racket (Figure 12.2).
• Correlational evidence supports the idea that guns foster aggressive behavior. For example, Seattle and Vancouver are virtually identical cities, with the exception of Vancouver's strict gun control

laws; the murder rate in Seattle is more than double that of Vancouver. Archer and his colleagues find in cross-cultural research that (1) the homicide rate is highly correlated with the availability of handguns; and (2) that American teens are far more likely to write conclusions to stories about conflicts that are "lethal, gun-laden, and merciless" than are teens in any of the other ten countries surveyed.

D. Endorsement, Imitation and Aggression

• If a respected person or institution endorses aggression, it will have an impact on the attitudes and behavior of a great many people.

• This is especially true for children. Children frequently learn to solve conflicts aggressively by imitating adults and their peers, especially when they see that the aggression is rewarded. The people that children imitate the most are their parents.

• A major cause of aggression is social learning. According to **social learning theory**, we learn social behavior (e.g., aggression) by observing others and imitating them. Children learn to solve conflicts aggressively by watching adults and their peers, especially when they see that aggression is rewarded, as it is in many sports.

• A large percentage of physically abusive parents were abused by their own parents when they were children. In support of the idea that this aggression is learned rather than inherited, Bandura postulated social learning theory (the theory that we learn social behavior by observing others and imitating them). In support of this theory, the famous Bobo doll experiments showed that children imitated novel aggressive behaviors modeled by adults.

E. Violence in the Media: TV, Movies, and Video Games

1. Effects on Children

• By the time the average American child finishes elementary school, he or she will have seen 8,000 murders and more than 100,000 other acts of violence on television.

• Studies have shown that 58% of TV programs contain violence, and of those, 78% showed no remorse, criticism, or penalty for the violence. Additionally, characters portrayed as heroes or desirable role models initiated 40% of the violent incidents.

• A number of long-term studies indicate that the more violence individuals watch on TV as children, the more violence they exhibit years later as teens and adults. This is correlational research and not conclusive about causality; however, reviews of the experimental research generally (but not always) suggests that watching violence does indeed cause aggressive behavior in children.

• For example, Liebert and Baron (1972) exposed a group of children to a violent cops-and-robbers show; while another group was exposed to a nonviolent sporting event show. After watching TV, the child was allowed to play in another room with a group of other children; those who had watched the violent program showed far more aggression.

• A later experiment (Josephson, 1987) showed that watching TV violence had the greatest effect on those children who were somewhat prone to violence to begin with. Thus watching one episode of violent TV may not increase the aggression of those who are not violent to begin with. However, a steady diet of violent TV over a long period may increase aggression in those who were not previously prone to it. A series of field studies by Leyens et al. supports this conclusion: in his studies, the great majority of children, even those without strong aggressive tendencies, who were exposed to a high degree of media violence over a long period, were more aggressive than those who watched more benign shows.

• At a 1995 congressional hearing, it was estimated that the average 12-year-old has witnessed more than 100,000 acts of violence on TV; this pervasion of violence may prime children to make aggressive responses.

• Playing violent video games seems to have the same kind of impact on children that watching TV violence does, as demonstrated in recent correlational and experimental research.

2. What about Adults?

• Adults as well as children may be influenced by violent television. For example, Phillips (1983, 1986) analyzed the homicide rate in the U.S. as it compared to the showing of heavyweight boxing on TV; he found a substantial pattern of correlations. Not everyone is influenced by violent TV, but some people are, with tragic results.

3. The Numbing Effect of TV Violence

• Repeated exposure to horrifying events has a numbing effect on our sensitivity to those events. Studies show that those who watch a good deal of TV did not react physiologically to a bloody boxing match, while those who did not watch TV did (Cline et al., 1973); and that those who were previously exposed to a violent police drama failed to become upset by an aggressive interaction that upset those who previously watched a volleyball game (Thomas et al., 1977). In a follow-up experiment, Thomas (1982) showed that college students exposed to TV violence not only were more physiologically aroused but also administered more powerful electric shocks to a fellow student, compared to the control group. Thus viewing media aggression desensitizes us to real-world aggression.

4. How Does Media Violence Affect Our View of the World?

• Gerbner et al. find that people who are heavy TV viewers (4 or more hours a day) view the world as a much more dangerous and hostile place than those who watch less.

5. Why Does Media Affect Viewers' Aggression?

• Five reasons have been suggested: (1) Watching TV violence may simply weaken previously learned inhibitions against aggression; (2) Watching TV violence might teach people new ways to aggress and inspire imitation; (3) TV violence may make feelings of anger more available and thus prime an aggressive response; (4) Watching violence reduces sensitivity and sympathy for victims, making it easier to live with violence and possibly to aggress; and (5) Since watching TV violence makes the world seem a more dangerous place, viewers are more likely to interpret strangers' behavior or ambiguous situations as having hostile intent.

F.   Does Violence Sell?

• In a study by Bushman & Bonacci (2002) they found that violence and sex impair the memory of viewers for advertising between the violent segments. In terms of sales, advertisers might be well advised to sponsor nonviolent shows.

G. Violent Pornography and Violence against Women

• During the past 25 years, nearly half of all rapes or attempts have been date rapes. Many occur because of adolescents' confused sexual **scripts**, or ways of behaving socially that we implicitly learn from the culture, which suggest that the man's role is to be persistent and the woman's role is to resist the man's sexual advances. Thus students tend to believe that when a woman says "no," she doesn't mean it. This has led several colleges to suggest that dating couples negotiate explicit contracts about sexual conduct at the beginning of dates, leading to criticism by social pundits.

• Coincident with this increase in date rape has been the increase in the availability of magazines, films, and videos depicting vivid, explicit sexual behavior.

•Scientific research on whether pornography increases rape is thus far inconclusive.

• Two presidential commissions have examined whether pornography contributes to violence against women. The 1970 commission concluded that sexually explicit material "in and of itself" does not increase violence; the 1985 commission concluded that it did. The 1985 conclusions may have been politically motivated, however.

• The authors suggest that an important distinction should be made between simple pornography and violent pornography. Studies by Donnerstein and Malamuth and their colleagues find that viewing violent pornography promotes greater acceptance of sexual violence towards women and almost

certainly is associated with actual aggressive behavior. For example, Donnerstein and Berkowitz (1981) showed male subjects either a violent pornographic film, a nonviolent pornographic film, or a violent nonpornographic film. After viewing the film, the subjects took part in an ostensibly unrelated experiment that gave them the opportunity to "shock" a female confederate. Those who watched the violent pornography gave the highest level of shocks, while those who watched the nonviolent pornography gave the lowest. Another study showed that a female confederate was shocked more than a male. Similarly, Malamuth (1981) showed men either a violent pornographic or a nonviolent erotic film and asked them to report their subsequent fantasies; those who watched the violent pornographic film created more violent sexual fantasies than those who watched the mutually consenting sex. Thus viewing pornographic violence against women does tend to focus aggressive feelings on women as targets and make people more accepting of this kind of violence.
• Data on the effects of nonviolent pornography are mixed. Meta-analysis shows a small but measurable effect of nonviolent pornography on violence towards women. However, men exposed to pictures of nude women engaged in nonsexual activities were actually less prone to commit violence than men in control conditions (Allen et al. 1995). Thus, only with respect to violent pornography are the problems clear.

IV. How to Reduce Aggression

A. Does Punishing Aggression Reduce Aggressive Behavior?
• For children, harsh punishment provides a model of aggression and does not provide a disincentive for transgressing the sanctions when the child is unsupervised. However, the threat of mild punishment, swiftly administered, does seem to reduce aggression.
1. Using Punishment on Violent Adults
• For adults, the research evidence on the effects of punishment on aggression is mixed. Laboratory experiments suggest that under ideal conditions—when the punishment is swift and certain—punishment can reduce aggression. But in real life, punishment occurs under anything but ideal conditions. Thus the societal data seem to indicate that severe punishment does not seem to deter violent crimes.

B. Catharsis and Aggression
• The common belief that one can "blow off steam" and "get it (anger) out of your system" is an oversimplification of Freud's psychoanalytic notion of **catharsis**. According to this idea, performing an aggressive act, watching others engage in aggressive behavior, or engaging in fantasy aggression relieves built-up aggressive energies and hence reduces the likelihood of further aggressive behavior.
• While there is some evidence that stifled feelings can produce illness, this does not mean that indiscriminate venting of feelings is healthy or useful.
1. The Effects of Aggressive Acts on Subsequent Aggression
• Despite the fact that some prominent psychologists believe in the catharsis hypothesis, controlled studies suggest that acting aggressively or viewing aggression increases, rather than decreases, subsequent aggression and hostility.
• Even direct aggression against the source of anger increases, rather than decreases, subsequent aggression. For example Geen et al. (1975) had students angered by a confederate. Half of the subjects had the opportunity to give shocks to the confederate on a first task; and then all subjects had the opportunity in a second task. The catharsis hypothesis predicts that those subjects who had already shocked the confederate would give fewer, less intense shocks the second time; in fact, they expressed even greater aggression the second time around.
• Overall, results of studies do not support the catharsis hypothesis.
2. Blaming the Victim of our Aggression
• The belief in catharsis may arise from the fact that venting aggression makes us feel better; however, feeling better does not reduce hostility.

• Committing aggression not only reduces the barriers against further aggression, but it leads to attempts to justify the aggression by blaming the victim of our aggression and believing that they deserved it. This dissonance reduction in turn increases the likelihood of further aggression.

• Blaming and derogating the victim is especially likely if the target was an innocent victim of your aggression (Glass, 1964; Davis & Jones, 1960). When the target is not totally innocent, the opportunity to aggress against the person leads to even greater hostility than when one is prevented from aggressing (Kahn, 1966).

• When people are angered, they frequently engage in overkill.

C. The Effect of War on General Aggression

• When a nation is at war, its people are more likely to commit aggressive acts against one another. The fact that a nation is at war (1) weakens the population's inhibitions against aggression, (2) leads to imitation of aggression, (3) makes aggressive responses more acceptable, and (4) numbs our senses to the horror of cruelty and destruction, making us less sympathetic toward the victims. Being at war serves to legitimize violence as a way to address difficult problems.

D. What Are We Supposed to Do with Our Anger?

• One way to control anger is by actively enabling it to dissipate, e.g., by counting to 10 or otherwise distracting oneself.

1. Venting versus Self-Awareness

• There is an important difference between being angry and expressing that anger in a violent and destructive manner. Expressing feelings of anger nonviolently and in a nonjudgmental manner is an assertive response that avoids the dangers of either violent expression or of repression of the feelings (Aronson, 2003).

• While expressing angry feelings to the person who caused them is probably best, expressing them to a third party may also be helpful. Work by Pennebaker (1990) indicates that repressing emotional stresses has negative effects on health, and that revealing the emotions to another person has beneficial effects. Further, these beneficial effects are due not simply to venting of feeling but also to the self-awareness that usually accompanies self-disclosure. Berkowitz and Troccoli (1990) found that those subjects experiencing discomfort and mild pain while listening to a target who were not given an opportunity to rate their feelings rated the target most negatively. Those participants in pain who were given the opportunity for expression were able to avoid being overly harsh.

2. Defusing Anger through Apology

• One way to reduce aggression in another person is for the person who caused the frustration to take responsibility, apologize, and indicate it won't happen again.

3. The Modeling of Nonaggressive Behavior

•Children exposed to models who behave nonaggressively when provoked, show a much lower frequency of aggression than children who were not exposed.

4. Training in Communication and Problem-Solving Skills

• In most societies, it is the people who lack proper social skills who are most prone to violent solutions to interpersonal problems. Thus one way to reduce violence is to teach people how to communicate anger and criticism constructively and how to negotiate and compromise. There is some evidence that such formal training can be an effective means of reducing aggression, and many schools are now training students in non-aggressive strategies for conflict reduction.

5. Building Empathy

• Baron (1976) had cars hesitate at a green light; just previous to the hesitation, a pedestrian had passed by in between the car that was stopped at the light and the one behind it. Half of the pedestrians were on crutches. Baron found that the drivers of the second car were significantly less likely to honk in this condition, presumably because the crutches evoked empathy.

Chapter 12

- In contrast, in situations where aggression is high, we tend to dehumanize our victims; this lowers inhibitions against aggression and makes continuing it more likely.
- If it is the case that most people must dehumanize their victims in order to commit extreme acts of aggression against them, then increasing empathy will make aggression more difficult. Research suggests that training students to take the perspective of the other or providing personal information about the victim leads to lower levels of aggression.

V. Could the Columbine Massacre Have Been Prevented?
- Aronson (2000) suggests that acts such as the Columbine massacre are not simply the result of individual pathology; these events instead may represent a pathological response to a general school atmosphere that includes exclusion, mockery, and taunting. If this is correct, then it should be possible to make schools safer by bringing about a change in the negative exclusionary atmosphere, following techniques such as those used in Olweus's program to decrease bullying in Norway and Norma Feshbach's program on increasing empathy among school children in Los Angeles.

LEARNING OBJECTIVES

After reading Chapter 12, you should be able to do the following:

1. Identify the critical feature that distinguishes aggressive from nonaggressive behavior. Explain why behavior that causes no physical harm to anyone can still be considered aggressive behavior. Distinguish between hostile and instrumental aggression. (p. 352)

2. Contrast the philosophy of Rousseau with the philosophies of Hobbes and Freud concerning people's natural inclinations to aggress. Define Freud's concepts of Eros and Thanatos, and describe his hydraulic theory. (p. 353)

3. Discuss animal studies which support the role of instinct and those which support the role of learning in the production of aggressive behavior. Discuss why aggression can be considered an optional strategy. (pp. 353-355)

4. Identify the importance of culture and social change in the degree of human aggression that exists using the examples of the Iroquois and regional differences in the U.S. (pp. 355-356)

5. Identify the relationship between the body and aggressive responses. Describe conditions when stimulation of the amygdala produces aggression and when it produces escape behavior. Identify the effects that serotonin has on impulsive aggression. Describe evidence that suggests the male sex hormone, testosterone, produces aggression. (p. 356)

6. Discuss the relationships among gender, culture, and aggressive behavior. Describe the relationship between gender and overt, versus covert, aggression. Describe the relationship between gender and aggressive behavior as a result of direct provocation. Contrast the large gender differences in lethal violence committed against intimate partners. (pp. 357-359)

7. Discuss the relationship between alcohol use and aggression. (p. 359)

320

Copyright © 2010 by Pearson Education, inc. All rights reserved.

8.   Describe anecdotal and experimental evidence that suggests people are more likely to behave aggressively when they experience pain or discomfort. Identify the environmental factor that has been linked to riots and violent crime. Discuss the prediction regarding global warming and violent crime. (pp. 359-360)

9.   Describe the frustration-aggression theory. Identify factors that accentuate frustration and thereby increase the probability of aggressive behavior. Discuss the mediating role of anger or annoyance in the frustration-aggression theory. Identify situational factors which might inhibit aggression even by somebody who has been angered. (pp. 361-362)

10.   Define relative deprivation and discuss its impact on frustration and subsequent aggression. (p. 362)

11.   Identify conditions when direct provocation is likely to evoke aggressive retaliation. (p. 363)

12.   Discuss the cognitive and behavioral effects of aggressive stimuli (e.g., guns) in the presence of angry individuals. Discuss evidence that the presence of guns increases the aggressive behavior of people in the real world. (pp. 363-364)

13.   Describe social learning theory and the basic procedure used by Bandura and his colleagues to demonstrate social learning in the laboratory. Discuss the consequences of exposing children to an aggressive model. (pp. 365)

14.   Discuss the effects of watching violence in the media. Identify the conclusions that can be drawn from correlational and experimental research on media violence and aggressive behavior in children and adults. Describe evidence that suggests repeated exposure to TV violence has a numbing effect on people. Identify the effects of watching a lot of television on people's views of the world. State five reasons why media violence produces aggression. (pp. 365-370)

15.   Discuss the effects of TV violence on recall of advertisements associated with those programs. (p. 370)

16.   Define scripts and describe the role they play in sexual relationships. Discuss the effects of viewing sexually explicit material, on the acceptance of sexual violence toward women and on aggressive behavior toward women. Compare these effects to the effects of viewing materials that combine sex and violence towards women. (pp. 370-372)

17.   Identify the conditions under which punishing aggression reduces aggressive behavior in children and adults. (pp. 372-373)

18.   Define catharsis. Describe evidence that "blowing off steam" by engaging in physical activities, by watching others engage in aggressive behavior, or by behaving aggressively increases rather than decreases hostile feelings. Explain how cognitive dissonance theory accounts for findings that aggression breeds subsequent aggression toward victims of one's aggression. Discuss the effects of war on the aggressive behavior of people.
(pp. 374-377)

19.   Identify the most effective means of dealing with pent-up anger. Contrast the effects of venting versus self-awareness on subsequent aggression. Identify the benefits and underlying process of expressing feelings in a nonviolent manner. (pp. 377-378)

20. Identify the most effective means of defusing anger that someone is experiencing as a consequence of your behavior. (p. 379)

21. Discuss the effects of training, reinforcing, and of modeling nonaggressive behaviors on aggression in children. Discuss the effects of empathy and empathy training on reducing aggression. (pp. 379-380)

22. Identify the benefits of teaching empathy in school. Discuss the possible effects of empathy training on preventing school shootings. Identify why it is important to look to the social situation when trying to understand why these tragic events happened. (p. 381)

23. Discuss the issue of whether the Columbine Massacre could have been prevented (pp. 381-383).

KEY TERMS

1. _____ Intentional behavior aimed at doing harm or causing pain to another person. (p. 352)

2. _____ Aggression stemming from feelings of anger and aimed at inflicting pain. (p.352)

3. _____ Aggression as a means to some goal other than causing pain. (p. 352)

4. _____ The instinct toward life, posited by Freud. (p. 353)

5. _____ According to Freud, an instinctual drive toward death, leading to aggressive actions. (p. 353)

6. _____ An area in the core of the brain that is associated with aggressive behaviors. (p. 356)

7. _____ A chemical in the brain that may inhibit aggressive impulses. (p. 357)

8. _____ A hormone associated with aggression. (p. 357)

9. _____ The idea that frustration—the perception that you are being prevented from attaining a goal—increases the probability of an aggressive response. (p. 361)

10. _____ An object that is associated with aggressive responses (e.g., a gun) and whose mere presence can increase the probability of aggression. (p. 363)

11. _____ The idea that we learn social behavior (e.g., aggression) by observing others and imitating them. (p. 365)

12. _____ Ways of behaving socially that we learn implicitly from our culture. (p. 369)

13. _____ The notion that "blowing off steam"—by performing an aggressive act, watching others engage in aggressive behaviors, or engaging in a fantasy of aggression—relieves built-up aggressive energies and hence reduces the likelihood of further aggressive behavior. (p. 374)

GUIDED REVIEW
PRACTICE TEST

1. Which of the following behaviors best demonstrates instrumental aggression?
    a) shooting clay pigeons with a shotgun
    b) intentionally tripping a classmate during recess
    c) running a stop sign, thereby causing an accident
    d) holding up a clerk while robbing a convenience store

2. The hydraulic theory of aggression maintains that:
    a) aggression will leak if the individual is not emotionally strong enough to restrain his/her aggressive urges.
    b) heated, frustrating situations heighten aggressive energy to the boiling point.
    c) people who pour out their aggressive energies are likely to flood others with aggressive urges.
    d) aggressive energy must be released to avoid build-up and an explosion resulting in illness.

3. There is much evidence to support the general contention held by most social psychologists that, for humans, innate patterns of behavior:
    a) are rigidly preprogrammed.
    b) are nonexistent.
    c) are modifiable by situational and social events.
    d) are incompatible with a social existence.

4. Research reveals that naturally occurring testosterone levels are higher among prisoners:
    a) with neurological disorders.
    b) convicted of violent crimes.
    c) with personality disorders.
    d) convicted of embezzlement.

5. Carlsmith and Anderson (1979) found that riots between 1967 and 1971 were far more likely to occur on:
    a) hot days than on cool days.
    b) rainy days than on sunny days.
    c) weekends than on weekdays.
    d) odd-numbered years than on even-numbered years.

6. Findings by Berkowitz and LePage (1967) that angry participants were more likely to deliver shocks to a fellow student when a gun was present in the room indicate that:
    a) the presence of weapons increases the probability that frustration will occur.
    b) the presence of weapons in and of itself is sufficient to trigger aggressive actions.
    c) the presence of weapons increases the probability an aggressive response will occur.
    d) all the above.

7. At recess, a boy can choose to play with one of four classmates. Which classmate should he AVOID if he wants to play a nonviolent game of basketball?
   a) Johnny, who tends to be aggressive and has just watched a television program hosted by a soft-spoken man on television.
   b) Rich, who is generally not aggressive and has just watched a violent G.I. Joe cartoon on television.
   c) Sam, who tends to be aggressive and has just watched a violent G.I. Joe cartoon on television.
   d) Tim, who is generally not aggressive and has just watched a television program hosted by a soft-spoken man on television.

8. Physical punishment may not curb aggressive actions by children because such punishment:
   a) is difficult for children to understand.
   b) is not supported by social norms.
   c) models aggressive behavior.
   d) provides insufficient justification for behaving nonaggressively.

9. Research shows that "blowing off steam" by engaging in competitive and aggressive games or by watching others do so:
   a) increases aggressive feelings.
   b) decreases aggressive feelings.
   c) evokes people's primary tendencies.
   d) inhibits aggressive behavior.

10. Dissonance arises when we aggress toward someone who is deserving of our retaliation because:
    a) our retaliations are often more hurtful than the act for which we are retaliating.
    b) we often fail to perceive that people are deserving of retaliation.
    c) we often underestimate the impact retaliation has on deserving victims.
    d) we do not like to think of ourselves as aggressive even when aggression is warranted.

11. If you are feeling angry with someone, what is the most effective way to deal with your anger?
    a) Keep your feelings to yourself.
    b) Express your anger in an aggressive manner.
    c) Observe violence among others.
    d) Calmly indicate that you are feeling angry and explain why.

12. Ohbuchi et al. (1989) found that participants liked a blundering experimental assistant better and were less likely to aggress toward him if:
    a) the experimenter insisted that the blunder had caused no harm.
    b) the assistant blamed his blunder on the experimenter.
    c) the assistant apologized for his blunder.
    d) the assistant allowed the participants to be in the experiment a second time.

13. According to Freud, "Thanatos" is the:
    a) life instinct that humans are born with.
    b) death instinct that drives aggressive actions.
    c) process by which memories are pushed into the unconscious.
    d) subconscious reenactment of the human evolutionary process.

14. Kuo's (1961) finding that a cat raised with a rat from birth refrained from attacking the rat or other rats suggests that:
   a) instincts may be inhibited by experience.
   b) aggressive behavior is not instinctive.
   c) raising different species of animals together lowers the animals' levels of testosterone.
   d) frustration is necessary to produce an aggressive response.

15. When the amygdala of a less-dominant monkey is stimulated in the presence of dominant monkeys, the less-dominant monkey exhibits:
   a) attack behavior.
   b) escape/avoidance behavior.
   c) no noticeable change in behavior.
   d) confusion and inconsistent behavior.

16. The theory that predicts you will act with the intention to hurt others when you are thwarted from attaining a goal is called:
   a) social learning theory.
   b) cathartic aggression theory.
   c) frustration-aggression theory.
   d) deprivation theory.

17. When the Iron Curtain in Eastern Europe crumbled, people expected the quality of their lives to dramatically improve. When economic reforms stalled, aggressive behavior resulted from:
   a) deprivation.
   b) social learning.
   c) dehumanization.
   d) relative deprivation.

18. Findings that children were more likely to beat up a Bobo doll after watching an adult do so led Bandura (1961, 1963) to conclude that:
   a) aggression may be learned by imitating aggressive models.
   b) there are striking differences in instinctive aggressive drives among children.
   c) watching aggressive behavior is intrinsically rewarding.
   d) observing aggression by adults unleashes children's inherent aggressiveness.

19. Which of the following best summarizes the effects of viewing sexually explicit material on aggression toward women?
   a) Viewing sexually explicit material, in and of itself, increases the likelihood of aggressive behavior toward women.
   b) Viewing materials that combine sex with violence increases the likelihood of aggressive behavior toward women.
   c) Viewing materials that combine sex with violence appears to be harmless.
   d) Viewing nonviolent material that depicts women as objects increases the likelihood of aggression toward women.

Chapter 12

20.   Geen et al. (1975) found that participants were most likely to shock an experimental accomplice who had angered them if:
a)   they had shocked the accomplice on a previous occasion.
b)   they had been unable to shock the accomplice on a previous occasion.
c)   they expected the accomplice to shock them later in the experiment.
d)   the experimenter had informed them that the shocks would facilitate learning by the accomplice.

21.   Pennebaker (1990) suggests that the beneficial effects of "opening up" and talking about one's feelings are the result of:
a)   blowing off steam.
b)   increased insight and self-awareness.
c)   revealing one's dependency on others.
d)   increased empathy with others.

22.   Evidence that people find it easier to aggress toward those they have dehumanized suggests that people will find it difficult to aggress toward people whom:
a)   they feel empathy toward.
b)   are dissimilar to them.
c)   have not provoked them.
d)   model aggressive behavior.

23.   According to social psychologists, voluntary behavior geared to cause either psychological or physical pain is called a(n):
a)   hostile action.
b)   aggressive action.
c)   violent action.
d)   antisocial action.

24.   An act of aggression arising from feelings of anger and intended to cause pain or injury is called _____ aggression.
a)   violent
b)   antisocial
c)   hostile
d)   instrumental

25.   The aggression exhibited by the Iroquois in the past and the regional differences in aggressive behavior in the U. S. today support the hypothesis that aggression can be:
a)   innate.
b)   instinctual.
c)   learned.
d)   universal.

26.   The chemical substance produced in the midbrain that seems to inhibit aggression is:
a)   dopamine.
b)   testosterone.
c)   norepinephrine.
d)   serotonin.

27. Which of the following best characterizes the relationship between gender differences and aggression?
    a) There are no gender differences in aggression.
    b) Boys engage in all types of aggression more than girls do.
    c) Girls engage in covert acts of aggression while boys engage in overt acts of aggression.
    d) Girls engage in overt acts of aggression while boys engage in covert acts of aggression.

28. Which of the following is FALSE regarding the relationship between gender differences and aggression?
    a) Women are less likely than men are to perceive an ambiguous situation as requiring aggression.
    b) Even when provoked, women continue to display significantly less aggression than men do.
    c) Women feel guiltier after committing overt acts of aggression than men do.
    d) In the last few decades, the number of nonviolent crimes committed by women has increased more than it has for men.

29. Of all the violent crimes against women in a typical year, some _____ percent were committed by their intimate male partners; for men, the figure is _____ percent.
    a) 50; 8
    b) 37; 5
    c) 33; 6
    d) 22; 3

30. The presence of which stimulus has been found to increase aggression?
    a) alcohol
    b) drugs
    c) baseball bat
    d) gun

31. Which of the following can increase frustration and therefore increase the likelihood of aggression?
    a) being close to a goal and being thwarted
    b) experiencing unexpected frustration
    c) experiencing legitimate frustration
    d) all the above

32. According to social psychologist Leonard Eron, how many murders and other acts of violence have U. S. children seen by the time they finish elementary school?
    a) 1,000 murders and 25, 000 other violent acts
    b) 3,000 murders and 50,000 other violent acts
    c) 5,000 murders and 75,000 other violent acts
    d) 8,000 murders and 100,000 other violent acts

Chapter 12

33.   Which of the following is true about children viewing media violence?
        a)   The more violence children watch on television, the more violence they show in their later years.
        b)   Children who watch violent programs engage in more acts of violence than do children who watch nonviolent programs.
        c)   Watching television violence increases violent behavior only in children who are violent already.
        d)   Both a and b are true.

34.   Which of the following is FALSE about adults and viewing media violence?
        a)   There exists a consistent relationship between viewing television violence and the viewer's antisocial behavior.
        b)   Men who watch more television show more physiological arousal when watching violence than do men who watch less television.
        c)   College students exposed to a lot of television violence give others more powerful shocks than do students who are exposed to nonviolent television.
        d)   People who watch more than four hours of television a day have a greater fear of being assaulted than do people who watch less than two hours a day.

35.   Which of the following is a reason why exposure to media violence can increase aggression?
        a)   It weakens inhibitions against violent behavior.
        b)   It might trigger imitation and give people ideas about how to engage in violent acts.
        c)   It increases angry feelings and primes aggressive responses to those feelings.
        d)   All the above are reasons.

36.   Evolutionary psychologists argue that aggression is genetically programmed into men because it enables them to perpetuate their genes.
        a)   True
        b)   False

37.   The evolutionary perspective theorizes that males aggress for what reasons?
        a)   Males behave aggressively to establish dominance over other males.
        b)   Males aggress "jealously" to ensure that their mates are not copulating with others.
        c)   both of the above
        d)   none of the above

38.   Chimpanzees and bonobos have _____ percent of their DNA in common with human beings.
        a)   35
        b)   50
        c)   77
        d)   98

39.   Wilson and Muller (2006) found that chimps kill each other at
        a)   a much lower rate than humans in hunter-gatherer societies kill each other.
        b)   about the same rate than humans in hunter-gatherer societies kill each other.
        c)   a much greater rate than humans in hunter-gatherer societies kill each other.
        d)   about the same rate as humans in metropolitan areas kill each other.

40.   Bonobos are often referred to as the _____ ape.
    a)   "make love, not war"
    b)   "don't call us, we'll call you"
    c)   "live and let live"
    d)   "whatever will be will be"

SHORT ANSWER REVIEW

Aggression is (1) _____ (p. 352) behavior aimed at doing harm or causing pain to another person. Hostile aggression is defined as having as one's (2) _____ (p. 352) the harming of another; instrumental aggression uses inflicting harm as a (3) _____ (p. 352) to some other end.

Over the centuries, philosophers and psychologists have argued about whether or not humans are aggressive by nature. Some argued that it is in human nature to be aggressive whereas others argued that humans (4) _____ (p. 353) aggressive behavior. Sigmund Freud theorized that humans are born with an (5) _____ (p. 353) toward life, which he called Eros, and an equally powerful instinct toward death, which he called Thanatos. According to Freud, the Thanatos leads to aggressive actions.

Evolutionary psychologists have argued that aggression is (6) _____ (p. 353) into men because it enables them to perpetuate their genes. Observations of other species suggest that animals are naturally aggressive. However, there is substantial variation in the degree of aggressiveness of our two closest animal relatives—chimpanzees and (7) _____ (p. 354-355). Social psychologists argue that although aggressive behavior may be hardwired into humans, it is influencecd by situational and cultural factors. Aggression is an (8) _____ (p. 355) strategy.

There is a great deal of variation in the levels of aggression of individuals living in different (9) _____ (p. 355). It is also the case that within a given society, for example the (10) _____ (pp. 356), the degree of aggressiveness can change across time due to changes in the situation faced by the tribe. In our own society there are some striking regional differences in aggressive behavior. For example, there is a "culture of (11) _____ (p. 356)" in the South. Multiple factors shape whether or not a culture tends to nurture aggressive behavior.

There are neural and chemical influences on aggression. An area in the brain called the (12) _____ (p. 356) is thought to control aggression. Evidence suggests that the chemical serotonin serves to (13) _____ (p. 357) aggressive behavior and that the hormone (14) _____ (p. 357) is positively correlated with aggressive behavior.

Men are much more likely than women to behave aggressively in (15) _____ (p. 358) situations. Men are also more likely to interpret a given situation as provocative. However, gender differences are (16) _____ (p. 358) when women are actually provoked. Crime statistics show that males commit violent crimes at much higher rates then females. Sex differences in aggressive behaviors tend to hold up across (17) _____ (p. 358). Within heterosexual couples husbands are far more likely to murder their wives than vice versa.

Alcohol can increase aggressive behavior because it serves as a disinhibitor—it reduces one's (18) _____ (p. 359). Research suggests that alcohol disrupts the way people usually process information so that they may respond to the most obvious aspects of a social situation and fail to pick up the more (19) _____ (p. 359) elements of the situation.

When people experience pain, they are far more likely to act aggressively. Discomfort, such as (20) _____ (p. 359), humidity, air pollution, and offensive odors increase the likelihood of hostile and violent behavior.

Many social situations lead to aggression including situations that cause frustration, such as traffic jams. The frustration-aggression theory states that frustration—the perception that you are being

(21) _____ (p. 361) from attaining a goal – increases the probability of an aggressive response. Frustration is more likely to produce aggression if one is thwarted on the way to a goal. Aggression also increases when the frustration is unexpected. Also, (22) _____ (p. 362) – the feeling that you have less than what you deserve or less than people similar to you have – can lead to frustration and aggressive behavior.

Individuals frequently aggress to reciprocate for the aggressive behavior of others. This response is reduced if there are mitigating circumstances. When convinced a provocation was (23) _____ (p. 363), most of us will not reciprocate.

Research suggests that the mere presence of an aggressive stimulus in a situation increases the degree of aggressive behavior. An aggressive stimulus is an object that is associated with aggressive responses [e.g. a (24) _____ (p. 363)] and whose mere presence can increase the probability of aggression. In a classic study, participants angered in the presence of a gun administered more intense electric shocks to their "victim" than those angered in the same setting in which a tennis racket was substituted for the gun.

Social learning theory holds that we learn social behavior (e.g., aggression) by observing others and (25) _____ (p. 365) them. People, especially children, learn to respond to conflict aggressively by observing aggressive behavior in adults and peers.

Most children are exposed to a great deal of violence through watching TV, movies, and playing violent video games. Long term studies show that the more TV violence observed by a child the greater the amount of violence they exhibit as (26) _____ (p. 366). Watching TV violence has the greatest impact on youngsters who are somewhat (27) _____ (p. 367) to violence to begin with. Even children who are not inclined toward aggression however, will become more aggressive if exposed to a

(28) _____ (p. 367) of violent films over a long period. Exposure to violent media has also been shown to increase violent behavior in adults. Studies have found that viewing television violence can subsequently numb people's reactions when they face real-life aggression. Watching media violence can also affect our view of the world. Heavy TV viewers have an exaggerated view of the degree of violence taking place outside their own home and have a much greater fear of being personally (29) _____ (p. 369). Research shows that viewing violence impairs the (30) _____ (p. 370) of viewers and, therefore, people are less likely to remember a product advertised on a violent TV program.

Almost half of all rapes or attempted rapes during the last three decades have not involved assaults by a stranger but are instances of "date rape," in which the victim is acquainted with or even dating the assailant. Scripts may contribute to this. Scripts are ways of behaving socially that we learn implicitly from our culture. The sexual scripts adolescents are exposed to suggest that the traditional female role is to resist the male's sexual advances and the male's role is to be (31) _____ (p. 370).

Over the past 25 years, a team of researchers has conducted careful studies, in both naturalistic and laboratory settings, to determine the effects of violent pornography. Exposure to violent pornography increases (32) _____ (p. 371) of sexual violence toward women and is almost certainly a factor associated with actual aggressive behavior toward women.

Social psychologists have investigated how to reduce aggression. One question that has been investigated is "Does punishing aggression reduce aggressive behavior?" If the punishment is itself aggressive, it actually (33) _____ (p. 372) such behavior to children and may engender greater aggressiveness in the child. Further, severe punishment may actually enhance the attractiveness of the transgression to the child. However, the threat of (34) _____ (p. 372) punishment—of a degree just powerful enough to get the child to stop the undesired activity temporarily—leads the child to try to justify his or her restraint and, as a result, can make the behavior less appealing. For punishment to serve as a deterrent to crime, it must be both prompt and certain.

The theory of (35) _____ (p. 374) would predict that venting one's anger or watching others behave aggressively would serve to make one less likely to engage in subsequent acts of aggression. Research shows the contrary: acting aggressively, or observing aggressive events (such as a football game), actually (36) _____ (p. 375) the likelihood of future aggressive behavior. Committing an overt act of aggression against a person changes your feelings about that person, increasing your negative feelings toward the target and making future aggression against that person more likely. At a national level, violent acts against another nation lead to increasingly negative attitudes towards that nation and greater willingness to inflict further violence because it triggers the tendency to justify that action. When a nation is at war, even one that is far away, its people are (37) _____ (p. 377) to commit aggressive acts against one another.

Typically, venting anger causes more harm than good. It is more effective to become aware of the anger and then to deal with it in ways that are more constructive. It is often the case that a cycle of anger and aggression can be diffused through apology. Children are less likely to act aggressively if they have been exposed to (38) _____ (p. 379) models. There is also some evidence that formal training on how to communicate anger or criticism in constructive ways, how to negotiate and compromise when conflicts arise, and how to be more sensitive to the needs and desires of others can be an effective means of reducing aggression. We are also less likely to aggress toward someone if we feel (39) _____ (p. 380) for them. Most people find it difficult to inflict pain on a stranger unless they can find a way to dehumanize their victim. Understanding the process of (40) _____ (p. 381) is the first step toward reversing it.

Chapter 12

ESSAY REVIEW

1. Describe how evolutionary psychologists explain aggressive behavior.

2. Discuss what is meant by "culture of honor" and identify where and why this culture originated.

3. Describe the relationship between alcohol and aggression.

4. Explain the relationship between being provoked and reciprocating. Why is it that sometimes people do not reciprocate when provoked?

5. Discuss the relationship between imitation and aggression. How does social learning theory explain aggression?

EXIT TESTS

EXIT TEST 1

1. Which of the following is an example of aggression?
    a) accidentally bumping into someone in a crowded store
    b) a girl calling her little sister "stupid"
    c) a man kicking his wife in bed while he is asleep
    d) dropping a piece of furniture on someone's foot while the two of you are moving it because you lost your grip on it

2. Nearly all organisms seem to have evolved strong inhibitory mechanisms that enable them to suppress aggression when it is in their best interest to do so.
    a) True
    b) False

3. Cross-cultural studies on human aggression have found that human cultures _____ in their degree of aggressiveness.
    a) vary widely
    b) do not vary at all
    c) vary only slightly
    d) that are "primitive" are very high

4. Which of the following people is most likely to behave aggressively in response to an insult?
    a) Matt, who is from the Northeast
    b) Al, who is from the Midwest
    c) Hank, who is from the South
    d) Charles, who is from the North

5. Women who change their sex and have their testosterone levels raised
    a) initially become more aggressive, but later levels of aggression decrease and return to what they were before testosterone levels were raised.
    b) have no change in aggressive behavior.
    c) become less aggressive.
    d) become more aggressive.

6. In a cross-cultural study by Archer & McDaniel (1995), women from _____ showed greater evidence of aggressiveness.
   a) Australia
   b) the United States
   c) Sweden
   d) Korea

7. In 1998, of the 3,419 women killed in the United States, _____ percent died at the hands of a husband, boyfriend, former husband, or former boyfriend.
   a) 37
   b) 32
   c) 35
   d) 48

8. In Phoenix, Arizona, drivers in non-air-conditioned cars are less likely to honk their horns in traffic jams than drivers in air-conditioned cars.
   a) True
   b) False

9. In a 1991 movie called *Fried Green Tomatoes*, a character named Evelyn Couch has found a parking space at a busy grocery store. Evelyn puts her turn signal on and prepares to pull into the space when two young women in a small car quickly pull into the space before her. Evelyn yells at the young women and explains that she was about to pull into the space. They reply "Face it lady, we are younger and faster." After the young women enter the grocery store Evelyn proceeds to repeatedly run her car into their car. Can Evelyn's behavior be explained by the frustration-aggression theory?
   a) No, because she was not frustrated.
   b) No, because she did not behave aggressively.
   c) Yes, because not getting the parking space frustrated her and led to her aggressive behavior.
   d) No, because the car was empty and no one was injured.

10. Rev. Jesse Jackson suggested that the frustration and aggression of the race riots of 1967 and 1968 occurred because of thwarted expectations.
   a) True
   b) False

EXIT TEST 2

1. Seattle, Washington, and Vancouver, British Columbia, are similar in many ways. How do they differ?
   a) Vancouver severely restricts handgun ownership; Seattle does not.
   b) The murder rate in Seattle is more than twice as high as that in Vancouver.
   c) The murder rate in Vancouver is more than twice as high as that in Seattle.
   d) both a and b are true

2. The people children imitate most are
   a) famous athletes.
   b) their parents.
   c) their peers.
   d) movie stars.

3. Children who are not inclined toward aggression will become more aggressive if exposed to a steady diet of violent films over a long period of time.
   a) True
   b) False

4. The text mentions that several years ago a man drove his truck through the window of a crowded cafeteria in Killeen, Texas, and then emerged from the cab and began shooting people at random. By the time the police arrived he had killed 22 people. What preceded this man's shooting spree?
   a) The man had been provoked by a coworker.
   b) The man had become frustrated when a bank had turned him down for a loan.
   c) Based on a ticket stub in his wallet, it can be assumed that he had recently watched *The Fisher King*, a film depicting a deranged man firing a shotgun into a crowded bar, killing several people.
   d) The man had received an injection of testosterone.

5. Studies have found that simply viewing television violence cannot numb people's reactions to violence when they face real-life aggression.
   a) True
   b) False

6. If you are advertising a product on television and you want viewers to remember your ad you should advertise during a show that is
   a) violent.
   b) sexually explicit.
   c) violent and sexually explicit.
   d) nonviolent and non-sexually explicit

7. _____ are ways of behaving socially that we learn implicitly from culture.
   a) Social schemas
   b) Scripts
   c) Cultural schemas
   d) Social interaction frameworks

8. In a meta-analysis by Allen et al. (1995) it was found that exposure to violent pornographic material produced _____ aggression against women.
   a) a high degree of
   b) a low degree of
   c) a moderate degree of
   d) no

9. Olweus studied bullying and a bullying intervention program in Norway. He found that 20 months after the program began, bullying had decreased by _____.
   a) one-fourth
   b) one-third
   c) one-half
   d) three-fourths

10. When a nation is at war it
  a) weakens the population's inhibitions against aggression and leads to imitation of aggression.
  b) makes aggressive responses more acceptable.
  c) numbs our senses to the horror of cruelty and destruction.
  d) all of the above.

STUDY ACTIVITIES

1. What evidence suggests that, among humans, innate patterns of aggression are modified by the surrounding culture?

2. Imagine that you are on a debate team opposing a team from the National Rifle Association, which maintains that "Guns don't kill, people do." Based on what you know about the effects of "aggressive stimuli," defend your position that guns do kill people.

3. What are the effects on children and adults of long-term exposure to television violence?

4. Describe the frustration-aggression theory. What produces frustration? What is the role played by anger in this theory? According to this theory, what factors determine the likelihood that aggression will result from frustration?

5. Outline steps you can take to reduce aggressive behavior in yourself and others.

6. What is the difference between hostile and instrumental aggression? Describe examples you have seen of these two types.

7. What roles do the amygdala and testosterone play in aggressive behavior? What effect does serotonin have on aggressive behavior? What research findings support the influence of testosterone on aggressive behavior?

8. What are the consequences of viewing violent pornography on attitudes about sexual violence toward women and on aggressive behavior toward women?

9. Explain which type of punishment is most likely to deter aggressiveness and why it works. Why doesn't fighting aggression with aggression work?

10. What effects does wartime have on a nation's aggressive behavior at home and on attitudes toward victims?

Chapter 12 Answers

Practice Test

1. D (p. 352)
2. D (p. 353)
3. C (pp. 354-355)
4. B (p. 357)
5. A (p. 360)
6. C (p. 363)
7. C (p. 365)
8. C (p. 372)
9. A (p. 374)
10. A (pp. 375-376)
11. D (pp. 377-378)
12. C (p. 379)
13. B (p. 353)
14. A (p. 354)
15. B (p. 356)
16. C (p. 361)
17. D (p. 362)
18. A (p. 365)
19. B (p. 371)
20. A (p. 375)
21. B (p. 378)
22. A (p. 380)
23. B (p. 352)
24. C (p. 352)
25. C (p. 356)
26. D (p. 357)
27. C (pp. 357-358)
28. B (pp. 357-358)
29. D (p. 358)
30. D (p. 363)
31. D (pp. 359-361)
32. D (p. 366)
33. D (pp. 366-367)
34. B (pp. 367-368)
35. D (pp. 369-370)
36. A (p. 353)
37. C (p. 353)
38. D (pp. 354-355)
39. B (p. 355)
40. A (p. 355)

Short Answer Review

1. intentional (p. 352)
2. goal (p. 352)
3. means (p. 352)
4. learn (p. 353)

5.   instinct (p. 353)
6.   genetically programmed (p. 353)
7.   bonobos (p. 354-355)
8.   optional (p. 355)
9.   cultures (p. 355)
10.   Iroquois (p. 356)
11.   honor (p. 356)
12.   amygdala (p. 356)
13.   inhibit (p. 357)
14.   testosterone (p. 357)
15.   provocative (p. 358)
16.   reduced (p. 358)
17.   cultures (p. 358)
18.   social inhibitions (p. 359)
19.   subtle (p. 359)
20.   heat (p. 359)
21.   prevented (p. 361)
22.   relative deprivation (p. 362)
23.   unintentional (p. 363)
24.   gun (p. 363)
25.   imitating (p. 365)
26.   teenagers and young adults (p. 366)
27.   prone (p. 367)
28.   steady diet (p. 367)
29.   assaulted (p. 369)
30.   memory (p. 370)
31.   persistent (p. 370)
32.   acceptance (p. 371)
33.   models (p. 372)
34.   mild (p. 372)
35.   catharsis (p. 374)
36.   increases (p. 375)
37.   more likely (p. 377)
38.   nonaggressive (p. 379)
39.   empathy (p. 380)
40.   dehumanization (p. 381)

Essay Review

1.   Your essay should include
   - Evolutionary psychologists argue that aggression is genetically programmed into men because it enables them to perpetuate their genes. (p. 353)
   - Males are theorized to aggress for two reasons: First, males behave aggressively to establish dominance over other males. The idea here is that the female will choose the male who is most likely to provide the best genes and the greatest protection and resources for their offspring. (p. 353)
   - Second, males aggress "jealously" to ensure that their mate(s) are not copulating with others. This ensures their paternity. (p. 353)

2.   Your essay on "culture of honor" should include:
- The "culture of honor" refers to an inclination to endorse violence for protection and in response to insults. (p. 356)
- This culture originated in the early South and in the old West. (p. 356)
- It may have begun with particular economic and occupational circumstances, especially in herding societies where protection of the herd was vital. If you own cattle, constant vigilance is impossible, therefore, to protect your cattle you would want to have the reputation as a person of honor who will behave aggressively against thieves and rustlers. (p. 356)

3.   Your essay on alcohol and aggression should include the following:
- Alcohol is a social lubricant that lowers our inhibitions against acting in ways frowned on by society, including acts of aggression. (p. 359)
- Alcohol often serves as a disinhibitor—it reduces our social inhibitions, making us less cautious than we usually are. (p. 359)
- Intoxicated people often respond to the earliest and most obvious aspects of a social situation and often miss the subtleties. Ambiguous situations might be misinterpreted as provocative. (p. 359)

4.   Your essay should include:
- Aggression frequently stems from the need to reciprocate after being provoked by aggressive behavior from another person. (p. 363)
- In research by Baron (1988) participants were provoked and then provided with an opportunity to retaliate. When provided with an opportunity to retaliate, they did so. (p. 363)
- People do not always reciprocate when provoked because they ask themselves whether or not the provocation was intentional. If they are convinced it was unintentional, they are not likely to reciprocate. (p. 363)

5.   Your essay on imitation and aggression should include the following:
- Children frequently learn to solve conflicts aggressively by imitating adults and their peers, especially when they see that the aggression is rewarded. The people that children imitate most are their parents. If the parents were abused as children, this can set a chain of abuse in motion. (p. 365)
- Social learning theory holds that we learn social behavior, including aggression, by observing others and imitating them. (p. 365)

Exit Test 1

1.   B (p. 352)
2.   A (p. 355)
3.   A (p. 355)
4.   C (p. 356)
5.   D (p. 357)
6.   A (p. 358)
7.   B (p. 358)
8.   B (p. 360)
9.   C (p. 361)
10.   A (p. 362)

Exit Test 2

1. D (p. 364)
2. B (p. 365)
3. A (p. 367)
4. C (p. 368)
5. B (p. 369)
6. D (p. 370)
7. B (p. 370)
8. A (pp. 371-372)
9. C (p. 374)
10. D (p. 377)

1. Cultures vary widely in their degree of aggressiveness. For instance, "primitive" tribes in Central Africa and New Guinea are far less aggressive than our "civilized" United States. Moreover, there is evidence of changes in the aggression within a culture over time. The Iroquois Indians were peaceful until the European influence brought them into economic competition with neighboring tribes. (pp. 355-356)

2. Berkowitz and LePage (1967) have demonstrated increased aggression by angered individuals in the presence of an aggressive stimulus (a gun) and concluded that the "trigger can also pull the finger" of individuals ready to aggress and who have no strong inhibitions against doing so. (pp. 363-364)

3. Children exposed to a steady diet of violent television are more likely to behave aggressively, even if they are not disposed to such behavior. Additionally, children who watch a lot of violence on TV are less sensitive to subsequent violence they observe. The effects of viewing television violence on aggressive behavior are similar for adults. (pp. 366-368)

4. Frustration is the feeling that you are being prevented from obtaining a goal. According to the frustration-aggression theory, frustration produces anger or annoyance and a readiness to aggress. Likelihood of aggressive behavior depends on: (1) how frustrated you are (frustration increases the closer the goal is), and (2) when the frustration is unexpected. (pp. 361-362)

5. The most effective means to reduce your own aggression when you are angry is to avoid engaging in aggressive behavior. Instead, express your anger calmly. To defuse aggression in someone who you have frustrated, apologize for your behavior. People can be taught nonaggressive behavior by imposing swift yet mild punishment, by exposing people to nonaggressive models and by reinforcing their nonaggressive communication and problem-solving behaviors. Finally, by building empathy in people, they are less likely to dehumanize individuals and behave aggressively toward them. (pp. 377-381)

6. Hostile aggression is aggression stemming from feelings of anger and aimed at inflicting pain. Instrumental aggression is a means to some goal other than causing pain. (p. 352)

7. The amygdala is an area in the core of the brain that is associated with aggressive behaviors. When the amygdala is stimulated, docile organisms become violent; similarly, when neural activity in that area of the brain is blocked, violent organisms become docile. Serotonin is a

chemical in the brain that may inhibit aggressive impulses. Laboratory animals injected with testosterone become more aggressive, and there is a parallel finding in humans. Women who have their testosterone levels increased become more aggressive and men who have their testosterone levels lowered become less aggressive. (pp. 356-357)

8.   Studies indicate that exposure to violent pornography promotes greater acceptance of sexual violence toward women and is almost certainly a factor associated with actual aggressive behavior toward women. A meta-analysis found that exposure to violent pornographic material produced a high degree of aggression against women. They also found that nonviolent pornographic material had a small but measurable effect on aggressive behavior against women. (pp. 370-372)

9.   The threat of mild punishment is most likely to deter aggression. This leads the person to try to justify his or her restraint and, as a result, can make the behavior less appealing. If punishment takes the form of an aggressive act, the punishers are actually modeling aggressive behavior for the person whose aggressive behavior they are trying to stamp out and might induce that person to imitate their action. (p. 372)

10. When a nation is at war it (1) weakens the population's inhibitions against aggression, (2) leads to imitation of aggression, (3) makes aggressive responses more acceptable, and (3) numbs our senses to the horror of cruelty and destruction, making us less sympathetic toward the victims. In addition, being at war serves to legitimize violence as a way to address difficult problems. (p. 377)

CHAPTER 13

Prejudice: Causes and Cures

CHAPTER 13 OVERVIEW

The first part of this chapter discusses how prejudice is a ubiquitous phenomenon; it affects us all. What varies across societies are the particular social groups which are the victims of prejudice and the degree to which societies enable or discourage discrimination. Prejudice is dangerous. It can be relentless and can escalate to extreme hatred. For the targets of relentless prejudice, the seeds of self-esteem are usually sown early in life. Often, but not always, prejudice leads to feelings of inferiority on the part of those who are the recipients of prejudiced expressions.

The intensity of the expression of prejudice in the United States has lessened over the last several decades. As would be predicted, the self-esteem of individuals in discriminated against groups has also improved. While this progress is real, prejudice is still a significant social problem.

The next section of the chapter defines prejudice. Social psychologists define **prejudice** as a hostile or negative attitude toward a distinguishable group of people based solely on their membership in that group. Stereotypes, while related to prejudice are different. While prejudice is defined in terms of a negative attitudinal and emotional response, stereotypes denote both the positive and negative traits that people assign to group members. A **stereotype** is a generalization about a group of people in which certain traits are assigned to virtually all members of the group, regardless of actual variation among group members. Stereotyping is a cognitive process, not an emotional one. Discrimination denotes actual behavior—it is the action component. **Discrimination** is defined as an unjustified negative or harmful action towards members of a group solely because of their membership in that group.

The next section of the chapter addresses the question "What Causes Prejudice?" No one knows for sure whether or not prejudice is part of our biological makeup. While social psychologists do not agree on whether or not humans are naturally prejudiced, most would agree that the specifics of prejudice must be learned. Even when young children pick up their parents' prejudices, they do not necessarily retain those prejudices in adulthood. As a broad-based and powerful attitude, prejudice has many causes.

The processes of social cognition are important in the creation and maintenance of stereotypes and prejudice. Categorization of people into groups leads to the perception of in-groups and out-groups. In-group bias refers to positive feelings and special treatments for people we have defined as being part of our own in-group and negative feelings and unfair treatment for others simply because we have defined them as being in the out-group. Another consequence of categorization is the perception of out-group homogeneity. **Out-group homogeneity** is the perception that individuals in the out-group are more similar to each other (homogeneous) than they really are, as well as more similar than the members of the in-group are.

Even people who are usually sensible and reasonable about most topics become relatively immune to rational, logical arguments when it comes to prejudice. There are two reasons for this, involving the affective and cognitive aspects of an attitude. First, it is primarily the emotional aspect of attitudes that makes a prejudiced person so hard to argue with; logical arguments are not effective in countering emotions. Second, an attitude tends to organize the way we process relevant information about the targets of that attitude. Stereotypes also tend to be persistent.

Devine's theory suggests that there is a two-step model of cognitive processing. This model can be applied to stereotypes. First, the automatic processing brings up the stereotype. In the second step controlled (or conscious) processing can refute or ignore it. According to the justification-suppression model of prejudice, most people struggle between their urge to express prejudice and their need to maintain a positive self-concept, both in their own eyes as well as the eyes of others. However, it requires energy to suppress prejudiced impulses. Because people are programmed to avoid the constant expenditure of energy, we are always on the lookout for information that will enable us to convince ourselves that there is a valid justification for holding a negative attitude toward a particular out-group. Once we find a valid justification for disliking this group, we can act against them and still feel as though we are not bigots—thus avoiding cognitive dissonance.

Another way that our cognitive processing perpetuates stereotypical thinking is through the phenomenon of illusory correlation. **Illusory correlation** is the tendency to see relationships, or correlations, between events that are actually unrelated. Illusory correlations are most likely to occur when the events or people are distinctive or conspicuous. Minority group members are, by definition, distinctive because fewer of them are present in the society. Other groups who are not distinctive in terms of numbers, such as women, may nonetheless become distinctive or conspicuous because of a nonstereotypical profession or talent. Distinctiveness leads to the creation of and belief in an illusory correlation. This illusory correlation is then applied to all members of the target group.

Researchers have found that when people are presented with an example or two that seems to refute their existing stereotype, most of them do not change their general belief. When people are bombarded with many examples that are inconsistent with the stereotype, they gradually modify their beliefs.

Just as we form attributions to make sense of one person's behavior, we also make attributions about whole groups of people. The fundamental attribution error applies to prejudice—we tend to overestimate the role of dispositional forces when making sense out of others' behavior. Stereotypes can be described as the **ultimate attribution error**—making negative dispositional attributions about an entire group of people.

Knowledge of stereotypes applying to a group to which one belongs can lead to stereotype threat. **Stereotype threat** is the apprehension experienced by members of a group that their behavior might confirm a cultural stereotype. Aronson and his colleagues reasoned that the effects of stereotype threat can be reversed by countering the stereotype. Research has shown performance-enhancing benefits of counter-stereotype mindsets.

When a member of an out-group behaves as we expect, it confirms and even strengthens our stereotype. When out-group members act nonstereotypically, we tend to make situational attributions about them, thereby maintaining our stereotypes.

It is hard for people who have rarely been discriminated against to fully understand what its like to be a target of prejudice. True empathy for targets of discrimination is difficult for those who have routinely been judges on the basis of their own merit and not their racial, ethnic, religious, or other group membership. When empathy is absent, it is sometimes hard to avoid falling into the trap of blaming the victim for his or her plight. **Blaming the victim** is the tendency to blame individuals (make dispositional attributions) for their victimization, typically motivated by a desire to see the world as a fair place. This belief in a just world can lead to derogation of a victim and the perpetuation of prejudice.

The **self-fulfilling prophecy** is a case whereby people (1) have an expectation about what another person is like, which (2) influences how they act toward that person, which (3) causes that person to behave in a way consistent with people's original expectations. Researchers have demonstrated the relevance of this phenomenon to stereotyping and discrimination.

Realistic conflict theory states that prejudice is the inevitable byproduct of real conflict between groups for limited resources—whether involving economics, power, or status. Competition for resources leads to derogation of and discrimination against the competing out-group. **Scapegoating** is a process whereby frustrated and angry people tend to displace their aggression from its real source to a convenient target—an out-group that is disliked, visible, and relatively powerless.

Institutionalized racism and institutionalized sexism are norms operating throughout the society's structure. **Institutional racism** refers to racist attitudes that are held by the vast majority of people living in a society where stereotypes and discrimination are the norm. **Institutional sexism** refers to sexist attitudes that are held by the vast majority of people living in a society where stereotypes and discrimination are the norm. **Normative conformity**, or the desire to be accepted and "fit in," leads many people to go along with stereotyped beliefs and not challenge them. **Modern racism** (outwardly acting unprejudiced while inwardly maintaining prejudiced attitudes) is an example of a shift in normative rules about prejudice: Nowadays, people have learned to hide their prejudice in situations where it would lead them to be labeled as racist. Subtle forms of prejudice can also be directed toward women.

The final section of this chapter addresses the question, "How Can Prejudice Be Reduced?" The most important way to reduce prejudice is through contact—bringing in-group and out-group members together. However, mere contact is not enough and can even exacerbate existing negative attitudes. Early desegregation of schools illustrates this fact. Instead, contact situations must include the following six conditions: **mutual interdependence** (the situation that exists when two or more groups need each other and must depend on each other to accomplish a goal that is important to each of them); a common goal; equal status; informal, interpersonal contact; multiple contacts; and social norms of equality. Traditional classrooms are highly competitive and do not have the characteristics mentioned above. Jigsaw classrooms, however, do have these characteristics and these classrooms have produced positive interpersonal outcomes.

CHAPTER 13 OUTLINE

I. Prejudice: The Ubiquitous Social Phenomenon
• Prejudice is ubiquitous; it affects all of us—majority group members as well as minority. People are prejudiced against many aspects of identity: nationality, ethnicity, gender, sexual preference, religion, appearance, physical state, and even professions and hobbies. Prejudice is dangerous. It can be relentless and can escalate to extreme hatred, to thinking of its members as less than human, to torture, to murder, and even to commit genocide.

A. Prejudice and Self-Esteem
• Prejudice is dangerous, fostering negative consequences from lowered self-esteem to
   genocide.
• Clark and Clark (1947) showed that African American children as young as 3 were already convinced that it was not desirable to be black, choosing to play with white rather than black dolls. This evidence led to the 1954 *Brown v. Board of Education* decision to desegregate schools.
• Goldberg (1968) showed that women had learned to consider themselves intellectually inferior to men, rating the same article higher when it was written by "John McKay" than by "Joan McKay."

B. A Progress Report
• Over the past 30 years, blatant discrimination has been reduced; the previous two findings no longer replicate. However, prejudice still exists in subtle—and sometimes blatant—forms.

II. Prejudice Defined
• Prejudice is an attitude, and thus has affective, cognitive, and behavioral components.
• Prejudice is a hostile or negative attitude toward a distinguishable group of people, based solely on their membership in that group. Prejudiced people direct their prejudice towards members of the group as a whole, ignoring distinguishing characteristics.

A. Stereotypes: The Cognitive Component
• Journalist Walter Lippman introduced the term stereotype in 1922. A **stereotype** is a generalization about a group of people in which identical characteristics are assigned to virtually all members of the group, regardless of actual variation among the members. Stereotypes are not necessarily emotionally laden and do not necessarily lead to discrimination. Frequently stereotyping is merely a way to simplify a complex world—Allport's (1954) "law of least effort."
1. Sports, Race, and Attribution
• The potential abuse engendered by stereotyping can be subtle as well as blatant, and involve positive as well as negative characteristics (e.g., the stereotype that African Americans are good basketball players). The abuse involves ignoring the overlap of distributions and ignoring individual differences in characteristics. For example, Stone et al. (1997) found that those students who believed a student was African American rated him as having better athletic ability than those who thought he was white, who rated him as having greater "basketball sense."
2. Stereotypes, Attribution, and Gender
• Gender stereotypes are still pervasive in our society. Women are seen as more nurturant and less assertive than men; this may be due to their involvement in the homemaker role. Evolutionary psychologists argue that the difference is due to a basis in the behaviors required for reproductive success. Whatever the cause of the difference, this stereotype does have some basis in truth. Work by Eagly, Wood, and Swim shows that there are indeed behavioral differences between men and women, such that women are more concerned with the welfare of others and men are more independent and dominant.
• Nonetheless, gender stereotyping often does depart from reality and can cut deeply. For example, people tend to see men's ability and women's motivation as responsible for their successes and men's lack of effort and women's lower ability as responsible for failure. These results, originally found in the 1970s, continued to be replicated in work in the late 1990s.
• Research shows that girls are more likely to blame themselves for their failures, while boys are likely to blame bad luck. Jacobs and Eccles (1992) showed that daughters of women who held gender stereotypic beliefs were most likely to hold such self-defeating beliefs themselves.

B. Discrimination: The Behavioral Component
• **Discrimination** is an unjustified negative or harmful action towards a member of a group, simply because of his or her membership in that group. For example, Bond et al. (1988) compared how white vs. black patients in a psychiatric hospital (run by an all-white staff) were treated. He found that, in the first 30 days of a stay, there appeared to be an assumption that blacks would be more violent than whites, as their offenses were more likely to be treated with physical restraints or drugs (Figure 13.1). However, eventually the staff did notice that there was no racial difference in violent incidents and began to treat whites and blacks equally.
1. Discrimination against Homosexuals
In the summer of 2003, the Supreme Court struck down state laws against sodomy, echoing the softening attitudes towards homosexuality in American society. In a study by Hebl, et al. (2002) confederates applied for jobs in the community. In some job interviews the confederates

portrayed themselves as homosexuals and in other interviews they did not. Hebl found that in the cases where the confederates were portrayed as homosexuals, the potential employers were less verbally positive and spent less time interviewing them. However, the employers did not formally discriminate against them (e.g., not calling them back as often for follow-up interviews as the other candidates).

III. What Causes Prejudice?

• Whether or not there is a biological root to prejudice is unknown. Most social psychologists would agree that the specifics of prejudice must be learned.

• Prejudices are easy to learn, although childhood prejudices are not necessarily maintained. For example, Rohan and Zanna (1996) found the greatest similarity of beliefs for parents and their children with egalitarian values. Children whose parents hold prejudices may be exposed to competing views and not hold their parents' prejudices.

• In the 1960s, a schoolteacher (Jane Elliot) in Riceville, Iowa, divided her class by eye color, telling the blue-eyed students that they were better than the brown-eyed students, and giving them special privileges; in less than half an hour, the formerly cohesive class was split along eye-color lines, with the blue-eyed students taunting and punishing the others, and the brown-eyed students feeling so low that their academic performance was depressed. The next day, the eye-color roles were reversed, and the day after that, the class was debriefed. Even 20 years later, the students claimed the exercise had a life-long impact (see *Eye of the Storm* and *A Class Divided* in the film list).

A. The Way We Think: Social Cognition

• One explanation for prejudice is that it is the inevitable byproduct of categorization, schemas, heuristics, and faulty memory processes in processing information.

1. Social Categorization: Us versus Them

• The first step in prejudice is the creation of group categorizations. Once we have mental categories, we group stimuli into them by similarities, downplaying differences between members of a group and exaggerating differences between members of different groups.

2. In-group bias

• *In-group bias* is the especially positive feelings and special treatment we reserve for people we have defined as being part of our *in-group* (the group with which a person identifies and of which he or she feels a member), and the negative feelings and unfair treatment we reserve for others simply because we have defined them as being in the *out-group* (groups which an individual does not identify with).

• Tajfel postulates that the underlying motive behind in-group bias is self-esteem maintenance and enhancement. To study this, he invented the minimal group paradigm, in which arbitrary groups were formed by putting strangers together on the basis of trivial criteria. Even in these minimal groups, people still displayed in-group bias by rating in-group members more highly, liking them better, and rewarding them more. People even preferred to take less money as a reward for their own group, if it meant beating the out-group, rather than taking more money but being beat by the out-group.

3. Out-Group Homogeneity

• Another consequence of social categorization is the **out-group homogeneity** bias, the perception that those in the out-group are more similar (homogenous) to each other than they really are, as well as more similar than the members of the in-group are (i.e., the belief that "they're all alike"). Quattrone and Jones (1980) showed that Rutgers and Princeton students watching videos of other students (purportedly from Rutgers or Princeton) making decisions would judge the student's selection as typical of others at his school, when the person went to the rival school, but not if they went to the student's own school (Figure 13.2).

Chapter 13

4. The Failure of Logic
• There are two reasons why it is almost impossible to get a person holding a deep-seated prejudice to change his or her mind. First, it is primarily the emotional aspect of attitudes that makes a prejudiced person hard to argue with; logic is not effective in countering emotions—people will ignore or distort any challenge to their belief. Second, people with strong prejudices have a firmly established schema for the target group(s); this will lead them to pay attention to, and recall more often, information that is consistent with their beliefs than that which is inconsistent. Thus stereotypes become relatively impervious to change.

5. The Persistence of Stereotypes
• Stereotypes reflect cultural beliefs—within a given society, they are easily recognized descriptions of members of a particular group. Even if we don't believe stereotypes, we can easily recognize them as common beliefs held by others.
• In a series of studies conducted at Princeton University over a span of 36 years (1933-1969), students were asked to assign traits to members of various ethnic and national groups. The participants could do so easily and to a large extent they agreed with each other.
• A quarter of a century later, Patricia Devine and Andrew Elliot (1995) showed that the stereotypes were not fading at all; virtually all the participants were fully aware of the negative stereotypes of African Americans, whether they believed them personally or not.

6. The Activation of Stereotypes
• Greenberg and Pyszczynski (1985) conducted a study to find out whether knowing a stereotype will affect the processing of information about a target person even for unprejudiced people. Observers watched a staged debate between a white and a black student; which student performed better in the debate was manipulated. Additionally, a planted confederate in the audience either made a racist remark, a nonracist remark, or no remark about the black student. When this student was the poorer debater, the racist remark activated the negative stereotype and led to lower ratings of him than in the other conditions (Figure 13.3). Similarly, Henderson-King and Nisbett (1997) found that it took only one negative action by one African American to activate the negative stereotype against blacks and discourage participants from wanting to interact with a different African American. These findings suggest that stereotypes exist in most of us, easily activated to have negative effects on the perception and treatment of out-group members.

7. Automatic and Controlled Processing of Stereotypes
• Patricia Devine (1989) developed a theory about how stereotypical and prejudiced beliefs affect information processing. Her theory is based on the distinction between automatic and controlled information processing. According to her theory, when we process information about another, a two-step process takes place: first the stereotypes that we know about are automatically triggered, then in the controlled process we decide whether or not to accept the stereotype; unprejudiced people will use the controlled process to override it. However, if a person is distracted, overwhelmed, or not attending, the controlled processing will not be initiated, and the stereotype will prevail (see Figure 13.4). In a test of this theory, Devine showed that high and low prejudiced Ss showed equal knowledge of the stereotype of African Americans; in a second part of the study, she displayed either stereotypical or nonstereotypical words to Ss subliminally; then she asked them to rate an ambiguous story about "Donald." Those Ss who had been subliminally exposed to the stereotypical words rated Donald more harshly, regardless of level of prejudice. Finally, in a third study, Devine showed that, when processing consciously, high prejudice students listed significantly more negative words than low prejudice students in describing black Americans.

8. The Justification-Suppression Model of Prejudice
• According to the justification-suppression model of prejudice, most people struggle between their urge to express prejudice and their need to maintain a positive self-concept, both in their own eyes as well as the eyes of others. However, it requires energy to suppress prejudiced impulses. Because people are programmed to avoid the constant expenditure of energy, we are always on the lookout for information that will enable us to convince ourselves that there is a

348
Copyright © 2010 by Pearson Education, inc. All rights reserved.

Prejudice: Causes and Cures

valid justification for holding a negative attitude toward a particular out-group. Once we find a valid justification for disliking this group, we can act against them and still feel as though we are not bigots—thus avoiding cognitive dissonance.

9. The Illusory Correlation

• An **illusory correlation** is the tendency to see relationships, or correlations, between events that are actually unrelated. Illusory correlations are most likely to occur when the events or people are distinctive or conspicuous; minority group members are so by definition. Once formed, an illusory correlation increases attention to confirming information and decreases attention to disconfirming information. The media create illusory correlations by their stereotypical presentations of women and minorities.

10. Can We Change Stereotypical Beliefs?

• Kunda and Oleson (1997) found that when people are presented with examples that strongly challenge their existing stereotypes, they tend to dismiss the disconfirming example as "the exception that proves the rule," and some actually strengthen their stereotypic belief.

• Researchers have found that when people are presented with an example or two that seems to refute their existing stereotype, most of them do not change their general belief. When people are bombarded with many examples that are inconsistent with the stereotype, they gradually modify their beliefs.

B. How We Assign Meaning: Attributional Biases

1. Dispositional versus Situational Explanations

• Stereotypes are negative dispositional attributions. Thomas Pettigrew has called our making dispositional attributions about a whole group of people the **ultimate attribution error**. Bodenhausen (1988) found that students were more likely to find a defendant guilty of a crime (ignoring extenuating circumstances) when his name was Carlos Ramirez than when it was Robert Johnson. In an earlier study, Bodenhausen and Wyer (1985) had found that when a crime was consistent with a group stereotype, Ss were less lenient in parole decisions, ignoring other relevant information, than when the crime was inconsistent with a group stereotype. Thus when people act in a way that confirms our stereotype, we make dispositional attributions and ignore possible situational causes.

2. Stereotype Threat

There is a statistical difference in academic test performance among various cultural groups in this country. One important reason for this is clearly situational and is based on a phenomenon called stereotype threat. **Stereotype threat** is the apprehension experienced by members of a minority group that they might behave in a manner that confirms an existing cultural stereotype. This worry, in turn, interferes with their ability to perform well in these situations. For example, Steele and Aronson found that when white and black students were told that a difficult test they were taking was just in the development phase and thus not valid, there were no differences in performance; but when the students were told that the same test was a valid measure of intellectual ability, the blacks performed more poorly than the whites.

• Stereotype threat applied to gender as well as race. Spencer et al. (1999) found a similar phenomenon among women taking math tests. Even white males can display the phenomenon— when compared to Asian males on a math exam (J. Aronson et al., 1999).

• Laboratory experiments have shown that when black students are exposed to successful African American role models, their performance improves.

C. Blaming the Victim

• **Blaming the victim** is the tendency to blame individuals (make dispositional attributions) for their victimization; ironically, it is motivated by a desire to see the world as a fair and just place where people get what they deserve. Believing that people get what they deserve leads one to blame victims for their outcomes. For example, Janoff-Bulman et al. (1985) presented students with a description of a woman's friendly behavior towards a man; students judged this behavior

349

as appropriate. Yet in another condition where the scenario ended with the woman being raped by the man, students rated the same behavior as inappropriate, as her having brought the rape on herself.

1. Self-Fulfilling Prophecies
• The **self-fulfilling prophecy** is a process in which we find confirmation and proof for our stereotypes by unknowingly creating stereotypical behavior in out-group members through our treatment of them.
• Word, Zanna, and Cooper (1974) conducted a set of experiments that demonstrates the phenomenon. In the first study, they asked white undergraduates to interview job applicants who were either white or black. The students tended to display discomfort when interviewing the African Americans: for example, they sat further away, stammered, and terminated the interview earlier. In a second experiment, the researchers varied the behavior of the interviewers so that they acted towards a job candidate either the way that the interviewers had acted towards whites or the way that the interviewers had acted towards blacks in the first study. They found that those applicants who had been interviewed in the way that African Americans had been interviewed were judged to be more nervous and less effective than the others (Figure 13.6) were.

D. Prejudice and Economic Competition: Realistic Conflict Theory
• **Realistic conflict theory** is the theory that limited resources lead to conflict between groups, and result in increased prejudice and discrimination.

1. Economic and Political Competition
• John Dollard (1938) was among the first to document the relationship between discrimination and economic competition in his classic study of prejudice in a small industrial town. At first, there was no discernable hostility toward the new German immigrants; prejudice flourished, however, as jobs grew scarce.
• Although correlational data is supportive of the theory, it still does not allow a causal inference. To allow this, an experiment is essential, such as that conducted by Sherif et al. (1961). In the classic "Robber's Cave" experiment, two groups of 12-year-old boys at a summer camp were randomly assigned to one of two groups, the Eagles or the Rattlers. In the first phase of the study, the groups were isolated and placed in situations designed to increase group cohesiveness. In the second phase of the study, the researchers set up a series of competitive activities in which the two groups were pitted against each other. Hostility between the two groups rapidly escalated. In the next phase of the study, researchers tried to eliminate hostility by eliminating competitive games and increasing contact. This failed to reduce the hostilities (the final resolution follows later in the chapter).

2. The Role of the Scapegoat
• **Scapegoating**, the tendency for individuals, when frustrated or unhappy, to displace aggression onto groups that are disliked, visible, and relatively powerless, may occur when people are frustrated (for example, by scarcity of resources) but there is no clear target to blame the frustration on. It may occur even in the absence of direct competition.
• In recent years homosexuals have become an increasingly convenient scapegoat.

E. The Way We Conform: Normative Rules
• Prejudice is created and maintained by many forces in the social world. Some operate within the individual and some operate on whole groups of people. One group level variable is conformity to normative standards or rules in society.

1. When Prejudice is Institutionalized
Institutionalized racism refers to the idea that racist attitudes are held by the vast majority of us because we live in a society where stereotypes and discrimination are the norm; **institutionalized sexism** is the idea that sexist attitudes are held by the vast majority of us for the same reason. In societies in which racism and sexism are institutionalized, **normative conformity** leads to the tendency to go along with the group in order to fulfill their expectations and gain acceptance.

Pettigrew (1958) argues that the greatest determinant of prejudice is this slavish conformity to social norms. For example, he showed that ministers in Little Rock, AK, in the 1950s were personally in favor of desegregation but kept these beliefs to themselves. Other studies show that people's prejudice and discrimination changes when they move to an area with different norms, or even, in a study of miners in West Virginia, when they are underground and when above. Over the past 50 years, American norms for attitudes such as that towards desegregation have changed drastically.

2. "Modern" Prejudice
• Although American norms have changed and the blatant expression of prejudice has diminished, prejudice is still with us. **Modern racism** is prejudice revealed in subtle, indirect ways because people have learned to hide prejudiced attitudes in order to avoid being labeled as racist. For example, many parents protest against their children being bussed only when the busing is interracial. Because of the nature of modern prejudice, it can best be studied using subtle or unobtrusive measures. For example, the bogus pipeline technique uses an impressive-looking machine labeled as a lie detector; the machine is a fake. People who are hooked up to the machine and believe that their true attitudes can be detected showed higher levels of racism and sexism than those completing the paper scales. However, sometimes racism and sexism still appear in overt behavior: for example, African Americans and females visiting a car dealership were given a higher price on a new car than white males.

3. Subtle and Blatant Prejudice in Western Europe
• Mertens & Pettigrew (1997) and Pettigrew & Meertens (1995) examined blatant and modern racism in France, the Netherlands, and Great Britain. They found that those who scored as racist on both scales wanted to send immigrants back; those who scored low on both wanted to improve their rights and were willing to take actions to do so, and those who scored as nonracist on the blatant scale but racist on the subtle scale did not want to take action to send immigrants back, nor were they willing to support any actions to help improve their rights.

F. Subtle Sexism
Subtle forms of prejudice can also be directed toward women. Many men have feelings of ambivalence toward women and as Glick and Fiske (2001) have shown this ambivalence can take one of two forms: *hostile sexism* or *benevolent sexism*. Hostile sexism suggests that women are inferior to men while benevolent sexism tends to hold stereotypically positive views of women.

IV. How Can Prejudice Be Reduced?
• The hope that prejudice can be reduced by education has proven naïve. Change requires more.

A. The Contact Hypothesis
• The contact hypothesis is the idea that merely bringing members of different groups into contact with each other will erode prejudice. This idea lay at the basis of the 1954 Supreme Court decision on school desegregation. For example, Deutsch and Collins (1951) had shown that white and black families randomly assigned to an integrated housing unit showed reductions in racism compared to those assigned to segregated units. However, things did not work so smoothly in school desegregation: there was tension and in more than half of the studies, prejudice actually increased, and in a quarter of the studies, the self-esteem of African American children was found to have decreased after desegregation. Mere contact does not work.

B. When Contact Reduces Prejudice: Six Conditions
• Allport (1954) suggested that six conditions are necessary for inter-group contact to reduce prejudice: (1) **mutual interdependence**, or the existence of situations where two or more groups need each other and must depend on each other in order to accomplish; (2) a common goal that is important to both of them; (3) equal status of group members; (4) having informal interpersonal

contact; (5) multiple contacts with several members of the out-group so that individuals can learn that their beliefs are wrong; and (6) social norms in place that promote equality. When these conditions are met, suspicious or even hostile groups will reduce their stereotyping, prejudice, and discrimination. Sherif's Robber's Cave study, described above, ultimately resolved the intergroup hostility by fostering each of these six conditions (Figure 13.7).

C. Why Early Desegregation Failed
• In most classrooms, the environment is very competitive; when minority students who have had deficient preparation are bussed in, they are guaranteed to lose the competition. The situation is ripe for the creation of self-fulfilling prophecies by both majority and minority group members. Thus Stephen (1978) found a general decrease in self-esteem of minority students following desegregation. To change the atmosphere of the classroom so that it meets the six conditions outlined above, Aronson and his colleagues developed the **jigsaw classroom.** This is a classroom setting designed to reduce prejudice and raise the self-esteem of children by placing them in small desegregated groups and making each child dependent on the other children in his or her group to learn the course material and do well in the class. Formal studies demonstrate that children in jigsaw classrooms perform better and show greater increases in self-esteem than those in traditional classrooms; further, they show more evidence of true integration and better abilities to empathize with and see the world through the eyes of others.

D. Why Does Jigsaw Work?
• Gaertner et al. (1990) suggest that the process is effective because it breaks down in-group and out-group categorization and fosters the notion of the class as a single group.
• Another reason is that it places people in a "favor-doing" situation, which leads people to like those they do favors for.
• A third reason why the jigsaw process is effective is that it encourages the development of empathy. Diane Bridgeman thus showed that 10-year-old students who had spent two months in a jigsaw classroom were more likely to successfully take the perspective of a story character and correctly answer questions from this character's point of view than were students who had not had the jigsaw classroom experience.
1. The Gradual Spread of Cooperative Learning
• The cooperative learning movement has been widely accepted by researchers as one of the most effective ways of improving race relations, building empathy, and improving instruction in schools. However, the educational system, like all bureaucracies, resists change, and the slowness of change can have tragic consequences.

LEARNING OBJECTIVES

After reading Chapter 13, you should be able to do the following:

1.   Describe the ubiquitous nature of prejudice. Identify what aspects of people's identities are targeted for prejudice. Discuss the consequences of prejudice for the self-esteem of the targets of prejudice. Describe the nature of prejudice today. Describe indications that prejudice has been reduced since the 1950s. (pp. 388-390)

2.   Define prejudice. Describe the affective component of prejudice. (pp. 390-391)

3.   Describe the cognitive component of prejudice. Identify why we develop stereotypes and what functions they serve. Discuss the effects of stereotypes on the relationships among sports, race, and attribution. Discuss the effects of gender stereotypes on attributions for achievement of men

and women. Identify the effects of gender stereotypes on young girls' performance in math and state the important influence on girls' perceptions of their math ability. (pp. 391-394)

4. Describe the behavioral component of prejudice and discuss findings that discrimination is unwittingly practiced today even among trained professionals. Discuss the prevalence of discrimination against homosexuals. (pp. 394-396)

5. Discuss conclusions drawn by social psychologists and evolutionary psychologists regarding the role of biology and learning in causing prejudice. Identify when parents and children are most likely to hold the same attitudes and values. Describe the classroom study conducted by Jane Elliot (1977) and the purpose it served. (pp. 396-397)

6. Describe the social cognition approach to the study of the causes of prejudice. Identify important consequences of social categorization that facilitate prejudice. Discuss the findings of research on minimal groups and the motives underlying in-group bias. Define out-group homogeneity. Describe how in-group bias and out-group homogeneity contribute to the formation and perpetuation of prejudice. (pp. 397-399)

7. Identify how affective and cognitive components of prejudice make prejudice resistant to change. Explain why logical arguments may not be effective at reducing prejudice. (pp. 399-401)

8. Identify why stereotypes are difficult to change. Explain why unwanted stereotypes persist. Describe Devine's two-step model of cognitive processing as it relates to stereotypes and prejudice. Describe the role of automatic processes in the activation of stereotypes and of controlled processes in disregarding the stereotype and reducing its effect on behavior. (pp. 401-403)

9. Describe research regarding the variability of people's automatic prejudice. Explain the justification-suppression model of prejudice. (pp. 402-405)

10. Describe how illusory correlations perpetuate stereotypic thinking. Identify why we are likely to perceive illusory correlations among minorities and unrelated events. Discuss how other cognitive factors such as the out-group homogeneity effect and stereotypes increase the negative effects of illusory correlations. (pp. 405-406)

11. Define the ultimate attribution error and discuss the influence of stereotyping in committing this error. (pp. 407-408)

12. Identify alternative explanations for the differences in academic test scores that are found between cultural groups in this country. Discuss the role of stereotype threat in producing these differences. Identify when stereotype threat applies to gender as well as ethnicity. (pp. 408-409)

13. Describe the results of laboratory experiments involving exposing black students to successful African American role models. Based on the results of Aronson et al. (2009), explain why Obama's election may or may not reduce stereotype threat. (p. 409)

14. Identify what is meant by "blaming the victim" and explain the typical motivation for this behavior. Describe the relevance of the self-fulfilling prophecy to stereotyping and discrimination both at the individual level and at the societal level. (pp. 409-411)

15. Describe realistic conflict theory as well as correlational and experimental support for this theory. Discuss scapegoat theory. Explain how frustration leads to the creation of a scapegoat. Identify characteristics of some groups that make them likely targets of scapegoating. (pp. 411-413)

16. Define institutionalized racism and institutionalized sexism. Discuss evidence that supports the role of normative conformity in prejudice. (pp. 414-415)

17. Describe modern racism. Identify the conditions that reveal modern racism and the consequences of these in the study of discrimination. Discuss research techniques necessary to reveal modern racist attitudes. Discuss the types of prejudice found in Western Europe. Describe the types of subtle sexism identified by Glick and Fiske.
(pp. 415-417)

18. Contrast the success of desegregation in housing projects studied by Deutsch and Collins (1951) with the initial failure of desegregation in schools nationwide. Define the contact hypothesis as stated by Allport (1954) and identify the six conditions necessary to reduce prejudice when there is contact between groups. Define mutual interdependence.
(pp. 417-419)

19. Explain why early attempts at desegregation failed. (pp. 419-420)

20. Define a jigsaw classroom. Describe how contact between students in the jigsaw classroom differs from contact in traditional classroom settings. Identify the advantages that have been gained by students learning in jigsaw classrooms. (pp. 420-421)

21. Discuss why the jigsaw classroom is effective. Identify what this and other cooperative learning environments encourage and its importance for interpersonal relations. (pp. 421-423)

KEY TERMS

1. _____ A hostile or negative attitude toward a distinguishable group of people, based solely on their membership in that group. (p. 391)

2. _____ A generalization about a group of people in which certain traits are assigned to virtually all members of the group, regardless of the actual variation among the members. (p. 391)

3. _____ Unjustified negative or harmful action toward a member of a group simply because of his or her membership in that group. (p. 394)

4. _____ The perception that individuals in the out-group are more similar to each other than they really are, as well as more similar than the members of the in-group are. (p. 398)

5. _____ The tendency to see relationships , or correlations, between events that are actually unrelated. (p. 405)

6. _____ The tendency to make dispositional attributions about an entire group of people. (p. 407)

7. _____ The apprehension experienced by members of a group that their behavior might confirm a cultural stereotype. (p. 408)

8. _____ The tendency to blame individuals (make dispositional attributions) for their victimization, typically motivated by a desire to see the world as a fair place. (p. 409)

9. _____ The case whereby people (1) have an expectation about what another person is like, which (2) influences how they act toward that person, which (3) causes that person to behave in a way consistent with people's original expectations. (p. 410)

10. _____ The idea that limited resources lead to conflict between groups and result in increased prejudice and discrimination. (p. 411)

11. _____ The tendency for individuals, when frustrated or unhappy, to displace aggression onto groups that are disliked, visible, and relatively powerless. (p. 413)

12. _____ Racist attitudes that are held by the vast majority of us because we are living in a society in which stereotypes and discrimination are the norm. (p. 414)

13. _____ Sexist attitudes that are held by the vast majority of us because we are living in a society in which stereotypes and discrimination are the norm. (p. 414)

14. _____ The tendency to go along with the group in order to fulfill the group's expectations and gain acceptance. (p. 414)

15. _____ Outwardly acting unprejudiced while inwardly maintaining prejudiced attitudes. (p. 415)

16. _____ The situation that exists when two or more groups need each other and must depend on each other in order to accomplish a goal that is important to each of them. (p. 418)

17. _____ A classroom setting designed to reduce prejudice and raise the self-esteem of children by placing them in small, desegregated groups and making each child dependent on the other children in the group to learn the course material and do well in the class. (p. 421)

GUIDED REVIEW

PRACTICE TEST

1. Once formed, stereotypes:
   a) easily change when contradictory information is encountered.
   b) develop into more elaborate and complex categories.
   c) deteriorate unless challenged by contradictory information.
   d) are resistant to change on the basis of new information.

2. According to Stipek and Galinski (1991), young girls attribute success in math to _____ and boys attribute success in math to _____.
   a) luck; hard work
   b) hard work; luck
   c) luck; ability
   d) ability; luck

3. According to Gordon Allport, stereotypes result:
    a) from our efforts to maximize our cognitive time and energy.
    b) from the breakdown of once normal cognitive processes.
    c) from conflicts that exist between groups when resources are limited.
    d) when individuals adhere to norms which foster prejudice.

4. Individuals emotionally involved in their beliefs about a target group are not likely to be persuaded by opposing arguments because:
    a) such individuals have amassed a large number of arguments to defend their position.
    b) attitudes based on emotions are not affected by logical arguments.
    c) arousal caused by emotional involvement interferes with normal cognitive processing.
    d) they are unable to process arguments and must rely on less persuasive peripheral cues.

5. According to Devine's (1989) two-step model of cognitive processing, simply knowing stereotypes that you do not believe affects your cognitive processing because:
    a) we are constantly aware of the stereotypes.
    b) we can recall the stereotypes at will.
    c) the stereotypes are inconsistent with our beliefs.
    d) the stereotypes are automatically activated.

6. According to Weber and Crocker (1983) people will gradually modify their stereotypical beliefs if you present them with two or three powerful disconfirming pieces of evidence.
    a) True
    b) False

7. When students read that a prisoner had committed a crime that matched the common stereotype of the offender, Bodenhausen and Wyer (1985) found that the students:
    a) ignored other information that was inconsistent with the stereotype and were harsher in their recommendations for parole.
    b) were puzzled by other information that was inconsistent with the stereotype and refrained from making any recommendations.
    c) dismissed the information that was consistent with the stereotype and were harsher in their recommendations for parole.
    d) made situational attributions for the crime and were more lenient in their recommendations for parole.

8. Defense attorneys who focus the jury's attention on the sexual histories of sexual assault victims are exploiting people's tendency to:
    a) make situational attributions.
    b) perceive out-group heterogeneity.
    c) blame the victim.
    d) convict rather than to acquit the accused.

9. Realistic conflict theory maintains that:
    a) abundant resources produces greed and negative feelings toward out-groups.
    b) conflict experienced within a group is likely to be attributed to members of an out-group.
    c) mutual interdependence among groups produces competition and negative feelings toward competing groups.
    d) limited resources produce competition and negative feelings toward competing groups.

10. Institutional racism and sexism arise when:
   a) people are angered or frustrated by social institutions.
   b) two or more groups must depend on each other in order to accomplish a common goal.
   c) negative stereotypes become the fundamental categories people use to organize their experiences.
   d) people live in a society where stereotypes and discrimination are normative.

11. Stereotypes result from our tendency to:
   a) present ourselves favorably.
   b) categorize people and events.
   c) reduce cognitive dissonance.
   d) maintain our self-esteem.

12. Prejudice is:
   a) any behavior aimed at physically or emotionally harming people who are members of a discernible group.
   b) a generalization about a group of people in which identical characteristics are assigned to virtually all members of the group.
   c) a hostile or negative attitude toward a distinguishable group of people, based solely on their membership in that group.
   d) the tendency to categorize people into groups, based on some specific characterization.

13. Attributing a higher level of motivation to successful females than to successful males may be one way of:
   a) implying that the successful female has less actual skill than her male counterpart.
   b) rationalizing the presence of the obstacles society imposes on women's endeavors to be successful.
   c) implying that the successful female is more emotional than her male counterpart.
   d) rationalizing the prejudice toward women that exists in our society.

14. The bigot's cry, "They all look alike to me," illustrates one consequence of social categorization called the:
   a) perception of out-group homogeneity.
   b) in-group bias.
   c) illusory correlation.
   d) ultimate attribution error.

15. Which of the following best describes the relationship between knowing and believing stereotypes?
   a) To know a stereotype is to believe the stereotype.
   b) You can know a stereotype without believing the stereotype.
   c) You can believe a stereotype without knowing the stereotype.
   d) Stereotypes have no impact unless they are both known and believed.

16. Illusory correlations are especially likely to be found between minorities and unrelated events because minorities are:
   a) powerless.
   b) outspoken.
   c) distinctive.
   d) victimized.

17. Furnham and Gunter (1984) have found that negative attitudes toward the poor and homeless are more prevalent among individuals who:
    a) score high on measures of self-esteem.
    b) tend to be high in self-awareness.
    c) believe we live in a "dog-eat-dog" world.
    d) have a strong belief in a "just world."

18. To demoralized and frustrated Germans who blamed Jews for troubles in Germany following World War I, the Jews provided a convenient:
    a) minimal group.
    b) scapegoat.
    c) out-group.
    d) stereotype.

19. Findings that people's prejudices change when they move to areas where norms are more or less prejudicial support the notion that prejudice is largely the result of:
    a) social cognition processes.
    b) an inheritable factor.
    c) competition.
    d) conformity.

20. Contact between majority and minority groups will reduce prejudice when members of the groups:
    a) interact voluntarily in an unstructured setting.
    b) have low expectations for increased intergroup harmony.
    c) compete for limited available resources.
    d) are of equal status and in pursuit of common goals.

21. The action or behavioral aspect of prejudice is:
    a) generalization.
    b) discrimination.
    c) stereotyping.
    d) none of the above.

22. Randall believes that the homeless man he sees every day when he goes to work is lazy and just does not want to work. In fact, Randall thinks all homeless people are lazy. When Randall makes dispositional attributions about an entire group of people he is committing the:
    a) fundamental attribution error.
    b) ultimate attribution bias.
    c) universal attribution error.
    d) ultimate attribution error.

23. Feeling apprehensive about confirming a negative cultural stereotype when working on a task can lead people to feel _____, which can result in _____ performance on the task.
    a) stereotype anxiety; poor
    b) stereotype threat; poor
    c) stereotype anxiety; improved
    d) stereotype threat; improved

24. Steele and Aronson (1995) found that when African American students are given a test that they are told measures their intellectual ability they perform _____ the white students do. When they are told that the test does not measure their intellectual ability they perform _____ the white students do.
    a)   worse than; better than
    b)   better than; worse than
    c)   worse than; as well as
    d)   as well as; as well as

25. Word, Zanna, and Cooper (1974) found that when African Americans are interviewed by whites, they are likely to perform less well than white interviewees. This is explained best by:
    a)   the ultimate attribution error.
    b)   scapegoating.
    c)   blaming the victim.
    d)   the self-fulfilling prophecy.

26. A situation where two or more groups need and depend on each other to accomplish a goal important to each of them defines:
    a)   common dependence.
    b)   common interdependence.
    c)   mutual dependence.
    d)   mutual interdependence.

27. All of the following are conditions of contact necessary to decrease stereotyping, prejudice, and discrimination EXCEPT which one?
    a)   equal status
    b)   social norms of equality
    c)   formal contact
    d)   a common goal

28. Which of the following is true about the jigsaw classroom and its effects?
    a)   Students depend on each other for the class material.
    b)   Students in jigsaw classrooms show a decrease in prejudice and stereotyping compared to students in traditional classrooms.
    c)   Students in jigsaw classrooms show an increase in self-esteem compared to students in traditional classrooms.
    d)   All the above are true.

29. Which of the following explains why the jigsaw classroom works to reduce prejudice, stereotyping, and discrimination?
    a)   It breaks down in-group versus out-group delineations.
    b)   It increases competitive strategies.
    c)   It encourages the development of empathy.
    d)   both a and c

30. In the jigsaw classroom, if one student in a group is having difficulty mastering his or her material, other members will benefit most if they:
    a)   pay more attention to students who have mastered the material already.
    b)   compete with the student for the teacher's praise.
    c)   encourage the student and ask friendly, probing questions.
    d)   complete the student's assignment for him/her.

31.   The phenomenon of modern prejudice refers to the finding that over the past 50 years:
        a)   the economic gap between minority and white Americans has become greater than ever.
        b)   radical hate groups have become more prevalent.
        c)   people have learned to hide their prejudice when it is socially unacceptable to express it.
        d)   the popularity of ultraconservative political groups has increased.

32.   Rochelle is walking across campus one night. As two males walk by, she feels her heart race. Her reaction demonstrates the _____ component of her prejudice.
        a)   stereotypical
        b)   affective
        c)   cognitive
        d)   behavioral

33.   In a study by Goldberg (1968), female college students read scholarly articles and evaluated them. For some students the article was signed by a male author (e.g. "John T. McKay") and for others, the same articles were signed by female authors (e.g. Joan T. McKay"). Goldberg found that female students
        a)   rated the articles much higher if they were attributed to a male author.
        b)   rated the articles much higher if they were attributed to a female author.
        c)   rated the articles the same whether the author was believed to be male or female.
        d)   rated the articles only slightly higher if they were attributed to a male author.

34.   Social categorization is both useful and necessary.
        a)   True
        b)   False

35.   Research by Patricia Devine and Andrew Elliot (1995) indicates that stereotypes are fading in American society.
        a)   True
        b)   False

36.   According to the justification-suppression model of prejudice most people struggle between their urge to express prejudice and their need to maintain a(n)
        a)   positive self-concept in their own eyes.
        b)   positive self-concept in the eyes of others.
        c)   accurate view of self.
        d)   both a and b

37.   One reason stereotypes are so insidious and persistent is the human tendency to make _____ attributions.
        a)   situational.
        b)   dispositional.
        c)   external.
        d)   peripheral.

38.   The tendency to blame victims for their victimization is typically motivated by the desire to see the world as
        a)   reliable.
        b)   perfect.
        c)   a fair and just place.
        d)   predictable.

39.   The prejudice, violence, and negative stereotyping directed against Chinese immigrants in the United States fluctuated wildly throughout the nineteenth century as a result of
    a)   changes in economic competition.
    b)   politics.
    c)   world conflict.
    d)   changes in immigration policies.

40.   Rodney does not tell his friends that he disagrees with their prejudicial attitudes because he wants to get along with them. Rodney's behavior illustrates
    a)   stereotype internalization.
    b)   normative conformity.
    c)   prejudicial acceptance.
    d)   prejudice internalization.

SHORT ANSWER REVIEW

Prejudice is a (1) _____ (p. 388) phenomenon, it affects us all. What varies across societies are the particular social groups which are the victims of prejudice and the degree to which societies enable or discourage discrimination. Prejudice is dangerous. It can be relentless and can escalate to extreme hatred. For the targets of relentless prejudice, the seeds of low (2) _____ (p. 389) are usually sown early in life. Often, but not always, prejudice leads to feelings of (3) _____ (p. 390) on the part of those who are the recipients of prejudiced expressions.

Social psychologists define prejudice as a (4) _____ (p. 391) or negative attitude toward a distinguishable group of people based solely on their membership in that group. Stereotypes, while related to prejudice are different. While prejudice is defined in terms of a negative attitudinal and emotional response, stereotypes denote both the positive and negative traits that people assign to group members. A (5) _____ (p. 391) is a generalization about a group of people in which certain traits are assigned to virtually all members of the group, regardless of actual variation among group members. Stereotyping is a cognitive process, not an emotional one. Discrimination denotes actual behavior—it is the action component. Discrimination is defined as an unjustified negative or harmful (6) _____ (p. 394) towards members of a group, solely because of their membership in that group.

No one knows for sure whether or not prejudice is part of our (7) _____ (p. 396) makeup. While social psychologists do not agree on whether or not humans are naturally prejudiced, most would agree that the specifics of prejudice must be (8) _____ (p. 396). Even when young children pick up their parents' prejudices, they do not necessarily (9) _____ (p. 396) those prejudices in adulthood. As a broad-based and powerful attitude, prejudice has many causes.

The processes of social cognition are important in the creation and maintenance of stereotypes and prejudice. Categorization of people into groups leads to the perception of in-groups and out-groups. (10) _____ (p. 397) refers to positive feelings and special treatments for people we have defined as being part of our own in-group and negative feelings and unfair treatment for others simply because we have defined them as being in the out-group. Another consequence of categorization is the perception of out-group homogeneity. Out-group homogeneity is the perception that individuals in the out-group are more (11) _____ (p. 398) to each other (homogeneous) than they really are, as well as more similar than the members of the in-group are.

Even people who are usually sensible and reasonable about most topics become relatively immune to (12) _____ (p. 399) when it comes to prejudice. There are two reasons for this, involving the affective and cognitive aspects of an attitude. First, it is primarily the emotional aspect of attitudes that makes a prejudiced person so hard to argue with; logical arguments are not effective in (13) _____ (p. 399). Second, an attitude tends to organize the way we process relevant information about the targets of that attitude. Stereotypes also tend to be persistent.

Devine's theory suggests that there is a two-step model of (14) _____ (p. 403). This model can be applied to stereotypes. First, the (15) _____ (p. 403) processing brings up the stereotype. In the second step controlled (or conscious) processing can refute or ignore it. According to the (16) _____ (p. 404), most people struggle between their urge to express prejudice and their need to maintain a positive self-concept, both in their own eyes as well as the eyes of others. However, it requires energy to suppress prejudiced impulses. Because people are programmed to avoid the constant expenditure of (17) _____ (p. 404), we are always on the lookout for information that will enable us to convince ourselves that there is a valid justification for holding a negative attitude toward a particular out-group. Once we find a valid justification for disliking this group, we can act against them and still feel as though we are not bigots—thus avoiding (18) _____ (p. 404).

Another way that our cognitive processing perpetuates stereotypical thinking is through the phenomenon of illusory correlation. Illusory correlation is the tendency to see (19) _____ (p. 405), or correlations, between events that are actually unrelated. Illusory correlations are most likely to occur when the events or people are distinctive or conspicuous. Minority group members are, by definition, distinctive because fewer of them are present in the society. Other groups who are not distinctive in terms of numbers, such as women, may nonetheless become distinctive or conspicuous because of a nonstereotypical profession or talent. (20) _____ (p. 405) leads to the creation of and belief in an illusory correlation. This illusory correlation is then applied to all members of the target group.

Researchers have found that when people are presented with an example or two that seems to (21) _____ (p. 406) their existing stereotype, most of them do not change their general belief. When people are bombarded with many examples that are inconsistent with the stereotype, they gradually (22) _____ (p. 406) their beliefs.

Just as we form attributions to make sense of one person's behavior, we also make attributions about whole groups of people. The fundamental attribution error applies to prejudice—we tend to overestimate the role of dispositional forces when making sense out of others' behavior. Stereotypes can be described as the (23) _____ (p. 407)—making negative dispositional attributions about an entire group of people.

Knowledge of stereotypes applying to a group to which one belongs can lead to stereotype threat. Stereotype threat is the (24) _____ (p. 408) experienced by members of a group that their behavior might confirm a cultural stereotype. Aronson and his colleagues reasoned that the effects of stereotype threat can be reversed by countering the stereotype. Research has shown performance-enhancing benefits of counter-stereotype mindsets. Laboratory experiments have shown that when black students are exposed to successful (25) _____ (p. 409) their performance improves.

It is hard for people who have rarely been discriminated against to fully understand what its like to be a target of prejudice. True (26) _____ (p. 409) for targets of discrimination is difficult for those who have routinely been judges on the basis of their own merit and not their racial, ethnic, religious, or other group membership. When empathy is absent, it is sometimes hard to avoid falling into the trap of blaming the victim for his or her plight. Blaming the victim is the tendency to blame individuals (make dispositional attributions) for their (27) _____ (p. 409), typically motivated by a desire to see the world as a fair place. This belief in a just world can lead to derogation of a victim and the perpetuation of prejudice.

The self-fulfilling prophecy is a case whereby people (1) have an expectation about what another person is like, which (2) influences how they act toward that person, which (3) causes that person to behave in a way (28) _____ (p. 410) with people's original expectations. Researchers have demonstrated the relevance of this phenomenon to stereotyping and discrimination.

(29) _____ (p. 411) states that prejudice is the inevitable byproduct of real conflict between groups for limited resources—whether involving economics, power, or status. Competition for resources leads to derogation of and discrimination against the competing out-group. Scapegoating is a process whereby frustrated and angry people tend to (30) _____ (p. 413) their aggression from its real source to a convenient target—an out-group that is disliked, visible, and relatively powerless.

Institutionalized racism and institutionalized sexism are norms operating throughout the society's structure. Institutional racism refers to racist attitudes that are held by the vast majority of people living in a society where stereotypes and discrimination are the (31) _____ (p. 414). Institutional sexism refers to sexist attitudes that are held by the vast majority of people living in a society where stereotypes and discrimination are the norm. (32) _____ (p. 414), or the desire to be accepted and "fit in," leads many people to go along with stereotyped beliefs and not challenge them. Modern racism (outwardly acting unprejudiced while (33) _____ (p. 415) maintaining prejudiced attitudes) is an example of a shift in normative rules about prejudice: Nowadays, people have learned to hide their prejudice in situations where it would lead them to be labeled as racist. Subtle forms of prejudice can also be directed toward women.

The most important way to reduce prejudice is through contact—bringing in-group and out-group members together. However, mere contact is not enough and can even exacerbate existing negative attitudes. Early desegregation of schools illustrates this fact. Instead, contact situations must include the following six conditions: (34) _____ (p. 418) (the situation that exists when two or more groups need each other and must depend on each other to accomplish a goal that is important to each of them); a common goal; equal status; informal, interpersonal contact; multiple contacts; and social norms of equality. Traditional classrooms are highly competitive and do not have the characteristics mentioned above. (35) _____ (pp. 420-421) however, do have these characteristics and these classrooms have produced positive interpersonal outcomes.

ESSAY REVIEW

1. Discuss the findings of research studies on prejudice and self-esteem from the 1940s to the 1960s. Have these results been replicated recently? Explain why they have or have not been replicated.

2. Discuss how Gordon Allport describes stereotyping.

3. Explain the role parents play in the development of prejudice. Are attitudes adopted from parents always life-long?

4   What is the first step in prejudice? Explain the in-group bias and out-group homogeneity.

5.   Why does logic fail when trying to argue with people who are prejudiced?

EXIT TESTS

EXIT TEST 1

1.   Clark and Clark (1947) conducted a study in which they found that African American children preferred playing with a white doll to a black doll. More recent studies
        a)   have replicated these results.
        b)   have found the same tendency but not as strong.
        c)   have found an even stronger preference for white dolls.
        d)   show that African American children are now just as content with black dolls as white dolls.

2.   Prejudice is a(n)
        a)   belief.
        b)   attitude.
        c)   behavior.
        d)   schema.

3.   Stereotyping is a _____ process.
        a)   cognitive
        b)   emotional
        c)   behavioral.
        d)   affective.

4.   Which of the following is an example of discrimination?
        a)   Believing that all professors are boring intellectuals.
        b)   Hating all lawyers.
        c)   Throwing away someone's job application because of his or her racial group.
        d)   Thinking that all politicians are greedy.

5.   A study by Bond et al. (1988) comparing the treatment of white and black patients in a psychiatric hospital run by an all-white professional staff found
        a)   physical and chemical restraints were used four times as often with black patients than with white patients.
        b)   a virtual lack of differences in the number of violent incidents committed by black and white patients.
        c)   that after several weeks the staff managed to overcome the effects of the existing stereotype.
        d)   all of the above.

6.   Unlike women, ethnic minorities, and people with disabilities, homosexuals are not protected by national laws banning discrimination in the workplace.
        a)   True
        b)   False

7. The specifics of prejudice
    a)   are inborn.
    b)   must be learned.
    c)   are the same in every culture.
    d)   all of the above.

8. We try to make sense out of our social world by grouping people according to
    a)   gender.
    b)   nationality.
    c)   ethnicity.
    d)   all of the above.

9. Being in the in-group leads you to treat the out-group unfairly because such tactics
    a)   keep you from being rejected by your group.
    b)   help you form group schemas.
    c)   build your self-esteem.
    d)   confirm your view of the world.

10. Shirley is a Baptist and she believes that all Catholics are alike. Shirley's belief illustrates
    a)   out-group homogeneity.
    b)   religious schema.
    c)   in-group homogeneity.
    d)   doctrinal schema.

EXIT TEST 2

1. It is primarily the _____ aspect of attitudes that make a prejudiced person so hard to argue with.
    a)   behavioral
    b)   cognitive
    c)   emotional
    d)   experiential

2. Devine's theory suggest a _____-step model of cognitive processing.
    a)   two
    b)   three
    c)   four
    d)   five

3. Because people are programmed to avoid the constant expenditure of energy, we are always on the lookout for information that will enable us to convince ourselves that there is a valid justification for holding a negative attitude toward a particular out-group.
    a)   True
    b)   False

4. There is a common belief that couples who haven't been able to have children will conceive a child after they adopt a child. This is an example of
    a)   a schema.
    b)   a stereotype.
    c)   an empirical fact.
    d)   an illusory correlation.

5. To refute an existing stereotype you should
    a) present one piece of contradictory evidence.
    b) present two examples of contradictory evidence.
    c) bombard the person with contradictory evidence.
    d) do nothing—stereotypes cannot be refuted.

6. The fundamental attribution error is the tendency to make dispositional attributions about an entire group of people.
    a) True
    b) False

7. Reconstructing situations after the fact to support our belief in a just world simply requires
    a) making a dispositional attribution to the victim.
    b) making a situational attribution to the victim.
    c) forming new schemas.
    d) making internal attributions about the perpetrator.

8. Realistic conflict theory maintains that limited resources lead to conflict between groups and results in increased prejudice and discrimination.
    a) True
    b) False

9. Sherif et al. (1961) aroused feelings of conflict and tension between two groups of boys at a summer camp by
    a) telling each group lies about the other.
    b) treating the two groups unequally.
    c) turning the leaders of each group of boys against each other.
    d) pitting them against each other in competitive games where prizes were awarded for the winning team.

10. Doctors, even African American doctors, are more likely to order more expensive, better diagnostic tests for white patients than for black patients even when they have the same insurance benefits. This is an example of
    a) out-group homogeneity.
    b) out-group prejudice.
    c) institutional racism.
    d) in-group discrimination.

STUDY ACTIVITIES

1. Why, according to Devine's two-step model of cognitive processing, are people who are high in prejudice more likely to express stereotypic thinking than people who are low in prejudice?

2. How does the self-fulfilling prophecy serve to perpetuate biased expectations produced by the ultimate attribution error?

3. Provide examples of modern racism.

4. Describe the process by which institutional racism and sexism is taught to members of society and is sustained within the society.

5. In what ways have children in jigsaw classrooms benefited from learning in this environment compared to children in traditional classrooms?

6. How is prejudice different from discrimination? What are the three components of a prejudiced attitude?

7. What role does human thinking have in the causes of prejudice? How does social categorization increase prejudice?

8. What is an illusory correlation? What factors lead to the formation of this type of correlation and how does this process promote prejudice?

9. What is the ultimate attribution error? What are the consequences of committing this error?

10. What is the scapegoat theory and when do people tend to scapegoat?

Chapter 13

Chapter 13 Answers

Practice Test

1. D (p. 391)
2. C (p. 394)
3. A (p. 391)
4. B (p. 399)
5. D (pp. 402-404)
6. B (p. 406)
7. A (p. 407)
8. C (p. 409)
9. D (p. 411)
10. D (p. 414)
11. B (p. 397)
12. C (p. 390)
13. A (p. 393)
14. A (p. 398)
15. B (p. 401)
16. C (p. 405)
17. D (p. 409)
18. B (p. 413)
19. D (pp. 414-415)
20. D (p. 419)
21. B (p. 394)
22. D (p. 407)
23. B (p. 408)
24. C (p. 408)
25. D (pp. 410-411)
26. D (p. 418)
27. C (p. 419)
28. D (pp. 420-421)
29. D (pp. 420-421)
30. C (p. 421)
31. C (pp. 415-416)
32. B (pp. 390-391)
33. A (p. 390)
34. A (p. 397)
35. B (p. 401)
36. D (p. 404)
37. B (p. 407)
38. C (p. 409)
39. A (p. 412)
40. B (p. 414)

Short Answer Review

1. ubiquitous (p. 388)
2. self-esteem (p. 389)
3. inferiority (p. 390)
4. hostile (p. 391)

5.   stereotype (p. 391)
6.   action (p. 394)
7.   biological (p. 396)
8.   learned (p. 396)
9.   retain (p. 396)
10. In-group bias (p. 397)
11. similar (p. 398)
12. rational, logical arguments (p. 399)
13. countering emotions (p. 399)
14. cognitive processing (p. 403)
15. automatic (p. 403)
16. justification-suppression model of prejudice (p. 404)
17. energy (p. 404)
18. cognitive dissonance (p. 404)
19. relationships (p. 405)
20. Distinctiveness (p. 405)
21. refute (p. 406)
22. modify (p. 406)
23. ultimate attribution error (p. 407)
24. apprehension (p. 408)
25. African American role models (p. 409)
26. empathy (p. 409)
27. victimization (p. 409)
28. consistent (p. 410)
29. Realistic conflict theory (p. 411)
30. displace (p. 413)
31. norm (p. 414)
32. Normative conformity (p. 414)
33. inwardly (p. 415)
34. mutual interdependence (p. 418)
35. Jigsaw classrooms (pp. 420-421)

Essay Review

1.   Your essay should include the following:
   - Kenneth Clark and Mamie Clark (1947) found that African American children preferred white dolls to black dolls. The great majority of the children rejected the black doll, feeling that the white doll was prettier and generally superior. (p. 389)
   - Philip Goldberg (1968) demonstrated that women had learned to consider themselves intellectually inferior to men. They rated the same articles higher if they were signed by a male author than if they were signed by a female author. Recent research has failed to replicate the above results. (p. 390)
   - Significant changes have taken place in American society since these studies were conducted. Blatant acts of overt prejudice and discrimination have decreased sharply and legislation of affirmative action has opened the door to greater opportunities for women and minorities. (p. 390)

2.   Your essay should include the following:
   - Gordon Allport described stereotyping as "the law of least effort." (p. 391)
   - According to Allport, the world is just too complicated for us to have a highly differentiated attitude about everything. Instead, we maximize our cognitive time and energy by developing elegant, accurate attitudes about some topics while relying on simple, sketch beliefs for others. (p. 391)
   - Given our limited capacity for processing information, it is reasonable for human beings to behave like "cognitive misers"—to take shortcuts and adopt certain rules of thumb in our attempt to understand other people. (p. 392)

3.   Your essay should include the following:
   - The specifics of prejudice must be learned. (p. 396)
   - Even when young children pick up their parents' prejudices, they do not necessarily retain those prejudices in adulthood. (p. 396)
   - When parents hold egalitarian attitudes and values, their adult children tend to hold these attitudes and values as well. But when parents hold prejudice-related attitudes and values, their adult children are less likely to hold the same views. (p. 396)

4.   Your essay should include the following:
   - The first step in prejudice is the creation of groups—putting some people into one group based on certain characteristics and others into another group based on their different characteristics. (p. 397)
   - In-group bias refers to positive feelings and special treatment for people we have defined as being part of our in-group and negative feelings and unfair treatment for others simply because we have defined them as being in the out-group. (pp. 397-398)
   - Out-group homogeneity is the perception that individuals in the out-group are more similar to each other (homogenous) than they really are, as well as more similar than members of the in-group are. (p. 398)

5.   Your essay should include:
   - It is primarily the emotional aspect of attitudes that make a prejudiced person so hard to argue with; logical arguments are not effective in countering emotions. (p. 399)
   - An attitude tends to organize the way we process relevant information about the targets of that attitude. Individuals who hold specific opinions about certain groups will process information about those groups differently from the way they process information about other groups. (p. 400)
   - Specifically, information consistent with their notions about these target groups will be given more attention, will be rehearsed more often, and will therefore be remembered better than information that contradicts these notions. (p. 400)
   - Whenever a member of a group behaves as we expect, the behavior confirms and even strengthens our stereotype. (p. 400)

Exit Test 1

1. D (p. 389)
2. B (p. 390)
3. A (p. 391)
4. C (p. 394)
5. D (p. 395)
6. A (p. 395)
7. B (p. 396)
8. D (p. 397)
9. C (p. 398)
10. A (p. 398)

Exit Test 2

1. C (p. 399)
2. A (p. 403)
3. A (p. 404)
4. D (p. 405)
5. C (p. 406)
6. B (p. 407)
7. A (pp. 409-410)
8. A (p. 411)
9. D (p. 412)
10. C (p. 414)

Study Activities

1. According to Devine (1989), stereotypes that we all know come to mind automatically when we encounter members of the stereotyped group. People who are low in prejudice are likely to suppress or override the stereotype by consciously telling themselves that the stereotype is inaccurate and unfair. People who are high in prejudice are less likely to entertain such thoughts consciously. Consequently, their thinking is more likely to be ruled by the stereotype. (pp. 402-404)

2. The ultimate attribution error is committed when we make dispositional attributions for entire groups of people and leads us to expect them to behave in stereotypic ways (for instance, lazy or stupid). Such biased expectancies are perpetuated by the self-fulfilling prophecy when we interact with out-group members in a manner that elicits behavior that confirms the stereotype. (pp. 407-408, 410-411)

3. Modern racism is prejudice revealed in subtle, indirect ways because people have learned to hide their prejudiced attitudes in order to avoid being labeled as racist. Modern racism can be revealed in voting trends. Also, consider the following example: while it is not acceptable to overtly criticize people on the basis of group membership, it is generally acceptable to laugh at jokes that do so. Racial jokes seem especially acceptable when the comedian is a member of the group he/she is derogating. (pp. 415-416)

4. When discrimination attains the status of a social norm, it is taught along with other social norms to members of society from their earliest years. The desire to "fit in" and to be liked by others ensures that people will exhibit normative conformity to society's rules. In this manner, institutional discrimination is sustained. (pp. 414-415)

5. Compared to students in traditional classrooms, students in jigsaw classrooms exhibit decreased prejudice and stereotyping, increased liking for group mates both within and across ethnic boundaries, increased liking for school, better performance on objective exams, increased self-esteem, intermingling, and empathy. (pp. 420-421)

6. Prejudice is an attitude, while discrimination is an action. Prejudice refers to the general attitude structure and its affective (emotional) component. A stereotype is the cognitive component and discrimination is the behavioral component. (pp. 390 & 394)

7. Prejudice is the inevitable byproduct of the way we process and organize information. Our tendency to categorize and group information, to form schemas and use them to interpret new or unusual information, to rely on potentially inaccurate heuristics (shortcuts in mental reasoning), and to depend on what are often faulty memory processes—all of these aspects of social cognition can lead us to form negative stereotypes and to apply them in a discriminatory way. The first step in prejudice is the creation of groups. This creates a sense of "us versus them." (p. 397)

8. Illusory correlation is the tendency to see relationships, or correlations, between events that are actually unrelated. Illusory correlations are most likely to occur when the events or people are distinctive or conspicuous. Minority group members are, by definition, distinctive. Distinctiveness leads to the creation of and belief in an illusory correlation. This illusory correlation is then applied to all members of the target group. (pp. 405-406)

9. The ultimate attribution error is the tendency to make dispositional attributions about an entire group of people. Relying too heavily on dispositional attributions often leads us to make attributional mistakes. (p. 407)

10. Scapegoat theory is a special case of the conflict-competition theory. When times are tough and things are going poorly, individuals have a tendency to lash out at members of an out-group with whom they compete directly for scarce resources. The research on scapegoating shows that individuals, when frustrated or unhappy, tend to displace aggression onto groups that are disliked, are visible, and are relatively powerless. (p. 413)

SOCIAL PSYCHOLOGY IN ACTION 1

Making a Difference with Social Psychology: Attaining a Sustainable Future

CHAPTER SPA 1 OVERVIEW

The first part of this chapter discusses applied research in social psychology. By its very nature, social psychology addresses both basic and applied questions about human behavior. Social psychologists have conducted a good deal of applied research on important social and psychological issues, such as how people can adopt a more sustainable lifestyle.

One of the most important lessons of social psychology is the value of conducting experiments to answer questions about social influence. This lesson is important when testing the effectiveness of interventions designed to solve an applied problem. There are examples of interventions that backfired and had negative effects because they were not adequately tested.

Social psychologists are in a unique position to find solutions to applied problems. First, the field of social psychology is a rich source of theories about human behavior that people can draw upon to devise solutions to problems. Second, social psychologists know how to perform rigorous experimental tests of these solutions to see if they work.

The next section of the chapter examines the use of social psychology to achieve a sustainable future. Social psychologists have adopted a variety of approaches to get people to act in more environmentally responsible ways. Energy conservation is a type of social dilemma called commons dilemma, a situation in which everyone takes from a common pool of goods that will replenish itself if used in moderation, but will disappear if overused. It is in any individual's interest to consume as much as possible, but if everyone acts that way, everyone loses – there are no resources left. It is notoriously difficult to resolve social dilemmas, as indicated by the difficulty of getting people to conserve water when there are droughts, recycle their waste goods, and clean up a common area in a dormitory or apartment. Social psychologists have studied the conditions under which people are most likely to act for the common good, such as encouraging people to communicate with each other. Communication works in two ways. First, when people make a public commitment to help it is harder to back down. Second, when people communicate they are more likely to establish a sense of group identity and solidarity, which makes them more likely to act for the good of the group.

Another approach is to remind people of both injunctive and descriptive norms against environmentally damaging acts, such as littering. Focusing people's attention on injunctive norms against littering—the idea that throwing trash on the ground is not a socially accepted behavior—is especially effective. The best way to communicate the descriptive norm against littering is to clean up all the litter in an environment to illustrate that "no one litters here." However, littering may be more likely to occur in a totally clean environment than in one containing a single piece of litter. The single piece of trash sticks out like a sore thumb, reminding people that no one has littered here except one thoughtless person.

A problem with some environmental social dilemmas is that it is not easy for people to keep track of how much of a resource they are using, such as gas, electricity, or water. One simple technique is to make it easier for people to know how much energy they are using, for example by providing them with water meters that are easy to read.

Researchers have demonstrated that a little competitiveness helps people conserve energy in the workplace. Units in a company that were competing with each other to conserve energy were more successful than units that were encouraged to save, but did not compete. It also works to arouse dissonance in people by making them feel that they are not practicing what they are preaching—for example, that even though they believe in water conservation, they are taking long showers. Sometimes the best way to change people's behavior is simply to make it easy for them to do so. Removing barriers that make pro-environmental behaviors difficult, such as instituting curbside recycling and providing people with recycling bins, has been shown to be effective.

The final section of this chapter addresses happiness and a sustainable life style. It is possible to adopt a sustainable life style and be a happy person. Happiness is partly genetic; some of us are born with a happier temperament than others. Environmental circumstances outside of our control, such as huge political upheavals in a country, can have a big impact on happiness. Nonetheless, research shows that there are things that people can control that influence their happiness. Perhaps the best predictor of whether someone is happy is the quality of his or her social relationships. Secondly, pursuing something in an enjoyable way often makes us happy and we may be even happier while we are pursuing something than when we get it. Finally, a good way to be happy and feel better about yourself is to help other people.

Research shows that the relationship between the amount of money people make and how happy they are is weak at best. Once people have the basic necessities of life, having more money doesn't increase happiness much at all. Further, people who are materialistic – those who place a high value on money and possessions – tend to be less happy than people who place less value on money and possessions. One reason for this is that people who are materialistic have less satisfying social relationships.

Research on affective forecasting has found that people often make systematic mistakes about what will make them happy in the future. People often strive for things that are unlikely to make them happier (e.g., earning lots of money) and overlook things that will make them happy (e.g., spending time with close friends and loved ones). The lesson from this is that people can achieve a sustainable life style without sacrificing the things that make people truly happy.

CHAPTER SPA 1 OUTLINE

I. Applied Research in Social Psychology
• Since its inception, the field of social psychology has been interested in applying what it knows to solve practical problems. Basic research is concerned primarily with theoretical issues. Applied research is concerned primarily with addressing specific real-world problems.

A. Capitalizing on the Experimental Method
• Only by conducting experiments (as opposed to observational or correlational studies) can we hope to discover what solutions will work best to solve problems such as getting people to reduce energy consumption.

1. Assessing the Effectiveness of Interventions
• Critical Incident Stress Debriefing (CISD) is a psychological intervention that has been widely implemented across the world to help people who have experienced traumatic events, such as rescue workers who witness multiple deaths in a natural disaster or plane crash. The basic idea of the program is to bring people together as soon as possible after the trauma for a three-to-four hour session, in which participants describe their experiences in detail and discuss their emotional reactions to the event. This cathartic experience is supposed to prevent later psychiatric symptoms and it is widely used.
• Experimental research has finally been conducted on CISD. The results provide no convincing evidence that psychological briefing techniques prevent post-traumatic stress disorders.
2. Potential Risks of Social Interventions

• Not only has CISD been found to be ineffective at preventing PTSD, it may, in fact, do harm. In one study, CISD participants were compared with a control group. Thirteen months after the intervention, the CISD group had a significantly higher incidence of post-traumatic stress disorder, scored higher on psychological measures of anxiety and depression, and reported significantly less contentedness with their lives.

• Other research has indicated that right after a traumatic event, when people are experiencing considerable negative emotions may not be the best time to focus on the event and discuss it with others. Instead, people are often quite resilient when left alone.

B. Social Psychology to the Rescue

• The field of social psychology is a rich source of theories about human behavior that people draw upon to devise solutions to problems. Social psychologists know how to perform rigorous experimental tests on these solutions to see if they work.

II. Using Social Psychology to Achieve a Sustainable Future

• Social psychologists have adopted a variety of approaches to get people to act in more environmentally responsible ways.

A. Resolving Social Dilemmas

• A *social dilemma* is a situation in which the most beneficial action for an individual will, if chosen by most people, have harmful effects on everyone. Of particular relevance is the *commons dilemma*, defined as a situation in which everyone takes from a common pool of goods that will replenish itself if used in moderation, but which will disappear if overused. Examples include the use of limited resources such as water and energy.

• Orbell et al. (1988) modeled the commons dilemma in a study where people, in groups of seven, were given $6 each and told that, if anyone donated their share to the pot, its amount would be doubled and distributed among the other six members. In this situation, if everyone donated their money, each would end up with $12; double what they started with. Most people, however, looked out for themselves, and as a result, everyone lost out. When Orbell et al. allowed the participants to talk among themselves for ten minutes, however, the number of people who donated money to the group increased from 38 to 79 percent. Communication, however, probably only works in small groups where everyone talks to each other.

B. Conveying and Changing Social Norms

• Littering is a significant social problem that costs millions in tax dollars every year. Cialdini and his colleagues used a technique reminding people of the social norms against littering in order to decrease it. Cialdini et al. made a distinction between injunctive norms, or socially sanctioned behaviors (people's perceptions of what behaviors are approved of by others), and descriptive norms, or peoples' perceptions of how other people are actually behaving in a given situation, regardless of what behaviors are socially sanctioned. Focusing people's attention on either of these norms reduces littering. For example, when Reno et al. (1993) made an injunctive norm salient by having a confederate pick up a fast-food bag from the ground and discard it in the trash, students who found handbills on their windshields were less likely to throw them on the ground. Cialdini et al. found that a single piece of litter on the ground in an otherwise clean environment made the norm against littering more salient and led to less littering than did a completely clean environment (Figure 14.2). However, when the floor was fully littered, a high percentage of Ss also littered, following the descriptive norm. Of the two kinds of norms, Cialdini et al. suggest that injunctive norms work better, since descriptive norms work only if everyone cooperates.

C. Keeping Track of Consumption

• A problem with some environmental social dilemmas is that it is not easy for people to keep track of how much of a resource they are using, such as gas, electricity, or water.

• Van Vugt and Samuelson (1999) compared two communities during a drought; the houses of one community had been equipped with water meters. The residents of these houses consumed less water than residents of unmetered houses.

• Graham, Koo, and Wilson (in press) found that students who kept track of the miles they saved drove their cars less than did students who did not keep track of the miles they saved. This finding is consistent with research showing that simply keeping track of one's behavior is the first step to changing it. Graham and colleagues (in press) also found that receiving concrete feedback about the savings turned out to be an effective way to get college students to drive their cars less.

D. Introducing a Little Competitiveness

• Siero et al. (1996) have found that by posting notices asking employees to take specific actions (e.g., closing windows during cold weather and turning off lights as they leave a room) and providing weekly feedback as to energy saved, modest improvement in energy conservation was achieved; but by providing social comparison information with another work group a week, a large improvement in conservation was achieved (Figure SPA-1.3).

E. Inducing Hypocrisy

• A third approach to resolving social dilemmas is to make people aware of inconsistencies in their publicly stated beliefs and their private behaviors.

• During a water shortage in California, University of California officials posted signs in the shower rooms of gyms, exhorting students to conserve water by taking briefer, more efficient showers. Fewer than 15% of the students complied, however. Increasing the size of the signs to make them more obvious only increased compliance to 19%, and led to several students taking even longer showers than usual, as a reaction against being told what to do. Aronson and his colleagues (Dickerson et al., 1992) applied the hypocrisy technique to this situation. One group was made mindful of their usage by answering a short questionnaire; another group was asked to sign their names to a public poster exhorting shorter showers; and a third group was asked to do both, making them feel hypocritical if they took long showers. This group took significantly shorter showers.

F. Removing Small Barriers to Achieve Big Changes

• Sometimes the best way to change people's behavior is simply to make it easy for them to do so.

• Even if we could get people not to litter, there is still a huge problem of what to do with our trash once it is collected and thrown away. The amount of trash that ends up in landfills needs to be reduced. Many cities encourage recycling to this end. However, the inconvenience of recycling leads to less than optimal compliance.

• The first approach to this problem is to try to change people's attitudes and values in a pro-environmental direction, with the assumption that their behavior will follow suit. And in fact, several studies find that people's attitudes to recycling are good predictors of their behavior.

• However, sometimes we act inconsistently with our attitudes despite our best intentions due to overwhelming inconvenience. Following Lewin's observation that big social changes can sometimes follow the removal of small barriers, a number of studies have found that removing some of the hassles involved with recycling (e.g., accepting commingled recyclables, or instituting curbside pickup) increases people's recycling behavior. For example, Guagnano et al. (1995) found in a field study that people's attitudes predicted behavior only when they did not possess a recycling bin; when they had the bin, people conformed even if they did not have strong pro-environmental attitudes.

• Thus two ways to get people to act in environmentally sound ways are to change people's attitudes, and to remove barriers to environmentally friendly actions.

• Holland, Aarts, and Langendam (2006) found that we can nudge people into doing the right things by getting people to form **implementation intentions,** which are people's specific plans about where, when, and how they will fulfill a goal.

III. Happiness and a Sustainable Life Style
• Consumption isn't nearly what it's cracked up to be when it comes to being happy. It is entirely possible to adopt a sustainable lifestyle and be a very happy person.

A. What Makes People Happy?
• Most psychologists agree that happiness is partly genetic; some of us are born with a happier temperament than others. Further, environmental circumstances outside of our control, such as huge political upheavals in a country, can have a big impact on happiness. Nonetheless, research shows that there are things that people can control that influence their happiness.

1. Satisfying Relationships
• Perhaps the best predictor of whether someone is happy is the quality of his or her social relationships.
• In one study, extremely happy college students were compared with their less-happy peers and the main thing that set them apart was that happy people spent more time with other people and were more satisfied with their relationships. Although this study is correlational, researchers generally agree that having high quality relationships is a major source of happiness.

2. Flow: Becoming Engaged in Something You Enjoy
• Although it can be incredibly gratifying to have our dreams come true, there is evidence that people are happier when they are working at something they enjoy and making progress.
• There are a couple of reasons for this. First, when people are working toward a goal they are often in a highly desired state called *flow*, which occurs when people are "lost" in a task that is challenging but attainable. Second, when people are working toward a goal but are not certain that they will obtain it, it is hard to think about anything else.

3. Helping Others
• A good way to be happy and feel better about yourself is to help other people.
• Helping others can make people happy in a couple of ways. First, it is a way of connecting people to others and enhancing social relationships, which is an important source of happiness. Second, people who help others are likely to come to view themselves in a more positive light, namely as the "kind of person" who is altruistic and cares about others.

B. Money, Materialism, and Happiness
• Research shows that the relationship between the amount of money people make and how happy they are is weak at best. People who are very poor and have trouble getting food and shelter are, not surprisingly, less happy than others. After people have all the necessities of life, however, having more money doesn't increase happiness much at all.
• There is clear evidence that people who are materialistic—those who place a high value on money and possessions—are less happy than people who place less value on money and possessions. One reason for this is that people who are materialistic have less satisfying social relationships.

C. Do People Know What Makes Them Happy?
• Research on affective forecasting has found that people often make systematic mistakes about what will make them happy in the future. One study of college freshman indicated that the most important reason for going to college was "to be able to make more money." Although there is nothing wrong with wanting to achieve a comfortable lifestyle, money itself does not make people happy.
• One of the best predictors of happiness is having satisfying social relationships, yet Americans are becoming increasingly isolated from each other. In 1985, about 75 percent of the people surveyed said that they had a close friend with whom they could talk about their problems, but by 2004, only half the people said they had such a friend.

LEARNING OBJECTIVES

After reading Chapter SPA 1, you should be able to do the following:

1.   Explain how social psychologists capitalize on the experimental method to solve applied problems. (p. 430)

2.   Discuss the importance of assessing the effectiveness of interventions. Identify the potential risks of social interventions. (pp. 430-432)

3.   Identify examples of social psychologists finding solutions to applied problems. (pp. 432-433)

4.   Identify conditions that decrease selfish behaviors and foster trust in response to social dilemmas in small groups and in large communities. (pp. 433-436)

5.   Differentiate between injunctive and descriptive norms. (pp. 433-434)

6.   Describe how Cialdini and colleagues have reduced littering by reminding people of norms. Identify how descriptive norms are most effectively communicated. Identify the limitation of using descriptive norms to communicate appropriate behavior. (pp. 434-435)

7.   Identify the benefit of making it easier for people to keep track of their energy consumption (p. 436)

8.   Discuss how introducing competitiveness can increase energy conservation in the workplace. (pp. 436-437)

9.   Explain how hypocrisy techniques have been used to increase water conservation. (pp. 437-438)

10.   Discuss how removing barriers can get people to recycle. Identify the strategy that may yield the best results. (pp. 438-439)

11.   Describe the research on what makes people happy. (pp. 440-441)

12.   Explain the relationship between money, materialism, and happiness. (p. 441)

13.   Discuss the results of research on affective forecasting. (p. 442)

KEY TERM

1.   _____   People's specific plans about where, when, and how they will fulfill a goal. (p. 439)

GUIDED REVIEW

PRACTICE TEST

1.   Social psychological questions are best tested with
   a)   surveys.
   b)   correlational studies.
   c)   case studies.
   d)   the experimental method.

2.   Research that is used to address specific real world problems is
   a)   basic.
   b)   applied.
   c)   both a and b.
   d)   neither a nor b.

3.   Unlike medical treatments, it is not necessary to test psychological and social "treatments" such as programs for energy conservation.
   a)   True
   b)   False

4.   Critical Incident Stress Debriefing (CISD) is widely used to help people who have experienced traumatic events. Research indicates it is
   a)   somewhat effective.
   b)   very effective.
   c)   not very effective, but not harmful.
   d)   ineffective and may in fact do harm.

5.   Though driving affords you greater personal freedom, the pollution created by millions of drivers represents a global problem. This situation is a classic example of a problem known as a(n):
   a)   high-density situation.
   b)   paradoxical affair.
   c)   social dilemma.
   d)   attributional spiral.

6.   Of particular relevance to energy conservation is the _____, a situation in which everyone takes from a common pool of goods that will replenish itself if used in moderation, but will disappear if overused.
   a)   high-density situation
   b)   paradoxical affair
   c)   commons dilemma
   d)   usage bias

SPA 1

7.   In a study by Orbell et al. (1988) participants were put in a situation in which, if everyone cooperated by donating money to the group, everyone could double their money. In this study
a)   most people looked out for themselves, and as a result, everyone lost.
b)   no one donated any money.
c)   most of the participants donated their money.
d)   everyone cooperated by donating their money.

8.   Orbell et al. (1988), in the study mentioned above, found that allowing the group to talk with each other for _____ minutes dramatically _____ the number of people who donated money to the group.
a)   10; decreased
b)   10; increased
c)   30; increased
d)   30; decreased

9.   Holland and colleagues (2006) found that office workers recycled more paper when
a)   their bosses asked them to directly.
b)   they were offered incentives for doing so.
c)   they were told most of their coworkers were recycling paper.
d)   they were provided with a recycling box that they could keep next to their desks.

10.   People's perceptions of how others are actually behaving in a given situation, regardless of what they ought to be doing are _____ norms.
a)   injunctive
b)   conjunctive
c)   descriptive
d)   global

11.   In California, $41 million of tax money is spent per year
a)   cleaning up litter.
b)   recycling.
c)   on water treatment.
d)   on cleaning up air pollution.

12.   Many college students believe that their peers are more in favor of drinking than they actually are.
a)   True
b)   False

13.   Littering is LEAST likely to occur in which of the following situations?
a)   an immaculately clean room
b)   a badly littered room
c)   a badly littered room with a sign prohibiting litter
d)   an otherwise clean room with a single piece of litter

14.   People's specific plans about where, when, and how to fulfill a goal are called _____.
a)   goal-directed plans
b)   implementation intentions
c)   goal action plans
d)   goal intentions

382
Copyright © 2010 by Pearson Education, inc. All rights reserved.

15. The difficulty of getting people to conserve water and energy and to recycle their waste goods demonstrates the difficulty of resolving:
    a) attributional biases.
    b) disjunctive tasks.
    c) social dilemmas.
    d) self-serving biases.

16. Which of the following is true about norms and reducing littering?
    a) Focusing people's attention on descriptive norms is the most effective way to reduce littering.
    b) Focusing people's attention on social norms is the most effective way to reduce littering.
    c) Focusing people's attention on gender norms is the most effective way to reduce littering.
    d) Focusing people's attention on injunctive norms is the most effective way to reduce littering.

17. You are most likely to feel social pressure to conform if you are exposed to a(n) _____ norm.
    a) injunctive
    b) descriptive
    c) peripheral
    d) elaborative

18. Which types of norms depend upon everyone's cooperation in order to be effective?
    a) injunctive norms
    b) descriptive norms
    c) nonsalient norms
    d) generosity norms

19. The findings of Graham and colleagues (in press), indicate that _____ is the first step to changing behavior.
    a) realizing there is a better way of doing things
    b) changing attitudes
    c) simply keeping track of it
    d) increasing motivation

20. Sharla and Bobby are having a big picnic at their house and they do not want people to throw litter on their lawn. According to research on descriptive norms, what should they do?
    a) clean their lawn carefully and make sure it is spotless
    b) plant one piece of distinctive looking trash on their lawn before guests arrive
    c) plant a lot of trash on their lawn before the guests arrive
    d) put some extra garbage cans in their yard

21. At one unit of a factory in the Netherlands, employees engaged in energy-saving behaviors when
    a) competition was introduced.
    b) employees were offered bonuses for reducing energy usage.
    c) employees were offered extra time off for reducing energy usage.
    d) employees were threatened with pay cuts if energy usage did not decrease.

22.	Administrators at the University of California were successful in getting students to reduce water usage by posting signs in the shower rooms asking students to take briefer showers.
a)	True
b)	False

23.	Which of the following is a strategy to decrease the negative effects of social dilemmas?
a)	allow people to communicate with each other
b)	allow people to monitor their own behaviors or rate of consumption
c)	introducing a little competitiveness
d)	all the above are effective strategies

24.	All of the following can increase recycling in a community EXCEPT which one?
a)	having residents sort the materials
b)	instituting curbside recycling
c)	adding more recycling bins in a community
d)	implementing a media campaign that targets people's attitudes toward recycling

25.	Several studies have found that people's attitudes toward recycling are good predictors of their recycling behaviors.
a)	True
b)	False

26.	Most psychologists agree that happiness is partly genetic.
a)	True
b)	False

27.	Perhaps the best predictor of whether someone is happy is
a)	how much money the person makes.
b)	how satisfied the person is with his or her career.
c)	the quality of his or her social relationships.
d)	the amount of material possessions the person has.

28.	*Flow* occurs when people are "lost" in a task that is challenging but attainable.
a)	True
b)	False

29.	Research shows that the relationship between the amount of money people make and how happy they are is very strong.
a)	True
b)	False

30.	Aronson and his colleagues' hypocrisy technique, having people preach behaviors that they are not practicing, has been found to increase:
a)	water conservation only.
b)	water conservation and recycling.
c)	recycling only.
d)	none of the above.

31.	People who are very poor and have trouble getting food and shelter are surprisingly happy.
a)	True
b)	False

32. People who are materialistic, who place a high value on money and possessions, are
    a)   much happier than less materialistic people.
    b)   slightly happier than less materialistic people.
    c)   no different in happiness than less materialistic people.
    d)   less happy than people who place less value on money and possessions.

33. People who are materialistic
    a)   have social relationships that are much more satisfying than those of most people.
    b)   have social relationships that are somewhat more satisfying than those of most people.
    c)   tend not to have any real social relationships.
    d)   have less satisfying social relationships.

34. Social psychologists conduct
    a)   only basic research.
    b)   only applied research.
    c)   both basic and applied research.
    d)   only experimental studies.

35. People are accurate in their assessment of whether an intervention has helped them, so such self-reports should be taken at face value.
    a)   True
    b)   False

36. What did Harvard psychologist Richard McNally and his colleagues conclude about psychological debriefing techniques?
    a)   there is no convincing evidence that they prevent post-traumatic stress disorders
    b)   they are very effective at preventing post-traumatic stress disorders
    c)   they are slightly effective at preventing post-traumatic stress disorders
    d)   they are very effective at preventing trauma-induced psychosis

37. A study on Critical Incident Stress Debriefing (CISD) found that 13 months after the intervention, the CISD group reported _____ contentedness with their lives compared to a control group.
    a)   significantly more
    b)   significantly less
    c)   slightly less
    d)   slightly more

38. Forcing people to talk about and relive traumatic experiences may make people
    a)   have more nightmares.
    b)   less likely to have nightmares about the trauma.
    c)   more likely to remember those experiences later.
    d)   less likely to remember those experiences later.

39. The Jigsaw Classroom technique
    a)   has never been scientifically tested.
    b)   has been scientifically tested but not proven effective.
    c)   is not widely used.
    d)   is a prototypical example of a successful social psychological intervention.

40.   In a study by Reno et al. (1993), in the control condition, in which there was no fast-food bag on the ground and the accomplice simply walked by, _____ percent of participants threw a handbill found on their windshield on the ground.
   a)   12
   b)   29
   c)   37
   d)   82

SHORT ANSWER REVIEW

By its very nature, social psychology addresses both basic and applied questions about human behavior. Since its inception, the field of social psychology has been interested in applying what it knows to solve (1) _____ (p. 430) problems.

One of the most important lessons of social psychology is the value of conducting experiments to answer questions about social (2) _____ (p. 430). This lesson is important when testing the effectiveness of interventions designed to solve an applied problem. There are examples of interventions that backfired and had negative effects (such as CISD) because they were not adequately (3) _____ (p. 431).

Social psychologists are in a unique position to find (4) _____ (p. 432) to applied problems. First, the field of social psychology is a rich source of (5) _____ (p. 432) about human behavior that people can draw upon to devise (6) _____ (p. 432) to problems. Second, social psychologists know how to perform rigorous (7) _____ (p. 432) tests of these solutions to see if they work.

Social psychologists have adopted a variety of approaches to get people to act in more environmentally (8) _____ (p. 432) ways. Energy conservation is a type of social dilemma (a conflict in which the most (9) _____ (p. 433) action for an individual will, if chosen by most people, have (10) _____ (p. 433) effects on everyone) called commons dilemma, a situation in which everyone takes from a common pool of goods that will (11) _____ (p. 433) itself if used in moderation but will (12) _____ (p. 433) if overused. It is in any individual's interest to consume as much as possible, but if everyone acts that way everyone loses – there are no resources left. It is notoriously difficult to resolve social dilemmas, as indicated by the difficulty of getting people to conserve water when there are droughts, recycle their waste goods, and clean up a common area in a dormitory or apartment. Social psychologists have studied the conditions under which people are most likely to act for the common good, such as encouraging people to communicate with each other.

Communication works in two ways. First, when people make a (13) _____ (p. 433) commitment to help, it is harder to back down. Second, when people communicate they are more likely to establish a sense of (14) _____ (p. 433) and solidarity, which makes them more likely to act for the good of the group.

Another approach is to remind people of both injunctive and descriptive norms against environmentally damaging acts, such as littering. Focusing people's attention on (15) _____ (p. 434) norms against littering—the idea that throwing trash on the ground is not a socially accepted behavior—is especially effective. The best way to communicate the (16) _____ (p. 434) norm against littering is to clean up all the litter in an environment to illustrate that "no one litters here." However, littering may be more likely to occur in a totally clean environment than in one containing one conspicuous piece of litter. The single piece of trash sticks out like a sore thumb, reminding people that no one has littered here except one (17) _____ (p. 434) person.

A problem with some environmental social dilemmas is that it is not easy for people to (18) _____ (p. 436) of how much of a resource they are using, such as gas, electricity, or water. One simple technique is to make it (19) _____ (p. 436) for people to know how much energy they are using, for example, by providing them with water meters that are easy to read.

Researchers have demonstrated that a little (20) _____ (p. 436) helps people conserve

energy in the workplace. Units in a company that were competing with each other to conserve energy

were more successful than units that were encouraged to save but did not compete. It also works to arouse

dissonance in people by making them feel that they are not practicing what they are preaching—for

example, that even though they believe in water conservation, they are taking long showers. Sometimes

the best way to change people's behavior is simply to make it (21) _____ (p. 438) for them to do

so. Removing barriers that make pro-environmental behaviors difficult, such as instituting curbside

recycling and providing people with recycling bins, has been shown to be effective.

It is possible to adopt a sustainable life style and be a happy person. Happiness is partly (22)

_____ (p. 440); some of us are born with a happier temperament than others. Environmental

circumstances outside of our control, such as huge political upheavals in a country, can have a big impact

on happiness. Nonetheless, research shows that there are things that people can control that influence their

happiness. Perhaps the best predictor of whether someone is happy is the quality of his or her (23)

_____ (p. 440). Secondly, pursuing something in an enjoyable way often makes us happy and we

may be even happier while we are pursuing something than when we get it. Finally, a good way to be

happy and feel better about yourself is to (24) _____ (p. 441) other people.

Research shows that the relationship between the amount of money people make and how happy

they are is (25) _____ (p. 441) at best. Once people have the basic necessities of life, having more

money doesn't increase happiness much at all. Further, people who are (26) _____ (p. 442) – those

who place a high value on money and possessions – tend to be less happy than people who place less

value on money and possessions. One reason for this is that people who are materialistic have less

satisfying social relationships.

Research on (27) _____ (p. 442) has found that people often make systematic mistakes about what will make them happy in the future. People often strive for things that are unlikely to make them happier (e.g., earning lots of money) and overlook things that will make them happy (e.g., spending time with close friends and loved ones). The lesson from this is that people can achieve a sustainable life style without sacrificing the things that make people truly happy.

ESSAY REVIEW

1. Identify the three points about social psychology made by Kurt Lewin, the person generally recognized as the founder of empirical social psychology.

2. Differentiate between basic and applied research. What did Kurt Lewin mean when he said "There is nothing so practical as a good theory."

3. Explain why social psychologists are in a unique position to find solutions to applied problems. Give an example of a successful social psychological intervention.

4. Identify factors that we cannot control that influence happiness and factors that we can control that influence happiness.

5. Explain what is meant by *flow* and why achieving a goal may decrease happiness.

EXIT TESTS

EXIT TEST 1

1. Implementing psychological interventions before they have been experimentally tested
   a)   is okay, because they are not as important as medical treatments.
   b)   is okay, as long as you have done a survey about it first.
   c)   can be a big waste of time, effort, and money.
   d)   saves a lot of money in the long run.

2. Social psychologists are in a unique position to find solutions to applied problems because
   a)   the field of social psychology is a rich source of theories about human behavior that people can draw upon to devise solutions to problems.
   b)   social psychologists know how to perform rigorous experimental tests of these solutions to see if they work.
   c)   both a and b.
   d)   neither a nor b.

3. Robert Cialdini and his colleagues have used the power of _____ to prevent people from littering.
    a) social norms
    b) subliminal messages
    c) logical reasoning
    d) persuasion

4. Which of the following illustrates the injunctive norm regarding littering?
    a) seeing someone drop a piece of litter on a heavily littered beach
    b) seeing someone pick up a piece of litter in a parking lot
    c) seeing a clean classroom with only one piece of litter on the floor
    d) all of the above

5. Descriptive norms work better at preventing littering than injunctive norms.
    a) True
    b) False

6. During a study on water consumption in the Hampshire region of England during a severe drought in the summer of 1995, researchers found that water conservation increased when
    a) competitiveness was introduced.
    b) hypocrisy was induced.
    c) barriers to water conservation were removed.
    d) houses were equipped with water meters that allowed residents to monitor how much water they were consuming.

7. Orbell et al. (1988) found that participants were most likely to donate money to a community pot, and thereby benefit everyone in the group, if they:
    a) were made to feel dissonance between being a nice person and being selfish.
    b) first heard a sermon about the Good Samaritan.
    c) interacted with other participants for ten minutes before having to decide whether or not to donate.
    d) All of the above interventions increased donations.

8. In a study by Graham and colleagues (in press), which students drove their cars the least?
    a) those who had the highest insurance rates.
    b) those who received feedback about how much money they had saved on gas and maintenance costs.
    c) those who received feedback about savings in air pollution.
    d) those who received feedback about how much money they had saved and feedback about savings in air pollution.

9. Graham and colleagues (in press) found that students who kept track of the miles they saved drove their cars less than did students in a control group who did not keep track of the miles they saved.
    a) True
    b) False

10. Sometimes the best way to change people's behavior is simply to make it easy for them to do so.
    a) True
    b) False

EXIT TEST 2

1.   A person's attitudes will always accurately predict his or her behavior.
    a)   True
    b)   False

2.   Which of the following have been found to increase recycling?
    a)   instituting curbside recycling
    b)   allowing residents to mix materials instead of having to sort them
    c)   increasing the number of recycling bins in a community
    d)   all of the above

3.   Guagnuano et al. (1995) conducted a natural experiment on recycling in Fairfax County, Virginia. They found that attitudes about recycling predicted behavior only when
    a)   there was a community recycling bin nearby the person's residence.
    b)   there was not a community recycling bin nearby the person's residence.
    c)   the person did not possess a curbside recycling bin.
    d)   they did possess a curbside recycling bin.

4.   Research indicates that happiness depends solely on our circumstances at the time.
    a)   True
    b)   False

5.   In a study by Diener and Seligman (2003), compared to their less-happy peers, happy college students
    a)   spent more time with other people and were more satisfied with their relationships.
    b)   had more money.
    c)   had better grades.
    d)   lived off campus.

6.   Which of the following people illustrates *flow*?
    a)   Carlos, who just completed a master's degree
    b)   Chen, who just started a new job today
    c)   Yolanda, who just finished a writing project
    d)   Carmen, who is engrossed in a remodeling project

7.   A good way to be happy and feel better about yourself is to
    a)   earn more money.
    b)   buy more stuff.
    c)   help other people.
    d)   sleep more.

8.   In a study by Lyubomirsky et al. (2005), college students in an experimental condition were asked to perform five acts of kindness toward others in one day. Students in a control group just went about their normal activities. The students who performed the acts of kindness were happier than the students in the control group and their elevated happiness was maintained for
    a)   2 hours.
    b)   2 days.
    c)   1 week.
    d)   several weeks.

9. Americans have become dramatically wealthier over time; however, happiness has remained remarkably stable.
   a) True
   b) False

10. When it comes to money and happiness
   a) money itself is a problem.
   b) money can contribute to happiness if it is used to obtain high quality social relationships, to pursue meaningful goals, and to help others.
   c) only people with more money than they need can truly be happy.
   d) people who place a high value on money and possessions are just as happy as everyone else.

STUDY ACTIVITIES

1. Define social dilemma and identify one that you face every day. Why is it a dilemma? How have you responded to the dilemma?

2. If you were a member of a local water conservation committee, how might you go about inducing community members to save water when they know that it is in their own immediate best interests to use all the water that they want?

3. At a local park, littering has become a serious problem. Describe techniques you could employ to evoke injunctive and descriptive norms against littering. Which kind of norm is most likely to be effective in the long run? Why?

4. Imagine you are a volunteer with the Red Cross and you learn from the local director that they are planning to implement a new intervention specifically designed for natural disaster survivors. You ask if the new program has been tested and find out that it has not. What would you recommend to the director regarding implementing this new intervention?

5. You are serving on a committee on your campus that is trying to reduce pollution by getting students to drive less. Based on the research by Graham and colleagues (in press) what recommendations would you make to the committee?

6. Applying the research conducted at a factory in the Netherlands (Siero et al., 1996), how could your college or university get professors to save more energy by turning off the lights in their classrooms and offices when the rooms are not in use?

7. You have been hired as a consultant by a large city to provide suggestions on how to increase recycling in that city. Describe what would your recommendations be.

8. Explain why happiness is not completely within our control.

9. Imagine you are working as a volunteer in a student counseling center on campus. A student comes in complaining of being unhappy. He states that his life feels empty. What could you encourage the student to do in order to increase his happiness?

10. Imagine you are talking with another student who says her main goal is to make a lot of money. She believes that if she can just get a high-paying job she will be able to have all the things she wants in life and will be happy. What information can you share with her about money, materialism, and happiness to give her a more accurate understanding of their relationship to each other?

Chapter SPA 1 Answers

Practice Test

1. D (p. 430)
2. B (p. 430)
3. B (p. 430)
4. D (p. 431)
5. C (p. 433)
6. C (p. 433)
7. A (p. 433)
8. B (p. 433)
9. D (p. 439)
10. C (pp. 433-434)
11. A (p. 434)
12. A (p. 435)
13. D (pp. 434-435)
14. B (p. 439)
15. C (p. 433)
16. D (p. 434)
17. A (p. 435)
18. B (p. 435)
19. C (p. 436)
20. B (pp. 434-435)
21. A (p. 436)
22. B (p. 437)
23. D (pp. 436)
24. A (pp. 438-439)
25. A (p. 438)
26. A (p. 440)
27. C (p. 440)
28. A (p. 441)
29. B (p. 441)
30. B (pp. 437-438)
31. B (p. 441)
32. D (p. 442)
33. D (p. 442)
34. C (p. 430)
35. B (p. 431)
36. A (p. 431)
37. B (p. 431)
38. C (p. 432)
39. D (p. 432)
40. C (p. 434)

Short Answer Review

1. practical (p. 430)
2. influence (p. 430)
3. tested (p. 431)
4. solutions (p. 432)
5. theories (p. 432)
6. solutions (p. 432)
7. experimental (p. 432)
8. responsible (p. 432)
9. beneficial (p. 433)
10. harmful (p. 433)
11. replenish (p. 433)
12. disappear (p. 433)
13. public (p. 433)
14. group identity (p. 433)
15. injunctive (p. 434)
16. descriptive (p. 434)
17. thoughtless (p. 434)
18. keep track (p. 436)
19. easier (p. 436)
20. competitiveness (p. 436)
21. easy (p. 438)
22. genetic (p. 440)
23. social relationships (p. 440)
24. help (p. 441)
25. weak (p. 441)
26. materialistic (p. 442)
27. affective forecasting (p. 442)

Essay Review

1. Kurt Lewin made the following points:
   - Social psychological questions are best tested with the experimental method. (p. 429)
   - These studies can be used to understand basic psychological processes and to develop theories about social influence. (p. 429)
   - Social psychological theories and methods can be used to address pressing social problems. (p. 429)

2. Your essay should include the following:
   - Basic research is concerned primarily with theoretical issues. (p. 430)
   - Applied research is concerned primarily with addressing specific real-world problems. (p. 430)
   - Lewin meant that to solve difficult social problems, we must first understand the underlying psychological dynamics of human nature and social influence. (p. 430)

3.   Your answer should include the following:
  - First, the field of social psychology is a rich source of theories about human behavior that people can draw upon to devise solutions to problems. (p. 432)
  - Second, social psychologists know how to perform rigorous experimental tests of these solutions to see if they work. (p. 432)
  - The Jigsaw Classroom is an example of a successful social psychological intervention. (p. 432)

4.   Your essay should include the following:
  - Factors that we cannot control include genetics and environmental circumstances. Most psychologists agree that happiness is partly genetic. Environmental circumstances outside of our control, such as huge political upheavals in a country, can have a big impact on happiness. (p. 440)
  - Factors that we can't control that influence happiness include having satisfying relationships with other people, pursuing something we love, and helping others. (p. 440)

5.   Your essay should include the following:
  - Flow occurs when people are "lost" in a task that is challenging but attainable. Flow is what we feel when we are highly absorbed in a task and have the sense that we are making progress. (pp. 440-441)
  - Flow is such a pleasurable and absorbing state that people often lose track of how much time has passed and exactly where they are. When people achieve their goal the flow stops. People may be very gratified with what they have accomplished, but they are no longer "lost" in the pursuit of their goal. (p. 441)
  - Also, when people are working hard toward a goal, but are not certain that they will obtain it, it is hard to think about anything else. The uncertainty about the outcome focuses their attention on the task and other matters fade from view. After the goal is obtained, however, people's thoughts invariably turn to other matters—such as how much homework they have and the fact that they need to do their laundry. (p. 441)

Exit Test 1

1.   C (p. 432)
2.   C (p. 432)
3.   A (p. 434)
4.   B (p. 434)
5.   B (p. 435)
6.   D (p. 436)
7.   C (p. 433)
8.   D (p. 436)
9.   A (p. 436)
10.   A (p. 438)

Exit Test 2

1.   B (p. 438)
2.   D (p. 438)
3.   C (pp. 438-439)
4.   B (p. 440)
5.   A (p. 440)

6.   D (pp. 440-441)
7.   C (p. 441)
8.   D (p. 441)
9.   A (p. 441)
10.   B (p. 441)

Study Activities

1.   A social dilemma is a situation in which the most beneficial action for you will, if chosen by most people, have harmful effects on everyone. Some common examples are driving to school, littering, and failing to conserve resources. (p. 433)

2.   The failure to conserve water is a classic social dilemma. In large groups, like an entire community, communication between members is an impractical means of resolving the dilemma. It may be possible to send committee members door-to-door, asking people to sign petitions condemning wastefulness while making them mindful of their own wasteful behavior. Because such hypocrisy arousing techniques require an initial behavior (e.g., signing the petition), they may also be of limited use on a large scale. Making it easy to keep track of consumption may be an effective strategy in this case. Your committee might decide, for instance, to have water meters installed that are easy to understand. (pp. 436 & 437)

3.   You might remind people of socially sanctioned behaviors (evoking injunctive norms) by using the waste can or by displaying anti-littering posters. You could change people's perceptions of people's littering behavior in the park (changing descriptive norms) by removing the litter. In the long run, evoking injunctive norms is likely to be most effective since the effectiveness of descriptive norms depends on everyone's cooperation. (pp. 433-435)

4.   You should inform the director that it is important to test the intervention before a wide-scale implementation. Only by experimentally testing the intervention can you know if it is effective. If it is implemented and it is not effective, it can waste time, money, and effort and may even have negative effects on people's lives. (pp. 430-432)

5.   Have students keep track of the miles they save when they avoid driving. Also, provide students with feedback about how much money they saved on gas and maintenance costs and feedback about savings in air pollution. (p. 436)

6.   The school could put up flyers asking faculty to turn off lights when they leave a room. They could also provide faculty with regular feedback on their behavior such as graphs showing how much they had improved their behaviors. The most improvement would result by introducing a little competitiveness, perhaps by providing feedback to each department or division on how it was doing compared to the other departments/divisions. (pp. 436-437)

7.   You should suggest a mass media campaign that targets people's attitudes and suggest ways to make recycling easy for residents. These suggestions could include increasing the number of recycling bins in the community, instituting curbside recycling, and allowing residents to mix materials, instead of having to sort them. (pp. 438-439)

8.   Happiness is not completely within our control because it is partly genetic; some of us are born with a happier temperament than others. Further, environmental circumstances outside of our control can have a big impact on happiness. (p. 477)

9.   You could encourage him to concentrate on improving his social relationships, to become engaged in something he enjoys and to do something to help others. (pp. 440-441)

10. Research shows that the relationship between the amount of money people make and how happy they are is weak at best. After people have the basic necessities of life, having money does not increase happiness much at all. Americans have become dramatically wealthier over time yet happiness has remained remarkably stable. (p. 441)

SPA 2

Social Psychology and Health

CHAPTER SPA 2 OVERVIEW

The first part of this chapter discusses the effects of stress on our psychological and physical health. People have been found to be surprisingly **resilient** when they experience negative events, often showing only mild, transient reactions, followed by a quick return to normal, healthy functioning. Nonetheless, stressful events can have debilitating effects on people's psychological and physical health. Some studies calculate the number of stressful events people are experiencing and use that to predict their health. Holmes and Rahe suggested that stress is the degree to which people have to change and readjust their lives in response to an external event. The more change that is required, the greater the stress we experience. This definition of stress applies to happy events as well, if the event causes big changes in one's daily routine.

Stress is best defined as the negative feelings and beliefs that arise whenever people feel unable to cope with demands from their environment. Negative life experiences are bad for our health. Stress caused by negative interpretations of events can directly affect our immune systems, making us more susceptible to disease.

Internal-external locus of control is the tendency to believe that things happen because we control them versus believing that good and bad outcomes are out of our control. People perceive negative events as stressful if they feel they cannot control them. In the last 40 years, college students have increasingly adopted an external locus of control, which is the tendency to believe that good and bad outcomes are out of their control. The less control people believe they have, the more likely it is that the event will cause them physical and psychological problems. Studies have found that a high sense of **perceived control**, defined as the belief that we can influence our environment in ways that determine whether we experience positive or negative outcomes, is associated with good physical and mental health. For example, the loss of control experienced by many older people in nursing homes can have negative effects on their health. It is important to note that the relationship between perceived control and disease is more important to members of Western cultures than members of Asian cultures. Even in Western societies, there is a danger in exaggerating the relationship between perceived control and health. Finally, for people living with serious illnesses, keeping some form of control even when their health is failing has benefits.

It is also important for people to have high **self-efficacy** in a particular domain, which is the belief in their ability to carry out specific actions that produce desired outcomes. People's level of self-efficacy has been found to predict a number of important health behaviors. Self-efficacy helps in two ways. First, it influences our persistence and effort at a task. Second, self-efficacy influences the way our bodies react while we are working toward our goals. In short, self-efficacy operates as a kind of self-fulfilling prophecy.

The way in which people explain the causes of negative events is also critical to how stressful those events will be. When bad things happen, learned helplessness can result. **Learned helplessness** is the state of pessimism that results from attributing a negative event to stable, internal, and global factors. If we think a negative event had a stable cause, we've made a **stable attribution** – we believe that the event was caused by things that will not change over time, as opposed to factors that can change over time. Explaining a negative event as due to an internal cause – that is making an **internal attribution** – means we believe that something about us caused the event, as opposed to factors that are external to us. Finally, explaining an event as due to a global cause – that is, making a **global attribution** – is the belief that the event is caused by factors that apply in a large number of situations, rather than factors that are specific and apply in only a limited number of situations. According to learned helplessness theory, making stable, internal, and global attributions for negative events leads to hopelessness, depression, reduced effort, and difficulty in learning. Learned helplessness theory is intimately related to attribution theory.

Optimistic people tend to react better to stress and are generally healthier than pessimists. Most people have been found to have an optimistic outlook on life. In fact, most people seem to be unrealistically optimistic about their lives. This kind of unrealistic optimism would be a problem if it caused people to make serious mistakes about their prospects in life but most people seem to have a healthy balance of optimism and reality monitoring.

The next section of the chapter addresses coping with stress. **Coping styles** refer to the ways in which people react to threatening events. Men are more likely to react to stress with a **fight-or-flight reaction**, responding to stress by either attacking the source of the stress or fleeing from it. Women are more likely to react to stress with a **tend-and-befriend reaction**, responding to stress with nurturant activities designed to protect oneself and one's offspring (tending) and creating social networks that provide protection from threats (befriending).

Social support, perceiving that others are responsive and receptive to one's needs, is very helpful for dealing with stress. There is some evidence that social support helps people physically as well as emotionally. When things are tough, the kind of social support that we get matters. Social support operates differently in different cultures. Some researchers focus on ways of coping with stress that everyone can adopt. Several studies show that "opening up" by discussing ones' stressors by writing or talking about one's problems, has long-term health benefits.

The final section of this chapter addresses prevention and promoting healthier behavior. Many serious health problems are preventable, if people adopt different habits and avoid risky behaviors. HIV infections are at crisis proportions, particularly in Sub-Saharan Africa. Most of these cases could have been avoided if people had used condoms during sexual intercourse, yet many people are not taking the precautions they should. People could improve their health behaviors in many other areas as well, such as the areas of alcohol consumption, smoking, and overeating. The number one and two causes of preventable deaths in the United States are tobacco use and obesity.

Social psychologists have designed many successful interventions to improve health habits. For example, many studies have succeeded in getting people to practice safer sex. They have used social psychological principles such as increasing self-efficacy and framing the message in terms of gains instead of losses. Fear appeals have not been found to be effective in promoting safer sex.

CHAPTER SPA 02 OUTLINE

•The chapter opens by presenting the story of Joanne Hill's experience of suffering an unimaginable amount of loss over a four-year period.

I. Stress and Human Health
• Stress can affect the body in dramatic ways.

A. Resilience
• Humans are remarkably resilient. **Resilience** refers to mild, transient reactions to stressful events, followed by a quick return to normal, healthy functioning.

1. Effects of Negative Life Events

• Hans Selye was a pioneer in stress research. He defined stress as the body's physiological response to threatening events. Later researchers have focused on what it is about an event that makes it threatening. For example, Holmes and Rahe (1967) devised the Social Readjustment Rating Scale quantifying the amount of stress due to different life events. The original Social Readjustment Rating Scale is a bit dated and it did not include events that many college students find stressful. The College Life Stress Inventory is a recently developed version for college students. This version is reproduced in the text.

• Research finds that the amount of life stress correlates with anxiety and illness. However, this is correlational research, and "third variables" may account for the findings.

• Additionally, inventories such as Holmes and Rahe's focus on stressors experienced by the middle class and under-represent stressors experienced by the poor and members of minority groups (e.g., poverty and racism). Jackson and Inglehart (1995) find that not only is there a negative correlation between the racism and financial strain experienced by minority groups and their health status; but there is also a negative correlation between the expression of racism by majority group members and health status (probably due to hostility, which is related both to racism and to coronary heart disease).

B. Perceived Stress and Health

• Another problem with the "counting" method of trying to quantify life stress is that it ignores subjective interpretations of events. While some situational variables are hazardous to health regardless of how one interprets them, other environmental events are open to interpretation. According to Richard Lazarus, it is subjective and not objective experiences that cause problems. In this model, **stress** can be defined as the negative feelings and beliefs that occur whenever people feel they cannot cope with demands from their environment.

• Cohen, Tyrrell, and Smith (1991, 1993) demonstrated that subjective levels of stress relate to illness: they had participants list the events that they felt were stressing them, and exposed them to a cold virus; the more stress they were experiencing, the more likely they were to get ill (Fig. SPA-2.1). Note that this is still a correlational design, however—it is not ethical to manipulate the amount of life stress that people experience over extended periods. However, Cacioppo and his colleagues have manipulated mild stressors in the lab over short periods of time and have found that even these lead to suppression of the immune system.

C. Feeling in Charge: The Importance of Perceived Control

• One of the things that determine whether or not a person interprets a situation as stressful is how much control they feel they have over events. **Internal-external locus of control** is the tendency to believe that things happen because we control them versus believing that good and bad outcomes are out of our control.

• Research by Jean Twenge and her colleagues (2204) has found that between the years 1960 and 2002, college students in the United States have scored more and more on the external end of the locus of control scale.

• Shelley Taylor's work on breast cancer victims showed that those who believed their cancer was controllable were better adjusted psychologically than those who didn't. **Perceived control**, or the belief that we can influence our environment in ways that determine whether we experience positive or negative outcomes, is important independent of the degree of actual control that we have. Again, though, note that this work on chronic illness is correlational.

1. Increasing Perceived Control in Nursing Homes

• Experimental work randomly assigns people to conditions of high or low perceived control. Studies of the elderly in nursing homes show that one consequence of entering a home is that people feel they have lost control of their lives. When Langer and Rodin (1976) tried to boost the perceived control of a group of residents by having them decide on which film to attend, choose

how to arrange their rooms, and taking responsibility for a house plant, they found that, in comparison with a group who was given the same privileges (movies, house plants) but with instructions that emphasized that others had control, residents who had received the control instructions felt happier, became more active, and experienced less mortality (Figure 15.3).
• Schulz (1976) conducted a study where nursing home residents either were or were not given control over when and for how long students would visit them; during the period of the visits, those who were given control were happier, healthier, more active and taking fewer medications than those in the comparison group. However, once the study ended and the students stopped visiting, those who had had temporary control had worse outcomes, with deteriorating health and happiness and increased mortalities.

2. Disease, Control, and Well-Being
• A cautionary note is that the relationship between perceived control and health is more important in Western than Asian cultures (Sastry & Ross, 1998). Even in Western societies, there is a danger in exaggerating the relationship between perceived control and health. Perceived control generally is associated with better health and adjustment to illness. However, when control is emphasized too much, people can blame themselves for their illness or their failure to recover from it, adding to the tragedy. Work by S. Thompson and her colleagues shows thatfocusing on having control over the consequences of disease (e.g., their emotional reactions), rather than the progress of the disease itself, helped adjustment.

D. Knowing You Can Do It: Self-Efficacy
• **Self-efficacy** is the belief in one's ability to carry out specific actions that produce desired outcomes (as opposed to a more general sense of control) (Bandura, 1986, 1997). Level of self-efficacy has been found to predict a number of health behaviors (quitting smoking, losing weight, lowering cholesterol, exercising regularly). Self-efficacy increases the likelihood of people engaging in healthier behaviors in two ways: influencing persistence and effort, and influencing the ways our bodies react when we are working towards goals (e.g., leading to lower anxiety and more optimal immune system response).
• Self-efficacy can be increased. In one study (Blittner, Goldberg, & Merbaum, 1978), participants in a quit-smoking program were told either that they had been selected for participation because they had shown great willpower and potential for quitting, or that they had been chosen randomly. People in the self-efficacy instructions group were most likely to have quit smoking at the end of the 14-week program (67%), compared to those in the treatment only (28%) and control (no treatment) condition (6%) (Figure 15.4). Self-efficacy for making a change in health behavior thus creates a self-fulfilling prophecy.

E. Explaining Negative Events: Learned Helplessness
• A second important determinant of how much stress people will subjectively experience from a negative life event is how the person explains the event to him or herself. **Learned helplessness** is the state of pessimism that results from explaining events due to stable, internal, and global factors (Figure 15.5). A **stable attribution** is the belief that the cause of an event is due to factors that will not change over time, as opposed to unstable factors that will change. An **internal attribution** is the belief that the cause of an event is due to things about you, as opposed to factors that are external to you; and a **global attribution** is the belief that the cause of an event is due to factors that apply in a large number of situations, as opposed to the belief that the cause is specific and applies in only a limited number of situations. Learned helplessness causes depression, reduced effort, and difficulty in learning new material.
• Wilson and Linville (1982, 1985) conducted a study with first-year college students. They assumed that many first-year students experience academic difficulties because of a damaging pattern of attributions that leads to learned helplessness. To combat this, students were given extensive information about the temporal instability of poor performance. Compared to a control group who did

not receive the information, students in the treatment condition improved their grades more the following year and were less likely to drop out of college. Other studies that have directly measured attributions have found that those who explain bad events in an optimistic way are in better health and perform better.

F. Optimism: Looking on the Bright Side
• Optimistic people tend to react better to stress and are generally healthier than pessimists.
• Most people have been found to have an optimistic outlook on life. In fact, most people seem to be unrealistically optimistic about their lives. Weinstein (1980), for example, found that most people estimated that good things were more likely, and bad things were less likely, to happen to them than to their peers.
• This kind of unrealistic optimism would be a problem if it caused people to make serious mistakes about their prospects in life but most people seem to have a healthy balance of optimism and reality monitoring.

II. Coping with Stress
• **Coping styles** are the ways in which people react to stressful events.

A. Gender Differences in Coping with Stress
• **Fight-or-flight response** refers to responding to stress by either attacking the source of the stress or fleeing from it.
• Taylor et al. (2000) pointed out that most of the research on fight-or-flight has been done on males, and argue that fight-or-flight is not a viable option for female organisms that may be pregnant, nursing, or tending young offspring. Instead, they posit that females **tend-and-befriend**, a response to stress with nurturant activities designed to protect oneself and one's offspring (tending) and creating social networks that provide protection from threats (befriending).
• It is easy to oversimplify gender differences. Although gender differences in coping do exist, the magnitude of these differences is not very large. Further, seeking social support can benefit both women and men.

B. Social Support: Getting Help from Others
• **Social support** is the perception that others are responsive and receptive to one's needs. This is an important aid in dealing with stress. Controlled studies suggest that social support may play a role in the course of life-threatening illnesses. Spiegel et al. (1989) conducted a study in which women with advanced breast cancer were randomly assigned to a social support condition or a control condition. Not only did the social support improve women's moods and reduce their fears, but it also lengthened their lives by an average of 18 months.
• Evidence also comes from cross-cultural studies: people who live in cultures that stress interdependence and collectivism suffer less from stress-related diseases, possibly because it is easier for them to obtain social support.

C. Opening Up: Making Sense of Traumatic Events
• James Pennebaker (1990) has conducted a number of studies that validate the cultural wisdom that it is best to "open up" about stress. In one study, students were asked to write for 15 minutes on four consecutive nights about either a traumatic event or about a trivial event. While writing about the traumatic event was upsetting in the short term, those who did so had fewer illnesses in the next six months. Pennebaker explains these and similar results as due to two factors. First, giving meaning to events means that people no longer need to spend as much energy thinking about it; second, having written may make people less likely to try to suppress thoughts about the event. Trying to suppress negative thoughts can lead to an obsession with those very thoughts that expressing them relieves.

III. Prevention: Promoting Healthier Behavior

• Another area emphasized by social psychologists working in the health arena is the issue of compliance, or getting people to change their health habits for the better.

A. Preventable Health Problems

• Many serious health problems are preventable, if people adopted different habits and avoided risky behaviors. For example, many cases of AIDS could have been avoided if people had used condoms during sexual intercourse. People could improve their health behaviors in many other areas as well, such as alcohol consumption, smoking, and overeating.

• Americans are doing a good job of improving one unhealthy habit, smoking cigarettes. Smoking rates have been declining steadily in the United States, nonetheless, tobacco use remains the number one cause of preventable deaths in the United States. The Number 2 cause of preventable deaths in the United States is obesity. A staggering 65 percent of Americans are overweight.

B. Social Psychological Interventions: Targeting Safer Sex

• Social psychologists have had considerable success in designing programs to get people to use condoms, quit smoking, drink less, and engage in a variety of preventive behaviors, such as using sunscreens.

• The key to getting people to change their behavior is instilling a sense of self-efficacy, which is the belief in one's ability to carry out specific actions that produce desired outcomes. A review of the more than 350 interventions designed to promote safer sex confirmed that it works to increase people's self-efficacy about condom use. Other approaches work as well, such as interventions based on the theory of planned behavior, which try to increase the (a) desirability of condom use; (b) perceived normative pressures to use condoms; and (c) perceptions that condom use is controllable. Another type of intervention that has been successful is one that frames the message in terms of gains instead of losses.

• Rothman and Salovey (1997) found that framing messages in terms of losses versus gains can make a big difference. When trying to get people to *detect* the presence of a disease, it is best to use a loss frame, emphasizing what they have to lose by avoiding this behavior. When trying to get people to engage in behaviors that will *prevent* disease, it is best to use a gain frame, emphasizing what they have to gain by engaging in these behaviors. A loss frame focuses people's attention on the possibility that they might have a problem that can be dealt with by performing detection behaviors; while a gain frame focuses people on their current good state of health and the fact that, to stay that way, it is best to engage in prevention.

LEARNING OBJECTIVES

After reading SPA 2, you should be able to do the following:

1. Explain the connection between stress and health. Define resilience. Describe attempts to show the connection between stress and health using the Social Readjustment Rating Scale which measures major life events. Identify problems associated with this approach. Identify solutions to these problems and the importance of studying subjective rather than objective stress. (pp. 448-453)

2. Define stress. Describe recent research that suggests stress lowers people's resistance to infectious disease. (pp. 452-456)

3.   Define internal-external locus of control. Describe correlational and experimental research that suggests perceived control is associated with better adjustment to chronic diseases, with greater immunity to disease, and with better health and adjustment. Define perceived control. Distinguish between the effects of a temporary and an enduring sense of control. Describe the relationship between culture and perceived control. (pp. 453-456)

4.   Define self-efficacy. Discuss the role that self-efficacy plays in one's health. Describe how self-efficacy can be increased. (pp. 456-461)

5.   Define learned helplessness. Describe the attributions for negative events that result in learned helplessness and depression. Identify and define each component of a pessimistic attribution style. Describe the link between learned helplessness and academic performance. Discuss the association between a pessimistic attribution style and health. (pp. 457-462)

6.   Discuss research on coping styles. Identify and explain gender differences in coping with stress. Define the stress responses of fight-or-flight and tend-and-befriend. Identify the problem with oversimplifying gender differences in coping with stress. (pp. 461-462)

7.   Define social support. Identify the health benefits of social support. Discuss cultural differences in the existence of social support and the consequences of these differences. (pp. 462-464)

8.   Discuss the effectiveness of "opening up" as a coping style. Explain why "opening up" can lead to better health. (pp. 464-465)

9.   Discuss how Americans could change their behaviors to prevent health problems. (pp. 465-468)

10.   Describe how social psychological principles can be applied to improve health by reducing HIV infections through getting people to use condoms. Describe how message framing can affect people's adherence to a persuasive communication. (pp. 465-468)

KEY TERMS

1.   _____   Mild, transient reactions to stressful events, followed by a quick return to normal, healthy functioning. (p. 448)

2.   _____   The negative feelings and beliefs that arise whenever people feel unable to cope with demands from their environment. (p. 452)

3.   _____   The tendency to believe that things happen because we control them versus believing that good and bad outcomes are out of our control. (p. 453)

4.   _____   The belief that we can influence our environment in ways that determine whether we experience positive or negative outcomes. (p. 454)

5.   _____   The belief in one's ability to carry out specific actions that produce desired outcomes. (p. 456)

6.   _____   The state of pessimism that results from attributing a negative event to stable, internal, and global causes. (p. 457)

7. _____ The belief that an event is caused by factors that will not change over time, as opposed to factors that will change over time. (p. 457)

8. _____ The belief that an event is caused by things about you, as opposed to factors that are external to you. (p. 458)

9. _____ The belief that an event is caused by factors that apply in a large number of situations rather than factors that are specific and apply in only a limited number of situations. (p. 458)

10. _____ The ways in which people react to threatening events. (p. 461)

11. _____ Responding to stress by either attacking the source of the stress or fleeing from it. (p. 461)

12. _____ Responding to stress with nurturant activities designed to protect oneself and one's offspring (tending) and creating social networks that provide protection from threats (befriending). (p. 462)

13. _____ The perception that others are responsive and receptive to one's needs. (p. 462)

GUIDED REVIEW

PRACTICE TEST

1. When people undergo a major upheaval in their lives, such as losing a spouse, their chance of dying increases.
   a) True
   b) False

2. Stress is the:
   a) state of pessimism that results from attributing a negative event to stable, internal, and global causes.
   b) inability to control the outcomes of one's efforts.
   c) awareness of heightened physiological arousal.
   d) negative feelings and beliefs that occur whenever people feel they cannot cope with demands from their environment.

3. Americans have begun to reject aspects of the traditional medical model, especially the submissive role expected of patients by many doctors. One reason why this new approach to medicine may be becoming more popular is that patients:
   a) gain a more objective conceptualization of health issues.
   b) benefit from greater perceived control over their illness.
   c) enjoy the status that is usually reserved for medical doctors.
   d) pay lower insurance costs when they make use of nontraditional medical approaches.

4.   Langer and Rodin (1976) found that nursing home residents were happier, more active, and lived longer when:
    a)   they were provided with interesting movies to watch.
    b)   their surroundings were beautified with plants.
    c)   they were given responsibility and control over decisions.
    d)   the staff made potentially stressful choices for them.

5.   An individual who exaggerates the role of perceived control in alleviating physical illness runs the risk of:
    a)   experiencing self-blame and failure if the illness persists.
    b)   experiencing stress by maintaining a perception that the course of the disease is unpredictable.
    c)   making unstable, external, and specific attributions if the illness persists.
    d)   all of the above

6.   If Ken believes that he flunked his English test because he's lazy and lacks intelligence, he is attributing his failure to _____ causes.
    a)   external, unstable, and specific
    b)   internal, stable, and global
    c)   external, stable, and specific
    d)   internal, unstable, and global

7.   Even though Rob did not do as well as he had hoped on his Graduate Record Exams (GRE), he strongly believes that he can succeed in graduate school and earn a doctorate. Rob's belief illustrates that he is high in
    a)   external attributions.
    b)   doctoral potential.
    c)   educational esteem.
    d)   self-efficacy.

8.   High positive correlations between scores on Holmes and Rahe's (1967) Social Readjustment Rating Scale and the likelihood of physical illness indicate that health problems are associated with:
    a)   people's interpretations of their social world.
    b)   a pessimistic attribution style.
    c)   learned helplessness.
    d)   changes in a person's life.

9.   Participants in a study by Cohen et al. (1991) who experienced low or high amounts of stress were exposed to a virus that causes the common cold. Results indicated that:
    a)   increasing participants' awareness of the virus made them more susceptible to catching a cold.
    b)   exposure to the virus is sufficient to trigger illness, regardless of the amount of stress experienced by participants.
    c)   participants who experienced high amounts of stress were more likely to catch a cold.
    d)   extraneous factors such as age, weight, and gender masked the relationship between stress and immunological response.

10.   According to Lazarus (1966), what is the most important influence on how stressful a person considers an event?
a)   the objective event itself
b)   the person's interpretation of the event
c)   the culture's interpretation of the event
d)   whether the event was positive or negative

11.   The unforeseen tragic results of the Schulz (1976) nursing home study suggest that institutions that strive to give their patients a sense of control should ensure that:
a)   patients are not overwhelmed by responsibilities.
b)   patients will not have to relinquish that control.
c)   certain restrictions on the amount of control are enforced.
d)   decisions are made for patients who do not want control.

12.   If you believe that the cause of an event is due to things about you, such as your ability or effort, you are making a(n) _____ attribution.
a)   specific
b)   internal
c)   stable
d)   global

13.   Which of the following factors is the most important determinant of learned helplessness?
a)   the individual's perceptions of the causes of events
b)   the accuracy of the individual's causal attributions
c)   the actual causes of events
d)   the individual's attributions for events that did not, but could have, occurred

14.   In recent studies by Harris and others, college students have been asked to estimate how likely a variety of events were to happen to them, compared to how likely these events were to happen to their peers. They found that
a)   everyone thought the good events were more likely to happen to them than their peers and that the negative events were less likely to happen to them than their peers.
b)   everyone thought the negative events were more likely to happen to them than their peers and that the good events were less likely to happen to them than their peers.
c)   everyone was very optimistic and expected good things to happen to themselves and their peers.
d)   everyone was very pessimistic and expected bad things to happen to themselves and their peers.

15.   Most people seem to have a healthy balance of optimism and reality monitoring.
a)   True
b)   False

16.   According to Pennebaker (1997), what is it about opening up that leads to better health?
a)   People who open up receive more social support.
b)   People who open up are less likely to have nightmares.
c)   People who write about negative events never think about them again.
d)   People who write about negative events construct a more meaningful narrative or story that explains the events.

17.   Which of the following is true regarding perceived control and failing health?
        a)   It is important for people to feel in control of something.
        b)   People's perceptions of control over the consequences of the disease influence
                psychological adjustment.
        c)   Maintaining a sense of control can improve one's psychological well-being.
        d)   All the above are true.

18.   Sondra and her family want her to quit smoking. If Sondra believes she can quit smoking, she has
        a sense of _____ regarding quitting smoking.
        a)   perceived control
        b)   self-efficacy
        c)   learned helplessness
        d)   perceived efficiency

19.   Which of the following is FALSE regarding self-efficacy?
        a)   People's sense of self-efficacy can predict the likelihood that they will quit smoking and
                exercise regularly.
        b)   A person high in self-efficacy in one area, say losing weight, will be high in other health-
                related domains, say quitting smoking.
        c)   People with high self-efficacy experience less anxiety while working on a difficult task
                compared to people with low self-efficacy.
        d)   People can instill a sense of self-efficacy in others.

20.   According to learned helplessness theory, when people make stable, internal, and _____
        attributions for negative events they run the risk of hopelessness, _____, reduced effort, and
        difficulty learning new tasks.
        a)   specific; schizophrenia
        b)   specific; depression
        c)   global; depression
        d)   external; heart disease

21.   People who explain negative events in optimistic rather than pessimistic ways:
        a)   are more depressed.
        b)   suffer from more short-term illnesses.
        c)   experience better coping.
        d)   experience all of the above.

22.   When we are feeling threatened, the body releases hormones such as norepinephrine and
        epinephrine that allow people to attack or to flee. This describes the _____ response to stress.
        a)   tend-or-flight
        b)   befriend-or-fight
        c)   tend-and-befriend
        d)   fight-or-flight

23.   Women may be more likely than males are to exhibit the _____ response to stress while males may
        be more likely than women are to exhibit the _____ response to stress.
        a)   flight-and-tend; fight-or-flight
        b)   fight-or-befriend; tend-and-befriend
        c)   tend-and-befriend; fight-or-flight
        d)   fight-or-flight; tend-and-befriend

24.   Spencer feels that people in his life are receptive and responsive to his needs. Spencer perceives
       _____ in his life.
       a)   perceived control
       b)   stress
       c)   social support
       d)   buffering

25.   According to research by Taylor and colleagues (in press), which of the following people, when
       under stress, would be least likely to seek social support?
       a)   Tran, who is from the China
       b)   Al, who is from Texas
       c)   Erin, who is from New York
       d)   Steve, who is from California

26.   Invisible support singles out the beneficiary as needy and as someone who can't help him- or
       herself.
       a)   True
       b)   False

27.   Rothman and his colleagues (1993) found that framing a message in terms of _____
       increases people's detection behaviors whereas framing a message in terms of _____
       increases people's prevention behaviors.
       a)   rewards; costs
       b)   costs; losses
       c)   gains; losses
       d)   losses; gains

28.   Based on research in health psychology, what advice is appropriate for someone whose family
       member just entered a nursing home?
       a)   Ask her is she would like to have a plant for which she must provide care.
       b)   Let her decide when she wants you to visit her.
       c)   Sign her up to watch a movie every Friday night.
       d)   Both a and b are appropriate.

29.   Thomas is a fourth grader who recently failed his test on multiplication. Since this is not the first
       test he has failed in math, he begins to believe that he is stupid and will not do well on any other
       math tests or even on tests in other subjects. Tomas may be experiencing ____.
       a)   learned helplessness
       b)   the actor observer bias
       c)   self-serving bias
       d)   self-efficacy

30.   Why does the coping strategy of "opening up" lead to improved health?
       a)   It may help people suppress negative thoughts.
       b)   It may help people explain a negative event.
       c)   It may help people understand a negative event.
       d)   both b and c

31. Maggie has recently survived a hurricane. For awhile afterwards she felt a little stressed but she has quickly returned to her normal activities and level of functioning. Which of the following terms best describe Maggie?
    a) optimistic
    b) resilient
    c) Type A personality
    d) Type B personality

32. Americans are doing a good job of improving one unhealthy habit, namely _____.
    a) over eating.
    b) excessive drinking.
    c) smoking cigarettes.
    d) not exercising.

33. _____ remains the number one cause of preventable deaths in the United States and _____ is the number two preventable cause.
    a) tobacco use; obesity
    b) tobacco use; excessive drinking
    c) obesity; tobacco use
    d) excessive drinking; obesity

34. According to your text, _____ percent of Americans are overweight.
    a) 35
    b) 40
    c) 52
    d) 66

35. A key to getting people to change their health-related behaviors is instilling a sense of _____.
    a) optimism
    b) self-efficacy
    c) stable attributions.
    d) external attributions.

36. A review of the more than 350 interventions designed to promote safer sex confirmed that it works to
    a) induce fear about contracting HIV.
    b) increase people's self-efficacy about condom use.
    c) induce fear about contracting any sexually transmitted disease.
    d) all of the above.

37. A person can die after eating a perfectly safe piece of fruit if he or she discovers that the fruit came from a forbidden supply.
    a) True
    b) False

38. A newer version of the Holmes and Rahe Social Readjustment Rating Scale has been developed specifically for _____.
    a) professionals
    b) children
    c) college students
    d) the elderly

39.   Although experiencing racism is stressful, it does not affect health.
    a)   True
    b)   False

40.   The statement "Many times, exam questions tend to be so unrelated to course work that studying is really useless." reflects
    a)   a global attribution.
    b)   resilience.
    c)   an internal locus of control.
    d)   an external locus of control.

SHORT ANSWER REVIEW

There is more to our physical health than germs and (1) _____ (p. 448)—we also need to consider the amount of stress in our lives and how we deal with that stress. People have been found to be surprisingly (2) _____ (p. 448) when they experience negative events, often showing only mild, transient reactions, followed by a quick return to normal, healthy functioning. Nonetheless, stressful events can have debilitating effects on people's psychological and physical health. Some studies calculate the number of stressful events people are experiencing and use that to predict their health. Holmes and (3) _____ (p. 450) suggested that stress is the degree to which people have to change and readjust their lives in response to an external event. The more change that is required, the greater the stress we experience. This definition of stress applies to happy events as well, if the event causes big changes in one's daily routine.

Stress is best defined as the negative feelings and beliefs that arise whenever people feel unable to (4) _____ (p. 452) with demands from their environment. Negative life experiences are bad for our health. Stress caused by negative interpretations of events can directly affect our immune systems, making us more susceptible to disease.

Internal-external locus of control is the tendency to believe that things happen because we (5) _____ (p. 453) them versus believing that good and bad outcomes are out of our control. People perceive negative events as stressful if they feel they cannot control them. In the last 40 years, college

students have increasingly adopted an (6) _____ (p. 453) locus of control, which is the tendency to

believe that good and bad outcomes are out of their control. The less control people believe they have,

the more likely it is that the event will cause them physical and psychological problems. Studies have

found that a high sense of perceived control, defined as the belief that we can (7) _____ (p. 454)

our environment in ways that determine whether we experience positive or negative outcomes, is

associated with good physical and mental health. For example, the loss of control experienced by many

older people in (8) _____ (p. 454) can have negative effects on their health. It is important to note

that the relationship between perceived control and disease is more important to members of (9)

_____ (p. 456) cultures than members of Asian cultures. Even in Western societies, there is a

danger in exaggerating the relationship between perceived control and health. Finally, for people living

with serious illnesses, keeping some form of control even when their health is failing has benefits.

It is also important for people to have high self-efficacy in a particular domain, which is the belief

in their ability to carry out specific (10) _____ (p. 456) that produce desired outcomes. People's

level of self-efficacy has been found to predict a number of important health behaviors. Self-efficacy

helps in two ways. First, it influences our (11) _____ (p. 457) and effort at a task. Second, self-

efficacy influences the way our (12) _____ (p. 457) react while we are working toward our goals.

In short, self-efficacy operates as a kind of self-fulfilling prophecy.

The way in which people explain the causes of negative events is also critical to how stressful

those events will be. When bad things happen, learned helplessness can result. Learned helplessness is the

state of (13) _____ (p. 457) that results from attributing a negative event to stable, internal, and

global factors. If we think a negative event had a stable cause, we've made a stable attribution—we

believe that the event was caused by things that will not change over (14) _____ (p. 457), as

opposed to factors that can change over time. Explaining a negative event as due to an internal cause—

that is making an internal attribution—means we believe that something about (15) _____ (p. 458) caused the event, as opposed to factors that are external to us. Finally, explaining an event as due to a global cause—that is, making a global attribution—is the belief that the event is caused by factors that apply in a (16) _____ (p. 458) number of situations rather than factors that are specific and apply in only a limited number of situations. According to learned helplessness theory, making stable, internal, and global attributions for negative events leads to hopelessness, depression, reduced effort, and difficulty in learning. Learned helplessness theory is intimately related to (17) _____ (p. 459).

No one always feels in control and sometimes it is difficult to avoid being (18) _____ (p. 461) after something bad happens. Coping styles refer to the ways in which people react to (19) _____ (p. 461) events. Men are more likely to react to stress with a fight-or-flight reaction, responding to stress by either attacking the source of the stress or fleeing from it. Women are more likely to react to stress with a (20) _____ (p. 462), responding to stress with nurturant activities designed to protect oneself and one's offspring (tending) and creating social networks that provide protection from threats (befriending).

Social support--the (21) _____ (p. 462) that other people are responsive to one's needs – is very helpful for dealing with stress. People who have someone to lean on deal better with life's problems and show improved health. Some researchers focus on ways of coping with stress that everyone can adopt. Several studies show that (22) _____ (p. 464), by writing or talking about one's problems, has long-term health benefits.

In addition to helping people reduce stress, it is important to find ways to help people change their health habits more directly. Many serious health problems are (23) _____ (p. 465), if people adopted different habits and avoided (24) _____ (p. 465) behaviors. HIV infections are at crisis proportions, particularly in Sub-Saharan Africa. Most of these cases could have been avoided if people had used (25) _____ (p. 465) during sexual intercourse, yet many people are not taking the precautions they should. People could improve their health behaviors in many other areas

as well, such as alcohol consumption, (26) _____ (p. 466), and overeating. The number one and

two causes of preventable deaths in the United States are tobacco use and (27) _____ (p. 466).

Social psychologists have designed many successful interventions to improve health habits. For

example, many studies have succeeded in getting people to practice safer sex. They have used social

psychological principles such as increasing (28) _____ (p. 467) and framing the message in terms

of gains instead of losses. (29) _____ (p. 468) have not been found to be effective in promoting

safer sex.

ESSAY REVIEW

1. Define stress and identify the factor that has been found to be important in determining what is stressful for people. What is meant by resilience?

2. Differentiate between internal and external locus of control. Describe what Twenge and her colleagues have learned about the locus of control of college students. What type of belief is associated with good mental and physical health?

3. Discuss the cultural differences in the relationship between perceived control and distress. Identify the danger in exaggerating the relationship between perceived control and health.

4. Define self-efficacy and identify how it helps predict a number of important health behaviors.

5. Describe what is meant by "opening up." What is it about opening up that leads to better health?

EXIT TESTS

EXIT TEST 1

1. Soon after a major earthquake in the Los Angeles area on January 17, 1994, there was an increase in the number of people who suddenly died of heart attacks.
    a) True
    b) False

2. Mild, transient reactions to stressful events, followed by a quick return to normal, healthy functioning describes _____.
   a) bounce back phenomenon
   b) self-efficacy
   c) resilience
   d) external attributions.

3. People who experience the loss of a loved one but do not show symptoms of extreme distress are in a state of denial.
   a) True
   b) False

4. One of the problems with inventories such as the Social Readjustment Rating Scale is that they
   a) never include enough items.
   b) put too much emphasis on stressors that only affect students.
   c) focus too much on stressors that only affect the poor.
   d) focus on stressors experienced by the middle class and underrepresent stressors experienced by the poor and members of minority groups.

5. According to Richard Lazarus, it is _____ not _____ stress that causes problems.
   a) objective; subjective
   b) subjective; objective
   c) short-term; long-term
   d) long-term; short-term

6. What was the important difference between the studies on control in nursing homes conducted by Langer and Rodin and the one conducted by Schulz?
   a) The residents in the Langer and Rodin study were given an enduring sense of control, whereas the residents in the Schulz study experienced control and then lost it.
   b) The residents in the Langer and Rodin study all had dementia, those is the Rodin study did not.
   c) The average age of the residents in the Langer and Rodin study was much younger than the average age of the residents in the Rodin study.
   d) The residents in the Langer and Rodin study lived in a nursing home in a large metropolitan area whereas the residents in the Rodin study lived in a nursing home in a rural area.

7. For people living with serious illnesses, keeping some form of control even when their health is failing
   a) has benefits only if they are still living at home.
   b) has benefits unless they are on hospice care.
   c) has benefits.
   d) has no benefits.

8. Kyle is high in self-efficacy but Bill is low in self-efficacy for calculus. If both Kyle and Bill get a poor grade on their first exam we can predict that
   a) they will both drop the course.
   b) they will both remain in the course.
   c) Kyle will stay in the class and try harder but Bill will drop the course.
   d) Bill will stay in the class and try harder but Kyle will drop the course.

SPA 2

9.   The belief that an event is caused by factors that apply in a large number of situations rather than
        factors that are specific and apply in only a limited number of situations is a(n)
        a)   external attribution.
        b)   internal attribution.
        c)   stable attribution.
        d)   global attribution.

10.   Learned helplessness theory is intimately related to
        a)   resilience.
        b)   attribution theory.
        c)   the fight or flight response.
        d)   the buffering hypothesis.

EXIT TEST 2

1.   If you have a friend who is under a great deal of stress, you should find a way to help him or her
        unobtrusively without making a big deal of it.
        a)   True
        b)   False

2.   _____ refers to the ways in which people react to threatening events.
        a)   Fight-or-flight response
        b)   Stress-reaction response
        c)   Coping styles
        d)   Stress orientation

3.   Smoking rates have been declining steadily in the United States.
        a)   True
        b)   False

4.   When something traumatic happens to you it is best to
        a)   bury it as deep as you can and never talk about it because talking about it will cause you
                to experience the pain all over again.
        b)   deny it ever happened.
        c)   fill your life with so much activity that you do not have time to think about it.
        d)   spend time thinking about the event and discussing it with others.

5.   One study found that only _____ percent of single, sexually active Americans never use condoms
        when having vaginal sex.
        a)   27
        b)   32
        c)   44
        d)   23

6.   Binge drinking is defined as _____ or more drinks on one occasion for men and _____ or more
        for women.
        a)   6; 3
        b)   5; 4
        c)   7; 5
        d)   4; 5

416

7.   Binge drinkers are more likely to have a number of health problems including
    a)   high blood pressure and heart disease.
    b)   meningitis.
    c)   sexually transmitted diseases.
    d)   all of the above.

8.   High positive correlations between scores on Holmes and Rahe's (1967) Social Readjustment Rating Scale and the likelihood of physical illness indicate that health problems are associated with:
    a)   people's interpretations of their social world.
    b)   a pessimistic attribution style.
    c)   learned helplessness.
    d)   changes in a person's life.

9.   If you want to promote safer sex your intervention should frame messages in terms of
    a)   gains.
    b)   losses.
    c)   both.
    d)   neither.

10.   In one study, a scary ad about AIDS led to
    a)   more cautious sexual behavior in a sample of heterosexual men.
    b)   more cautious sexual behavior in a sample of gay men.
    c)   riskier sexual behavior in a sample of gay men.
    d)   riskier sexual behavior in a sample of heterosexual men.

STUDY ACTIVITIES

1.   Describe means of improving people's health that have been suggested by social psychologists.

2.   Imagine that you have just become the director of a home for the elderly. Describe the conditions that you would implement at the home to make residents happier and healthier.

3.   A researcher who is interested in the effects of relationship dissolution on people's self-esteem is surprised to find no correlation between the recency of people's romantic breakups and measures of self-esteem. As a social psychologist, what explanation for these apparently unexpected findings might you offer?

4.   Imagine that you are a clinical psychologist and a client comes to you complaining about persistent though not severe depression. Using what you know about learned helplessness theory, suggest changes in the way your client explains events that will alleviate the melancholia.

5.   Your friends Richard and Janet have just been going through a very stressful time. Explain how each is likely to deal with their stress.

6.   One of your friends at school was recently the victim of a violent crime but has not really spoken much about it. What would you suggest your friend do to help him or her cope with the event?

SPA 2

7. Your neighbor works at a college counseling center. He is surprised at how many students come in during their first semester feeling very hopeless about their performance in their classes and thinking about dropping out of school. How would you explain this phenomenon to him?

8. Your sister wants to quit smoking but is not sure she can. What advice can you give her to help her increase her chances of success?

9. You have been hired to develop a public service announcement to encourage people to practice safe sex by wearing condoms. How should you frame your message?

10. You are a psychologist working in a university wellness center. In order to develop programs to better meet the needs of the students, you and a coworker have been asked to conduct a study to discover how prevalent stress is amongst the students on your campus. Your coworker suggests using the Social Readjustment Rating Scale. How would you reply?

Chapter 15 Answers

Practice Test

1. A (p. 448)
2. D (p. 452)
3. B (p. 454)
4. C (p. 454)
5. A (p. 456)
6. B (pp. 457-458)
7. D (p. 456)
8. D (p. 450)
9. C (p. 452)
10. B (p. 452)
11. B (pp. 455-456)
12. B (p. 458)
13. A (pp. 457-458)
14. A (p. 461)
15. A (p. 461)
16. D (p. 465)
17. D (pp. 454-456)
18. B (p. 456)
19. B (pp. 456-457)
20. C (pp. 457-459)
21. C (p. 462)
22. D (pp. 461-462)
23. C (p. 462)
24. C (p. 462)
25. A (p. 464)
26. B (p. 464)
27. D (pp. 467-468)
28. D (pp. 454-456)
29. A (p. 457)
30. D (p. 465)
31. B (p. 448)
32. C (p. 466)
33. A (p. 466)
34. D (p. 466)
35. B (p. 467)
36. B (p. 467)
37. A (p. 448)
38. C (p. 450)
39. B (p. 450)
40. D (p. 458)

Short Answer Review

1. disease (p. 448)
2. resilient (p. 448)
3. Rahe (p. 450)
4. cope (p. 452)

5.	control (p. 453)
6.	external (p. 453)
7.	influence (p. 454)
8.	nursing homes (p. 454)
9.	Western (p. 456)
10.	actions (p. 456)
11.	persistence (p. 457)
12.	bodies (p. 457)
13.	pessimism (p. 457)
14.	time (p. 457)
15.	us (p. 458)
16.	large (p. 458)
17.	attribution theory (p. 459)
18.	pessimistic (p. 461)
19.	threatening (p. 461)
20.	tend-and-befriend reaction (p. 462)
21.	perception (p. 462)
22.	opening up (p. 464)
23.	preventable (p. 465)
24.	risky (p. 465)
25.	condoms (p. 465)
26.	smoking (p. 466)
27.	obesity (p. 466)
28.	self-efficacy (p. 467)
29.	Fear appeals (p. 468)

Essay Review

1.	Your essay should include the following:
	- Stress is defined as the negative feelings and beliefs that occur whenever people feel unable to cope with demands from their environment. (p. 452)
	- The factor that has been found to be important in determining what is stressful for people is our subjective interpretations of our situation. (p. 452)
	- Resilience refers to a mild, transient reaction to stressful events, followed by a quick return to normal, healthy functioning. (p. 448)

2.	Your essay on locus of control should include:
	- An internal locus of control is the tendency to believe that things happen because we control them. An external locus of control is the tendency to believe that good and bad outcomes are out of our control. (p. 453)
	- Twenge et al. (2004) have found that between the years 1960 and 2002, college students in the United States have scored more and more on the external end of the locus of control scale. (p. 453)
	- Studies have found that a high sense of perceived control, defined as the belief that we can influence our environment in ways that determine whether we experience positive or negative outcomes, is associated with good physical and mental health. (p. 454)

3.   Your essay on perceived control and health should include:
- The relationship between perceived control and distress is more important to members of Western cultures that members of Asian cultures. One study found that Asians reported that perceived control was less important to them than Westerners did and that there was less of a relationship between perceived control and psychological distress in Asians than in Westerners. (p. 456)
- The researchers argue that in Western cultures, where individualism and personal achievement are prized, people are more likely to be distressed if they feel that they cannot personally control their destinies. A lowered sense of control is less of an issue in Asian cultures, they argue, because Asians place greater value on collectivism and putting the social group ahead of individual goals. (p. 456)
- The danger in exaggerating the relationship between perceived control and health is that sometimes people blame themselves for their illnesses, even to the point where they do not seek effective treatment. If people do not get better, they may blame themselves for failing to recover. (p. 456)

4.   Your essay on self-efficacy should include:
- Self-efficacy is the belief in one's ability to carry out specific actions that produce desired outcomes. (p. 456)
- Self-efficacy helps to predict a number of important health behaviors in two ways. First, it influences our persistence and effort at a task. Second, self-efficacy influences the way our bodies react while we are working toward our goals. People with high self-efficacy experience less anxiety while working on a difficult task, and their immune systems function more optimally. (p. 456)

5.   Your essay on opening up should include:
- Opening up refers to spending time thinking about a traumatic event and discussing it with others. Writing about traumatic events is also a way of opening up. (p. 464)
- People who write about negative events construct a more meaningful narrative or story that explains the events. After an event is explained, people do not have to think about it as much. Further, people might be less inclined to try to suppress thoughts about the event. Trying to suppress negative thoughts can lead to a preoccupation with those very thoughts because the act of trying not to think about them can actually make us think about them more. Writing about or confiding in others about a traumatic event may help people gain a better understanding of the event and thus move forward with life. (p. 465)

Exit Test 1

1.   A (p. 448)
2.   C (p. 448)
3.   B (p. 448)
4.   D (p. 450)
5.   B (p. 452)
6.   A (p. 455)
7.   C (p. 456)
8.   C (pp. 456-458)
9.   D (p. 458)
10.   B (p. 459)

SPA 2

Exit Test 2

1.   A (p. 464)
2.   C (p. 461)
3.   A (p. 466)
4.   D (pp. 464-465)
5.   D (p. 465)
6.   B (p. 466)
7.   D (p. 466)
8.   A (pp. 450-452)
9.   A. (p. 467)
10.   C (p. 468)

Study Activities

1.   Stress, which lowers the responsiveness of our immune system and makes us more susceptible to disease, can be reduced by increasing people's sense of control and by getting them to explain negative events in a more optimistic way. (pp. 459-465)

2.   Research finds that giving residents a sense of control over their lives increases both happiness and health. As director, you should stress to residents that they have the ability to make decisions about their lives at the home and should present them with options from which they can choose. You must be careful, however, not to repeal these changes once implemented. Research finds that instilling a sense of control and then revoking it has more negative consequences than never instilling it in the first place.
(pp. 454-456)

3.   Situations themselves have less impact on people than do people's interpretations of the situations. If people who have recently broken up are as likely to interpret the event negatively as positively (e.g., they finally got out of an unsatisfying and suffocating relationship), then we would expect the correlation to be low. Rather than measuring the recency of breakups, the researcher should have measured how the participants felt about the breakups. (pp. 452-453)

4.   According to learned helplessness theory, depression may result from explaining negative events as due to internal, stable, and global causes. You would recommend that your client adopt an optimistic attributional style and explain negative events with external, unstable, and specific attributions. (pp. 457-459)

5.   Richard is more likely to show the fight-or-flight response by either attacking the source of the stress or fleeing from it. Janet is more likely to show the tend-and-befriend response by responding with nurturant activities designed to protect her and her offspring and by creating social networks that provide protection from threats. (pp. 461-462)

6.   You should suggest to your friend that he or she open up about the crime and what happened. You should suggest your friend talk to others about the experience and/or write about it. (pp. 464-465)

7.   You should explain to your neighbor that when people have an external locus of control they believe that good and bad outcomes are out of their control. Research shows that college students have been increasingly scoring toward the external end of the locus of control scale. (p. 453)

8.   You should tell your sister that she should believe in herself and that it is important for her to believe that she can quit smoking. Our self-efficacy can predict the likelihood that we will be able to successfully quit smoking. (pp. 456-457)

9.   Your message should be framed in terms of gains (e.g., "If you use condoms, you can stay healthy and avoid sexually transmitted diseases") instead of losses (e.g., "If you don't use condoms, you could get AIDS"). (p. 467)

10.   You should explain to your coworker that the original Social Readjustment Rating Scale did not include events that many college students find stressful. You should suggest that you use a version that was recently developed specifically for college students, The College Life Stress Inventory. (p. 450)

Social Psychology in Action 3

Social Psychology and the Law

CHAPTER SPA 3 OVERVIEW

This chapter applies basic psychological processes to the study of the legal system. The first part of the chapter examines eyewitness testimony. The American legal system assigns a great deal of significance to eyewitness testimony. Eyewitness testimony is often of questionable accuracy, because of the way people naturally observe and remember unexpected events.

The problem is that our minds are not like video cameras, which can record an event, store it over time, and play it back later with perfect accuracy. **Acquisition** refers to the process whereby people notice and pay attention to information in the environment. Because people cannot perceive everything that is happening around them, they acquire only a subset of the information that is available in the environment. **Storage** refers to the process by which people store in memory the information they have acquired from the environment. **Retrieval** refers to the process by which people recall information stored in their memories. Eyewitnesses can be inaccurate because of problems at any of these three stages. For example, research on **own-race bias** shows that people find it more difficult to recognize members of other races than members of their own race. In addition, research has shown that memories are reconstructed. **Reconstructive memory** is the process whereby memories of an event become distorted by information encountered after the event occurred. Research on reconstructive memory indicates that errors in **source monitoring**—whereby people try to identify the source of their memories--can occur when people become confused about where they saw or heard something. Recognizing the problems people have retrieving information from memory, social psychologists have issued guidelines for how police lineups should be conducted.

There is no guaranteed way of telling whether a witness is making an accurate or inaccurate identification. Numerous studies have shown that a witness's confidence is only weakly related to his or her accuracy. There is some evidence, however, that people who identify a suspect from an array of pictures within 10 seconds and express very high confidence in their choice are especially likely to be correct.

Even if witnesses have very accurate memories for what they see, they might deliberately lie when on the witness stand. Humans are not very good at telling whether another person is lying. The **polygraph** is a machine that measures people's physiological responses. Polygraph operators attempt to tell if someone is lying by observing that person's physiological responses while answering question. The polygraph can detect lying at above-chance levels, but is not perfect and often yields inaccurate results.

Two general approaches have been tried to improve the accuracy of eyewitness testimony. The first involves hypnosis, however, there is no hard evidence that people's memories improve when they are hypnotized. The second way people have tried to increase the eyewitness accuracy is with the use of the cognitive interview. The **cognitive interview** is a technique whereby a trained interviewer tries to improve eyewitnesses' memories by focusing their attention on the details and content of the event. Unfortunately, this technique has not proved to be any better than hypnosis; in fact, it may increase errors and confabulations of memory, especially when used with children.

How valid are **recovered memories**; the sudden recollection of events, such as sexual abuse that had been forgotten or repressed? Though recovered memories may be true in some instances, they can also be the result of **false memory syndrome**, whereby people come to believe the memory is true when it actually is not. False memories are especially likely to occur when another person suggests to us that an event really occurred.

The next section of this chapter examines the group processes of juries. Juries are of particular interest to social psychologists because the way they reach verdicts is directly relevant to social psychological research on group processes and social interaction. One study found that judges who presided over criminal jury trials disagreed with the verdict rendered by the jury a full 25 percent of the time. The jury system is not a perfect system and based on research in social psychology. There are ways we might expect it to go wrong.

People often construct theories and schemas to interpret the world around them and the same is true of jurors. Some psychologists suggest that jurors decide on one story that best explains all the evidence; they then try to fit this story to the possible verdicts they are allowed to render, and if one of those verdicts fits well with their preferred story, they are likely to vote to convict on that charge. Lawyers typically present the evidence in one of two ways. In the first, called *story order,* they present the evidence in the sequence in which the events occurred, corresponding as closely as possible to the story they want the jurors to believe. In the second, called *witness order,* they present witnesses in the sequence they think will have the greatest impact, even if this means that events are described out of order. Juries are thus most swayed by lawyers who present the evidence in a way that tells a consistent story.

The interrogation techniques used by the police can sometimes produce false confessions. The video recording of interrogations is a safeguard against this, though focusing the camera solely on the suspect increases the likelihood that viewers will think he or she voluntarily confessed.

During deliberations, jurors with minority views are often pressured into conforming to the view of the majority; thus verdicts usually correspond to the initial feelings of the majority of jurors. In a study of more than 200 juries in actual criminal trials, researchers found that in 97 percent of the cases, the jury's final decision was the same as the one favored by a majority of the jurors on the initial vote. However, one study found that people on a jury who have a minority point of view often convince the majority to change their minds about the specific verdict to render.

The final section of this chapter addresses the question "Why do people obey the law?" It is important to find ways of preventing people from committing crimes. **Deterrence theory** holds that people refrain from criminal activity if they view penalties as severe, certain, and swift. Deterrence theory may be correct about crimes that are the result of rational thought but is unlikely to apply to crimes of passion that are not rational, such as many murders. There is no evidence, for example, that the death penalty deters murders, and there is even some evidence that it increases the murder rate. People are more likely to obey the law if their sense of **procedural justice** is high; that is, if they believe that the procedures used to determine their guilt or innocence are fair.

CHAPTER SPA 3 OUTLINE

I. Eyewitness Testimony
• The American legal system assigns a great deal of significance to eyewitness testimony. For example, in the Adams/Harris case described at the beginning of the chapter (and in the documentary film *Thin Blue Line*), Adams was convicted largely on the basis of eyewitness testimony, despite greater circumstantial evidence against Harris.
• Experiments confirm that jurors rely heavily on eyewitness testimony; unfortunately, jurors overestimate eyewitness accuracy. According to the Innocence Project, there have been over 180 cases in which someone has been exonerated with DNA evidence after being convicted of a crime, and in 75 percent of these cases, the conviction was based on faulty eyewitness identification.
• In a study by Lindsay et al. (1981), participants witnessed a theft in which the thief was either very, moderately, or not very difficult to identify in a lineup, based on the amount of visual information about him presented. The more visual information provided, the greater the number of Ss who correctly identified him; however, visual information had little impact on how accurate the witnesses believed themselves to be (Figure SPA-3.1).

A. Why Are Eyewitnesses Often Wrong?
• In order for someone to be an accurate eyewitness, he or she must successfully complete three stages of memory processing, **acquisition**, or noticing and attending to the particular information out of all of the information available; **storage**, or storing the information in memory; and **retrieval**, or recalling the information stored in their memories (Figure 16.2). Only a subset of the information available at one phase makes it to the next stage in the process; eyewitnesses can be inaccurate because of problems at any stage.

1. Acquisition
• A number of factors limit the amount of information about a crime that people take in, such as how much time they have to watch an event and the nature of the viewing conditions. Crimes usually occur under the very conditions that make acquisition difficult: quickly, unexpectedly, and under poor viewing conditions, such as at night.
• Geoffrey Loftus and Erin Harley calculated the amount of detail that is lost in the perception of a face as distance increases. When the researchers showed photographs to research participants, they found that accuracy in identification began to drop with the simulated distance exceeded 25 feet. At 34 feet only 75 percent of the participants recognized the face, and at 77 feet, only 25 percent of the participants did so.
• When eyewitnesses are the victims of a crime, they will be terribly afraid. The more stress people are under, the worse their memory for people involved in and the details of a crime. If a weapon is involved, attention focuses on the weapon rather than on the person wielding it. Additionally, perception is heavily colored by our expectations.
• Finally, the information that we take in is influenced by familiarity with it; unfamiliar things are more difficult to recognize than familiar things. For example, people are better at recognizing faces that are of the same race that they are, a phenomenon known as **own-race bias**.
• An explanation for own-race bias is that, in attending to members of one's own race, people focus on individuating information, while attending to members of other races, people focus on those characteristics that distinguish that face from their own race.

2. Storage
• Memories are not like photographs in an album that merely fade with time, rather they can be distorted by information encountered after an event has occurred, a phenomenon known as **reconstructive memory**.
• Elizabeth Loftus has studied this phenomenon extensively. In one study, she showed students 30 slides depicting different states of a car accident; different slides were shown to different groups

of students (for example, one group saw a "Stop" sign and another, a "Yield" sign. Students were either asked questions about what they had seen or asked misleading questions about what they hadn't seen (e.g., someone who had seen a yield sign was asked if they saw the stop sign). While 75% of those who were asked about the sign they actually saw correctly identified the photograph they had seen, only 41% of those asked the misleading question were able to do so. Other studies have found that misleading questions can change people's minds about many other details. Thus the way that police and lawyers question witnesses can change the witnesses' reports of what they saw.

• Misleading questions can change people's minds about what they saw. Though some controversy exists, most researchers suggest that misleading questions cause a problem with **source monitoring**, the process by which people try to identify the source of their recollections. People often get mixed up about where they heard or saw something, mistakenly believing that a man looks familiar because they saw him at the scene of a crime when in fact he looks familiar because they saw his picture in the paper. This may have occurred in the identification of "John Doe No. 2" in the Oklahoma City bombing.

3. Retrieval

• Often criminals are convicted on the basis of eyewitnesses selecting them from a criminal lineup. However, the results of the lineup depend strongly on who else is included in the lineup. Witnesses will pick out of the lineup the person who most resembles the criminal even if the resemblance is not strong.

• To avoid this "best guess" problem, social psychologists recommend that police follow these five steps: (1) make sure that everyone in the lineup resembles the witness's description of the suspect; (2) tell the witness that the person suspected of the crime may or may not be in the lineup; (3) do not always include the suspect in an initial lineup—this provides a way to test witness reliability; (4) make sure that the person conducting the lineup does not know which person in the lineup is the suspect; (5) present pictures of people sequentially rather than simultaneously, to prevent witnesses comparing and choosing on the basis of resemblance even when the criminal is not in the lineup (6) present witnesses with both photographs and sound recordings of their voices, as this increases correct identifications; (7) don't use composite face programs; and (8) don't count on witnesses knowing whether their selections were biased.

B. Judging Whether Eyewitnesses Are Mistaken

• Ronald Cotton was sentenced to life in prison on the basis of Jennifer Thompson's complete confidence that he was her rapist. However, a few years later, another man, Bobby Poole, bragged in prison that he was the rapist. Although Thompson did not recognize him, subsequent DNA testing showed that Poole was the rapist. Cotton was released after serving 11 years for a crime he did not commit.

1. Does Certainty Mean Accuracy?

• The U.S. Supreme Court has ruled that the amount of confidence witnesses exhibit is a good indicator of their accuracy (*Neil v. Biggers*, 1972). However, numerous studies have shown that confidence and accuracy are not strongly related. There is only a weak relationship between confidence and accuracy, and it is dangerous to assume that because a witness is confident, he or she is correct. Things that influence people's confidence are not necessarily the same things that influence their accuracy.

2. Responding Quickly

• Dunning and Stern (1994) compared the process by which both accurate and inaccurate witnesses made identifications; accurate witnesses said the face just "popped out" at them, while inaccurate witnesses systematically compared them.

3. The Problem with Verbalization
• Research by Schooler and Engstler-Schooler (1990) suggests that there may have been something about making an identification slowly and deliberately that made people less accurate, in particular the processes of trying to put an image of a face into words. Those students who wrote a detailed description of a robber before trying to identify him from a lineup were less accurate than those who did not do so. The very process of translating an image into words is difficult and impairs memory for the face.

C. Judging Whether Witnesses Are Lying
• Another reason eyewitness testimony may be inaccurate is that witnesses may deliberately lie. Studies examining people's ability to detect deception find that people's ability is only slightly better than chance. People with a good deal of experience (e.g., law enforcement officials and clinical psychologists with considerable experience with defendants) are no more accurate at detecting deception than college students.

1. Can Polygraph Machines Tell if People are Lying?
• A **polygraph** is a machine that measures people's physiological responses (e.g., heart rate); when these machines are used in lie detection, polygraph operators attempt to tell if someone is lying by observing how that person responds physiologically while answering questions.
• One study found that the polygraph reveals whether someone is lying or telling the truth at levels better than chance. The accuracy rate, averaging over dozens of studies, was .86—that is, people were correctly labeled as lying or telling the truth 86 percent of the time. This still allows for a substantial number of errors, including false positives, where people who are telling the truth are incorrectly labeled as liars.
• Researchers continue to try to develop better lie detectors, using such measures as patterns of brain waves, involuntary eye movements, and blood flow in the face using high-definition thermal imaging technology. So far none of these measures has proved to be any better than a polygraph.

D. Can Eyewitness Testimony Be Improved?
• Two general approaches have been tried to improve eyewitness testimony, but neither has been very successful. The first involves hypnosis. Research suggests hypnosis improves confidence but not accuracy of memories. The second involves the use of the **cognitive interview**, a technique whereby a trained interviewer tries to improve eyewitnesses' memories by focusing their attention on the details and the context of the event. Although initial research seemed promising, subsequent research finds that this technique may increase errors and confabulations, especially when used with children. One reason may be that repeatedly imagining an event increases *source monitoring* errors. As of yet there is no definitive way to improve eyewitnesses' memory other than avoiding the pitfalls discussed in this chapter.

E. The Recovered Memory Debate
• **Recovered memories** are recollections of a past event, such as sexual abuse, that had been forgotten or repressed; a great deal of controversy surrounds the accuracy of such memories.
• The focus of the controversy is whether recovered memories are sufficient evidence that past abuse occurred. Many academic psychologists have their doubts about recovered memories because of empirical demonstrations of **false memory syndrome**, where the memory is objectively false but which people believe occurred. This is especially likely to occur when another person suggests that the events occurred.
• While the evidence for repression and recovery is sparse, there may be instances in which people do suddenly remember traumatic events that really did occur. Thus claims of abuse should be taken seriously. Unfortunately, it is difficult to distinguish accurate memories from false ones in the absence of corroborating evidence.

II. Juries: Group Processes in Action

• The jury tradition is longstanding in English and American law; despite this tradition, the jury system has often come under attack. One study found that judges who presided over criminal jury trials disagreed with the verdict rendered by the jury a full 25 percent of the time. The jury system is not a perfect system and based on research in social psychology, there are ways we might expect it to go wrong.

A. How Jurors Process Information during the Trial

• Pennington and Hastie (2000, 1992) suggest that jurors decide on one story that best explains all the evidence and then try to fit this story to the possible verdicts they are allowed to render; if one of the verdicts fits their preferred story, they are likely to convict. This explanation has important implications for how lawyers present their cases. Lawyers typically present their evidence either in *story order* or in *witness order* (the sequence they believe will have the greatest impact). The Pennington and Hastie work suggests that jurors are most likely to believe work presented in story order (Table 16.1). These researchers suggest that one reason the conviction rate in felony trials in America is so high (about 80%) is that in real trials, prosecutors usually use the story order while defense attorneys usually use the witness order.

B. Confessions: Are They Always What They Seem?

• Confessions are not always what they seem. Research has shown the interrogation process can go wrong in ways that elicit false confessions, even to the point where innocent suspects come to believe that they actually did commit the crime. One problem is that police investigators are often convinced that the suspect is guilty, and this belief biases how they conduct the interrogation. They ask leading questions, isolate suspects and put them under considerable stress, claim that an eyewitness has identified the suspect, and sometimes make false promises. After many hours of prolonged interrogation innocent people can become so psychologically fatigued that they don't know what to think, and may even come to believe that they are guilty.

• One solution to coerced confessions is requiring that interrogations be videotaped, so a jury can view the recording and judge for themselves whether the defendant was coerced into admitting things he or she didn't do. Almost all videos of interrogations focus on the suspect, rather than on the interrogator asking the questions. Research by Dan Lassiter (2004) showed that when the camera focused only on the suspect, people thought the confession was voluntary.

C. Deliberations in the Jury Room

• In a study of more than 200 juries in actual criminal trials, researchers found that in 97% of the cases, the jury's final decision was the same as the one favored by a majority of jurors on the initial vote. However, the process of deliberation makes people consider the evidence more systematically, and minority opinion often does change people's minds about the extent of guilt (e.g., first-degree murder versus second-degree versus manslaughter). Pennington and Hastie (1990) found that people on a jury who have a minority point of view often do convince the majority to change their minds about the specific verdict to render.

III. Why Do People Obey the Law?

A. Do Severe Penalties Deter Crime?

• **Deterrence theory** argues that people refrain from criminal activity because of the threat of legal punishment, as long as the punishment is perceived as relatively severe, certain, and swift. This theory assumes that people know what the penalties are for crimes, and that they have good control over their behavior and make rational decisions about whether or not to commit the crime after reflecting about the consequences. For many crimes, these assumptions do not hold.

• Research on drunk-driving laws (a behavior where people for the most part are making rational decisions about how much they can drink and still drive) finds that although increasing the severity of penalties was not related to lower fatality rates, an increased certainty of being caught was.
• On the other hand, there is no evidence that the death penalty prevents murders. Opponents of the death penalty point out that most murders are crimes of passion that are not preceded by rational consideration of the consequences, so that the death penalty does not act as a deterrent. Furthermore, many innocent people have been sentenced to death. Proponents of the death penalty argue that the lack of relationship between the penalty and the crime is due to the slow lag of the justice system, and that there would be a relationship if justice were administered swiftly. However, studies have found that executions are followed by an increase rather than a decrease in murders, possibly due to the modeling of aggressive behavior.

B. Procedural Justice: People's Sense of Fairness
• People do not only obey the law because they fear being caught and punished but, more importantly, because of their moral values about what constitutes good behavior. People will obey a law if they believe it is just, regardless of their belief about how likely they are to be caught if they break it. Thus rather than focusing on increasing penalties for crimes (which requires police officers for deterrence), politicians might focus on increasing people's beliefs that the laws are fair and just.
• **Procedural justice** is defined as people's judgments about the fairness of the procedures used to determine outcomes, such as whether they are guilty or innocent of a crime. People who feel they have been treated fairly are more likely to comply with the law than those who feel they have been treated unfairly. Research by Tyler (1990) shows that people prefer to receive a fair hearing in court, even if they end up being penalized, to having the case arbitrarily dismissed (with no penalty). Procedural justice is more important to people than positive outcomes.

LEARNING OBJECTIVES

After reading Chapter SPA 3, you should be able to do the following:

1. Discuss jurors' reliance on eyewitness testimony and their tendency to overestimate the accuracy of eyewitnesses. Identify why the accuracy of such testimony is overestimated. (pp. 474-475)

2. Identify biases in memory processing that lead to inaccurate eyewitness testimony. Distinguish among acquisition, storage, and retrieval. (pp. 475-481)

3. Identify situational factors that influence acquisition. Discuss the effect of previous expectancies on the acquisition of information. (pp. 476-478)

4. Discuss the influence of familiarity on memory. Define own-race bias and discuss its significance in eyewitness testimony. (p. 478)

5. Contrast the notion that memories are stored in our minds as static photographs with the notion that memories are actively reconstructed. Define reconstructive memory. Identify the role of misleading questions in reconstructive memory. Discuss how misleading questions alter what is stored in witnesses' memories. Define source monitoring and discuss its importance. (pp. 478-480)

6. Identify the role of retrieval in identifying a suspect from a police lineup. List the eight steps that social psychologists recommend to reduce the likelihood that witnesses will mistakenly pick an innocent individual out of a lineup when that person resembles the suspect. (pp. 480-481)

7. Discuss why the confidence of a witness does not necessarily equal the accuracy of his/her testimony. Identify the significance of responding quickly. Describe the problem with verbalization. (pp. 482-483)

8. Contrast the ability of novices and experts to detect deception. (pp. 484-485)

9. Describe the controversy over the use of the polygraph. Discuss the results of research on the accuracy of polygraph tests. Discuss the attempts to develop better lie detectors and their accuracy. (p. 485)

10. Identify ways to improve the accuracy of eyewitness testimony. Define the cognitive interview technique. Discuss the effectiveness of these strategies. (pp. 486-487)

11. Define recovered memories and the false memory syndrome and discuss the controversy surrounding these topics. (pp. 487-488)

12. Discuss why the use of the jury system in legal proceedings is relevant to social psychology. Describe the strategy jurors use to process information during a trial. Identify the implications for such a strategy on how lawyers present their cases. Distinguish between story order and witness order presentations of evidence. State the consequences of using each type of presentation both for prosecutors and defense lawyers. (pp. 488-489)

13. Discuss the reasons why confessions are not always what they seem. Why are confessions sometimes videotaped and does videotaping confessions achieve this objective? (pp. 489-491)

14. Identify the role of group processes and social interactions in the way juries reach verdicts. Discuss the role of conformity in the process of jury deliberation. Identify the effects minorities are likely to have on the process of jury deliberation and on the sentence rendered. (pp. 491-492)

15. Discuss why people generally obey laws. Examine the theory that severe penalties prevent crime. Define deterrence theory and identify its assumptions and limitations. (pp. 492-495)

16. Define procedural justice and discuss its role in people's adherence to laws and attitudes toward the legal system. (p. 495)

KEY TERMS

1. _____ The process by which people notice and pay attention to information in the environment; because people cannot perceive everything that is happening around them, they acquire only a subset of the information available in the environment. (p. 475)

2. _____ The process by which people store in memory information they have acquired from the environment. (p. 475)

3. _____ The process by which people recall information stored in their memories. (p. 475)

4. _____ The fact that people are better at recognizing faces of their own race than those of other races. (p. 478)

SPA 3

5. _____ The process whereby memories of an event become distorted by information encountered after the event occurred. (p. 479)

6. _____ The process whereby people try to identify the source of their memories. (p. 480)

7. _____ A machine that measures people's physiological responses (e.g., their heart rate); polygraph operators attempt to tell if someone is lying by observing that person's physiological responses while answering questions. (p. 485)

8. _____ Recollections of a past event, such as sexual abuse, that had been forgotten or repressed. (p. 487)

9. _____ Remembering a past traumatic experience that is objectively false but nevertheless accepted as true. (p. 487)

10. _____ The hypothesis that the threat of legal punishment causes people to refrain from criminal activity as long as the punishment is perceived as relatively severe, certain, and swift. (p. 493)

11. _____ People's judgments about the fairness of the procedures used to determine outcomes, such as whether they are innocent or guilty of a crime. (p. 495)

GUIDED REVIEW

PRACTICE TEST

1. The process whereby people notice and attend to information in the environment is called _____ and the process of keeping that information in memory is called _____.
   a) acquisition; storage
   b) learning; acquisition
   c) learning; storage
   d) attention; retrieval

2. It is very likely that witnesses to real crimes will give inaccurate testimony because:
   a) eyewitnesses feel that criminals will seek revenge for testimony that convicts them.
   b) emotions experienced while witnessing the crime will be evoked during testimony and interfere with recall.
   c) crimes usually occur under the very conditions that make acquisition difficult.
   d) arousal interferes with the storage of memories.

3. A cognitive process where memory for an event becomes distorted by information that is encountered after the event occurs is called:
   a) acquisition.
   b) storage.
   c) retrieval.
   d) reconstructive memory.

4. Witnesses are less likely to identify an innocent individual as a criminal when they view pictures of people presented:
   a) simultaneously.
   b) sequentially.
   c) repeatedly.
   d) on a single occasion.

5. Which of the following is true about why people obey the law?
   a) People who perceive that the procedures used to determine outcomes in court are fair will be more likely to obey the law than people who do not.
   b) Perceived procedural justice is a better explanation for why people obey the law than is deterrence theory.
   c) The death penalty prevents murders.
   d) Both a and b are true.

6. To avoid the "best guess" problem in a lineup you should tell the witnesses that the person suspected of the crime may or may not be in the lineup.
   a) True
   b) False

7. Composite face programs have been found to be very effective and police should continue to use them.
   a) True
   b) False

8. Since jurors decide upon a "best story" to explain the evidence, a good lawyer would present her witnesses:
   a) in order of ascending credibility.
   b) in order of descending credibility.
   c) in an manner which reveals the order of the events as they occurred.
   d) in a manner which leads to a startling and dramatic revelation.

9. Jurors tend to put a lot of faith in eyewitness testimony because:
   a) eyewitnesses are in a position of high status in the courtroom.
   b) jurors have a natural bias toward conviction.
   c) normative pressures to side with the eyewitness are high in the courtroom.
   d) they assume that the witness's confidence is a good indicator of accuracy.

10. Retrieval is the process by which people:
    a) notice and pay attention to a subset of information available in the environment.
    b) store information in memory that they have acquired from the environment.
    c) rehearse information so that it will not be immediately forgotten.
    d) recall information that is stored in their memories.

11. Which of the following coincides with the own-race bias?
    a) Sheila, an African American woman, is better at recognizing white faces than Black or Asian faces.
    b) Juan, an African American man, is better at recognizing Asian faces than white or Black faces.
    c) Steve, a white man, is better at recognizing white faces than Black or Asian faces.
    d) Lily, an Asian woman, is better at recognizing Black faces than Asian or white faces.

12. Why are people likely to give inaccurate accounts of events when asked misleading questions?
    a)   the questions change what people are willing to report
    b)   people assume that the misinformation presented in the question came from their own memories
    c)   the misinformation presented in the question conflicts with stored information and produces dissonance
    d)   the questions bias acquisition

13. Joe believes that he has nothing to lose by taking a polygraph test in order to be considered for a part-time sales job at a local pharmaceutical company. In fact, the probability that Joe will be mistakenly identified as a liar even though he tells the truth is:
    a)   2 percent.
    b)   5 percent.
    c)   14 percent.
    d)   35 percent.

14. Researchers continue to try to develop better lie detectors using brain waves, involuntary eye movements, and blood flow to the face. So far these measures have been found to be
    a)   much less effective than the polygraph.
    b)   no better than the polygraph.
    c)   a little more effective than the polygraph.
    d)   much more effective than the polygraph.

15. There is _____ that people's memory improves when they are hypnotized.
    a)   no hard evidence
    b)   strong evidence
    c)   correlational data proving
    d)   strong anecdotal evidence

16. The presence of minority opposition in a jury increases the likelihood that:
    a)   a guilty verdict will be rendered.
    b)   the facts in the case will be carefully considered.
    c)   self-awareness among jurors will be high.
    d)   a not guilty verdict will be rendered.

17. According to your text, which of the following has been used to increase the accuracy of eyewitness testimony?
    a)   the cognitive interview
    b)   exposure to pretrial publicity
    c)   memory enhancing drugs
    d)   inducing belief in the just world hypothesis

18. In a study by Elke Geraerts and her colleagues (2007), which group provided no corroborating evidence of their childhood sexual abuse?
    a)   those who had never forgotten the abuse
    b)   those who recovered their memories of abuse outside of therapy
    c)   those who recovered their memories of abuse in therapy
    a)   none of the above; all were able to provide some corroborating evidence

19. A memory of a past trauma that is objectively false but is believed to have occurred defines the:
    a)   recovered memory syndrome.
    b)   deception memory syndrome.
    c)   implicit memory syndrome.
    d)   false memory syndrome.

20. Since people pay less attention to features that characterize the individual in cross-race people and instead focus on facial characteristics of the entire group, they are likely to commit ____ when trying to recognize these faces.
    a)   the ultimate attribution error
    b)   the fundamental attribution error
    c)   source monitoring
    d)   the own-race bias

21. When people get confused about where and when they heard or saw something, they are having problems with:
    a)   source monitoring.
    b)   recall.
    c)   acquisition.
    d)   cognitive monitoring.

22. All of the following are social psychologists' recommendations to police regarding lineups EXCEPT which one?
    a)   the person conducting the lineup should not know which person in the lineup is the suspect
    b)   ask witnesses how confident they are that they can identify the suspect before they are given feedback about their lineup performance
    c)   present witnesses with either photos of people or sound recordings of people suspected of the crime
    d)   tell the witnesses that the person suspected of the crime may or may not be in the lineup

23. Regarding judging whether eyewitnesses are accurate, which of the following is correct?
    a)   The confidence level of the eyewitness is a good indication of how accurate an eyewitness is.
    b)   Eyewitnesses who take less time identifying the defendant are correct more often than are eyewitnesses who take more time.
    c)   Eyewitnesses who put a face of a suspect into words are more accurate than are those who do not verbalize the suspect's facial features.
    d)   All of the above are correct

24. Confessions are not always what they seem because
    a)   police officers may ask leading questions during interrogations.
    b)   suspects may be isolated and put under considerable stress.
    c)   police may claim than an eyewitness has identified the suspect.
    d)   all of the above.

25. Almost all videos of interrogations
    a) focus on the suspect.
    b) focus on the interrogator asking the questions.
    c) focus equally on the suspect and the interrogator asking the questions.
    d) Focused entirely on the suspect in the past but now, because of research, focus on the suspect and interrogator equally.

26. In research by Dan Lassiter (2004) under which condition were people most likely to believe that a videotaped confession was least voluntary (the most coerced)?
    a) when the camera focused only on the interrogator
    b) when the camera focused only on the suspect
    c) when the camera focused equally on the suspect and the interrogator
    d) none of the above—the focus of the camera made no difference in these beliefs

27. A technique to improve eyewitnesses' memories that has them focus their attention on the details and context of the event by asking them to recall the event several times and by asking them to create a mental picture of the scene is called:
    a) source retrieval.
    b) retrieval.
    c) cognitive interview.
    d) constructive interview.

28. Which of the following is true regarding how lawyers present information to the jury in a trial and its effects?
    a) Prosecutors usually present evidence in the witness order.
    b) Defense attorneys usually present evidence in the witness order.
    c) Juries are more likely to convict the defendant when the prosecutor uses the story order.
    d) Both b and c are true.

29. Deterrence theory proposes that people obey the law because of the threat of legal punishment, as long as the punishment is perceived as:
    a) severe.
    b) certain.
    c) swift.
    d) all the above.

30. Recollections of past events that had been forgotten or repressed, but have been recalled many years later, are known as:
    a) retrieved cognitions.
    b) recovered memories.
    c) false memories.
    d) transactive memories.

31. People's judgments about the fairness of the procedures used to determine outcomes, such as whether they are innocent or guilty of a crime describes
    a) procedural justice.
    b) judicial perceptual stance.
    c) a fairness cognition system.
    d) personal procedural bias.

32. In a study by Rod Lindsay et al. (1981) jurors
    a) underestimated the accuracy of the witnesses, especially in the condition where the thief was difficult to identify.
    b) underestimated the accuracy of the witnesses, especially in the condition where the thief was easy to identify.
    c) overestimated the accuracy of the witnesses, especially in the condition where the thief was difficult to identify.
    d) overestimated the accuracy of the witnesses, especially in the condition where the thief was easy to identify.

33. When Loftus and Harley (2005) showed photographs of celebrities photographed from varying distances to research participants they found that at 77 feet _____ percent of the participants recognized the face.
    a) 15
    b) 25
    c) 27
    d) 31

34. The text tells the story of a social psychologist named Alan who is an expert on social perception. One day Alan discovered the murdered body of his neighbor in her home and he went back to his home to call the police. Unlike most people, Alan was able to recall the murder scene with amazing detail.
    a) True
    b) False

35. Which of the following accurately explains why the own-race bias occurs?
    a) selective memory
    b) stereotypes
    c) When people examine different-race faces, they are drawn more to individuating features rather than to features that distinguish that face from their own race
    d) When people examine different-race faces, they are drawn more to features that distinguish that face from their own race, rather than individuating features.

36. Once a memory has been stored it cannot be altered.
    a) True
    b) False

37. Numerous studies have shown that a witness's confidence is only weakly related to his or her accuracy.
    a) True
    b) False.

38. We should be more willing to believe a witness who says, "I knew it was the defendant as soon as I saw him in the lineup," particularly if they made their judgment in _____ or less.
    a) 2 minutes
    b) 1 minute
    c) 10 seconds
    d) 15 seconds

39.   Most people are not very accurate at detecting lies but people with a lot of experience in dealing with liars (e.g., law enforcement agents and employees of the CIA) are much more accurate at detecting deception.
    a)   True
    b)   False

40.   Research has proven that all recovered memories are inaccurate.
    a)   True
    b)   False

SHORT ANSWER REVIEW

The American legal system assigns a great deal of significance to eyewitness testimony. Eyewitness testimony is often of questionable accuracy, because of the way people naturally observe and remember unexpected events. Unfortunately, jurors tend to (1) _____ (p. 474) the accuracy of eyewitnesses.

The problem is that our minds are not like (2) _____ (p. 475), which can record an event, store it over time, and play it back later with perfect accuracy. Acquisition refers to the process whereby people notice and pay attention to information in the environment. Because people cannot perceive everything that is happening around them, they acquire only a (3) _____ (p. 475) of the information that is available in the environment. Storage refers to the process by which people store in memory information they have acquired from the environment. Retrieval refers to the process by which people recall information stored in their memories. Eyewitnesses can be inaccurate because of problems at any of these three stages. For example, research on own-race bias shows that people find it more (4) _____ (p. 478) to recognize members of other races than members of their own race. In addition, research has shown that memories are reconstructed. Reconstructive memory is the process whereby memories of an event become (5) _____ (p. 479) by information encountered after the event occurred. Research on reconstructive memory indicates that errors in (6) _____ (p. 480) – whereby people try to identify the source of their memories--can occur when people become confused about where they saw or heard something. Recognizing the problems people have retrieving information from memory, social psychologists have issued guidelines for how police lineups should be conducted.

There is no sure fire way of telling whether a witness is making an accurate or inaccurate identification. Numerous studies have shown that a witness's confidence is only (7) _____ (p. 482) to his or her accuracy. Although there is some evidence that people who identify a suspect from an array of pictures within 10 seconds and express very high confidence in their choice are especially likely to be correct.

Even if witnesses have very accurate memories for what they saw, they might deliberately lie when on the witness stand. Humans are not very good at telling whether another person is lying. The polygraph is a machine that measures people's (8) _____ (p. 485). Polygraph operators attempt to tell if someone is lying by observing that person's physiological responses while answering question. The polygraph can detect lying at above-chance levels, but is not perfect and often yields inaccurate results.

Two general approaches have been tried to improve the accuracy of eyewitness testimony. The first involves hypnosis however, there is no hard evidence that people's memories improve when they are hypnotized. The second way people have tried to increase the eyewitness accuracy is with the use of the cognitive interview. The cognitive interview is a technique whereby a trained interviewer tries to improve eyewitnesses' memories by (9) _____ (p. 486) on the details and content of the event. Unfortunately, this technique has not proved to be any better than hypnosis; in fact, it may (10) _____ (p. 486-487) errors and confabulations of memory, especially when used with children.

How valid are recovered memories, the sudden recollection of events, such as sexual abuse that had been forgotten or (11) _____ (p. 487)? Though recovered memories may be true in some instances, they can also be the result of false memory syndrome, whereby people come to believe the memory is true when it actually is not. False memories are especially likely to occur when another person (12) _____ (p. 487) to us that an event really occurred.

Juries are of particular interest to social psychologists because the way they reach verdicts is directly relevant to social psychological research on group processes and social interaction. One study found that judges who presided over criminal jury trials disagreed with the verdict rendered by the jury a full (13) _____ (p. 488) percent of the time. The jury system is not a perfect system and based on research in social psychology, there are ways we might expect it to go wrong.

People often construct theories and schemas to interpret the world around them and the same is true of jurors. Some psychologists suggest that jurors decide on one (14) _____ (p. 489) that best explains all the evidence; they then try to fit this story to the possible verdicts they are allowed to render, and if one of those verdicts fits well with their preferred story, they are likely to vote to convict on that charge. Lawyers typically present the evidence in one of two ways. In the first, called, (15) _____ (p. 489) they present the evidence in the sequence in which the events occurred, corresponding as closely as possible to the story they want the jurors to believe. In the second, called, (16) _____ (p. 489) they present witnesses in the sequence they think will have the greatest impact, even if this means that events are described out of order. Juries are thus most swayed by lawyers who present the evidence in a way that tells a consistent story.

The interrogation techniques used by the police can sometimes produce false (17) _____ (p. 490). The video recording of interrogations is a safeguard against this, though focusing the camera solely on the (18) _____ (p. 491) increases the likelihood that viewers will think he or she voluntarily confessed.

During deliberations, jurors with minority views are often pressured into conforming to the view of the majority; thus verdicts usually correspond to the initial feelings of the majority of jurors. In a study of more than 200 juries in actual criminal trials, researchers found that in (19) _____ (p. 491) percent of the cases, the jury's final decision was the same as the one favored by a majority of the jurors on the (20) _____ (p. 491) vote. However, one study found that people on a jury who have a minority point of view often convince the majority to change their minds about the specific verdict to render.

"Why do people obey the law?" It is important to find ways of preventing people from committing crimes. (21) _____ (pp. 491-492) holds that people refrain from criminal activity if they view penalties as severe, certain, and swift. Deterrence theory may be correct about crimes that are the result of (22) _____ (p. 493) but is unlikely to apply to (23) _____ (p. 493) crimes of passion that are not rational, such as many murders. There is no evidence, for example, that the (24) _____ (p. 493) deters murders, and there is even some evidence that it (25) _____ (p. 493) the murder rate. People are more likely to obey the law if their sense of (26) _____ (p. 495) is high; that is, if they believe that the procedures used to determine their guilt or innocence are fair.

ESSAY REVIEW

1. Explain why familiarity is an important factor in memory processing. Define own-race bias and explain why it occurs and what consequences this bias has on eyewitness testimony.

2. Discuss how well people can detect deception. Do those working in the field of law enforcement do better than others at detecting deception?

3. Explain the relationship between accuracy and certainty of eyewitness accounts. Is it a good idea for law enforcement officials and jurors to assume that a witness who is very confident is also correct?

4. Describe what a polygraph machine is designed to do and how it does it? What is the assumption behind the use of the polygraph? How accurate, on average, are polygraphs at detecting when someone is lying? Does failing a polygraph test always mean that one is lying?

5. Identify recovered memories and false memory syndrome. Describe how they are relevant to the issue of eyewitness testimony?

EXIT TESTS

EXIT TEST 1

1. If an eyewitness fingers you as the culprit of a crime, you are
    a) quite unlikely to be convicted unless there is considerable circumstantial evidence indicating you are guilty.
    b) quite likely to be convicted, even if considerable circumstantial evidence indicates that you are innocent.
    c) unlikely to be convicted unless DNA evidence indicates you are guilty.
    d) quite likely to be convicted, even if DNA evidence indicates that someone else is guilty.

2. Jurors tend to _____ the accuracy of eyewitnesses.
    a) slightly underestimate
    b) greatly underestimate
    c) accurately estimate
    d) overestimate

3. _____ refers to a process involved when an eyewitness notices and pays attention to information in the environment while a crime is being committed.
    a) Acquisition
    b) Storage
    c) Retrieval
    d) Reconstructive memory

4. Kyle was working as a teller in a bank when a robber came in and pointed a gun at him, demanding he hand over all his cash. Kyle is most likely to remember well the ·
    a) facial features of the robber.
    b) customers in the bank.
    c) gun.
    d) clothes the robber was wearing.

5. Elizabeth Loftus and her colleagues have found that misleading questions can change people's minds about which of the following?
    a) how fast a car was going
    b) whether broken glass was at the scene of an accident
    c) whether a traffic light was green or red
    d) all of the above

6. Lucy tells her daughter about a new product she has learned about, stating she learned about it from a television commercial. Her daughter informs Lucy that she was the one who told her mother about the product a few days ago. Lucy has experienced an error in
    a) source labeling.
    b) source monitoring.
    c) procedural memory.
    d) sensory memory.

7. Identification errors from lineups are the most common cause of wrongful convictions in the United States.
    a) True
    b) False

8. Studies by Schooler and Engstler-Schooler (1990) show that putting an image of a face into words
   a) consistently improves memory, but only slightly.
   b) greatly improves memory.
   c) can make people's memory worse.
   d) has no effect on memory.

9. There is some evidence that people can deliberately act in ways that reduce the validity of the results of polygraph tests, such as biting their tongue and doing mental arithmetic.
   a) True
   b) False

10. There is some evidence that when people are under hypnosis
    a) their memory is slightly improved.
    b) their memory is greatly improved.
    c) they are less susceptible to suggestion.
    d) they are more susceptible to suggestion, coming to believe that they saw things that they did not.

EXIT TEST 2

1. Researchers have now proven that the cognitive interview reliably improves the accuracy of eyewitness reports.
   a) True
   b) False

2. If a person suddenly remembers being abused as a child the
   a) person's memory should be accepted on faith.
   b) person should be hypnotized to see if he or she can remember more details.
   c) claim should be taken seriously and investigated fully.
   d) claim should be ignored.

3. If you are a prosecuting attorney trying a case you should use _____ order to increase your chances of getting a conviction.
   a) story
   b) witness
   c) shock value
   d) believability

4. In research by Dan Lassiter (2004) under which condition were people most likely to believe that a videotaped confession was voluntary (not coerced)?
   a) when the camera focused only on the interrogator
   b) when the camera focused only on the suspect
   c) when the camera focused equally on the suspect and the interrogator
   d) none of the above—the focus of the camera made no difference in these beliefs

5. Research by Kassin (2007, 2008) has shown that the interrogation process can go wrong in ways that elicit false confessions. One problem is that
    a) suspects are often easily confused.
    b) suspects fear wrongful conviction so they confess in order to get a lesser sentence.
    c) suspects are usually on drugs and do not realize what they are doing.
    d) police investigators are often convinced that the suspect is guilty, and this belief biases how they conduct the interrogation.

6. The crime rate has been increasing in the United States.
    a) True
    b) False

7. In the blackout of 2003, the crime rate was actually lower in New York, Detroit, and Cleveland than on typical summer days.
    a) True
    b) False

8. There is no evidence that the death penalty prevents murder. This is based on comparing murder rates in
    a) American states that have the death penalty with those that do not.
    b) American states before and after they adopted the death penalty.
    c) other countries before and after they adopted the death penalty.
    d) all of the above.

9. According to your text it would be best to try to prevent crimes by
    a) hiring more police.
    b) installing more video cameras to monitor the behavior of people in public places.
    c) convincing people that the law is just and fair.
    d) increasing the penalties for breaking the law.

10. Whether a person accused of assault will repeat the crime in the future depends on whether the person is arrested or threatened with mild punishment.
    a) True
    b) False

STUDY ACTIVITIES

1. As a social psychologist, you have been contracted by a defense attorney to give your expert opinion on eyewitness accuracy following testimony by a woman who swears that she saw the defendant murder someone. What would you tell the court?

2. If juries usually stick with the verdict favored by the initial majority of jurors, why should we insist that juries deliberate until they reach consensus on that verdict?

3. Describe the three stages of memory processing that an eyewitness must successfully complete in order to give accurate testimony.

4. What reasons exist to explain why people obey the law? What are aspects of the legal system that help keep people from committing crimes?

5.   Define reconstructive memory and source monitoring. Discuss the effects misleading questions have on source monitoring.

6.   You are a psychologist that has been hired by a local police department to increase the accuracy of lineup identifications. Describe what your suggestions would be.

7.   Explain why the confidence of one's testimony is not always a good estimate of the accuracy of one's testimony. Describe the consequences of trying to put a face into words for the accuracy of identifying the face.

8.   Describe the methods that have been used in the attempt to improve the accuracy of eyewitness testimony. Discuss the success of these methods.

9.   Describe the two orders lawyers use to present evidence and identify which order is more effective? How do individual jurors process evidence during a trial? Given these findings, why may the felony conviction rate in America be as high as it is?

10.   Discuss the benefits of jury deliberations. How are jury members with minority opinions influential in jury deliberation?

Chapter SPA 3 Answers

Practice Test

1. A (p. 475)
2. C (p. 477)
3. D (p. 479)
4. B (p. 481)
5. D (pp. 492-495)
6. A (p. 481)
7. B (p. 481)
8. C (p. 489)
9. D (pp. 482-483)
10. D (p. 475)
11. C (p. 478)
12. B (pp. 478-480)
13. C (p. 485)
14. B (p. 485)
15. A (p. 486)
16. B (pp. 491-492)
17. A (p. 486)
18. C (p. 488)
19. D (p. 487)
20. D (p. 478)
21. A (p. 480)
22. B (p. 481)
23. B (pp. 482-483)
24. D (pp. 489-490)
25. A (p. 491)
26. A (p. 491)
27. C (p. 486)
28. D (p. 489)
29. D (pp. 492-493)
30. B (p. 487)
31. A (p. 495)
32. C (p. 475)
33. B (p. 477)
34. B (p. 477)
35. D (p. 478)
36. B (p. 479)
37. A (p. 482)
38. C (p. 483)
39. B (pp. 484-485)
40. B (p. 487)

Short Answer Review

1. overestimate (p. 474)
2. video cameras (p. 475)
3. subset (p. 475)
4. difficult (p. 478)

5.   distorted (p. 479)
6.   source monitoring (p. 480)
7.   weakly related (p. 482)
8.   physiological responses (p. 485)
9.   focusing their attention (p. 486)
10. increase (pp. 486-487)
11. repressed (p. 487)
12. suggests (p. 487)
13. 25 (p. 488)
14. story (p. 489)
15. story order (p. 489)
16. witness order (p. 489)
17. confessions (p. 490)
18. suspect (p. 491)
19. 97 (p. 491)
20. initial (p. 491)
21. Deterrence theory (pp. 492-493)
22. rational decision processes (p. 493)
23. impulsive (p. 493)
24. death penalty (p. 493)
25. increases (p. 493)
26. procedural justice (p. 495)

Essay Review

1.   Your essay should include the following:
   - Even if we notice a person or event we might not remember it very well, if we are unfamiliar with it. For example, people are better at recognizing faces that are of the same race as they are, a phenomenon known as own-race bias. (p. 478)
   - Own-race bias is due to the fact that people have more contact with members of their own race, allowing them to learn better how to distinguish one individual from another. (p. 478)
   - There is evidence that when people examine same-race faces, they pay close attention to individuating features that distinguish that face from others, such as the height of cheekbones or the contour of the forehead. When people examine different-race faces, however, they are drawn more to features that distinguish that face from their own race, rather than individuating features. Thus, an eyewitness is likely to be more accurate in identifications of people of their same race and more likely to make a mistake if the perpetrator is of a different race.
   (p. 478)

2.   Your essay on detecting deception should include the following:
   - People are not very good at detecting deception. Bond and DePaulo (2006) found that on average, people were correct only 54 percent of the time in telling lies from truths. (p. 484)
   - People with a lot of experience with liars (e.g., law enforcement agents and employees of the CIA) are no more accurate at detecting deception than college students. (p. 485)

3.   Your essay should include the following:
- Numerous studies have shown that a witness's confidence is only weakly related to his or her accuracy. When law enforcement officials and jurors assume that a witness who is very confident is also correct, they can make serious mistakes. (p. 482)
- One reason that confidence is not always a sign of accuracy is that the things that influence people's confidence are not necessarily the same things that influence their accuracy. After identifying a suspect, for example, a person's confidence increases if he or she finds out that other witnesses identified the same suspect and decreases if he or she finds out that other witnesses identified a different suspect. This change in confidence cannot influence the accuracy of the identification the person made earlier. (pp. 482-483)

4.   Your essay on the polygraph machine should include the following:
- The polygraph machine is designed to detect if someone is lying. (p. 485)
- It measures people's physiological responses. Polygraph operators attempt to tell is someone is lying by observing that person's physiological responses while answering questions. (p. 485)
- The assumption is that when people lie, they become anxious, and this anxiety can be detected by increases in heart rate, breathing rate, and so on. (p. 485)
- Polygraphs are accurate 86% of the time. (p. 485)
- No, failing a polygraph does not necessarily mean a person is lying because it could be a false positive. (p. 485)

5.   Your essay should include the following:
- Recovered memories are recollections of a past event, such as sexual abuse, that had been forgotten or repressed. (p. 487)
- False memory syndrome refers to remembering a past traumatic experience that is objectively false but nevertheless accepted as true. (p. 487)
- The accuracy of recovered memories cannot be accepted on faith. Claims of sexual abuse should be investigated fully and when sufficient evidence of guilt exists the person responsible for the abuse should be prosecuted. (p. 487)
- There may be instances in which people do suddenly remember traumatic events that really did occur. Unfortunately, it is very difficult to distinguish the accurate memories from the false ones in the absence of corroborating evidence. For this reason, claims of abuse cannot be taken on faith, especially if they are the result of suggestions from other people. (p. 487)

Exit Test 1

1.   B (p. 474)
2.   D (p. 474)
3.   A (p. 475)
4.   C (p. 477)
5.   D (pp. 479-480)
6.   B (p. 480)
7.   A (p. 480)
8.   C (p. 483)
9.   A (p. 485)
10.   D (p. 486)